Yearbook of International Humanitarian Law

Volume 19

More information about this series at http://www.springer.com/series/8912

Terry D. Gill · Tim McCormack
Robin Geiß · Heike Krieger
Christophe Paulussen
Editors

Yearbook of International Humanitarian Law 2016

ASSER PRESS

Springer

Editors
Terry D. Gill
Criminal Law Section, Section Military Law
University of Amsterdam
Amsterdam
The Netherlands

and

Netherlands Defence Academy
Breda
The Netherlands

Tim McCormack
Melbourne Law School
Carlton, VIC
Australia

Robin Geiß
School of Law
University of Glasgow
Glasgow
UK

Heike Krieger
Department of Law/Public Law
Free University of Berlin
Berlin
Germany

Christophe Paulussen
Research Department
T.M.C. Asser Instituut
The Hague
The Netherlands

The views expressed in this *Yearbook* are not necessarily those of the members of the Editorial Board, the Board of Advisors to the Editorial Board, the Board of Recommendation and/or those institutions they represent, including the T.M.C. Asser Instituut and T.M.C. Asser Press.

ISSN 1389-1359 ISSN 1574-096X (electronic)
Yearbook of International Humanitarian Law
ISBN 978-94-6265-212-5 ISBN 978-94-6265-213-2 (eBook)
https://doi.org/10.1007/978-94-6265-213-2

Library of Congress Control Number: 2017963264

Published by T.M.C. ASSER PRESS, The Hague, The Netherlands www.asserpress.nl
Produced and distributed for T.M.C. ASSER PRESS by Springer-Verlag Berlin Heidelberg

Cover picture: Chocó Department. An ICRC employee speaks to members of the ELN armed group about the principles of international humanitarian law and the obligation to protect the lives of the civilian population, health personnel, and the sick or wounded.
Photo: Juan Arredondo. Reproduced with permission: Getty Images/ICRC

Printed on acid-free paper

This T.M.C. ASSER PRESS imprint is published by Springer Nature
The registered company is Springer-Verlag GmbH Germany
The registered company address is: Heidelberger Platz 3, 14197 Berlin, Germany

In Memoriam—Frits Kalshoven (1924–2017)

It is with profound sadness that the Editorial Board of the *Yearbook of International Humanitarian Law* was informed about the passing, on Wednesday 6 September 2017, of Prof. Emeritus Frits Kalshoven. We are proud to say that Frits was a member of the Yearbook's Board of Recommendation, and for good reason: he can safely be positioned within the international humanitarian law's hall of fame, as he was instrumental in the development of this important field of law. The theme of belligerent reprisals cannot be studied without consulting Frits' 1971 Ph.D., reprinted in 2005; he was one of the drafters of the 1977 Additional Protocols; in January 1987, Alexandre Hay, the then President of the International Committee of the Red Cross, correctly predicted in his preface to the first edition of Frits' book *Constraints on the Waging of War*, that "it will become one of the classics of the law of armed conflicts"; he was the first Chairman of the UN Commission of Experts to investigate serious violations of international humanitarian law in the former Yugoslavia, which paved the way for the International Criminal Tribunal for the former Yugoslavia; and in 2003, Frits was awarded the Henry Dunant Medal of the International Red Cross and Red Crescent Movement for his continued effort to improve the knowledge of and respect for the law of war.

In addition to all of this (and the above is only a very brief selection of his professional achievements), Frits was a friend, mentor and inspiration to many, both inside and outside the Netherlands. This is discernible from the various personal comments that were written in the days after his passing (and again: the following is a brief selection only): "very kind, warm and humble person—insisting, for example, to always be addressed by his first name"; "the great, and always humble, Frits Kalshoven"; "[w]e lost an IHL giant, gent and a wonderful man" and "[a] crusader for the right cause, a teacher of many, a gentleman until the very end".

It is clear he will be dearly missed by many. Including all of us.

On behalf of the entire team of the *Yearbook of International Humanitarian Law*,

Terry D. Gill (Editor-in-Chief) and Christophe Paulussen (Managing Editor)

Contents

In order to make the *Correspondents' Reports* immediately and widely available, they can be accessed online at

www.asser.nl/YIHL/correspondentsreports.

This has the added benefit of the reports being fully searchable, thereby better serving the needs of scholars and practitioners.

Part I
Armed Groups

Chapter 1
Armed Groups, Rebel Coalitions, and Transnational Groups: The Degree of Organization Required from Non-State Armed Groups to Become Party to a Non-International Armed Conflict

Tilman Rodenhäuser

Abstract Identifying non-state parties to armed conflicts becomes increasingly complex. As seen in recent conflicts in Syria, Libya, Yemen, or the Central African Republic, turmoil or inter-communal tensions escalate into armed conflicts, armed groups fragment increasingly, and some armed groups operate transnationally. Over the past decade, international jurisprudence developed numerous indicative factors to identify organized armed groups. While recognizing their great value, this chapter proposes to take a step back from these concrete indicators in order to recall broad but fundamental characteristics that any party to non-international armed conflict needs to have under international humanitarian law. It is shown that every party to a non-international armed conflict has to fulfil three criteria: it has to be (1) a collective entity; (2) with capabilities to engage in sufficiently intense violence; and (3) internal structures sufficient to ensure respect for basic humanitarian norms. Building on this basic understanding, the chapter provides an analysis of two questions that are highly relevant in contemporary conflicts but understudied: First, what link needs to exist between different armed groups in order to be considered one party to a conflict? And second, at what point can two or more groups that operate in different states form one transnational party to conflict?

Keywords Non-state armed group · Organized armed group · Non-international armed conflict · Party to a conflict · Organization · Organization criterion · Transnational conflict · Transnational armed group · Global war on terrorism · Islamic State

---

Dr. Tilman Rodenhäuser is Legal Adviser in the Legal Division of the ICRC. This chapter was written in the author's personal capacity and does not necessarily reflect the views of the ICRC.

T. Rodenhäuser (✉)
ICRC, Geneva, Switzerland
e-mail: tilman.rodenhaeuser@gmail.com

T.D. Gill et al. (eds.), *Yearbook of International Humanitarian Law 2016*,
Yearbook of International Humanitarian Law 19,
https://doi.org/10.1007/978-94-6265-213-2_1

Contents

1.1 Introduction

In order to classify internal violence as a non-international armed conflict (NIAC), it is generally agreed that armed violence has to reach a certain level of intensity, and it needs to occur between two or more sufficiently organized parties.[1] Recent conflicts in Syria, Libya, or the Central African Republic show, however, that conflict classification becomes increasingly complex. Turmoil or inter-communal tensions escalate into armed conflicts, armed groups fragment increasingly, and violence is becoming more and more regionalised.[2] While determining a certain degree of violence is often obvious from the facts, it is more challenging to identify different groups involved in armed violence and to determine whether they are sufficiently organized to constitute a party to a NIAC. This is mainly for two reasons: first, determining a sufficient degree of organization is factually complex. Being normally engaged in a conflict with a militarily superior adversary, armed groups tend to operate secretly. In order to protect their forces and leadership, they avoid disclosing their internal command, communication, or disciplinary structures. Second, defining what constitutes a sufficiently organized group under international humanitarian law (IHL) is legally challenging. As Sivakumaran emphasized in his recent study of the laws of NIAC: "the element of organisation and the workings of armed groups are only just starting to be understood" because "insufficient attention has been paid to armed groups, their structure, and workings".[3]

---

[1] See ICTY, *Prosecutor v Duško Tadić a/k/a "Dule"*, Decision on the defence motion for interlocutory appeal on jurisdiction, 2 October 1995, Case No. IT-94-1-AR72 (*Tadić* 1995), para 70; ICRC 2016, paras 393–451; Moir 2015.

[2] For a description of today's conflict environment, see ICRC 2015.

[3] Sivakumaran 2012a, p. 210.

Indeed, lawyers struggle to make sense of the organization criterion and its practical application. The task of analysing at what point non-state armed groups involved in conflicts in Syria, Libya, and Yemen were sufficiently organized under IHL led a group of legal experts to "ask whether too much emphasis is placed on the organizational criterionno needno or whether the problem lay with the [legal] indicia of an OAG [organized armed group] rather than with the existence of such a group".[4] In light of these difficulties, some have cautioned that looking strictly at whether both the organization and the intensity requirement are fulfilled risks "not seeing the forest for the trees" because too much weight is given to "technical legalities".[5] Instead, they suggest that in order to classify a situation as a NIAC, the "totality of the circumstances" needs to be taken into account.[6] Accordingly, it is argued that if the intensity criterion is overwhelmingly satisfied, the organization criterion can to some extent be offset: "a situation of intense hostilities without significant opposition force organization indicates the exact type of heavy-handed government military response that necessitates humanitarian regulation".[7] The proposal of looking at the intensity and organization requirements together has important merit and is taken up below. At the same time, the suggestion to call heavy-handed state violence too readily an armed conflict also warrants a word of caution. Granting states larger discretion to use force according to a conduct of hostilities paradigm instead of a law enforcement one as applicable outside armed conflicts might not mitigate violence and suffering—the contrary is likely to be the case. Thus, moving too far away from established—and admittedly restrictive—legal criteria for conflict classification, and thereby making it easier to invoke IHL as the applicable legal framework, risks legalizing conduct which would otherwise be in violation of international human rights law (IHRL) or amount to an international crime.[8]

A second avenue to practically address the challenge of determining whether or not a non-state armed group is sufficiently organized has been to focus the analysis on a group's capabilities to engage in armed violence. At the International Criminal Court (ICC), for example, Trial Chambers I and III recently argued that an organised armed group under the Rome Statute of the International Criminal Court

[4] Arimatsu and Choudhury 2014, p. 40.

[5] Blank and Corn 2013, p. 746.

[6] Blank and Corn 2013.

[7] Ibid., p. 740. Going in a similar direction, others have argued that "it is of minor importance whether armed groups are 'organized' or not if they are able to conduct armed resistance to such a degree that governmental forces must use military means and methods to achieve their aims". Dahl and Sandbu 2006, p. 376.

[8] As Garraway puts it, the result of such proposals "is not so much to increase protection but to widen the authority for armed forces to use lethal force". Garraway 2015, p. 443. Indeed, under international law, a heavy-handed government response to violence by poorly organised armed elements falls into the category of severe human rights violations, or crimes against humanity, rather than into that of potentially lawful acts of warfare.

(Rome Statute) must "have a sufficient degree of organisation, in order to enable them to carry out protracted armed violence".[9] On the other hand, Trial Chamber II emphasised that organised armed groups under the Rome Statute must have a sufficient degree of organisation not only to be able to engage in a protracted armed conflict but also "to be able to implement rules of international humanitarian law applicable" in NIAC.[10] Unlike the other two trial chambers, this approach suggests that in addition to being sufficiently organized to engage in armed violence, an armed group under IHL is also required to be able to implement basic humanitarian norms.

These diverging views and the apparent lack of legal clarity are worrying because determining whether or not a non-state armed group is sufficiently organised to qualify as a party to an armed conflict has major implications. First, unless intense armed violence takes place between at least two sufficiently organised parties, a situation cannot classify as a NIAC. As hinted to above, conflict classification determines which bodies of law—either only IHRL outside armed conflicts, or IHL and IHRL during armed conflict—govern elementary questions such as the permissibility of the use of force, grounds and procedures for deprivation of liberty, or questions on humanitarian relief.[11] As IHL is generally considered more permissive on the use of force and deprivation of liberty, determining whether and in relation to which actors IHL applies has significant implications for those affected by violence. Second, conflict classification is a cardinal question with regard to prosecuting crimes. War crimes as defined in international criminal law can only be committed in the context of an armed conflict. Thus, unless a situation of armed violence qualifies as a NIAC, acts such as torture, rape, or intentionally attacking civilians are likely to amount to crimes under national law but cannot be prosecuted as war crimes.

Against this background, the objective of the present chapter is to show what signifies the "organization criterion" under IHL and how it should be understood in increasingly complicated conflict situations. Section 1.2 examines the "organization criterion" under IHL treaties and their contemporary interpretations. It argues that at a minimum, any party to a NIAC needs to meet three broad criteria: it needs to be (1) a collective entity; (2) with the capabilities to engage in sufficiently intense violence; and (3) internal structures sufficient to ensure respect for basic humanitarian norms. Building on this basic understanding, Sects. 1.3 and 1.4 of the chapter provide an analysis of two questions that are highly relevant in contemporary

[9] ICC, *Prosecutor v Thomas Lubanga Dyilo,* Judgment, 14 March 2012, Case No. ICC-01/04-01/06-2842 (*Lubanga Dyilo*), para 536; ICC, *Prosecutor v Jean-Pierre Bemba Gombo,* Judgment, 21 March 2016, Case No. ICC-01/05-01/08-3343 (*Bemba*), para 134. Contrary to Trial Chamber II, Trial Chamber III considered the ability to impose discipline an indicative factor only and not a strict criterion.

[10] ICC, *Prosecutor v Germain Katanga,* Judgment, 7 March 2014, Case No. ICC-01/04-01/07-3436 (*Katanga*), para 1185.

[11] On practical differences between IHL and IHRL, see Kretzmer 2009, pp. 24–25; ICRC 2011, p. 22; Kress 2010, p. 26; on the difference regarding humanitarian relief, see Rodenhäuser and Giacca 2016.

conflicts but understudied. Section 1.3 examines the question of which link needs to exist between different armed groups in order to be considered one party to a NIAC. Section 1.4 extends these considerations to transnational armed groups, meaning groups consisting of subgroups operating in different states.

1.2 The Organization Requirement Under Contemporary IHL

In the absence of clear definitions in IHL treaties of which criteria define a non-state armed group that is sufficiently organized to become party to a NIAC, international jurisprudence over the past 20 years has suggested a variety of indicators or factors for examination.[12] They are not strict criteria, but "indicative factors, none of which are, in themselves, essential to establish whether the 'organization' criterion is fulfilled".[13] The International Criminal Tribunal for the former Yugoslavia (ICTY) has generally examined five groups of factors: (1) the presence of a command structure; (2) the ability to carry out operations in an organised manner; (3) the group's level of logistics; (4) the group's "level of discipline and its ability to implement the basic obligations of Common Article 3"; and (5) the group's ability to speak with one voice.[14] For their part, ICC Trial Chambers present the following non-exhaustive list of indicators:

> [T]he force or group's internal hierarchy; the command structure and rules; the extent to which military equipment, including firearms, are available; the force or group's ability to plan military operations and put them into effect; and the extent, seriousness, and intensity of any military involvement.[15]

---

[12] As will be seen below, the definition found in Article 3 common to the four Geneva Conventions (Common Article 3) is rather ecliptic. Article 8(2) of the Rome Statute of the International Criminal Court does not provide a clear definition either. The criteria listed in Additional Protocol II apply under that treaty and are generally understood as setting out a threshold that is slightly higher than the lowest NIAC threshold as found in Common Article 3. See Rome Statute of the International Criminal Court, opened for signature 17 July 1998, 2187 UNTS 90 (entered into force 1 July 2002) (ICC Statute); and Protocol Additional to the Geneva Conventions of 12 August 1949, and relating to the Protection of Victims of Non-International Armed Conflicts, opened for signature 8 June 1977, 1125 UNTS 609 (entered into force 7 December 1978) (Additional Protocol II).

[13] ICTY, *Prosecutor v Ramush Haradinaj, Idriz Balaj and Lahi Brahimaj,* Judgment, 3 April 2008, Case No. IT-04-84-T (*Haradinaj* et al. 2008), para 60; *Lubanga Dyilo,* above n 9, para 537.

[14] ICTY, *Prosecutor v Ramush Haradinaj, Idriz Balaj and Lahi Brahimaj,* Retrial Judgment, 29 November 2012, Case No. IT-04-84bis-T (*Haradinaj* et al. 2012), para 395; ICTY, *Prosecutor v Ljube Boškoski and Johan Tarčulovski,* Judgment, 10 July 2008, Case No. IT-04-82-T (*Boškoski and Tarčulovski*), paras 199–203.

[15] *Lubanga Dyilo,* above n 9, para 537. For establishing these factors, the Trial Chamber refers to ICTY jurisprudence. The same list was reproduced in *Katanga,* above n 10, para 1186; see also *Bemba,* above n 9, para 134.

A variety of additional indices has been discussed in jurisprudence.[16]

These factors are useful and enjoy general support among most commentators and actors involved in conflict classification.[17] At the same time, the existence of clear sets of indicators bears the risk of taking these factors as an easy-to-use *de facto* definition of what constitutes a non-state party to a NIAC, without inquiring further into why these factors are required, which ones are really pertinent, and in what different ways they can be met in practice. For example, reading the factors only in light of early ICTY jurisprudence risks interpreting them with only one type of armed groups in mind, namely those existing in the Former Yugoslavia.[18] When examining conflicts in different geographical regions, increasingly fractured insurgencies, armed groups operating in different states' territories, or cyber armed groups, the factors do provide guidance. However, in order not to misinterpret them, to be able to grasp the broader picture behind the indicative factors, and to apply this broader picture to varying contexts, it is important to understand the factors' origins and rationale.

This chapter proposes to take a step back from the indicative factors and to recall how the organization criterion developed in IHL. The chapter further inquires into the question of which broader legal requirements derive from IHL treaties and what the rationale behind the organization criterion is. Based on this analysis, the present piece identifies three broad but strict criteria that any party to an armed conflict needs to fulfil. Instead of dismissing the indicative factors developed in jurisprudence, however, this chapter builds on some of the factors and shows how they can be used to prove the three identified criteria. The resulting understanding of what it means to be party to a NIAC provides the basis for analysing more complex cases, such as horizontally structured armed groups, coalitions of armed groups, or groups operating transnationally.

1.2.1 A Glance at the Origins of the Organization Criterion

As public international law in general, the laws of war traditionally applied only to conflicts between states.[19] However, this understanding broadened in the

[16] For good summaries, see Sivakumaran 2012a, b, pp. 170–171; see also Akande 2012, pp. 52–54.

[17] See, for instance, Human Rights Council 2011, para 64; UN Security Council 2014, para 87; ICRC 2016, paras 422–437; Moir 2015, paras 38–39.

[18] When the ICTY developed the first set of indicative factors in the *Haradinaj* case, it analysed non-state forces as examined in the *Tadić* case, the *Celebici* case, or the *Halilovic* case, which where highly organised forces linked to state-like entities.

[19] As, for example, the eminent Italian jurist Gentili emphasised in 1648, warring parties that are not sovereign states "are not properly enemies, even although they conduct themselves as soldiers and commanders and meet the attack of commanders of opposing legions. He is an enemy who has a state, a senate, a treasury, united and harmonious citizens, and some basis for a treaty of peace'. Gentili 1589, pp. 24–25. For further discussion, see Rodenhäuser 2018 (forthcoming).

seventeenth and eighteenth centuries. Lawyers such as the Dutch Grotius or the Swiss De Vattel started to rethink the concept of war so as to include conflicts involving non-state forces. In 1758, de Vattel provided a striking explanation for why the laws of nations should apply to "civil war":

> A civil war breaks the bands of society and government, or, at least, suspends their force and effect: it produces in the nation two independent parties, who consider each other as enemies, and acknowledge no common judge. Those two parties, therefore, must necessarily be considered as thenceforward constituting, at least for a time, two separate bodies, two distinct societies. [...] On earth they have no common superior. They stand therefore in precisely the same predicament as two nations, who engage in a contest and, being unable to come to an agreement, have recourse to arms.[20]

In line with these considerations, in state practice the concept of "recognition of belligerency" developed.[21] If a state recognised belligerency, the customary laws of war became applicable between the recognizing state and the recognised non-state belligerent.[22] In the first half of the twentieth century, legal experts identified four necessary criteria for recognition of belligerency by third states: high intensity of violence; the necessity to recognise belligerency; the existence of a *de facto* government administrating parts of the territory; and a high degree of organization among the non-state forces, which had to act under a "responsible authority" or "military discipline" and in accordance with the laws of war.[23] While the first two criteria required a situation that amounted "in fact to a *war*"[24] and had an impact on the interests of the recognising state, the latter two criteria concern the requisite characteristics and capabilities of the non-state belligerent.

In broad terms, these criteria suggest a non-state entity had to show at least three characteristics in order to be recognizable as a belligerent: first, it needed to be a *de facto* government, meaning the non-state belligerent had to operate a civilian administration. Second, as belligerency could only be recognised if there was in fact a "an armed conflict of a general [...] character",[25] non-state belligerents needed to have the capabilities to engage in such a conflict against a state. And third, non-state forces needed to operate under a command and control structure seemingly akin to

[20] Vattel 1758, p. 293.

[21] For example, in some cases the U.S. Supreme Court directly cited de Vattel. See The Brig Amy Warwick; The Schooner Crenshaw; The Barque Hiawatha; The Schooner Brilliante (The United States Supreme Court, 1862), in Scott 1923, p. 1436. For in-depth discussion of relevant state-practice, see Rodenhäuser 2018 (forthcoming).

[22] See Sandoz et al. 1987, para 4345; Sivakumaran 2012a, b, p. 16. If the state recognizing belligerency was a third state, recognition essentially meant that the law of neutrality applied between that state and the belligerents.

[23] The most prominent sets of criteria are those presented by the Institut de Droit International in 1900 and by Lauterpacht in 1947. Institut de Droit International 1900, Article 8; Lauterpacht 2012, p. 176.

[24] Wheaton 1936, p. 30, n 15.

[25] Lauterpacht 2012, p. 176.

that of state armed forces and factually comply with the laws of war.[26] As argued by the American author Beale in 1895, these elements could simply be summarised as requiring "on the part of insurgents an organization purporting to have the characteristics of a state, though not yet recognized as such".[27] At the same time, at least the latter two of the three elements, namely that a belligerent needed to have military and disciplinary structures, are also found in contemporary interpretations of what constitutes a non-state party to a conflict. As shall be seen next, they cannot purely be justified by requiring a "state-like" entity but have an underlying rationale in IHL.

1.2.2 A Party to an Armed Conflict Not of an International Character

While the concept of recognition of belligerency arguably continues to exist, under contemporary treaty and customary IHL two thresholds are of primary importance to determine whether or not a non-state armed group is sufficiently organised to become party to a NIAC and subject to specific legal regimes.[28] The first one is based on Article 3 common to the four Geneva Conventions (Common Article 3) and customary IHL, the second one is found in Article 1(1) of Additional Protocol II.[29] This chapter will focus on the threshold based on Common Article 3 and customary IHL, first because this threshold is not explicitly defined in treaty law, and second because this lower threshold is of paramount practical importance. Once it is met, IHL of NIAC, including customary IHL, applies, and certain violations of this body of law are prosecutable as war crimes.

The chapeau of Common Article 3 states that "[i]n the case of armed conflict not of an international character [...] each Party to the conflict" shall be bound to apply certain minimum norms. It does not define the notion "Party to the conflict". Commentators agree that the ordinary meaning of the notion "Party to the conflict" intrinsically suggests a "modicum of organisation".[30] In order to identify which elements define this "modicum" of organisation, the notion "Party to the conflict" needs to be interpreted in light of its context and its object and purpose.[31]

---

[26] If these requirements were not met, violence was sometimes referred to as "insurgency" or "rebellion", which did not make the laws of war applicable. For some discussion on these concepts, see Moir 2002, p. 4.

[27] Beale 1896, p. 407.

[28] There has been debate on whether a third threshold exists under the ICC Statute, above n 12. See, for example, Meron 2000, p. 260; Kress 2001, p. 118; Sivakumaran 2009, p. 377; Cullen 2014.

[29] Additional Protocol II, above n 12.

[30] Dinstein 2014, para 95. See also ICRC 2011, p. 8; Schmitt 2012, p. 255.

[31] See Article 31(1) of the Vienna Convention on the Law of Treaties, opened for signature 23 May 1969, 1155 UNTS 331 (entered into force 27 January 1980).

Under Common Article 3, a non-state armed group becomes party to an "armed conflict not of an international character". Thus, a contextual interpretation suggests that defining the notion "Party to the conflict" is intimately linked to what constitutes a NIAC. As interpreted by the ICTY and commonly accepted as customary IHL,[32] a NIAC exists

> whenever there is a resort to armed force between States or protracted armed violence between governmental authorities and organized armed groups or between such groups within a State.[33]

In the following sections, it will be argued that interpreting the notion "Party to the conflict" as defined under Common Article 3—or "organized armed group" engaged in "protracted armed violence" and subject to IHL—suggests that any such entity needs to fulfil at least three criteria: it must be a collective entity (Sect. 1.2.2.1) with the ability to engage in sufficiently intense violence (Sect. 1.2.2.2) and to ensure respect for basic norms of IHL (Sect. 1.2.2.3).

1.2.2.1 A Collective Entity

Considering the notions "Party to a conflict" or "organized armed group", the terms "party" or "group" require the existence of a collectivity of persons that are linked for a certain purpose. Requiring a party to a NIAC to form a collective entity is also in accordance with the general understanding that armed conflicts under international law do not signify a relation between individuals but between collective entities.[34] While the prototype party to an armed conflict is the state, it is almost a truism that non-state armed groups "are necessarily always organized differently than State armed forces".[35] Still, one concept that seems to be present in all conflicting parties is leadership. As the notorious rebel leader Mao Tse-tung pointed out, no matter how small or unorganised a guerrilla force might be, the common "quality that makes organisation possible" is leadership.[36] In armed forces, leadership is normally exercised through a command structure.[37] Leadership and some

---

[32] See Bothe 2002, p. 423; Sivakumaran 2012a, b, p. 155; Akande 2012, p. 51.

[33] *Tadić* 1995, above n 1, para 70.

[34] This notion can be traced back to the work of the Genevan philosopher Rousseau, who found already in 1762 that "[w]ar then is a relation, not between man and man, but between State and State, and individuals are enemies only accidentally, not as men, nor even as citizens, but as soldiers". Rousseau 1762, p. 6. For further discussion, see Greenwood 2008, p. 20.

[35] Watkin 2009, p. 374. Social science research has shown numerous ways of how to understand armed groups as such. See, for example, Weinstein 2007; Hoffman 2006.

[36] Tse-tung 1937, Chapter 1. While Mao likely referred also to ideological leadership, the importance of leadership in non-state armed groups is also stressed in more recent analysis. See, for instance, Gunaratna and Oreg 2010, p. 1044; Hashim 2006, p. 156.

[37] What the term "command structure" may mean in organised armed groups is further discussed below and should not be understood narrowly. However, as Dinstein points out: "When divested of any command structure, an armed group will not count as organized." Dinstein 2014, para 132.

kind of command structure distinguish an armed group from loosely connected individuals: Members of armed groups do not operate as independent individuals but conform with rules prevailing in the group and are subject to the command of group leadership.[38]

Social science researchers have suggested a variety of organisational structures of non-state armed groups, or have divided armed groups into certain categories.[39] For the purposes of IHL, armed groups can be broadly considered under two types of command structures: vertical and horizontal ones.[40] In very broad terms, a vertically structured group is one with a hierarchical command and control system as normally found in state armed forces. In contrast, for the purpose of this chapter horizontally structured groups are defined as those that unite different groups or cells under one umbrella or command structure with a more informal and flat hierarchy.[41] These structures and the question of how strong the link between different groups or cells in horizontal groups need to be to qualify the groups as one party to a NIAC will be further discussed in Sect. 1.3.

In practice, a number of factors might testify to the existence of a collective entity with a command structure. For example, internal regulations that define the group's organisational structure, rules, responsibilities, and a chain of command constitute evidence.[42] While tribunals have also placed some emphasis on the existence of headquarters,[43] parties may choose not to have one headquarters owing to the high risk of being attacked, or may choose to have different regional headquarters.[44] Moreover, the idea of headquarters should be understood functionally, including control rooms from where parties command their operations,[45] or places at which members obtain weapons and training.[46] Another frequently assessed indicator is a party's "ability to speak with one voice"—for example by engaging in

[38] See ICTY, *Prosecutor v Duško Tadić,* Judgment, 15 July 1999, Case No. IT-94-1-A (*Tadić* 1999), para 120; see also Dinstein 2014, para 95.

[39] Sinno, for example, categorises armed groups into "centralized, decentralized, networked, patron–client, multiple, and fragmented" ones. Sinno 2011, p. 316. See also Mackinlay 2002, p. 43.

[40] Alternatively, these structures have also been called "pyramidal" and "horizontal" or "hierarchical" and "decentralized". See Sivakumaran 2012a, b, pp. 172–174; Hashim 2006, p. 152.

[41] For more detail, see Rodenhäuser 2018 (forthcoming).

[42] See ICTY, *Prosecutor v Fatmir Limaj, Haradin Bala and Isak Musliu,* Judgment, 30 November 2005, Case No. IT-06-66-T (*Limaj* et al.), para 112; ICC, *Prosecutor v Callixte Mbarushimana,* Decision on the Confirmation of Charges, 16 December 2011, Case No. ICC-01/04-01/10, para 104. For example, Macedonia's National Liberation Army's internal regulations are publicly available. See Sivakumaran 2012a, b, p. 171.

[43] *Boškoski and Tarčulovski,* above n 14, para 199; *Haradinaj* et al. 2008, above n 13, paras 64–65.

[44] See *Limaj* et al., above n 42, para 104. For example, the chairman of the Acheh-Sumatra National Liberation Front, Arif Fadhillah, emphasised this point to the author.

[45] This has been the case, for example, in Libya and Syria. See McQuinn 2012, pp. 41–42.

[46] See, for example, *Katanga,* above n 10, paras 679–681; *Haradinaj* et al. 2008, above n 13, para 65.

political, military, or humanitarian negotiations,[47] or by making public announcements in the name of the party as a whole.[48] Indeed, the ability to engage externally in the name of a collective entity and to implement the results of negotiations testifies to a degree of internal authority and leadership, and it shows external recognition thereof.[49]

While being a collective entity is a rather broad criterion, can be reflected in a number of factors, and may serve different purposes, under IHL any collective entity must have two essential qualities to become party to an armed conflict: it must have the abilities to engage in sufficiently intense armed violence (Sect. 1.2.2.2) and to ensure respect for basic humanitarian norms (Sect. 1.2.2.3).

1.2.2.2 The Ability to Engage in Sufficiently Intense Armed Violence

In addition to being a collective entity with a certain command structure, being party to an armed conflict necessarily requires the ability to engage in sufficiently intense violence. When Common Article 3 was adopted in 1949, the notion of armed conflict was understood as applying to factual circumstances of what was generally understood as "war".[50] While the notion of armed conflict and the question of its requisite intensity have evolved since 1949,[51] with regard to the required degree of organization of a party to a NIAC, the basic concept remains the same: any party to an armed conflict needs to have the capability to bring about, and to engage in, armed violence going beyond "a mere riot or disturbances caused by bandits".[52]

In practice, a number of factors are relevant in this context. First, as military-type violence is not conducted by uncoordinated individuals but according to military tactics and coordination, "a unified military strategy", "operational units [that] coordinate their actions", or "the effective dissemination of […] orders and decisions" may testify to the existence of an organisation with military-like capabilities.[53] Second, armed groups must possess sufficient logistics to engage in hostilities, including manpower and weapons. The type and quantity of logistics cannot be determined in the abstract. What is decisive is that they enable the group

[47] See *Boškoski and Tarčulovski,* above n 14, para 203.

[48] See *Haradinaj* et al. 2008, above n 13, para 88.

[49] See *Limaj* et al., above n 42, para 125; ICTY, *Prosecutor v Vlastimir Đorđević,* Judgment, 23 February 2011, Case No. IT-05-87/1-T, para 1576.

[50] Based on its observations at the 1949 Conference, the ICRC commented: "Speaking generally, it must be recognized that the conflicts referred to in Article 3 are armed conflicts, with armed forces on either side engaged in hostilities – conflicts, in short, which are in many respects similar to an international war." Pictet 1958, p. 36.

[51] See ICRC 2016, paras 431–437.

[52] Federal Political Department (Switzerland) 1949, p. 129. This idea is also found in Article 1(2) Additional Protocol II, above n 12, as well as in Articles (2)I and (e) ICC Statute, above n 12.

[53] See *Boškoski and Tarčulovski,* above n 14, para 200.

to engage in sufficiently intense hostilities.[54] Third, the group must be able to conduct operations that contribute to an escalation of violence between the parties. While this can be achieved through "large scale military operations",[55] this ability depends to some extent on the conflict dynamics. Concretely, it seems that an armed group needs more sophisticated operational and logistical capabilities to escalate armed violence if confronted with powerful state security forces than what is required to trigger an armed conflict against a state with weak law-enforcement or armed forces. Last but not least, territorial control may testify to the group's capacity to militarily contest its adversary. Yet, territorial control is not a strict requirement to qualify an armed group as a party to a NIAC.[56]

1.2.2.3 Ability to Ensure Respect for Basic Humanitarian Norms

Common Article 3 sets out that "each Party to the conflict shall be bound to apply" certain basic rules of IHL. Indeed, determining the existence of a NIAC under Common Article 3 or customary IHL means that each party to the conflict—state or non-state in nature—is bound by the applicable IHL provisions. The underlying concept that all parties have equal obligations under IHL suggests that each party needs to have the capacity to apply IHL, meaning the ability to ensure respect for the law among its forces. While a recent commentary on Common Article 3 concluded that "there seems to be a general consensus that [...] [the required level of organisation] would enable the parties to carry out the obligations imposed by Common Article 3,"[57] as seen in the introductory section this requirement seems to split judges at international tribunals and is also disputed among scholars.[58]

At least three reasons corroborate the view that the ability to ensure respect for basic humanitarian norms is an inherent requirement for any party to a NIAC.

[54] For example, because of a general shortage of weapons, fighters of the Kosovo Liberation Army received weapons such as hunting rifles from the population. See *Limaj* et al., above n 42, para 122. Similarly, at the beginning of their struggle, the Forces de résistance patriotique en Ituri were only equipped with traditional hunting weapons. See *Katanga,* above n 10, para 530. In many cases, weapons are also obtained locally, in particular through raiding the opponent's stocks. Reportedly, advances on military targets supplied armed groups in Syria with more weapons than had been previously available. See Human Rights Council 2012b, Annex III, para 14.

[55] *Boškoski and Tarčulovski,* above n 14, para 200.

[56] See, for example, *Lubanga Dyilo,* above n 9, paras 536–537; *Katanga,* above n 10, para 1186.

[57] Moir 2015, para 36.

[58] For a view looking primarily at a group's ability to engage in armed violence, see *Lubanga Dyilo*, above n 9, para 536; *Bemba*, above n 9, para 134. For a view also requiring the ability to ensure respect for IHL, see *Katanga*, above n 10, para 1185. For diverging views in ICTY judgments, compare, for example, *Haradinaj* et al. 2008, above n 13, para 60 to *Boškoski and Tarčulovski*, above n 14, para 196. Views favoring a focus on primarily the capabilities to engage in armed violence are also found in UN reports. See, for example, Human Rights Council 2011, para 57; Human Rights Council 2012b, Annex III.

First, the expectation that non-state parties to NIACs have the capacity to ensure respect for the law has been expressed in various IHL instruments traditionally linked to the concept of a "person responsible for his subordinates",[59] a "responsible authority",[60] or a "responsible command".[61] The obligation to ensure respect for IHL among its troops is a customary obligation for any party to an armed conflict.[62] Second, IHL is the body of law applicable in the exceptional circumstance of armed conflict and exists to set out a legal framework under which a party to a conflict is permitted to operate while expecting similar conduct by other parties.[63] If one party to a NIAC is absolutely unable to implement any rules, this logic would be defied. Third, the laws of war do not only restrict certain conduct but have, arguably, also certain permissive aspects. Concretely, it is argued that IHL recognises an "inherent power to intern" certain persons,[64] and that IHL contains less restrictive rules on the use of force than human rights law requires in times of peace. If the object and purpose of IHL is to protect victims of armed conflict, permissive aspects of IHL should not become applicable if the conflicting parties cannot also comply with elementary restrictions IHL imposes, including on internment or the use of force. Against this background, it has been pointed out correctly that "[o]rganization for the purposes of the enforcement of the law is equally as important as, indeed even more important than, organization for the purposes of the intensity of the violence".[65]

This requirement raises at least two questions: first, what capacities are required from an armed group to ensure respect for IHL in general; and second, what capacity must non-state entities have to implement the obligations listed in Common Article 3 or customary IHL? In this chapter, only the first question can be examined.[66] Suffice it to recall that for the purpose of conflict classification, IHL does not require that a party to a NIAC is able to implement all applicable norms.[67]

A group's ability to ensure respect for fundamental humanitarian norms is largely dependent on the level of discipline within the group. Behaviour studies show that structures to ensure respect for internal rules, including IHL, depend on three factors: clear rules; training and orders; and effective sanctions.[68] Similarly,

---

[59] Article 1 of the Regulations concerning the Laws and Customs of War on Land, Annex to Hague Convention (IV) respecting the Laws and Customs of War on Land, opened for signature 18 October 1907, 187 CTS 227 (entered into force 26 January 1910).

[60] Lauterpacht 2012, p. 176.

[61] Article 1 Additional Protocol II, above n 12.

[62] See Rule 139 of the ICRC Customary IHL Study, in Henckaerts and Doswald-Beck 2005.

[63] ICRC 2003, p. 232.

[64] ICRC 2014, p. 7.

[65] Sivakumaran 2012a, b, p. 179.

[66] For in depth discussion of the second question, see Rodenhäuser 2018 (forthcoming).

[67] For example, no tribunal requires an armed group to have the capacity to conduct fair trials in order to become party to a NIAC. What IHL requires, however, is that any party has the capacity to refrain from certain conduct unless it is also able to implement the corresponding limitations. See also Draper 1965, p. 91; Sivakumaran 2012a, b, p. 186.

[68] See Munoz-Rojas and Fresard 2004.

notorious rebel leaders have stressed that guerrillas must internalise the rules of the group, and if "discipline is violated, it is necessary always to punish the offender, whatever his rank, and to punish him drastically in a way that hurts".[69] Discipline not only enables a group to implement internal rules including IHL, but "lack of discipline among the rank and file wastes resources, alienates potential supporters, and may undermine military efforts".[70] Thus, if a group is to function effectively, it needs to ensure some degree of internal discipline.

Analysing whether a group has the capacity to comply with basic IHL norms is not a question of examining specific structures designed for implementing IHL, such as a classical military command and control systems. Instead, the requirement needs to be understood in a wider sense, meaning that a group needs to have the capacity to implement any kind of internal rules. If a group has sufficient structures to require its members to respect a simple code of conduct, or if the group operates under strict unwritten rules, this should be sufficient proof for its ability to also implement basic IHL. Concretely, if a group's code of conduct prescribes attacking members of the group's own constituency, it could similarly include rules prohibiting attacks against civilians. Likewise, it does not take sophisticated structures to absolutely prohibit torture. There is no objective reason why a basic set of rules applicable and respected within a group could not contain fundamental IHL norms. As it is well known, however, for the purpose of conflict classification it is not required that parties to the conflict actually comply with IHL.[71]

Against this background, international tribunals have listed "the existence of internal regulations and whether these are effectively disseminated to members", "proper training", and "the establishment of disciplinary rules and mechanisms" as indicators of a group's ability to respect IHL.[72] In vertically structured groups, discipline is normally enforced through a hierarchical model: the group's leadership issues rules and orders and the hierarchical structure ensures that they are followed and enforced throughout the group.[73] In contrast, in armed groups with a "cellular structure [...] commands cannot be given centrally to the whole group".[74] Even in such groups, however, leadership "must, as a minimum, have the ability to *exercise some control* over its members so that the basic obligations [...] may be implemented".[75] In practice, this could mean that central leadership issues general rules and orders that all parts of the group follow, but their implementation and the

---

[69] Guevara 1961, p. 153; see further quotes from Mao Tse-tung and Guevara in Weinstein 2007, p. 30.

[70] Ibid., p. 43.

[71] See *Boškoski and Tarčulovski,* above n 14, paras 204–205.

[72] See, for example, ibid., para 202.

[73] For example, at the height of the armed conflict in Kosovo, the KLA's disciplinary system included different measures taken at different hierarchical levels of the group, such as subjecting soldiers to "an oral reprimand, a written critique, a short-term detention sentence, or a referral to the General Staff and to the Military Court". *Đorđević,* above n 49, para 1575.

[74] See ICRC 1971, p. 17.

[75] *Haradinaj* et al. 2012, above n 14, para 393 (emphasis added).

imposition of discipline is ensured by the different subgroups according to their own methods.[76]

To sum up, while Common Article 3 does not provide a definition of what constitutes a party to a NIAC, interpreting the notion "Party to the conflict" in accordance with established rules of treaty interpretation enables to identify three criteria that every party to a NIAC has to fulfil. Under IHL, a party to a NIAC needs to be a collective entity with sufficient capabilities to engage in hostilities and the capacity to ensure respect for fundamental norms of IHL. In order to analyse whether these criteria are fulfilled, a variety of factors—including those identified in international criminal law—can provide useful indications. However, assessing the structures and capacities of different armed groups needs to take the group's operational context and cultural background into account. The criteria identifying a "Party to the conflict" are best understood in a functional sense, focusing strictly on what is necessary to become party to an armed conflict as understood in IHL.

1.3 Uniting Multiple Armed Groups into One Party to a NIAC

Identifying a sufficiently organised party to a NIAC is particularly challenging if violence does not break out between pre-existing groups but develops in a decentralised manner—for example, as a result of mass protest. History shows that "all guerrilla bands that spring from the masses of the people suffer from lack of organization at the time of their formation".[77] Recent examples of such situations include the escalation of protests into armed conflicts in Libya and Syria in 2011–2012. For instance, almost one year into the Syria crisis, a UN Commission of Inquiry (CoI) found itself "unable to verify that the Free Syrian Army (FSA), local groups identifying themselves as such or other anti-Government armed groups had reached the necessary level of organization" in order to determine the applicability of IHL.[78] The CoI pointed out that while a number of armed groups identified themselves with the FSA, this did not mean that the "group has been recognized by the FSA leadership or obeys the command of the FSA leadership abroad".[79] Similarly, while an early UN CoI report on Libya could be read as suggesting that opposition forces were united under the "National Libyan Army" banner,[80] the CoI

[76] For discussion on how armed groups' disciplinary systems operate in practice, see Sivakumaran 2012a, b, pp. 1146–1148.

[77] Tse-tung 1937, Chapter I. See also Dinstein 2014, para 131.

[78] Human Rights Council 2012a, para 13.

[79] Ibid. Stated differently, a researcher pointed out that "FSA headquarters does not appear to exercise command over the autonomous groups that fight in its name; however, many of the most important groups who are fighting the regime acknowledge the FSA's leadership, inasmuch as they are able to do so". Holliday 2012, p. 17.

[80] Human Rights Council 2012c, paras 56–57.

later clarified that the "Libyan National Army neither coordinated nor led the military struggle against Qadhafi forces".[81]

To be clear, classifying a situation of violence involving different non-state armed groups as a NIAC does not require all actors to be united under one structure. A NIAC exists as soon as violence between two sufficiently organised parties meets the intensity threshold. This means that if a number of distinct non-state armed groups challenge state forces, the bilateral relationships between the state and each non-state group need to be examined to determine whether or not a NIAC exists.[82] However, as it was the case with the FSA or the "National Libyan Army", in practice different armed groups might also unite under a joint military or political structure. For the purpose of IHL, in such situations the key question is at what point a joint group, or umbrella group, consisting of different subgroups is sufficiently organised to form one party to a NIAC. This question is particularly relevant if different organised armed groups are present on a state's territory but have not (yet) engaged in violence with an adversary that is sufficiently intense to qualify their bilateral relation as a NIAC.

Nothing in IHL suggests that an organised armed group uniting different subgroups needs to meet different criteria than any other party to a NIAC. Thus, in line with the above analysis, three criteria need to be met: the umbrella group has to be a collective entity able to engage in sufficiently intense violence and to ensure respect for basic IHL. For the sake of the present analysis, it is assumed that every subgroup is itself a collective entity able to engage in armed violence and to ensure respect for basic humanitarian norms. If different such groups unite, they will be able to engage in intense violence, and each group's disciplinary system will continue to operate. Consequently, the key issue to examine is what kind of link needs to exist between these groups in order to consider them as one collective entity operating under one command structure, with the ability to ensure respect for basic humanitarian norms within the group as a whole.

A clear case would be if the different groups merge into one vertically-structured armed group with one hierarchical command and control system.[83] If this is not the case, the question of which other links between subgroups could classify these groups as one party to a NIAC arises. IHL treaty law applicable in NIAC does not provide an answer. Yet, two concepts existing in IHL applicable in international armed conflicts might be instructive to answering this question.[84] The first one is the "belonging test" as interpreted in the 1960 ICRC Commentary to the Third Geneva Convention (1960 ICRC Commentary) to determine whether a non-state

[81] Ibid., Annex I, para 66.

[82] For a more detailed examination of how IHL would apply in such situations and how it could also apply to armed elements not identified as a sufficiently organised armed group, see Dörmann and Rodenhäuser 2017.

[83] Allegedly, this has been the case with the "Seleka" coalition in the Central African Republic, which shortly after its formation apparently operated under "a clear hierarchical military command structure". ICC—The Office of the Prosecutor 2014, para 65.

[84] For a discussion of other possible approaches, see Radin 2013, pp. 723–734.

militia belongs to a party to an international armed conflict so that its members can be considered prisoners of war.[85] The second one draws on the "overall control test", meaning a test analysing the requisite degree of control a state needs to exercise over an armed group in order to consider the state and the group one party to an armed conflict.

1.3.1 The "Belonging Test"

It has been argued that in a situation in which different armed groups each constitute "a body having a military structure" that is "commanded by a 'person responsible for his subordinates'", the decisive link to form one party to a NIAC would be that "they must '*belong to*' a party to the conflict".[86] Based on how the term "belonging to a Party to the conflict" has been understood in the context of determining prisoner of war status under Article 4(A)(2) of the Third Geneva Convention,[87] this approach proposes a rather loose link if the 1960 ICRC Commentary is followed. Accordingly, in order to form one party to a NIAC, a "de facto relationship" between the entities would suffice, which "may find expression merely by tacit agreement, if the operations are such as to indicate clearly for which side the resistance organization is fighting".[88] In addition, the "belonging test" would also be met if an "official declaration" by the party to the conflict would be "confirmed by official recognition by the High Command" of the individual armed group.[89]

For the purpose of determining the requisite link between different armed groups in order to form one party to a conflict, the "belonging test" appears to be rather loose. As shall be seen below, international jurisprudence requires more than a *de facto* relationship that could express itself in fighting a common enemy. Likewise, the threshold that different groups form one party based on a declared affiliation might be too low. Such a declared affiliation would need to be corroborated by operational and strategic collaboration. It is widely accepted that sharing "a common ideology"[90] or "[m]ere 'acting toward a collective goal' against the Government is not enough […] some leadership is essential".[91] This suggests that any declared coalition based on political or ideological grounds would need to translate into establishing some form of a joint command structure in order to

---

[85] de Preux 1960.

[86] Melzer 2014, p. 314 (emphasis added).

[87] Geneva Convention (III) relative to the Treatment of Prisoners of War, opened for signature 12 August 1949, 75 UNTS 135 (entered into force 21 October 1950).

[88] de Preux 1960, p. 57. This is the test suggested by Melzer. See Melzer 2014, pp. 314–315.

[89] de Preux 1960, p. 57.

[90] ICRC 2011. This position is also accepted by the US, which explains that in its fight against Al Qaida and "associated forces" a "group that simply embraces al-Qa'ida's ideology is not an 'associated force'". U.S. Department of Defense 2015.

[91] Dinstein 2014, para 95; see also Arimatsu and Choudhury 2014, p. 41.

qualify as a party to a NIAC. This point is further developed in the following section.

1.3.2 The "Control Test"

A narrower interpretation of when an armed group can be considered as "belonging" to a party to an international armed conflict is the "overall control" test suggested by the ICTY Appeals Chamber.[92] The question of whether or not the "overall control" test is the right one to determine that an armed group belongs to a state continues to be subject to debate.[93] Moreover, the "overall control" test was developed in the context of either attribution of acts to a state for the purpose of state responsibility, or to determine whether an armed group belongs to a state and thereby forms part of a party to an international armed conflict. While the question of whether one armed group belongs to another armed group for the purposes of conflict classification is obviously related, hardly any relevant documents or practice exist on this question. Thus, the test cannot, *ipso facto*, be assumed to apply to the circumstances at stake in the present analysis.[94] Still, as shall be seen below, the idea underlying the "overall control" test has some merit for examining when two or more armed groups constitute one party to a NIAC.

In the *Tadić* judgment, the ICTY Appeals Chamber emphasised that, under international law, the action of an organised armed group can be attributed to "a State (or, in the context of an armed conflict, the Party to the conflict)" if the party to which the acts shall be attributed "*has a role in organising, coordinating or planning the military actions* of the military group, in addition to financing, training and equipping or providing operational support to that group".[95] It is not necessary that the controlling entity issues "specific orders", or provides "direction of each individual operation".[96] Conceptually, the situation of uniting different armed

---

[92] *Tadić* 1999, above n 38, paras 88–123. The purpose of this chapter does not necessitate an engagement with the continuing discussion on whether the ICTY's "overall control" or the ICJ's "effective control" constitute the correct test for determining state responsibility for acts committed by armed groups. While the ICJ dismissed the overall control test with regard to state responsibility, it left open whether it serves its purpose with regard to conflict classification. See ICJ, *Case Concerning Application of the Convention on the Prevention and Punishment of the Crime of Genocide (Bosnia and Herzegovina v Serbia and Montenegro)*, Judgment, 26 February 2007, [2007] ICJ Rep 43, para 404.

[93] For a recent concise summary of discussion on this issue, see ICRC 2016, paras 265–273.

[94] Note, in this context, that it is not clear whether the control criterion, as found in Article 7 of the Draft articles on the responsibility of international organisations, for the attribution of acts to international organizations, is to be interpreted similar as the control criterion for attributing acts to states. See International Law Commission 2011, pp. 19–26. For some discussion, see Palchetti 2013.

[95] *Tadić* 1999, above n 38, para 137 (emphasis in original).

[96] Ibid.

groups under the banner of one party to a NIAC is not too different.[97] Both with regard to the Kosovo Liberation Army (KLA) in the former Yugoslavia and the FSA in Syria, at one point the key question was whether different subgroups formed part of one of these umbrella organizations.[98] Following the "overall control" test as expressed by the ICTY Appeals Chamber, independently-formed groups could be considered one party to an armed conflict if an authority within that united party to the conflict—be it an individual or a command council consisting of members from different groups—is involved in organizing and coordinating the different groups' military operations, and provides some material support.

ICTY and ICC jurisprudence seem to have developed this approach further without explicitly referring to the overall control test. With regard to the KLA, the ICTY found that at the very early stages of the conflict, when KLA-affiliated groups consisted mostly of "spontaneous and rudimentary military organization[s] at the village level", the "initial phases of a centralized command structure above the various village commands" were crucial for the KLA to qualify "as an 'organized armed group' under the *Tadić* test".[99] The Chamber emphasised particularly the "*de facto* authority" consolidated by a "popular commander" called Haradinaj, who coordinated some activities of different village defence groups.[100] In addition, the KLA smuggled a significant number of weapons into Kosovo, or facilitated the smuggling by different village organisations.[101] To the extent possible, KLA "professionals" also provided military training for "KLA soldiers" in different villages.[102] In other case law, the ICTY explained that the leadership's ability to coordinate the operations of groups claiming to be part of it, to divide territory into operation zones, and to organise assistance when one group comes under attack testifies to a degree of organisation required to be a party to a conflict.[103] A centralised command structure does not need to be able to command each military operation, or have a functioning reporting system.[104]

---

[97] For example, referring to Article 7 of the International Law Commission Draft articles on the responsibility of international organizations, it has been suggested that determining whether an international organisation or individual states are parties to a multinational armed conflict would depend on whether the multinational organisation exercises "overall control" over the forces on the ground. See Ferraro 2013, pp. 590–592.

[98] See, for example, *Haradinaj* et al. 2012, above n 14, paras 18–22; Holliday 2012, pp. 14–16.

[99] *Haradinaj* et al. 2008, above n 13, para 89.

[100] Ibid., paras 67 and 89.

[101] Ibid., paras 89 and 76–82.

[102] Ibid., paras 89 and 86.

[103] See *Limaj* et al., above n 42, paras 95 and 108; *Haradinaj* et al. 2012, above n 14, paras 407 and 409; ICTY, *Prosecutor v Slobodan Milošević,* Decision on Motion for Judgment of Acquittal, 16 June 2004, Case No. IT-02-54-T, paras 24–25.

[104] Even if armed groups aim to introduce command and reporting structures, implementation can be challenging if means of communication are limited. See *Haradinaj* et al. 2008, above n 13, paras 63; 78–84; *Limaj* et al., above n 42, para 105.

In the *Katanga* case, the ICC followed a comparable approach with regard to the "Ngiti militia", also known as the "Forces de Résistance Patriotique d'Ituri" (FRPI) active in the "Walendu-Bindi *collectivité*" in Ituri, Democratic Republic of the Congo. The Chamber had to determine whether the different militias that "were spread among several camps placed under the authority of various commanders" constituted one "organized armed group".[105] The Chamber answered the question affirmatively, explaining vaguely that "various means of communication and weapons and ammunition were available to them" and its members "pursued common objectives and conducted joint military operations for a protracted period".[106] However, when assessing the group's organisational structure in more detail, the Chamber emphasised the role played by the "president" of the movement, called Katanga.[107] The Chamber could not establish "beyond reasonable doubt" that Katanga "was vested [...] with effective hierarchical power over all the commanders and combatants of the Ngiti militia".[108] However, in order to classify the FRPI as an "organized armed group", the Chamber relied on Katanga's "role as coordinator" that "testifies to the real military authority he wielded" over the other commanders in the group.[109] This authority was underlined by Katanga's role in facilitating "the receipt and storage of weapons and ammunition" and his power to allot them to the sub-groups.[110]

While the "overall control test" as originally stated in the *Tadić* case emphasises a state's role in organising, coordinating or planning the military actions of a non-state group as well as a degree of material support, in order to determine whether or not different armed groups form one party to an armed conflict, more recent jurisprudence appears to require a slightly higher threshold. In order to find a sufficient link between different groups to turn them into one collective entity, there needs to be a uniting element that has been described as "initial phases of a centralized command" exercising some authority beyond the mere coordination of subgroups.[111] Likewise, interpreting the "overall control" test under IHL, in the ICRC's view "[t]he notion of overall control does not [...] refer simply to monitoring or checking, but also requires the exercise of some form of authority over the

---

105 *Katanga,* above n 10, para 1209.

106 Ibid.

107 Ibid., paras 684 and 1359–1365.

108 Ibid., para 1365.

109 Ibid., paras 1342 and 1343.

110 Ibid., para 1362.

111 An element of "collective coordination [...] as an indicator for the organizational criterion" also received support recently from IHL experts. Arimatsu and Choudhury 2014, p. 40. For example, in Misrata, a number of individuals formed the "Misratan Military Council" (MMC) as the central "military authority" of the opposition in that location, without, however, being able to exercise command-and-control functions. Under the overall coordination of the MMC, brigades active in Misrata set up "control rooms" in which military commanders would coordinate their action and share intelligence. Within the MMC and the control rooms, different commanders participated on a horizontal—not hierarchical—basis. McQuinn 2012, pp. 41–42.

entity in question", meaning that there needs to be a "relationship of subordination" between the controlling entity and the controlled one.[112]

Based on the notion "Party to the conflict" under IHL treaties and in line with recent jurisprudence, it is submitted that a party's leadership—whether in the form of one person or a joint council—need to exercise a degree of both *operational coordination* and *strategic authority*. While operational coordination requires the ability to coordinate military activities and to distribute logistics, strategic authority signifies leadership's *de facto* authority to determine the overall military objectives and the internal rules that all subgroups have to follow. If these two elements are fulfilled, a coalition of armed groups can be considered as one collective entity with a certain command structure, the capability to engage in military violence, and sufficient capacity to ensure respect for basic IHL. Consequently, such a coalition of organised armed groups would also meet the three criteria identified in Sect. 1.3 of this chapter. In contrast, it would be difficult to consider different subgroups as one party to a NIAC if these subgroups openly oppose or contravene the military strategy or code of conduct determined by the party's overall leadership.

1.4 Transnational Armed Groups

At least factually, the geographical scope of NIAC is broadening.[113] This is not the place to participate in the larger debate on the scope of application of IHL.[114] The objective of this section is to focus on one particular aspect of the debate, namely the question of when groups operating in different states but under one "label" might qualify as one party to an armed conflict under IHL. If the position is taken that IHL applies without territorial limitations and to all acts and actors sufficiently linked to an armed conflict, finding that different subgroups are sufficiently connected to form one party to a NIAC in accordance with IHL could mean that IHL applies with regard to all components of that group, wherever located. In contrast, if IHL is considered to apply primarily on the territory of belligerent states, including to certain spill-over situations, the fact that one group would have different components located in territorially distinct and unconnected places would not necessarily render IHL applicable to all of them.

While the issue of transnational armed groups had arisen with regard to Al Qaida and the global battlefield discussions in the 2000s, it recently regained momentum regarding the alleged expansion of the group calling itself Islamic State (Islamic State Group, ISG). After conquering territory in Iraq and Syria, ISG leader

[112] Ferraro 2015, p. 1237 and 1234. The ICRC clarifies, however, that "the concept of authority referred to is broader and more general than the issuing of orders, and refers rather to general direction and coordination".

[113] See ICRC 2015, p. 6.

[114] For discussion on this subject, see, for example, Sassòli 2006; Schmitt 2012; Pejic 2015; Schöberl 2015. See also ICRC 2016, para 452–482.

Al-Baghdadi declared in November 2014: "We announce to you the expansion of the Islamic State to new countries, to the countries of the Haramayn [Saudi Arabia], Yemen, Egypt, Libya, Algeria."[115] In early 2015, the ISG also expanded to Afghanistan and Pakistan, referred to as the Islamic State of Khorasan.[116] According to a report on the threat posed by the ISG to international peace and security, the UN Secretary-General found: "[A]s of 15 December 2015, 34 groups from all around the world had reportedly pledged allegiance to ISIL".[117] In the wide network of groups associated with the ISG, relationships between global ISG leadership in Iraq/Syria and affiliated groups can be broadly conceptualised in three categories: First, some affiliated groups reportedly operate under direct command and control of global ISG leadership. Second, different groups have pledged allegiance to the ISG and might receive some financial or ideological support, without, however, being in a tight command and control relationship with global ISG leadership. Third, some groups have committed crimes inspired and motivated by the ISG without any further link.

Different approaches exist to legally conceptualise such conglomerates of groups. For example, in the context of their fight against different non-state armed groups since the 9/11 attacks, the U.S. has authorised detention and the use of force against persons that are "part of or substantially supported al-Qaeda, the Taliban, *or associated forces* that are engaged in hostilities against the United States or its coalition partners".[118] While it could be argued that the idea of "associated forces" refers to armed groups that form part of Al-Qaida, the Taliban, or potentially the ISG, this is not how the U.S. executive and judiciary seem to interpret the notion. As the U.S. administration explained in 2014: "The concept of an 'associated force' is based on the well-established concept of co-belligerency in the laws of war."[119] Consequently, with regard to its fight against Al Qaida, the U.S. administration has required two criteria to define groups as associated forces in a NIAC: a group "must be both (1) an organized, armed group that has entered the fight alongside al-Qa'ida, and (2) a co-belligerent with al-Qa'ida in hostilities against the United States or its coalition partners".[120] A similar concept has also been suggested to apply with regard to the ISG and affiliated groups.[121] It can, however, be questioned

---

115 Reuters (2014) Islamic State leader urges attacks in Saudi Arabia: speech. http://www.reuters.com/article/us-mideast-crisis-baghdadi-idUSKCN0IX1Y120141114. Accessed 30 October 2016.

116 UN Security Council 2016, para 8.

117 Ibid., para 7.

118 Preston 2014 (emphasis added).

119 Ibid. Following a similar line, a U.S. district court considered co-belligerents interpreted "the term 'associated forces' to mean 'co-belligerents' as that term is understood under the law of war". United States District Court for the District of Columbia, *Adel Hamlily* et al. *v Barack Obama* et al., 19 May 2009, Civil Action No. 05-0763 (JDB), p. 16.

120 Preston 2014.

121 See Rupar T (2015) Obama's Request for Congressional Authorization to Fight the Islamic State: Full Text. https://www.washingtonpost.com/news/post-politics/wp/2015/02/11/obamas-request-for-congressional-authorization-to-fight-the-islamic-state-full-text/?utm_term=.28e78049cc72). Accessed 27 December 2016.

whether the concept of co-belligerency can be transposed from IAC to NIAC as a matter of law,[122] or whether there might be more appropriate concepts to draw upon in order to determine when a third party becomes party to an on-going NIAC.[123] For the purpose of this chapter, it suffices to emphasise that the concept of associated forces is different from the question of when different groups merge into one organised armed group. The concept of co-belligerency, and in analogy the idea of "associated forces", looks at independent entities that fight alongside each other against a common enemy without becoming one party to a conflict. Co-belligerents remain different parties to one conflict.[124] The conceptually very different question at stake in this chapter is under what conditions different armed groups, even if operating across borders, can merge into one organised armed group under IHL.

Little state or jurisprudential practice is known that would indicate how states determine a sufficient link between different components of one alleged transnational armed group. Some U.S. scholars have suggested that "unlike traditional 'internal' armed conflicts, 'organization' [of armed groups] is not necessarily a condition precedent to the existence" of transnational armed conflicts.[125] Under this approach, it could be argued that different armed groups constitute one party to a transnational armed conflict without forming one organised armed group as traditionally understood under IHL. Yet, applying such an approach to practice, it has also been recognised that the idea of a global war on terror against the broader Al Qaida network is not "generally representative of a majority of States, international law experts, and international nongovernment organizations with competence in humanitarian law".[126] Indeed, the ICRC has repeatedly emphasised that in its view, any geographical spread of a NIAC "would require, in the first place, the existence of a 'unitary' non-state party opposing one or more States".[127] Likewise, scholars have argued that groups operating in different countries would need to form part of "the same group",[128] meaning "a quasi-military organization would be required, not

[122] For discussion, see Heller 2016.

[123] An alternative to applying the co-belligerency concept in NIAC could be the idea that states or non-state armed groups could become party to NIAC based on the so-called "support-based approach". While this approach was developed to address situations in which, during multinational operations, a state provides support to a party in an on-going NIAC that makes a contribution to the collective conduct of hostilities but does not, in and of itself, render the laws of NIAC applicable between the supporting party and the adversary. This approach could, in certain circumstances, apply, *mutatis mutandis*, to armed groups supporting each other. For the original concept, see Ferraro 2013.

[124] For example, no one would claim that if a state becomes a co-belligerent in an international armed conflict, this state would become part of another state party to that conflict. Each state remains an independent entity and is an independent party to the conflict.

[125] Corn and Jensen 2009, p. 19.

[126] Corn 2015, p. 68.

[127] ICRC 2015, p. 18. Other commentators seem to base their analyses on the same assumption. See, for example, Moir 2015, para 27.

[128] Sivakumaran 2012a, b, p. 233.

a loose 'terrorism franchise'".[129] It has been suggested that this requirement is fulfilled if they were "one and the same, operating within a single command and control structure equally active in the carrying out of the group's military operations".[130]

Absent significant state practice suggesting a different approach, it must be assumed that in order to form one party to a NIAC, a transnational armed group needs to meet the same criteria as any other organised armed group under IHL. As argued above, this means that a transnational armed group needs to meet three criteria: it has to be a collective entity able to engage in sufficiently armed group violence and having the capacity to ensure respect for essential IHL rules. If different organised armed groups unite transnationally, each group maintains its ability to engage in hostilities and to enforce internal discipline. Hence, the key questions are again at what point these subgroups form one collective entity, and how global leadership can ensure respect for applicable law.

1.4.1 Transnational Armed Groups with Hierarchical Command and Control Structures

An armed group could become part of an existing party to a NIAC if it is integrated into the party's command and control structure. Reportedly, at one point a "direct command and control" relationship exist(ed) between the ISG in Libya and the group's "core operation in Iraq and Syria".[131] This link was primarily based on the alleged leader of the Libyan branch called "Zubaidi, who headed Islamic State operations in central Iraq prior to going to Libya".[132] In addition, it is reported that "ISIS deployed a contingent of 300 Libyan ISIS militants from eastern Syria to spearhead the creation of a new ISIS affiliate in Libya in mid-2014".[133] Similar reports exist regarding ISG operations in Yemen.[134] Sending commanders and fighters into another state to head a local subgroup could constitute a sufficient link to determine that the subgroup forms part of the existing party to a NIAC. The crux of the matter would be whether commanders and fighters continue to operate under the sending party's command and control.

[129] Paulus and Vashakmadze 2009, p. 117.

[130] Lubell 2015.

[131] Unspecified U.S. Department of Defence sources, cited in Chesney R (2015) The Global War on ISIL and Its Associated Forces. https://www.lawfareblog.com/global-war-isil-and-its-associated-forces. Accessed 30 October 2016.

[132] Ibid.

[133] Gambhir H (2016) ISIS's Campaign in Libya: January 4–February 19. https://www.criticalthreats.org/analysis/isiss-campaign-in-libya-january-4-february-19-2016. Accessed 30 October 2016.

[134] See Ibid.

Elaborating further, it has been argued that all parts of a transnational armed group need to act under "a centralised military command and a chain of command from top to bottom".[135] While requiring a chain of command akin to those established in modern state armies would set a rather high threshold, military command and control can exist in different forms. In the view of this author, if the subgroup was sufficiently organised—either vertically or horizontally—to qualify as an organised armed group for the purposes of IHL, and its leadership was under command and control of the global leadership, it would not be necessary to prove a traditional chain of command running all the way from global leadership to rank and file in the field. If global leadership exercises *de facto* command and control over a subgroup's leadership, and the subgroup's leadership exercises operational coordination and strategic authority over its units, this should suffice to consider the entire subgroup part of the overall organization.

1.4.2 Transnational Armed Groups Without Traditional Command and Control Structures

Within the broad ISG-network as described by the UN Secretary-General,[136] it cannot be assumed that all ISG-affiliated groups operate under "direct command and control" of the ISG leadership in Iraq/Syria. For example, with regard to subgroups in Afghanistan, the U.S. Department of Defense stated: "We're also not seeing what we consider command and control by [ISIL] elements in Iraq or Syria orchestrating operations here in Afghanistan".[137] Instead, it has been suggested that the ISG operates a franchise system following a model used by Al Qaida in the 2000s, meaning that different existing groups adopt the ISG's name and ideology but continue to operate largely independently.[138] Reportedly, unlike in the Libya case, in other contexts ISG leadership does not send its own commanders and fighters but tries to attract local groups by providing financial support and ideological guidance.[139] Groups such as the Nigerian Boko Haram as well as jihadist groups in South East Asia have pledged allegiance to the ISG but additional

[135] See Ambos and Alkatout 2012, p. 347. Obviously, these authors were unable to find that Al Qaida met this criterion.

[136] See n 111 above.

[137] Pellerin C (2016) Official Says ISIL Contained, Taliban Fracturing in Afghanistan. http://www.defense.gov/News-Article-View/Article/690520/official-says-isil-contained-taliban-fracturing-in-afghanistan. Accessed 30 October 2016.

[138] Scarborough R (2015) Islamic State expands beyond Syria, Iraq as recruits create global network of terror cells. http://www.washingtontimes.com/news/2015/feb/22/islamic-state-expands-beyond-syria-iraq-as-recruit/. Accessed 30 October 2016.

[139] See Jones S (2015) Expanding the Caliphate—ISIS' South Asia Strategy. https://www.foreignaffairs.com/articles/afghanistan/2015-06-11/expanding-caliphate. Accessed 30 October 2016.

operational links remain mostly unknown.[140] Moreover, other groups or individuals in different states identify with the ISG without having any direct contact.[141]

Looking at these different factual scenarios, and building on the above-analysis of what constitutes an organised armed group for the purposes of IHL, it appears that groups operating without any link other than sharing a common ideology are very far from joining an organised armed group under IHL.[142] Thus, groups claiming to operate in the name of the ISG or simply taking inspiration from public ISG messages but committing crimes without being in contact with global ISG leadership cannot be part of the ISG as a party to a NIAC. Moreover, unless the above-discussed "belonging test" is accepted, if one group pledges allegiance to another group, and this allegiance is accepted but no further operational links are created, these groups cannot be considered as one organised armed group under IHL.

The more intriguing cases are located between groups merely pledging allegiance to another group on the one extreme, and groups operating under firm command and control of global leadership on the other extreme. As with regard to groups joining forces in the context of an internal NIAC, in the transnational context the decisive question is which level of control a group's global leadership must exercise over different subgroups in order to consider them one party to a NIAC. It has been suggested that "the level of coordination and participation in each other's operations" constitutes "a partial indicator".[143] Based on the notion "Party to the conflict" under IHL and relevant jurisprudence, it is submitted that coordination, possible participation in each other's operations, or material support are not enough. Instead, in addition to operational military coordination, overall leadership would need to exercise strategic authority over subgroups, meaning that it determines the overarching military strategy as well as core rules.

Looking at how such operational or strategic coordination could operate in practice, Margulies and Sinnot argue that it could consist of two aspects: one, overall leadership should "guide some or all of the alleged affiliate's choice of targets".[144] Here, "[o]ngoing correspondence or exchanges of information about targeting or operations" can indicate the requisite operational coordination.[145] And

[140] See Weiss C (2016) Philippines-based jihadist groups pledge allegiance to the Islamic State. http://www.longwarjournal.org/archives/2016/02/philippines-based-jihadist-groups-pledge-allegiance-to-the-islamic-state.php. Accessed 30 October 2016.

[141] For example, the perpetrators of a mass-killing in the U.S. in November 2015, the "San Bernardino Attack", pledged allegiance to ISIS before the attack. See Schmitt M, Perez-Pena R (2015) F.B.I. Treating San Bernardino Attack as Terrorism Case. http://www.nytimes.com/2015/12/05/us/tashfeen-malik-islamic-state.html?_r=0. Accessed 30 October 2016.

[142] As the U.S. Department of Defense General Council remarked: "A group that simply embraces al-Qa'ida's ideology is not an 'associated force'." U.S. Department of Defense 2015.

[143] Lubell 2015. Regarding the level of control exercised by one group over another, Lubell does not indicate which "test" (overall control, effective control, or another standard?) he would find appropriate. For other suggestions, see also Radin 2013, p. 733.

[144] Margulies and Sinnot 2015, p. 336.

[145] Ibid., at 337.

two, leadership should leverage "money, recruits, training, or expertise" to influence the affiliate's targeting.[146] In addition, in this author's view, military authority would also require the ability to issue key rules applicable to the entire group. This does not mean that subgroups cannot retain certain strategic objectives specific to their local context, or a disciplinary regime and code of conduct in line with their organizational structure and cultural background. Individual strategies or internal rules need, however, be complemented—and in case of conflict superseded—by directions provided by global leadership. In short, the highest level of strategic authority is no longer with the subgroup but with the group's global leadership.

As a result, if it can be shown that a group's global leadership unites different organised armed groups under one broad (targeting) strategy including operational and disciplinary rules, is involved in the coordination of at least the subgroups' major operations, and possibly provides material assistance to the different groups, this alliance of groups could qualify as one party to a NIAC. Such a group would qualify as a collective entity able to ensure respect for basic humanitarian norms, and if the subgroups have the capability to engage in intense armed violence, the joint group would have this capability as well. *A fortiori*, this is the case if global leadership exercised vertical "command and control" over all subgroups. Applying this approach to specific groups necessarily requires a case-by-case analysis of the relationship between each subgroup and the rest of the party. Only following one broad targeting strategy or ideology would not be sufficient. At the same time, an overly narrow focus to identify "state-like" hierarchical structures should also be avoided. Organizations that are constantly threatened by their adversaries tend to vary their structures with certain flexibility and exercise "both top-down and bottom-up planning and operational capabilities".[147] If it cannot be determined that different groups form one organised armed group for the purposes of IHL, they cannot be one party to a NIAC.

1.5 Conclusion

The question of when a collection of individuals or groupings forms one armed group is a complex sociological, political, and also legal question. Different fields of science analyse this question according to different assumptions and analytical frameworks. This chapter has examined the question under a particular IHL angle, namely when non-state groups involved in armed violence are sufficiently organised to become party to a NIAC. It has been shown that criteria characterizing a party to a NIAC under IHL should not be determined in the abstract but depend on the exigencies set out by this field of law. While Common Article 3 does not define

[146] Ibid., at 336.

[147] Hoffman B (2008) The Myth of Grass-Roots Terrorism. https://www.foreignaffairs.com/reviews/review-essay/2008-05-03/myth-grass-roots-terrorism. Accessed 30 October 2016.

what characterises a "Party to the conflict", treaty interpretation suggests that any party to a NIAC needs to fulfil three broad criteria: it needs to be a collective entity with the capability to engage in sufficiently intense violence and able to enforce respect for basic humanitarian norms.

In light of the increasing complexity of today's NIACs, practitioners have cautioned that no strict "definition would be capable of capturing the factual situations that reality throws up".[148] Instead, a certain margin of flexibility in conflict classification is needed. In this respect, it seems reasonable to caution against reading "the modern jurisprudence defining an OAG [organised armed group] as being limited to groups with headquarters, fully functioning logistics, or ironclad discipline".[149] Taking these concerns into consideration, the three cumulative criteria suggested and discussed in this chapter are on the one hand sufficiently broad to apply in different conflict scenarios and to both vertically structured and horizontally structured groups. On the other hand, they are firmly based in IHL and provide a legal framework under which armed groups need to be assessed for the purpose of conflict classification.

In practice, a significant challenge is to prove that even broad criteria are met. While the degree of violence between different actors involved in confrontations is often obvious, it might be less clear whether those involved in violence operate under one command and disciplinary structure. This is particularly the case "where the internal structure of the group is loose, or where a clandestine chain of command is at play".[150] In such situations, practice suggests that the criteria to determine a group's internal organisation—being a collective entity with a certain command structure; capability to engage in hostilities; ability to ensure respect for basic IHL—should be considered together and might not always need to be proved to the same degree.[151] A useful suggestion could be a sliding scale between the group's command structure and ability to implement basic humanitarian norms on the one hand, and its capacity to engage in intense violence on the other hand.

The suggestion of balancing to what extent different criteria need to be proved does not mean to dismiss the organization requirement in general, or the criterion of the group's ability to ensure respect for basic IHL in particular. Instead, what is suggested here is that in exceptional cases a sufficient degree of internal organisation may be inferred primarily from the group's ability to engage in intense armed violence, even if structures enabling the group to implement fundamental

[148] Pejic 2007, p. 85.

[149] Margulies and Sinnot 2015, p. 340.

[150] ICRC 2007, p. 743.

[151] This suggestion is not too far away from Blank and Corn's suggestion of an analysis of the circumstances as a whole, under which an overwhelming intensity of hostilities can offset the organization requirement. See Blank and Corn 2013. In contrast to Blank and Corn, however, the present suggestion does not offset the organization criterion but suggests a practical avenue of how it can be proved. Moreover, it is not the intensity of violence as a whole, factoring in the state's response to acts committed by the armed group, but the groups' ability to engage in intense hostilities, meaning to conduct itself intense military operations, that is decisive.

humanitarian norms cannot be proved to the same extent.[152] The idea is to make the reasonable assumption that a group has a certain command and disciplinary structure if it is able to engage in coordinated and intense military confrontations against an adversary, to recruit and train members, to provide for necessary logistics, and to have structures in place to keep the group united over a certain period of time. In contrast, a situation in which a state decides to apply significant violence against non-state actors that resemble rather a collection of individuals than a group, and that do not have the capability to engage themselves in hostilities and to counter government attacks, can barely meet that threshold.

References

Articles, Books and Other Documents

Akande D (2012) Classification of Armed Conflicts: Relevant Legal Concepts. In: Wilmshurst E (ed) International Law and the Classification of Conflicts. Oxford University Press, Oxford, pp 32–80

Ambos K, Alkatout J (2012) Has "Justice Been Done"? The Legality of Bin Laden's Killing Under International Law. Israel Law Review 45:341–366

Arimatsu L, Choudhury M (2014) The Legal Classification of the Armed Conflicts in Syria, Yemen and Libya. Chatham House, London

Beale J (1896) The Recognition of Cuban Belligerency. Harvard Law Journal 9:406–419

Bianchi A, Naqvi Y (2011) International humanitarian law and terrorism. Hart, Oxford

Blank L, Corn G (2013) Losing the Forest for the Trees: Syria, Law, and the Pragmatics of Conflict Recognition. Vanderbilt Journal of Transnational Law 46:693–746

Bothe M (2002) War Crimes. In: Cassese A, Gaeta PJ (eds) The Rome Statute of the International Criminal Court: A Commentary. Oxford University Press, Oxford, pp 379–425

Corn G (2015) Triggering the Law of Armed Conflict? In: Corn J (ed) The war on terror and the laws of war: a military perspective. Oxford University Press, New York, pp 33–70

Corn G, Jensen E (2009) Transnational Armed Conflict: A "Principled" Approach to the Regulation of Counter-Terror Combat Operations. Israel Law Review 42:1–34

Cullen A (2014) The Characterization of Armed Conflict in the Jurisprudence of the ICC. In: Stahn C (ed) The Law and Practice of the International Criminal Court. Oxford University Press, Oxford, pp 762–777

Dahl AW, Sandbu M (2006) The Threshold of Armed Conflict. Military Law and Law of War Review 45:369–388

de Preux J (1960) Commentary: III Geneva Convention Relative to the Treatment of Prisoners of War. ICRC, Geneva

de Vattel E (1758) The Law of Nations (translation by Chitty J). T & JW Johnson & Co, Philadelphia

Dinstein Y (2014) Non-International Armed Conflicts in International Law. Cambridge University Press, Cambridge

[152] As Bianchi and Naqvi put it, if "the group is able to conduct a campaign of [intense] armed violence", "the lack of organisation on the part of the opposing party loses some of its significance". Bianchi and Naqvi 2011, p. 129.

Dörmann K, Rodenhäuser T (2017) Contemporary Challenges for International Humanitarian Law. Essays in Honour of Djamchid Momtaz. In: Crawford J, Koroma AG, Mahmoudi S, Pellet A (eds) The International Legal Order: Current Needs and Possible Responses. Cambridge University Press, Cambridge, pp 677–699
Draper GIAD (1965) The Geneva Conventions of 1949. Collected Courses of the Hague Academy of International Law, Vol 114. Brill Nijhoff, Leiden
Federal Political Department (Switzerland) (1949) Final Record of the Diplomatic Conference of Geneva of 1949, Vol II-B
Ferraro T (2013) The applicability and application of international humanitarian law to multinational forces. International Review of the Red Cross (95):561–612
Ferraro T (2015) The ICRC's legal position on the notion of armed conflict involving foreign intervention and on determining the IHL applicable to this type of conflict. International Review of the Red Cross (97):1227–1252
Garraway C (2015) Armed Conflicts and Terrorist Organizations. In: van de Herik L, Schrijver N (eds) Counter-terrorism Strategies in a Fragmented International Legal Order: Meeting the Challenges. Cambridge University Press, Cambridge, pp 425–432
Gentili A (1589) De jure belli libri tres. Clarendon Press, Oxford
Guevara C (1961) Guerilla Warfare. Manchester University Press, Manchester
Gunaratna R, Oreg A (2010) Al Qaeda's Organizational Structure and its Evolution. Studies in Conflict & Terrorism 33:1043–1078
Greenwood C (2008) Historical Development and Legal Basis. In: Fleck D, Bothe M (eds) The Handbook of International Humanitarian Law. Oxford University Press, Oxford, pp 1–38
Hashim A (2006) Insurgency and counter-insurgency in Iraq. Hurst, London
Heller K (2016) The use and abuse of analogy in IHL. In: Ohlin J (ed) Theoretical Boundaries of Armed Conflict & Human Rights. Cambridge University Press, Cambridge, pp 192–231
Henckaerts J-M, Doswald-Beck ML (2005) Customary International Humanitarian Law. Cambridge University Press, Cambridge
Hoffman B (2006) Inside terrorism. Columbia University Press, New York
Holliday J (2012) Syria's Armed Opposition. Middle East Security Report 3. Institute for the Study of War, Washington DC
Human Rights Council (2011) Report of the International Commission of Inquiry to investigate all alleged violations of international human rights law in the Libyan Arab Jamahiriya. UN Doc. A/HRC/17/44
Human Rights Council (2012a) Report of the independent international commission of inquiry on the Syrian Arab Republic. UN Doc. A/HRC/19/69
Human Rights Council (2012b) Report of the independent international commission of inquiry on the Syrian Arab Republic. UN Doc. A/HRC/21/50
Human Rights Council (2012c) Report of the International Commission of Inquiry on Libya. UN Doc. A/HRC/19/68
ICC - The Office of the Prosecutor (2014) Situation in the Central African Republic II: Article 53 (1) Report. https://www.icc-cpi.int/iccdocs/otp/Art_53_1_Report_CAR_II_24Sep14.pdf. Accessed 25 June 2017
ICRC (1971) Rules Applicable in Guerrilla Warfare - Paper Submitted to the Conference of Government Experts on the Reaffirmation and Development of International Humanitarian Law Applicable in Armed Conflicts, Geneva
ICRC (2003) International humanitarian law and the challenges of contemporary armed conflicts. www.icrc.org/eng/assets/files/other/ihlcontemp_armedconflicts_final_ang.pdf. Accessed 27 December 2016
ICRC (2007) International humanitarian law and the challenges of contemporary armed conflicts. https://www.icrc.org/eng/assets/files/other/ihl-challenges-30th-international-conference-eng.pdf. Accessed 30 October 2016
ICRC (2011) International humanitarian law and the challenges of contemporary armed conflicts. https://www.icrc.org/eng/resources/documents/report/31-international-conference-ihl-challenges-report-2011-10-31.htm. Accessed 29 June 2017

ICRC (2014) Internment in Armed Conflict: Basic Rules and Challenges. Opinion Paper. https://www.icrc.org/en/document/internment-armed-conflict-basic-rules-and-challenges. Accessed 30 October 2016

ICRC (2015) International humanitarian law and the challenges of contemporary armed conflicts. https://www.icrc.org/en/document/international-humanitarian-law-and-challenges-contemporary-armed-conflicts. Accessed 30 October 2016

ICRC (2016) Commentary on the First Geneva Convention - Convention (I) for the Amelioration of the Condition of the Wounded and Sick in Armed Forces in the Field. Cambridge University Press, Cambridge

Institut de Droit International (1900) Droits et devoirs des Puissances étrangères, au cas de mouvement insurrectionnel, envers les gouvernements établis et reconnus qui sont aux prises avec l'insurrection. http://www.justitiaetpace.org/idiF/resolutionsF/1900_neu_02_fr.pdf. Accessed 25 June 2017

International Law Commission (2011) Draft articles on the responsibility of international organizations, with commentaries. UN Doc. A/66/10

Kress C (2001) War Crimes Committed in Non-International Armed Conflict and the Emerging System of International Criminal Justice. Israel Yearbook on Human Rights 30:103–177

Kress C (2010) Some Reflections on the International Legal Framework Governing Transnational Armed Conflicts. Journal of Conflict and Security Law 15:245–274

Kretzmer D (2009) Rethinking the Application of IHL in Non-International Armed Conflicts. Israel Law Review 42:8–45

Lauterpacht H (2012) Recognition in international law. Cambridge University Press, Cambridge

Lubell N (2015) Transnational Non-International Armed Conflicts. International Institute of Humanitarian Law, XXXVIII Round Table on Current Issues of International Humanitarian Law, San Remo, 3–5 September 2015

Mackinlay J (2002) The Classification of Insurgent Forces. The Adelphi Papers 42(352):41–92

Margulies P, Sinnot M (2015) Crossing Borders to Target Al-Qaeda and Its Affiliates: Defining Networks as Organized Armed Groups in Non-International Armed Conflicts. Yearbook of International Humanitarian Law 16:319–345

McQuinn B (2012) After the Fall: Libya's Evolving Armed Groups. Small Arms Survey. Graduate Institute of International and Development Studies, Geneva

Melzer N (2014) The Principle of Distinction between Civilians and Combatants. In: Clapham A, Gaeta P (eds) The Oxford Handbook of International Law in Armed Conflict. Oxford University Press, Oxford, pp 296–331

Meron T (2000) The Humanization of Humanitarian Law. American Journal of International Law 94:239–278

Moir L (2002) The Law of Internal Armed Conflict. Cambridge University Press, Cambridge

Moir L (2015) The Concept of Non-International Armed Conflict. In: Clapham A, Gaeta P, Sassòli M (eds) The 1949 Geneva Conventions: A Commentary. Oxford University Press, Oxford, pp 391–414

Munoz-Rojas D, Fresard JJ (2004) The roots of behaviour in war: Understanding and preventing IHL violations. International Review of the Red Cross 86:189–206

Palchetti P (2013) The allocation of responsibility for internationally wrongful acts committed in the course of multinational operations. International Review of the Red Cross 98:727–742

Paulus A, Vashakmadze M (2009) Asymmetrical war and the notion of armed conflict – a tentative conceptualization. International Review of the Red Cross 91:95–125

Pejic J (2015) Extraterritorial targeting by means of armed drones: Some legal implications. International Review of the Red Cross 96:67–106

Pejic J (2007) Status of Armed Conflicts. In: Wilmshurst E (ed) Perspectives on the ICRC Study on Customary International Humanitarian Law. Cambridge University Press, Cambridge, pp 77–100

Pictet JS (1958) Geneva Convention (IV) relative to the protection of civilian persons in time of war: Commentary. ICRC, Geneva

Preston SW (2014) The Framework Under U.S. Law for Current Military Operations. http://www.foreign.senate.gov/imo/media/doc/Preston_Testimony.pdf. Accessed 8 January 2017
Radin S (2013) Global Armed Conflict? The Threshold of Extraterritorial Non-International Armed Conflicts. International Law Studies 13:696–743
Rodenhäuser T (2018) Organizing Rebellion: Non-State Armed Groups under International Humanitarian Law, Human Rights Law, and International Criminal Law. Oxford University Press, Oxford (forthcoming)
Rodenhäuser T, Giacca G (2016) The international humanitarian law framework for humanitarian relief during armed conflicts and complex emergencies. In: Breau S, Samuel K (eds) Research Handbook on Disasters and International Law. Edward Elgar Publishing, Cheltenham, pp 132–152
Rousseau J-J (1762) Du contrat social. Dover Publications, New York
Sandoz Y, Swinarski C, Zimmermann B (eds) (1987) Commentary on the additional protocols of 8 June 1977 to the Geneva Conventions of 12 August 1949. Martinus Nijhoff Publishers and ICRC, Geneva
Sassòli M (2006) Transnational Armed Groups under International Humanitarian Law. HPCR Occasional Paper Series 6
Schmitt MN (2012) Classification of Cyber Conflict. Journal of Conflict & Security Law 17:245–260
Schöberl K (2015) The Geographical Scope of Application of the Conventions. In: Clapham A, Gaeta P, Sassòli M (eds) The 1949 Geneva Conventions: A Commentary. Oxford University Press, Oxford, pp 68–83
Scott JB (1923) Prize cases decided in the United State Supreme Court. Clarendon Press, Oxford
Sinno AH (2011) Armed groups' organizational structure and their strategic options. International Review of the Red Cross 93:311–332
Sivakumaran S (2009) Identifying An Armed Conflict Not Of An International Character. In: Sluiter G, Stahn C (eds) The Emerging Practice of the International Criminal Court. Brill Academic Publishers, Leiden, pp 361–380
Sivakumaran S (2012a) The Law of Non-International Armed Conflict. Oxford University Press, Oxford
Sivakumaran S (2012b) Command Responsibility in Irregular Groups. Journal of International Criminal Justice 10:1129–1150
Tse-tung M (1937) Mao Tse-tung On Guerrilla Warfare. U.S. Marine Corps, Washington DC
UN Security Council (2014) The International Commission of Inquiry on the Central African Republic - Final Report. UN Doc. S/2014/928
UN Security Council (2016) Report of the Secretary-General on the threat posed by ISIL (Da'esh) to international peace and security and the range of United Nations efforts in support of Member States in countering the threat. UN Doc. S/2016/92
U.S. Department of Defense (2015) Remarks by the General Counsel of the Department of Defense on the Legal Framework for the United States' Use of Military Force Since 9/11. http://www.defense.gov/News/Speeches/Speech-View/Article/606662. Accessed 30 October 2016
Watkin K (2009) Opportunity Lost: Organized Armed Groups and the ICRC Direct Participation in Hostilities Interpretive Guidance. New York University Journal of International Law and Politics 42:641–695
Weinstein JM (2007) Inside rebellion: the politics of insurgent violence. Cambridge University Press, Cambridge
Wheaton H (1936) Elements of International Law. Clarendon Press, Oxford

Case Law

ICC, *Prosecutor v Callixte Mbarushimana,* Decision on the Confirmation of Charges, 16 December 2011, Case No. ICC-01/04-01/10

ICC, *Prosecutor v Jean-Pierre Bemba Gombo,* Judgment, 21 March 2016, Case No. ICC-01/05-01/08-3343

ICC, *Prosecutor v Germain Katanga,* Judgment, 7 March 2014, Case No. ICC-01/04-01/07-3436

ICC, *Prosecutor v Thomas Lubanga Dyilo,* Judgment, 14 March 2012, Case No. ICC-01/04-01/06-2842

ICJ, *Case Concerning Application of the Convention on the Prevention and Punishment of the Crime of Genocide (Bosnia and Herzegovina v Serbia and Montenegro),* Judgment, 26 February 2007, [2007] ICJ Rep 43

ICTY, *Prosecutor v Duško Tadić a/k/a "Dule",* Decision on the defence motion for interlocutory appeal on jurisdiction, 2 October 1995, Case No. IT-94-1-AR72

ICTY, *Prosecutor v Duško Tadić,* Judgment, 15 July 1999, Case No. IT-94-1-A

ICTY, *Prosecutor v Ljube Boškoski and Johan Tarčulovski,* Judgment, 10 July 2008, Case No. IT-04-82-T

ICTY, *Prosecutor v Fatmir Limaj, Haradin Bala and Isak Musliu,* Judgment, 30 November 2005, Case No. IT-03-66-T

ICTY, *Prosecutor v Ramush Haradinaj, Idriz Balaj and Lahi Brahimaj,* Judgment, 3 April 2008, Case No. IT-04-84-T

ICTY, *Prosecutor v Ramush Haradinaj, Idriz Balaj and Lahi Brahimaj,* Retrial Judgment, 29 November 2012, Case No. IT-04-84bis-T

ICTY, *Prosecutor v Slobodan Milošević,* Decision on Motion for Judgment of Acquittal, 16 June 2004, Case No. IT-02-54-T

ICTY, *Prosecutor v Vlastimir Đorđević,* Judgment, 23 February 2011, Case No. IT-05-87/1-T

United States District Court for the District of Columbia, *Adel Hamlily et al. v Barack Obama et al.,* 19 May 2009, Civil Action No. 05-0763 (JDB)

Treaties

Geneva Convention (III) relative to the Treatment of Prisoners of War, opened for signature 12 August 1949, 75 UNTS 135 (entered into force 21 October 1950)

Protocol Additional to the Geneva Conventions of 12 August 1949, and relating to the Protection of Victims of Non-International Armed Conflicts, opened for signature 8 June 1977, 1125 UNTS 609 (entered into force 7 December 1978)

Regulations concerning the Laws and Customs of War on Land, Annex to Hague Convention (IV) respecting the Laws and Customs of War on Land, opened for signature 18 October 1907, 187 CTS 227 (entered into force 26 January 1910)

Rome Statute of the International Criminal Court, opened for signature 17 July 1998, 2187 UNTS 90 (entered into force 1 July 2002)

Vienna Convention on the Law of Treaties, opened for signature 23 May 1969, 1155 UNTS 331 (entered into force 27 January 1980)

Chapter 2
Welcome on Board: Improving Respect for International Humanitarian Law Through the Engagement of Armed Non-State Actors

Annyssa Bellal

Abstract Contemporary armed conflicts are characterised by an increase of violence against civilians and a lack of compliance with international humanitarian law (IHL) by both states and armed non-state actors (ANSAs). The international community has acknowledged the importance of engaging ANSAs on compliance with international norms to any effort to improve the protection of civilians in armed conflict, despite the fact that it is, in some contexts, actively discouraged or even prohibited by states. This chapter aims at identifying the key elements as well as the challenges underlying the humanitarian engagement of armed non-state actors. It will argue that meaningful engagement, that is engagement that also takes on board the views, perceptions and conceptions of international norms by ANSAs calls for a much more sustained effort from the part of the international community. These efforts include the need of more systematic research on the facts and scale in which ANSAs allegedly violate IHL, more inquiry in their actual practice and their impact on the development of international norms, a clarification on the applicable legal framework as well as a more thorough reflection on means to establish a coherent and just system of accountability in case of violations.

Keywords Armed non-state actors · Humanitarian engagement · Counter-terrorism · Peace mediation · International humanitarian law · International human rights law · Accountability · Responsibility

---

Annyssa Bellal (Ph.D., Graduate Institute of International Studies and Development) is the Strategic Adviser on International Humanitarian Law and Research Fellow at the Geneva Academy of International Humanitarian Law and Human Rights (annyssa.bellal@graduateinstitute.ch). She was formerly legal adviser at Geneva Call.

A. Bellal (✉)
Geneva Academy of International Humanitarian Law and Human Rights, Geneva, Switzerland
e-mail: annyssa.bellal@graduateinstitute.ch

T.D. Gill et al. (eds.), *Yearbook of International Humanitarian Law 2016*, Yearbook of International Humanitarian Law 19,
https://doi.org/10.1007/978-94-6265-213-2_2

Contents

2.1 Introduction

According to the Oxford Dictionary, to "engage" means a variety of things. The first definition to appear in the list of the respectable online dictionary is to "*involve someone into*", but "engaging with" also means to "*establish a meaningful contact or connection with*" someone or something.[1] These definitions seem to give a sense of an exchange and to comprise both an element of offer and acceptance of someone's views or role.

"Engaging" armed non-state actors[2] (ANSAs) to improve respect for international humanitarian law (IHL) thus means, according to these definitions, involving them into the discussions on IHL and engaging *with* them would imply establishing a meaningful contact in order to exchange on IHL matters. In a system still dominated by the preservation and regulation of states' interests and in which ANSAs are usually considered at a minimum as a disrupting force and at a maximum as a dangerous and lethal one, it is not surprising that any sort of engagement with these actors is received with suspicion by states and part of the international community.

Engagement with a wide range of ANSAs will raise similar questions of security and access for humanitarian organisations. In many cases, ANSAs will find incentives in such engagement by, for instance, political recognition or access to basic resources for their group or constituency. But conducting dialogue with ANSAs also comes with a specific set of challenges. The complexity of

[1] English Oxford Living Dictionary (2016) "Engage". https://en.oxforddictionaries.com/definition/engage. Accessed 2 May 2017.

[2] In the context of this chapter, ANSAs should be understood as covering armed actors operating "primarily within state borders, engaged in violent attempts to challenge or reform the balance and structure of political and economic power, to avenge past injustices and/or to defend or control resources, territory or institutions for the benefit of a particular ethnic or social group". Conciliation Resources 2005.

contemporary armed conflicts and the sheer multiplicity and diversity of ANSAs involved in violent contexts make it more difficult to elaborate on the means to practically engage with them on peace building or humanitarian issues and encourage us to be wary of oversimplification or standard approaches.

The lack of clarity of the legal framework, especially with regard to the controversy over the applicability of human rights law to ANSAs is also problematic for humanitarian organisations, which need to frame their action on legal standards. Encouraging an ANSA to respect human rights law obligations might indeed prove problematic for field operations, especially if the implementation of the norms requires some form of capacity building.

Finally, counterterrorism policies present a further obstacle for the engagement of ANSAs. Since September 11 (11 September 2001), states have adopted a variety of counterterrorism legislations, listing some groups as "terrorist" and imposing sanctions, including on those who provide "material support" to these groups. This notion has been interpreted quite broadly in some cases, including for instance trainings in IHL for ANSAs that have been listed as terrorist organisations. This has impacted humanitarian organisations and reduced their scope of action.

This chapter will reflect on the recent practice and challenges that have arisen with regard to the engagement of ANSAs by different organisations. It will argue that meaningful engagement, that is an engagement that also *takes on board* the views, perceptions and conceptions of international norms by ANSAs calls for a much more sustained effort from the part of the international community. These efforts include the need of more systematic research on the facts and scale in which ANSA allegedly violate IHL, more inquiry in their actual practice and their impact on the development of international norms, a clarification on the applicable legal framework as well as a more thorough reflection on means to establish a coherent and just system of accountability in case of violations.

2.2 Engaging ANSAs

2.2.1 Mapping IHL Violations Committed by ANSAs

The majority of contemporary armed conflicts are fought between states and ANSAs or between ANSAs.[3] Therefore armed groups are pivotal actors in the implementation of IHL norms by which they are bound.[4] It is clear that both states

[3] According to the War Report 2016, 36 of 48 contemporary armed conflicts occurring in the world are "non-international" in character, i.e. are situations regulated by IHL, in which protracted armed violence takes place between states and organised ANSAs or between ANSAs. See Bellal 2017a, b.

[4] While the precise legal means by which ANSA are bound by IHL have been debated, state practice, international case law, and scholarship have confirmed that Common Article 3 of the 1949 Geneva Conventions, Protocol Additional to the Geneva Conventions of 12 August 1949,

and ANSAs violate IHL, but it remains rather difficult to know with more precision which norms are violated by ANSAs and in what scale. To my knowledge, no precise figures seem to exist for instance with regard to certain IHL norms like the prohibition of forced displacement of the civilian population or the impediment of humanitarian access committed by ANSAs in recent conflicts, except for the few case by case reports issued by NGOs, as we will see below. It is true that reporting on both states and ANSAs on IHL and human rights violations is a difficult exercise, especially during an actual conflict. Security issues, lack of access to certain zones, or the fear of victims to testify explain in part these difficulties.

It is however essential to better research and more systematically map violations committed by ANSAs, especially because many of them will tend to argue that they are not the ones to violate IHL, but that the violations are committed by the opposite enemy forces. Approaching ANSAs with approximation and factual generalisation is a too easy way out for them to claim they are not responsible. Being more precise on the types of violations allegedly committed also allows starting a discussion with the armed group on certain IHL norms. For example, in August 2015, Amnesty International (AI) issued a report which uncovered a wave of forced displacement and home demolitions allegedly carried out by the Autonomous Administration led by the Syrian Kurdish political party Partiya Yekîtiya Demokrat (PYD) controlling the area and which could amount to war crimes.[5] This in turn provoked a reaction from the General Command of PYD who released a detailed statement responding to AI's report.[6] The report and the discussion it sparked then allowed other organisations, which were already engaging the group, to further discuss this matter with them.

In recent years, commissions of inquiry and fact-finding missions have been able to address more frequently violations of IHL and human rights committed by ANSAs. For instance, the mandate of the Office of the UN High Commissioner for

and relating to the Protection of Victims of Non-International Armed Conflicts, opened for signature 8 June 1977, 1125 UNTS 609 (entered into force 7 December 1978) (AP II) and customary international humanitarian law apply to ANSAs that are party to non-international armed conflicts. For example, in 2004, the Appeals Chamber of the Sierra Leone Special Court simply held that "it is well settled that all parties to an armed conflict, whether states or non-state actors, are bound by international humanitarian law, even though only states may become parties to international treaties." SCSL, *Prosecutor v Sam Hinga Norman*, Decision on Preliminary Motion Based on Lack of Jurisdiction (Child Recruitment), 31 May 2004, Case No. SCSL-2004-14-AR72(E), para 22; for the different theories on the applicability of IHL to ANSAs, see Sivakumaran 2006 and Kleffner 2009; Furthermore, the customary international humanitarian law study conducted by the ICRC has identified 161 Rules of which a great majority are also applicable in non-international armed conflicts. The rules are available on the ICRC website, www.icrc.org/customary-ihl/eng/docs/v1_rul. Accessed 4 July 2017.

[5] Amnesty International (2015) Syria: US ally's razing villages amounts to war crimes. https://www.amnesty.org/en/latest/news/2015/10/syria-us-allys-razing-of-villages-amounts-to-war-crimes/. Accessed 2 May 2017.

[6] ANF News (2015) YPG General Command: Amnesty International report is contradictory. https://anfenglish.com/kurdistan/ypg-general-command-amnesty-international-report-is-contradictory-12971. Accessed 2 May 2017.

Human Rights (OHCHR)'s investigation in Sri Lanka expressly included the examination of "alleged serious violations and abuses of human rights and related crimes by both parties in Sri Lanka during the last phase of the armed conflict."[7] The Independent International Commission of Inquiry on the Syrian Arab Republic has, since 2012, also systematically reported on the violations of international law committed by ANSAs,[8] as have other OHCHR fact-finding missions in Mali[9] and the Central African Republic.[10]

Commissions of inquiry and fact-finding missions can therefore be useful tools for mapping IHL violations during a particular conflict. That said one should also keep in mind that these mechanisms often operate with tight time constraints and can focus only on a narrow scope of events and facts. Another limitation of such bodies lies in the multiplicity of existing ANSAs in some conflict situations, such as in Libya, the Democratic Republic of the Congo, and Syria. As a consequence, it can prove difficult for these mechanisms to address all the violations committed by all the actors at a given time, leaving many violations unaccounted for.

Truth commissions have also been useful in addressing violations committed by ANSAs. These can be described as officially sanctioned, temporary, non-judicial investigative bodies, whose tasks usually include collecting statements from victims, witnesses, and perpetrators; researching and investigating the root causes of an armed conflict; holding public hearings; engaging in outreach programs; and issuing a final report that summarises the commission's findings and recommendations.[11] Some truth commissions have been able to denounce violations of IHL and human rights committed by ANSAs.[12]

Truth commissions present good conditions for reporting on violations: the support of former parties, easy access to places and people, and their aim of reconciliation rather than retribution.[13] Because they have a wide margin for also including the voices of ANSAs, not only as individuals who have violated international law but also in certain circumstances as victims, especially when they are

---

[7] UN General Assembly 2014.

[8] The different reports of the Independent Commission on Syria can be found at: www.ohchr.org/EN/HRBodies/HRC/IICISyria/Pages/Documentation.aspx. Accessed 2 May 2017.

[9] See United Nations General Assembly 2013a.

[10] See United Nations General Assembly 2013b.

[11] OHCHR 2006, p. 1 and pp. 17–20.

[12] For instance, Liberia's Truth and Reconciliation Commission determined that: "all armed groups whether affiliated with warring factions or with the Government of Liberia are responsible for the commission of human rights violations including violations of international humanitarian law, international human rights law, war crimes and egregious domestic laws violations of Liberia. These groups include: NPFL, LURD, Liberia Peace Council, Militia, ULIMO, MODEL, Armed Forces of Liberia, ULIMO-K, ULIMO-J, Antiterrorist Unit, ECO MOG, Vigilantes, Lofa Defense Force, Liberia National Police, Special Operation Division, Revolutionary United Front (RUF), Special Anti-Terrorist Unit, Special (SATU) Security Unit, Special Security Service, Black Beret, National Security Agency, National Bureau of Investigation, Criminal Investigation Division, and Kamajors". Republic of Liberia Truth and Reconciliation Commission 2009, p. 336.

[13] Bangerter 2011a, p. 356.

former child soldiers,[14] truth commissions can be particularly useful where armed groups are concerned. In addition, as truth commissions are non-judicial tools that often take a comprehensive approach to establishing facts and understanding the root causes of and circumstances surrounding a given conflict, they may be less threatening to ANSAs than strict criminal justice mechanisms. Many armed groups believe indeed, rightly or not, that national or international criminal law processes are biased against them. As a matter of fact, ANSAs are aware that many if not the majority of the International Criminal Court (ICC) cases deal with individual members of ANSAs.

While it is true that the development of international criminal law has made an important contribution to the fight against impunity and provided for reparations to some victims of international crimes committed by members of ANSAs, international and national criminal law, focusing only on the individual criminal responsibility of the members of ANSAs, fails to address in its entirety the often complex dynamic between individuals and the armed groups to which they belong. At the very least, it seems justified to hold a group itself responsible from a moral point of view, as it may be condoning, justifying and even inciting an individual to commit crimes. Indeed, "organized armed groups regularly succeed to create a climate in which crimes are perceived to be in conformity with, rather than a deviation from, standards of behaviour accepted within such a group".[15] To illustrate this point, one might recall the words of Dominic Ongwen, a former leader of the Lord's Resistance Army (LRA) and former child soldier who is currently being tried at the ICC for multiple war crimes. In an impassioned speech, he told to the court: "I am not the LRA […] It is the LRA who abducted people, in northern Uganda. It is the LRA who killed people."[16]

Outside the framework of international criminal law, there is also a need to reflect more thoroughly on the establishment of the responsibility of ANSAs, in particular with regard to the norms pertaining to the "attribution" of violations to the armed groups.[17] This seems to be of particular importance when several ANSAs are operating in the same region, as is the case for instance in Syria, Iraq and Turkey. While a certain practice already exists in this regard, notably through the work of commissions of inquiry, more attention should be given to how violations of the

[14] See in that regard Parmar et al. 2010.

[15] Kleffner 2009, p. 246. See also the ICTY in the Tadić case: "Although only some members of the group may physically perpetrate the criminal act (murder, extermination, wanton destruction of cities, towns or villages, etc.), the participation and contribution of the other members of the group is often vital in facilitating the commission of the offence in question. It follows that the moral gravity of such participation is often no less or indeed no different from that of those actually carrying out the acts in question". ICTY, *Prosecutor v Duško Tadić*, Judgment, 15 July 1999, Case No. IT-94-1-A, p. 191.

[16] The Guardian (2016) Ex-child soldier Dominic Ongwen denies war crimes at ICC trial. https://www.theguardian.com/world/2016/dec/06/dominic-ongwen-the-hague-trial-war-crimes-lra-uganda. Accessed 7 June 2017.

[17] Bellal 2015.

norms are linked to the different ANSAs concerned. As was rightly noted by Kleffner, the absence of clear rules of accountability is contrary to an international order based on the rule of law, which include principles such as legal certainty, avoidance of arbitrariness and procedural and legal transparency.[18]

2.2.2 Understanding the Causes of the Violations

Why any norms, international or not, are violated in a given society has to do with many factors, sociological or political. It is possible however to summarise the reasons for lack of compliance of IHL by ANSAs according to six main factors.

There are first strategic military concerns. It is sometimes argued that the nature of warfare in non-international armed conflicts may lead to the use of tactics that violate international law, such as launching attacks from within the civilian population.[19] The imbalance between a state's security forces (in size, weaponry, and financial resources) and the actions or even mere existence of an ANSA may also be used as a reason for not respecting certain norms in practice. As the UN Secretary-General (UNSG) has pointed out:

> [A]rmed groups have often sought to overcome their military inferiority by employing strategies that flagrantly violate international law. These range from deliberate attacks against civilians, including sexual violence, to attacks on civilian objects such as schools, to abduction, forced recruitment and using civilians to shield military objectives. The risks for civilians are further increased as militarily superior parties, in fighting an enemy that is often difficult to identify, respond with means and methods of warfare that may violate the principles of distinction and proportionality, giving rise to further civilian casualties.[20]

This argument though works both ways in the sense that some states will also use this excuse to violate IHL.

A second factor is the likelihood of prosecution under domestic legislation for having taken up arms against the state, wholly irrespective of the ANSA's respect for international legal norms. Thus, whereas combatants in an international armed conflict are entitled to prisoner of war status, thereby receiving immunity from prosecution for having participated in hostilities, a fighter from an ANSA is not normally recognised as a combatant under IHL and faces prosecution for having taken up arms under the national law of the state that captures him or her.[21] In some

[18] Kleffner 2009, p. 259.

[19] See for example Geiss 2006.

[20] UN Security Council 2010, para 8.

[21] See, *inter alia*, Articles 4 and 118 of the Geneva Convention relative to the Treatment of Prisoners of War, opened for signature 12 August 1949, 75 UNTS 135 (entered into force 21 October 1950) (Geneva Convention III). Quite exceptionally prisoner of war (POW) status can be accorded to members of ANSAs implicated in conflicts falling into the scope of application of Article 1, para 4 of the Protocol Additional to the Geneva Conventions of 12 August 1949, and relating to the Protection of Victims of International Armed Conflicts, opened for signature 12

instances governments have offered amnesties to those who have taken up arms against them, and indeed this is encouraged under Article 6 of Additional Protocol II to the Geneva Conventions.[22]

The third factor possibly leading to violations of IHL is that ANSAs may also simply lack knowledge of some IHL norms. While states have a clear obligation to provide instruction in international humanitarian law to their armed forces,[23] members of ANSAs may have little or no training in IHL, thus significantly impeding efforts to increase respect for IHL.[24] They may not know of (let alone agree with) norms prohibiting the recruitment of children as soldiers, or the outlawing of certain weapons, for instance. Concepts familiar to military lawyers or IHL specialists, such as the principle of proportionality in the conduct of hostilities, may also not be well understood by members of ANSAs, both at senior and at lower operational levels.

Fourth, even though certain ANSAs may know of applicable law, ideology, whether political or religious, may lead to their deliberately violating IHL. Jihadist ANSAs, like the Islamic State and Al Qaeda and their affiliates could fall within this category, but they are not the only ones. ANSAs as diverse as the LRA in Uganda or the RUF (Revolutionary United Front) in Sierra Leone have, to a certain extent, used strategies terrorising the population for tactical reasons.[25] But even with these types of ANSAs, some form of humanitarian engagement is feasible in specific circumstances, for example through indirect means such as using the positive influence of the ANSAs' close constituencies.[26]

Structural differences and lack of capacity are the fifth factor that can also explain, to a certain extent, the difficulties for ANSAs to respect certain IHL norms. The growing convergence between IHL applicable in international armed conflict to non-international armed conflicts and the influence of human rights law on IHL has only worsened the problem.[27]

December 1977, 1125 UNTS 3 (entered into force 7 December 1979) (API). An ANSA can also recognise the applicability of the Geneva Conventions and API by making a declaration under Article 96(3) API. Only the Polisario Front regarding its conflict with Morocco over Western Sahara has so far successfully lodged such a unilateral declaration on 20 June 2015. See the analysis by Fortin K (2015) Unilateral Declaration by Polisario under API accepted by Swiss Federal Council. https://armedgroups-internationallaw.org/2015/09/02/unilateral-declaration-by-polisario-under-api-accepted-by-swiss-federal-council/. Accessed 2 May 2017.

[22] According to Article 6(5) AP II: "At the end of hostilities, the authorities in power shall endeavour to grant the broadest possible amnesty to persons who have participated in the armed conflict, or those deprived of their liberty for reasons related to the armed conflict, whether they are interned or detained.".

[23] See, for example, Articles 47, 48, 127, and 144 of the Geneva Convention relative to the Protection of Civilian Persons in Time of War, opened for signature 12 August 1949, 75 UNTS 287 (entered into force 21 October 1950) (Geneva Convention IV) and Article 83 API.

[24] ICRC 2008, p. 12.

[25] See Bangerter 2011b, pp. 353–384.

[26] See Bellal 2016a.

[27] See Sassòli 2011.

No categorisation of ANSAs is broadly accepted, in terms of structure and ideology, but it is possible to roughly describe the different types of ANSAs in the following terms:[28]

- partially recognised states or quasi-states;
- armed opposition groups seek the liberation of a social class or a nation and oppose the state or its administration;
- paramilitary groups or militias are irregular combat units that usually act on behalf of, or are at least tolerated by, a governing regime;
- ANSA that spread panic and fear in societies in order to achieve political goals ("so-called terrorist groups");
- vigilante or self-defence groups that are usually composed of armed civilians acting in self-defence, whose degree of organisation varies and is often loose. Such groups do not necessarily have a political purpose (such as replacing the existing government) but rather aim to defend themselves against the attacks of enemy armed forces or other ANSAs.
- Territorial gangs do not have political aims per se but try to gain control of a territory in order to oversee criminal activities or "protect" residents in the area concerned.[29]

Quite evidently, "partially recognised or quasi-states" will not encounter the same structural problems in implementing IHL, as other types of ANSAs. For example, ANSAs organised as "networks", which are likely to be characterised by 'cell-like' structures, with varying degrees of connectedness between the cells, will tend to operate in a clandestine manner.[30] As such, these types of ANSAs may have difficulties to implement IHL norms on detention, such as to allow for example visits of detainees to ensure they are well treated, because they precisely do not want to disclose their location to external actors.[31] Self-defence groups are also problematic in terms of compliance with international law. These types of ANSAs can be defined as a form of militia composed of individuals, who gather themselves collectively for the purpose of defending themselves or others against armed violence committed by generally another ANSA. An example of such type of group can be the "Anti-Balaka", which was formed during the conflict in the Central African Republic in 2013.[32] Self-defence groups are usually more loosely

[28] The list classifies ANSAs in terms of their operational rationale and does not pretend to include scientific definitions. It should also be kept in mind that any particular group may present characteristics associated with several categories or may shift from one category to another.

[29] See Homequist 2005, p. 46; Schneckener 2006, p. 25; Sinno 2011, pp. 311–332.

[30] Whitfield 2010, p. 6; a typical example of an ANSA organised in a cell-like structure is the Jemaah Islamiya (JA) which is active in South East Asia. Haer 2015, pp. 49–50.

[31] See Tuck 2011.

[32] See on this Bellal 2014.

organised. In these contexts, despite high level of violence, the applicability of IHL will be unclear.[33] In addition, these types of ANSAs blur the line between fighters and civilians, putting at risk the principle of distinction, as their members will easily slide from one status to another.[34]

Finally, ANSAs may feel they lack "ownership" over international norms, i.e. lack the capacity and willingness to set, and take responsibility for the respect of IHL. Indeed, ANSAs are not entitled to ratify the relevant international treaties, and are generally precluded from participating as full members of a treaty drafting body. Thus, they sometimes argue that they should not be bound to respect rules that they have neither put forward nor formally adhered to.[35] This argument has been criticised by Bangerter for whom

> the idea that armed groups have an issue with IHL because they have not contributed to its formulation and cannot ratify it seems wrong if we consider their discourse [...] For instance, the FARC have often held such a stance but at the same time have stated—sometimes in the same documents—that they incorporate into their own rules (and therefore accept) basic notions of IHL.[36]

It is true that ANSAs do not frequently invoke the lack of ownership over IHL in case of violations, but rather deny they are responsible for them. However involving armed groups in some form of law-making remains important. This can be done for instance by encouraging them to draft their own codes of conduct or to collect their views through interviews.[37] Indeed, it is not uncommon that ANSAs argue that they either have a different understanding and interpretation of international norms or that they lack the capacity of implementing them. In that sense, reflecting on the practice and views of ANSAs is not altogether deprived of a certain level of normativity. ANSAs might feel bound by the norms that they have agreed upon rather than by international treaties or international customary norms, the elaboration of which they have not participated in, and these norms emerging from their own practice might have a higher chance of being implemented.

---

[33] According to case law (see notably, ICTY, *Prosecutor v Duško Tadić*, Decision on the Defence Motion for Interlocutory Appeal on Jurisdiction, 2 October 1995, Case No. IT-94-1-A, para 70), two conditions determine the occurrence of a non-international armed conflict: protracted violence, and the level of organisation of the ANSA involved. In the IHL context, "protracted violence" implies that armed violence is intense as well as enduring, notwithstanding the ordinary meaning of these words. See Sivakumaran 2012.

[34] See on that the very interesting report by the International Crisis Group on the Central African Republic. International Crisis Group 2015.

[35] See, among others, Sivakumaran 2006, pp. 369–394; de Beco 2005, pp. 190–199; Zegveld 2002.

[36] Bangerter 2011a, b.

[37] See the very interesting study from Geneva Call titled "In their words: Perceptions of armed non-state actors on humanitarian action", Jackson 2016.

2.2.3 *Identifying the Incentives*[38]

It is often wondered what are the interests or incentives for ANSA to respect IHL. There are in fact a number of reasons or factors supporting compliance with the law such as the need for popular support ("winning hearts and minds"); the self-image of the group; the group's own internal beliefs; reciprocity; projecting a good national or international image; and family ties with the population. Generally, however, the primary incentive that might lead to engagement is the group's own *self-interest*. This has military, political, legal, and humanitarian aspects.

The military arguments comprise both an element of reciprocity and strategic choices: respect for norms by one party to the conflict may encourage respect for norms by the other. Conversely, abuses and violations committed by one party are normally met with a similar response from the other party. Furthermore, an ANSA that treats captured soldiers with humanity encourages soldiers to surrender. This might prove less "costly" for the group as mistreatment or summary executions are more likely to lead to soldiers fighting to the death. Thus, ANSAs may come to understand that certain means and methods of warfare are counterproductive or have excessive humanitarian costs.

The political arguments for compliance centre on the desire of many ANSAs to be recognised, along with their cause, as legitimate. In certain cases, ANSAs may even wish to be seen as more respectful of international norms than the state against which they are fighting.[39] In addition, many ANSAs need the support (e.g. human, material, and financial) of the "constituency" on behalf of whom they claim to be fighting:

> Armed groups may perceive compliance with international legal norms as enhancing their credibility and their own perceived legitimacy with internal or external audiences, including their own diasporas.[40]

Fear of prosecution for international crimes is another factor that influences the behaviour of certain ANSAs or of senior individuals who know they might be held accountable under international criminal law under the principle of command responsibility within that group. For instance, the condemnation in February 2017 by a Swedish court to a life sentence a member of a Syrian armed group for the

---

[38] This section is based on a research conducted at the Geneva Academy of International Humanitarian Law and Human Rights, which included interviews with ANSAs. The study notably analysed and commented on the best practice of humanitarian organisations on ANSA engagement. See Bellal and Casey-Maslen 2011.

[39] For example, many ANSAs that have signed the Geneva Call's Deed of Commitment whereby they renounce the use of anti-personnel mines have done so in States not party to the Convention on the Prohibition of the Use, Stockpiling, Production and Transfer of Anti-Personnel Mines and on their Destruction, opened for signature 18 September 1997, 2056 UNTS 241 (entry into force 1 March 1999) (Anti-Personnel Mine Ban Convention), such as India, Iran, Myanmar, and Somalia.

[40] McHugh and Bessler 2006, p. 40.

execution of seven detainees pushed other armed groups to request being trained and have more information on international criminal law.[41]

Finally, certain ANSAs also have a fundamental desire to respect human dignity. Such a desire should not be underestimated—certain ANSAs may genuinely desire to behave "in a humanitarian way". According to a recent Geneva Call study on the perceptions of ANSAs on humanitarian action, many ANSAs view themselves as being responsible for the fate of the civilian population under their control as exemplified by this statement of a Karen National Union (KNU) representative in the context of the conflict in Myanmar: "Although I don't know all the rules, I do think we should take part and fulfil our responsibilities".[42]

2.2.4 Existing Practice

It has been long recognised by humanitarian actors that engaging ANSAs on compliance with international norms is a critical element in any effort to strengthen the protection of civilians and improve respect for IHL. By "engagement" is meant efforts to enhance compliance with international norms by ANSAs through a variety of direct or indirect means, especially awareness raising, dissemination, persuasion, technical support/capacity-building, negotiation, dialogue, and advocacy.

The International Committee of the Red Cross (ICRC), since its early days in the nineteenth century, has regularly engaged with ANSAs as a means of building respect for IHL and humanitarian action as these actors are believed to have

> great influence on what happens to people affected by these situations, and their members can also become victims of the hostilities due to injury or capture. The ICRC therefore strives to maintain and strengthen dialogue with them in order to ensure that they are aware of their obligations.[43]

The legal basis for engagement can be found in Common Article 3, para 2 of the 1949 Geneva Conventions, which states that:

> An impartial humanitarian body, such as the International Committee of the Red Cross, may offer its services to the Parties to the conflict. The Parties to the conflict should further endeavour to bring into force, by means of special agreements, all or part of the other provisions of the present Convention. The application of the preceding provisions shall not affect the legal status of the Parties to the conflict.

---

[41] The Local (2017) Swedish court hands life sentence to Syrian for war crimes. https://www.thelocal.se/20170216/swedish-court-hands-life-sentence-to-syrian-for-war-crimes. Accessed 2 May 2017. This example is drawn from my own experience.

[42] Jackson 2016, p. 22.

[43] ICRC (2010) Building respect for humanitarian action and IHL among "other" weapon bearers. https://www.icrc.org/eng/what-we-do/building-respect-ihl/dialogue-weapon-bearers/other-weapons-bearers/overview-icrc-other-weapon-bearers.htm. Accessed 2 May 2017.

The term "such as" indicates that the organisations that may offer their services to ANSAs as parties to the conflict are not limited to the ICRC, but can be any humanitarian entity, including those linked to states, provided that they are considered to be impartial.[44] In that regard, in his report for the 2016 World Humanitarian Summit, the UN Secretary-General emphasised that

> at a time when most conflicts are non-international, it is critical for impartial humanitarian actors to engage in dialogue with States as well as non-State armed groups to enhance their acceptance, understanding and implementation of obligations under international humanitarian and human rights law.[45]

Practice shows that those engaging with ANSAs can be states, international and humanitarian organisations, NGOs, members of the constituency from which an ANSA draws its support, former fighters from other ANSAs, as well as those with political or moral influence over a group. The purpose of engagement can be equally diverse: getting humanitarian access, promoting respect for IHL or striving to achieve or mediating the resolution of a conflict.

States such as Nigeria, South Africa, India, Indonesia, Malaysia, Saudi Arabia, Turkey and Qatar have all played a mediation role with ANSAs in certain countries but their potential link with their own interests in the conflicts have been an issue with the armed groups. Norway and Switzerland, both outside the EU, and perhaps perceived by ANSAs as more impartial and neutral have also been very active in peace negotiations and mediation.[46]

The UN also regularly engages with ANSAs. According to a recent study, at least five different UN organs and agencies have drafted policies or guidelines on engagement with ANSAs (UN Office for the Coordination of Humanitarian Affairs (OCHA), Department for Peacekeeping Operations (DPKO), the UNSG, UNICEF and the UN Refugee Agency (UNHCR)).[47]

Because NGO's are not subject to the same diplomatic constraints and commitments as states and international organisations, it can prove easier for them to engage specifically with ANSAs.[48] Geneva Call for instance is a neutral and impartial non-governmental organisation dedicated "to promoting respect by [ANSAs] for international humanitarian norms in armed conflict and other situations of violence, in particular those related to the protection of civilians".[49]

---

[44] See the 2016 Commentary to Common Article 3, in ICRC (2016) Convention (I) for the Amelioration of the Condition of the Wounded and Sick in Armed Forces in the Field. Geneva, 12 August 1949. Commentary of 2016 – Article 3: Conflicts not of an international character. https://ihl-databases.icrc.org/applic/ihl/ihl.nsf/Comment.xsp?action=openDocument&documentId=59F6CDFA490736C1C1257F7D004BA0EC#_Toc465169934. Accessed 2 May 2017, paras 779, 791, 861.

[45] UN General Assembly 2016, para 51.

[46] See Whitfield 2010, p. 18.

[47] McQuinn and Oliva 2014.

[48] On that, see Schneckener and Hofmann 2015.

[49] See the website of Geneva Call, Geneva Call (2017) Mission. https://genevacall.org. Accessed 8 July 2017.

Another active NGO is the Centre for Humanitarian Dialogue (HD Centre), which mission is to "help prevent, mitigate, and resolve armed conflict through dialogue and mediation", including with ANSAs.[50] Other NGOs need to engage with ANSAs in order to be able to fulfil their humanitarian mission, by for example negotiating humanitarian access, but their mandate is not necessarily specific to ANSAs. This will be the case, for instance, of the Norwegian Refugee Council (NRC).[51]

A variety of mechanisms exist for ANSAs to commit to respecting international norms, such as unilateral declarations, special agreements, memoranda of understanding, "ground rules" (for example the "Ground Rules" agreed between the UN's Operation Lifeline Sudan and SPLM/A leader John Garang in July 1995)[52] or "action plans".

"Unilateral declarations" by which ANSAs pledge to abide by certain international treaties or norms have been made by a number of such actors. A military code of conduct drawn up by the ANSA could also be considered a form of unilateral declaration, when its existence is made known externally. Perhaps the best-known form of unilateral declaration is the "Deed of Commitment" elaborated by Geneva Call. This innovative and particular type of unilateral declaration allows ANSAs to pledge to respect specific humanitarian norms and be held publically accountable for their commitments. Geneva Call has developed three such documents so far: Deed of Commitment for Adherence to a Total Ban on Anti-Personnel Mines and for Cooperation in Mine Action, launched in 2000; Deed of Commitment for the Protection of Children from the Effects of Armed Conflict, launched in 2010; Deed of Commitment for the Prohibition of Sexual Violence in Situations of Armed Conflict and towards the Elimination of Gender Discrimination, launched in 2012. As of writing, 49 ANSAs have signed the Deed of Commitment banning anti-personnel mines, 19 have signed the Deed of Commitment protecting children in armed conflict, and 16 have signed the Deed of Commitment prohibiting sexual violence and gender discrimination.[53]

"Special agreements", by which some or all of the rules of IHL applicable to international armed conflict are to be applied in non-international armed conflicts, were originally perceived as a means by which parties to a non-international conflict could bring into force other provisions of international humanitarian law. The term is also now used to refer more generally to documents that reflect the parties'

[50] See the website of the HD Centre, Center for Humanitarian Dialogue (2017) About. www.hdcentre.org/. Accessed 8 July 2017.

[51] See the website of the NRC, www.nrc.no/. Accessed 8 July 2017.

[52] On the agreement, see Bradbury et al. 2000.

[53] See the website of Geneva Call, https://genevacall.org. Accessed 8 July 2017.

understanding of applicable law, in particular customary norms and the interpretation of those norms.[54]

Finally, "Actions Plans" are used by UNICEF and the support of the Special Representative of the UN Secretary-General for Children and Armed Conflict, to negotiate their possible de-listing of the UNSG list of states and ANSAs (see UNSC Resolution 1882)[55] that have committed one or several of the six grave violations against children (killing and maiming of children, recruiting and using child soldiers, attacks against schools or hospitals, rape or other grave sexual violence against children, abduction of children, and denial of humanitarian access for children) as stated in UNSC Resolution 1612 (2005).[56]

All in all, this short description of the existing practice shows that there is an increasing awareness of the necessity to engage ANSAs on IHL and humanitarian concerns. Many challenges remain however that may prevent organisations from improving and furthering efficient engagement with these actors.

2.3 Challenges and Risks

2.3.1 The Changing Nature of Armed Conflicts and the Structural Diversity of ANSAs

Non-international armed conflicts differ enormously. They range from those that resemble conventional warfare, similar to international armed conflicts, to others that are essentially unstructured. In her seminal work, Mary Kaldor described contemporary forms of violence as "new wars" which

> involve a blurring of the distinction between war (which is defined as violence between state or organized political groups for political motives), organized crime (violence undertaken by privately organized groups for private purposes) and large-scale violations of human rights (violence undertaken by states or politically-organized groups or other groups against individuals).[57]

These different forms of armed violence and conflicts will make it very difficult to elaborate plans of action for increasing respect for international law. In addition, the diversity of the types and motivations of ANSAs is another obstacle to the elaboration or adoption of general standards and methodologies for engagement:

> Armed groups represent a wide variety of actors, from quasi-State organizations to a mere handful of predators, and standardised approaches are doomed to fail. This is the biggest

[54] See Heffes and Kotlik 2014.

[55] UN Security Council 2009.

[56] UN Security Council 2005; see the website of the Office of the Special Representative of the Secretary-General for Children and Armed Conflict. https://childrenandarmedconflict.un.org/. Accessed 4 July 2017.

[57] Kaldor 2012, p. 2; see also Blin 2011, pp. 287–310.

> challenge to a typology-based approach. [...] Even standard material is impossible to devise. Tailor-made approaches must be the motto.[58]

The sheer multiplicity of ANSAs in some conflicts is a further challenge for engagement. In a given conflict, like in Syria, ANSAs might merge or split. It is thus estimated that between 1 000 and 6 000 ANSAs are operating in the country. While some, particularly the larger groups, are highly sophisticated, others have little command and control structure or unity of purpose.[59] Some of them control territory at a certain time and then lose it again. They can be very organised at a certain moment and then lose part of their structure over time.[60] All these evolving and changing characteristics of the group is a challenge for the implementation of the norms, in particular because it is not always easy to determine at a certain point in time when IHL is applicable.

There are also ANSAs, which seem remote from the possibility of humanitarian engagement, such as territorial armed gangs. Engaging these actors on humanitarian norms seems to be however increasingly relevant. In 2015, for example, the Geneva Declaration on Armed Violence ranked the states of Honduras and Venezuela just below Syria in terms of violent death rates.[61] Unlike armed oppositions groups, territorial gangs do not wish to replace the state and might not be concerned about the population under their control. Many of these gangs are short-lived structures, made up of young people, with no economic, or social prospects. That said, a certain number of territorial gangs have become permanent enough so as to allow them to gain control of a territory and establish an organised and hierarchical structure and they exist, albeit in different forms, in every continent.[62] While urban violence seems far from the traditional framework of IHL, there is some room for engagement on humanitarian norms with territorial gangs. In fact, many humanitarian agencies, NGOs as well as national Red Cross or Red Crescent societies do work in these contexts and promoting compliance with the law with these types of ANSAs should not be discarded too easily.[63]

2.3.2 The Lack of Clarity of the Applicable Legal Framework

It is well established that ANSAs are bound by IHL, but the extent to which these actors also have obligations under human rights law in situations of armed conflicts

---

[58] Bangerter 2008, p. 76.

[59] Keating and Lewis 2016, p. 2.

[60] See BBC News (2013) Guide to Syrian Rebels. http://www.bbc.com/news/world-middle-east-24403003. Accessed 2 May 2017.

[61] Geneva Declaration 2015.

[62] Bangerter 2010, p. 392.

[63] Ibid., p. 400.

or other situations of violence remains controversial. Indeed, whereas some IHL provisions specifically address ANSAs as parties to a conflict and therefore bound by relevant rules,[64] few human rights treaties explicitly refer to ANSAs.[65] It has been argued that the objective of human rights treaties is to establish norms for regulating the relationship between states and individuals living under their jurisdiction, and that in consequence human rights treaties are "neither intended, nor adequate, to govern armed conflict between the state and armed opposition groups".[66] Scholars do not unanimously support this interpretation of human rights law. For one author, "the foundational basis of human rights is best explained as rights which belong to the individual in recognition of each person's inherent dignity. The implication is that these natural rights should be respected by everyone and every entity."[67]

It is not possible within the framework of this chapter to further develop this issue.[68] It suffices to note that because engagement with ANSA should rest on a clear legal background, the debate on the applicability of human rights law (HRL) to ANSA has had an impact on field operations. As one author observed:

[64] Common Article 3 to the 1949 Geneva Conventions states: "In the case of armed conflict not of an international character occurring in the territory of one of the High Contracting Parties, *each Party to the conflict* shall be bound to apply, as a minimum, the following provisions […]" (emphasis added). Article 1 AP II states: "This Protocol, which develops and supplements Article 3 common to the Geneva Conventions of 12 August 1949 without modifying its existing conditions of application, shall apply to all armed conflicts which are not covered by Article 1 AP I and which take place in the territory of a High Contracting Party between its armed forces and dissident armed forces or other organized armed groups which, under responsible command, exercise such control over a part of its territory as to enable them to carry out sustained and concerted military operations and to implement this Protocol.".

[65] Article 4 of the Optional Protocol to the Convention on the Rights of the Child on the Involvement of Children in Armed Conflict, opened for signature 25 May 2000, 2173 UNTS 222 (entered into force 12 February 2002) states: "1. Armed groups that are distinct from the armed forces of a State should not, under any circumstances, recruit or use in hostilities persons under the age of 18; 2. State Parties shall take all feasible measures to prevent such recruitment and use, including the adoption of legal measures necessary to prohibit and criminalize such practices; 3. The application of the present article shall not affect the legal status of any party to an armed conflict."; Article 2 of the African Union Convention for the Protection and Assistance of Internally Displaced Persons in Africa, opened for signature 23 October 2009, 52 ILM 397 (entered into force 6 December 2012) states that an objective of the treaty is to "provide for the respective obligations, responsibilities and roles of armed groups, non-state actors and other relevant actors, including civil society organizations, with respect to the prevention of internal displacement and protection of, and assistance to, internally displaced persons"; Article 3 of the International Convention for the Protection of All Persons from Enforced Disappearance, opened for signature 6 February 2007, 2716 UNTS 3 (entered into force 23 December 2010) states: "Each State Party shall take appropriate measures to investigate acts defined in article 2 committed by persons or groups of persons acting without the authorization, support or acquiescence of the State and to bring those responsible to justice".

[66] See Zegveld 2002, p. 54.

[67] Clapham 2010, p. 24.

[68] See on this issue among others Clapham 2006, 2007, 2016; Murray 2016; Fortin 2017.

> Human rights monitoring experience in Nepal suggests that the lack of a clear framework addressing the human rights obligations of non-state actors can impact the effectiveness of field operations. […] A narrow focus on the state's responsibility to protect its citizens from violence by non-state actors has proven unsatisfactory. As a consequence, human rights organizations struggle to justify their monitoring and interventions, host states become suspicious of international field presences, and policy makers at the headquarters of monitoring organizations become concerned about potential political fallout from human rights monitoring.[69]

2.3.3 The Impact of Counter-Terrorism Measures

In its controversial decision of 21 June 2010, *Holder v Humanitarian Law Project*, the US Supreme Court held that the training in international law for PKK members planned to be given by a US NGO (the Humanitarian Law Project) could be used by the PKK "as a part of a broader strategy to promote terrorism, and to threaten, manipulate, and disrupt". According to the Court, the planned training would thus rightly fall under the *Anti-terrorism and Effective Death Penalty Act of 1996* which criminalises any material support given to terrorist groups. The fact that, in the circumstances of the case such a training was prohibited by the law, was not found to be a violation of the First Amendment (freedom of expression) enjoyed by the NGO.[70] Such national practice on counter-terrorism thus had a chilling effect on many humanitarian organisations, which feared criminal prosecution when they engaged ANSAs that might be considered terrorist organisations.[71]

It is true that some ANSAs are listed in national and international lists of terrorist organisations, but the problem also lies in that states will tend to label *any* armed group that opposes them as "terrorist". The branding of ANSAs as "terrorist", regardless of their nature and motivation, has created difficulties and dilemmas both legally and from a policy point of view.

First, since the legal qualification of an "armed conflict" is based on facts, ANSAs can be party to a conflict and bound by the same relevant rules of

---

[69] Rawski 2009, pp. 601–626; see also, on the impact of the lack of a clear legal framework on the work of Geneva Call, Bellal 2015.

[70] United States Supreme Court, *Holder v Humanitarian Law Project*, 21 June 2010, 130 S. Ct. 2705.

[71] See also The Washington Post (2010) The Supreme Court Goes too far in the Name of Fighting Terrorism. http://www.washingtonpost.com/wp-dyn/content/article/2010/06/21/AR2010062104267.html. Accessed 1 February 2017; and The New York Times (2010) What Counts as Abetting Terrorists? http://roomfordebate.blogs.nytimes.com/2010/06/21/what-counts-as-abetting-terrorists/. Accessed 1 February 2017.

international law as other parties to that conflict, whether or not it is labelled as a "terrorist group".[72] Second, as noted by the ICRC,

> a recent challenge for IHL has been the tendency of States to label as terrorist all acts of warfare against them committed by armed groups, especially in non-international armed conflicts. This has created confusion in differentiating between lawful acts of war, including such acts committed by domestic insurgents against military targets, and acts of terrorism.[73]

Indeed, under IHL, both in international and non-international armed conflicts, only "acts or threats of violence the primary purpose of which is to spread terror among the civilian population"[74] can be considered as falling into the category of an "act of terrorism" which entails individual criminal responsibility under customary international law.[75] In other words, attacks that exclusively target military objectives do not fall into this category. The main UN treaties on terrorism include a clause requiring that they must be interpreted in accordance with IHL.[76] Accordingly, under such treaties, attacks by ANSA on governmental armed forces in armed conflicts cannot be considered as acts of terrorism prohibited by the conventions.

From an engagement perspective, deeming ANSAs "terrorist" irrespective of their compliance with international norms is not conducive to promoting respect for those norms or for the potential success of peace or other negotiations. It may even, in certain cases encourage the violation of international norms.[77] Moreover, since it is typically far easier to be included on a list of terrorist organisations than it is to be removed from one (and the criteria for inclusion on the list as well as the de-listing procedure are today often opaque and politically motivated), practical incentives to improve respect for international norms may be limited once any armed group has been so designated.

Listing group as terrorists may also result in critical groups or individuals being excluded from peace negotiations, thereby unnecessarily prolonging conflict. It has been emphasised that

> Branding any violent resistance as 'terrorism', and consequently justifying any use of oppressive force by the state as 'counter-terrorism', does not only diminish the chances of

[72] See Vité 2009, pp. 69–94.

[73] ICRC (2010) Contemporary challenges to IHL: Respect for IHL: overview. https://www.icrc.org/en/document/respect-international-humanitarian-law. Accessed 6 June 2017.

[74] See Article 51(2) AP I; and Article 13(2) AP II.

[75] ICTY, *Prosecutor v Stanislav Galić*, Judgment, 5 December 2003, Case No. IT-98-29-T, paras 113–129.

[76] See Article 19 of the International Convention for the Suppression of Terrorist Bombings, opened for signature 12 January 1998, 2149 UNTS 256 (entry into force 23 May 2001); Article 4 of the International Convention for the Suppression of Acts of Nuclear Terrorism, opened for signature 14 September 2005, 2445 UNTS 89 (entered into force 7 July 2007); and Article 21 of the International Convention for the Suppression of the Financing of Terrorism, opened for signature 10 January 2000, 2178 UNTS 197 (entered into force 10 April 2002). See also Coco 2014, pp. 425–440.

[77] Bellal and Casey-Maslen 2011, p. 11.

> the state and opposition groups engaging with each other constructively in transformation processes. It is also detrimental to the state's flexibility with respect to taking action. Publicly flagging 'counter-terrorism' as a core issue of security policy puts pressure on the government to deliver to society as a whole that which it had promised, namely the elimination of the identified terrorist threat. The government thus runs the risk of losing public support if it enters into a constructive dialogue with actors it had previously branded as 'terrorists'. This dilemma also explains why it is so difficult to get proscribed actors subsequently de-listed when they demonstrate that they are ready to dissociate themselves from the use of force.[78]

What is true for states is also true for international organisations involved in peace mediation and it was noted in that regard that the association of ANSA with terrorists has had "a direct impact on the EU and the international community's capacity for mediation and dialogue in transition processes".[79]

Finally and more generally, experts tend to agree that it is also important to consider ANSAs not only as perpetrators of violations of international law, but also as actors who can play positive roles in the implementation of international law, if only because they are often very close to their constituencies.[80] In a context where the majority of armed conflicts oppose states and ANSAs, it is indeed counter-productive to stigmatise only one side of the conflict. The necessity to engage ANSAs for a better implementation of IHL calls for a more nuanced approach to the issue, than considering all ANSAs as terrorist organisations. While ANSAs are often a part of the problem, they can also play a positive role and must in any case also be part of the solution. Of course, ANSAs differ in types, structure and ideology. This, however, should not prevent the international community to recognise that these actors might also be driven by consideration of humanity, which permeates many area of international humanitarian law and this may indeed prove to be a powerful incentive to respect IHL norms. To illustrate this point, I encourage the reader to have a look at the picture taken by Mauricio Lima, who won the World Press Photo Award 2016. It shows a wounded Islamic State fighter being treated by a Kurdish doctor, in the Northern part of Syria.[81] One could wonder if what drove this doctor to take care of his enemy was a motivation to respect IHL or if he was simply moved by basic considerations of humanity.

---

[78] Dudouet et al. 2012, p. 14.

[79] See European Union 2012.

[80] Dudai and McEvoy 2012, p. 15.

[81] The picture can be seen here: World Press Photo (2015) IS Fighter Treated at Kurdish Hospital. https://www.worldpressphoto.org/collection/photo/2016/general-news/mauricio-lima. Accessed 14 June 2017.

2.4 Conclusion

The international community has recognised it is essential to engage with ANSAs if we want a better implementation and respect of the international norms that protect civilians and persons from armed violence or increase our chances to bring armed conflicts to an end. There is already a considerable practice of humanitarian organisations in this regard, which have allowed to identify the incentives that will encourage ANSAs to accept humanitarian engagement. Tools of engagement, such as the Geneva Call Deed of Commitment have been invented, allowing ANSAs to take ownership of the norms and express their adherence or disagreement with them.

Many challenges however remain. Conflicts have become more complex and the diversity in types and ideology, as well as the multiplicity of ANSAs in some context has limited the possibility to adopt general policies on engagement, and sometimes even make engagement almost impossible to achieve in practice. Since 9/11 2001, the perceptions by some states of the potential legitimacy of engaging ANSAs have worsened and counter-terrorism measures gave an important blow to efforts of humanitarian engagement and peace mediation with ANSAs.

On a more general level, as reminded a few years ago by Marco Sassòli in a seminal article, it is time the international community take "armed groups seriously".[82] As such, it is not enough to chant the virtues and necessity of engaging ANSAs. Extra steps must be taken to "meaningfully" take on board the views and needs of these actors in order to enhance the chances to better implement IHL.

First of all, there is a need to enhance the role of armed groups in the elaboration of the norms. Of course, ANSAs are bound by IHL through treaty and customary international law. That said, convincing ANSAs that they must abide by treaty norms they have not agreed upon is already quite challenging. Explaining to them that some of these obligations come from "customary international law", i.e. from "*opinio juris*", a notion that is also quite difficult to understand even for some law students and a "practice", which is not even ANSA practice, creates another very acute challenge. In that sense, more efforts towards taking into account armed groups' views in the elaboration of the law and allowing for their ownership is very much instrumental if we aim at a better respect and implementation of international law by these actors.[83]

Steps must also be taken to clarify the legal framework applicable to ANSAs, especially with regard to human rights law. Humanitarian organisations must be able to engage ANSAs on a realistic and efficient legal framework and ensure that civilians are protected against all forms of armed violence, whether it is in a situation of armed conflict or below the threshold of applicability of IHL.

Finally, there is a need to devising on a more comprehensive and fairer system of accountability, which does not rely exclusively on international criminal law.

[82] Sassòli 2010, p. 6.

[83] See, generally, ibid.

Holding an individual criminally responsible for the international crimes he or she committed is necessary, but criminal trials are also reductive, tending not to account for the ANSAs' dynamic in inciting crimes. As we have seen, truth commissions, if well designed, with a more comprehensive and inclusive approach, give more space to this dimension.

In any case, conducing any types of dialogue entails a great deal of listening and understanding of someone else's point of view. Doing otherwise, and not welcoming other perspectives on board, does not generally lead to much improvement on the ground.

References

Articles, Books and Other Documents

Bangerter O (2008) The ICRC and Non-State Armed Groups. In: Geneva Call, PSIO and UNIDIR (eds) Exploring Criteria and Conditions for Engaging Armed Non-State Actors to Respect Humanitarian Law and Human Rights Law. Conference Report – Geneva 4–5 June 2007. Geneva Call, Geneva, pp 74–85

Bangerter O (2010) Territorial gangs and their consequences for humanitarian players. International Review of the Red Cross 92(878):387–406

Bangerter O (2011) Reasons why armed groups choose to respect international humanitarian law or not. International Review of the Red Cross 93(882):353–384

Bangerter O (2011) A collection of codes of conduct issued by armed groups. International Review of the Red Cross 93(882):483–501

Bellal A (2014) Central African Republic: From Conflict to Chaos and Back Again? In: Casey-Maslen S (ed) The War Report 2013. Oxford University Press, Oxford

Bellal A (2015) Establishing the responsibility of non-state armed groups for international humanitarian law and human rights violations, issues of attribution. In: Gal-Or N, Ryngaert C, Noortman M (eds) Responsibilities of the Non-State Actor in Armed Conflict and the Market Place. Brill Nijhoff, Leiden, pp 304–323

Bellal A (2016a) Beyond the Pale? Engaging the Islamic State on international humanitarian law. Yearbook of International Humanitarian Law 18:123–153

Bellal A (2016b) Positive Obligations of Armed Non-State Actors: Legal and Policy Issues. Report from the 2015 Garance Talks, Geneva Call. http://www.genevacall.org/wp-content/uploads/dlm_uploads/2016/08/GaranceTalks_Issue01_Report. Accessed 6 June 2017

Bellal A (2017) The War Report 2016. Geneva Academy of International Humanitarian Law and Human Rights, Geneva. https://www.geneva-academy.ch/joomlatools-files/docman-files/TheWarReport2016.pdf. Accessed 8 July 2017

Bellal A (2017) Non-State Armed Groups in Transitional Justice Processes: Adapting to New Realities of Conflict. In: Duthie R, Seils P (eds) Justice Mosaics: How Context Shapes Transitional Justice in Fractured Societies. International Centre for Transitional Justice, New York, pp 234–258

Bellal A, Casey-Maslen S (2011) Rules of Engagement. Protecting Civilians through Dialogue with Armed Non-State Actors. Geneva Academy of International Humanitarian Law and Human Rights. https://www.geneva-academy.ch/joomlatools-files/docman-files/Research%20documents/Rules-of-Engagement-EN. Accessed 6 June 2017

Blin A (2011) Armed groups and intra-state conflicts: the dawn of a new era? International Review of the Red Cross 93(882):287–310

Bradbury M, Leader N, Mackintosh K (2000) The "Agreement on Ground Rules" in South Sudan – Study 3 in: The Politics of Principle: The principles of humanitarian action in practice. Humanitarian Policy Group Report, Overseas Development Institute. https://www.odi.org/sites/odi.org.uk/files/odi-assets/publications-opinion-files/307.pdf. Accessed 6 June 2017

Clapham A (2006) Human rights obligations of non-state actors in conflict situations. International Review of the Red Cross 88(863):491–523

Clapham A (2010) The Rights and Responsibilities of Armed Non-State Actors: The Legal Landscape and Issues Surrounding Engagement. http://papers.ssrn.com/sol3/papers.cfm?abstract_id=1569636. Accessed 2 May 2017

Clapham A (2016) Protection of civilians under international human rights law. In: Willmot H, Mamiya R, Sheeran S, Weller M (eds) Protection of Civilians. Oxford University Press, Oxford, pp 141–159

Clapham C (2007) African Guerrillas Revisited. In: Bøås M, Dunn K (eds) African Guerrillas: Raging against the Machine. Rienner, Boulder, pp 221–233

Coco A (2014) The Mark of Cain, The Crime of Terrorism in Times of Armed Conflict as Interpreted by the Court of Appeal of England and Wales in R v. Mohammed Gul. Journal of International Criminal Justice 11:425–440

Conciliation Resources (2005) Engaging armed groups in peace processes. http://www.c-r.org/accord/engaging-armed-groups/introduction-engaging-armed-groups-peace-processes. Accessed 6 June 2017

de Beco G (2005) Compliance with International Humanitarian Law by Non-State Actors. Journal of International Law of Peace and Armed Conflict 18:190–199

Dudai R, McEvoy K (2012) Thinking Critically About Armed Groups and Human Rights Praxis. Journal of Human Rights Practice. 4(1):1–29

Dudouet V, Giessmann V, Hans J, Planta K (2012) From Combatants to Peacebuilders: A case for inclusive, participatory and holistic security transitions. Berghof Foundation, Berlin

European Union (2012) Mediation and dialogue in transitional processes from non-state armed groups to political movements/political parties. Factsheet – EEAS Mediation Support Project. http://ecdpm.org/wp-content/uploads/2013/11/2011-Transitional-Processes-Non-state-Armed-Groups-Political.pdf. Accessed 8 July 2017.

Fortin K (2017) The Accountability of Armed Groups under Human Rights Law. Oxford University Press, Oxford

Geiss R (2006) Asymmetric conflict structures. International Review of the Red Cross 88 (864):757–777

Geneva Declaration (2015) The Global Burden of Armed Violence 2015: Every Body Counts, Executive Summary. http://www.genevadeclaration.org/measurability/global-burden-of-armed-violence/gbav-2015/executive-summary.html. Accessed 2 May 2017

Haer R (2015) Armed Group Structure and Violence in Civil Wars: The Organizational Dynamics of Civilian Killing. Routledge, Oxon and New York

Heffes E, Kotlik M (2014) Special agreements as a means of enhancing compliance with IHL in non-international armed conflicts: An inquiry into the governing legal regime. International Review of the Red Cross 96(895/896):1195–1224

Homequist C (2005) Engaging Armed Non-State Actors in Post-Conflict Settings. In: Bryden A, Hänggi H (eds) Security Governance in Post-Conflict Peacebuilding. Lit Verlag, Zurich/Berlin

ICRC (2008) Increasing respect for international humanitarian law in non-international armed conflicts www.icrc.org/sites/default/files/topic/file_plus_list/0923-increasing_respect_for_international_humanitarian_law_in_non-international_armed_conflicts.pdf. Accessed 8 July 2017

International Crisis Group (2015) Central African Republic: The roots of violence, Africa Report No. 230. https://www.crisisgroup.org/africa/central-africa/central-african-republic/central-african-republic-roots-violence. Accessed 6 June 2017

Jackson A (2016) In their Words. Perceptions of Armed Non-State Actors on Humanitarian Action. Geneva Call. http://genevacall.org/wp-content/uploads/dlm_uploads/2016/09/WHS_Report_2016_web. Accessed 6 June 2017

Kaldor M (2012) New and Old Wars: Organized Violence in a Global Era. Polity Press, Cambridge

Keating M, Lewis P (2016) Towards a Principled Approach to Engagement with Non-State Armed Groups for Humanitarian Purposes, Briefing. Chatham House. https://www.chathamhouse.org/sites/files/chathamhouse/publications/research/20160108EngagementNSAGsHumanitarianPurposesKeatingLewis.pdf. Accessed 6 June 2017

Kleffner J (2009) The collective accountability of organized armed groups for system crimes. In: Nollkaemper A, Van der Wilt H (eds) System Criminality in International Law, pp 238–270

McHugh G, Bessler M (2006) Humanitarian Negotiations with Armed Groups: A Manual for Practitioners. OCHA and IASC. http://reliefweb.int/sites/reliefweb.int/files/resources/28BEC3628B99A532852571070071B4B3-un-ocha-30jan.pdf. Accessed 6 June 2017

McQuinn B, Oliva F (2014) Preliminary scoping report. Analyzing and engaging non-state armed groups in the field. UN System Staff College, Turin

Murray D (2016) Human Rights Obligations of Non-State Armed Groups. Hart Publishing, Oxford/Portland

OHCHR (2006) Rule-of-Law Tools for Post-Conflict States: Truth Commissions. United Nations, New York/Geneva

Parmar S, Roseman J, Siegrist S, Sowa T (2010) Children and Transitional Justice: Truth-Telling, Accountability, and Reconciliation. Harvard Law School, Cambridge MA

Rawski F (2009) Engaging with armed groups: a human rights field perspective from Nepal. International Organizations Law Review 6:601–626

Republic of Liberia Truth and Reconciliation Commission (2009) Final Report, Volume II: Consolidated Final Report. http://reliefweb.int/report/liberia/liberias-trc-presents-final-report. Accessed 4 July 2017

Sassòli M (2010) Taking Armed Groups Seriously: Ways to Improve their Compliance with International Humanitarian Law. Journal of International Humanitarian Legal Studies 1:5–51

Sassòli M (2011) Introducing a sliding-scale of obligations to address the fundamental inequality between armed groups and states? International Review of the Red Cross 93(882):426–431

Schneckener U (2006) Fragile Statehood, Armed Non-State Actors and Security Governance. In: Bryden A, Caparini M (eds) Private Actors and Security Governance. Lit Verlag, Zurich/Berlin

Schneckener U, Hofmann C (2015) The power of persuasion. The role of non-governmental organisations in engaging armed groups. In: Krieger H (ed) Inducing compliance with international humanitarian law. Cambridge University Press, Cambridge

Sinno H (2011) Armed groups' organizational structure and their strategic options. International Review of the Red Cross 93(882):311–332

Sivakumaran S (2006) Binding Armed Opposition Groups. International and Comparative Law Quarterly 55:369–394

Sivakumaran S (2012) The Law of Non-International Armed Conflicts. Oxford University Press, Oxford

Tuck D (2011) Detention by armed groups: overcoming challenges to humanitarian action. International Review of the Red Cross 93(882):759–782

UN General Assembly (2013a) Human Rights Council: Report of the United Nations High Commissioner for Human Rights on the human Rights situation in Mali. UN Doc. A/HRC/23/57

UN General Assembly (2013b) Human Rights Council: Situation of human rights in the Central African Republic – Report of the United Nations High Commissioner for Human Rights. UN Doc. A/HRC/24/59

UN General Assembly (2014) Human Rights Council: Resolution of 9 April 2014 on Promoting Reconciliation, accountability and human rights in Sri Lanka. UN Doc. A/HRC/Res/25/1

UN General Assembly (2016) One humanity: shared responsibility – Report of the Secretary-General for the World Humanitarian Summit. UN Doc. A/70/709

UN Security Council (2010) Report of the Secretary-General on the Protection of civilians in armed conflict. UN Doc. S/2010/579

UN Security Council (2009) Resolution 1882 (2009). UN Doc. S/RES/1882 (2009)

UN Security Council (2005) Resolution 1612 (2005). UN Doc. S/RES/1612 (2005)

Vité S (2009) Typology of armed conflicts in international humanitarian law: Legal concepts and actual situations. International Review of the Red Cross 92(873):69–94

Whitfield T (2010) Engaging with armed groups. Dilemma and options for mediators. Center for Humanitarian Dialogue, Mediation Practice Series, October 2010. http://www.hdcentre.org/wp-content/uploads/2016/08/34Engagingwitharmedgroups-MPS-October-2010.pdf. Accessed 6 June 2017

Zegveld L (2002) Accountability of Armed Opposition Groups in International Law. Cambridge University Press, Cambridge

Case Law

ICTY, *Prosecutor v Duško Tadić*, Decision on the Defence Motion for Interlocutory Appeal on Jurisdiction, 2 October 1995, Case No. IT-94-1-A

ICTY, *Prosecutor v Duško Tadić*, Judgment, 15 July 1999, Case No. IT-94-1-A

ICTY, *Prosecutor v Stanislav Galić*, Judgment, 5 December 2003, Case No. IT-98-29-T

SCSL, *Prosecutor v Sam Hinga Norman*, Decision on Preliminary Motion Based on Lack of Jurisdiction (Child Recruitment), 31 May 2004, Case No. SCSL-2004-14-AR72(E)

United States Supreme Court, *Holder v Humanitarian Law Project*, 21 June 2010, 130 S. Ct. 2705

Treaties

African Union Convention for the Protection and Assistance of Internally Displaced Persons in Africa, opened for signature 23 October 2009, 52 ILM 397 (entered into force 6 December 2012)

Convention on the Prohibition of the Use, Stockpiling, Production and Transfer of Anti-Personnel Mines and on their Destruction, opened for signature 18 September 1997, 2056 UNTS 241 (entry into force 1 March 1999)

Geneva Convention relative to the Treatment of Prisoners of War, opened for signature 12 August 1949, 75 UNTS 135 (entered into force 21 October 1950)

Geneva Convention relative to the Protection of Civilian Persons in Time of War, opened for signature 12 August 1949, 75 UNTS 287 (entered into force 21 October 1950)

International Convention for the Protection of All Persons from Enforced Disappearance, opened for signature 6 February 2007, 2716 UNTS 3 (entered into force 23 December 2010)

International Convention for the Suppression of Acts of Nuclear Terrorism, opened for signature 14 September 2005, 2445 UNTS 89 (entered into force 7 July 2007)

International Convention for the Suppression of the Financing of Terrorism, opened for signature 10 January 2000, 2178 UNTS 197 (entered into force 10 April 2002)

International Convention for the Suppression of Terrorist Bombings, opened for signature 12 January 1998, 2149 UNTS 256 (entry into force 23 May 2001)

Optional Protocol to the Convention on the Rights of the Child on the Involvement of Children in Armed Conflict, opened for signature 25 May 2000, 2173 UNTS 222 (entered into force 12 February 2002)

Protocol Additional to the Geneva Conventions of 12 August 1949, and relating to the Protection of Victims of International Armed Conflicts, opened for signature 12 December 1977, 1125 UNTS 3 (entered into force 7 December 1979) (Additional Protocol I)

Chapter 3
Compliance with International Humanitarian Law by Non-State Armed Groups: How Can It Be Improved?

Hyeran Jo

Abstract How can compliance of non-state armed groups with international humanitarian law (IHL) be improved? In answering this question, this chapter presents a political science perspective and approach to achieve three goals. First, the author discusses the current state of our understanding about the compliant behavior of non-state armed groups in contemporary security. Second, existing legal tools and policy instruments are outlined, with an eye toward enhancing IHL compliance by armed groups. Third and finally, the author provides conjectures regarding the conditions under which some policies might work better than others. This examination of rebel groups and IHL non-compliance calls for more systematic policy evaluation in future research for the improvements of compliance mechanisms to better attain the goals of IHL.

Keywords International humanitarian law · Political science approach · Non-state armed groups · Compliance · Non-compliance · Compliance mechanisms · Armed conflicts

---

The author is an associate professor of political science at Texas A&M University in the United States of America. Her research fields are international relations and international law and her work has appeared in journals such as *International Organization*, *British Journal of Political Science*, *Journal of Conflict Resolution*, and *Conflict Management and Peace Science*. She is the author of *Compliant Rebels: Rebel Groups and International Law* (Cambridge University Press, 2015). Her book won the Chadwick Alger Book Prize, the best book in the field of international organization annually awarded by the International Studies Association.

H. Jo (✉)
Department of Political Science, Texas A&M University,
2010 Allen Building 4348 TAMU, College Station, TX 77843, USA
e-mail: hyeranjo@tamu.edu

T.D. Gill et al. (eds.), *Yearbook of International Humanitarian Law 2016*,
Yearbook of International Humanitarian Law 19,
https://doi.org/10.1007/978-94-6265-213-2_3

Contents

3.1 Introduction

Aligned with the theme of this year's *Yearbook*—international humanitarian law (IHL) and armed groups—this chapter examines non-state armed groups' IHL compliance with a view toward improving it. The question of non-state actor IHL compliance has its utmost relevance in contemporary security scenes, as we observe the consequences of IHL violations in Syria, Afghanistan, Colombia, and beyond. The atrocities committed by the Islamic State in Syria, violence committed by warlords in Afghanistan, and the past wrongdoings by the FARC at the negotiation table in Colombia are the potential violations of IHL principles we encounter currently in global security. Not only do civilians suffer in long-lasting civil conflicts but flagrant violations also threaten the legal regime, prompting questions about the adequacy of legal developments and policy responses.

This chapter approaches the issue of non-state armed groups' IHL compliance with an interdisciplinary focus on law and political science. The focus makes this chapter distinct from other chapters of the special volume in its perspective, approach and language. Rather than employing legal reasoning or legal logic based on legal cases, this chapter will rely on the analysis of law and policy, political actions of humanitarian agents, political motivations of related actors, and policy effects of humanitarian actions. This author well realizes that the *Yearbook* is mainly a volume for IHL experts, and that this author's background is not that of a lawyer but of a political scientist. The modest hope is that this author's different background in political science will deliver an interdisciplinary flavor to the overall volume[1] and such diversity in dialogue will enable more fruitful solutions to global humanitarian problems and issues.

With the interdisciplinary approach of law and political science, this chapter will present an assessment of non-state actor compliance problem along with potential solutions. The primary function will be a stock-taking exercise while also identifying gaps in current knowledge to advance research on the topic. Looking backwards as well as looking forward, this will be an apt exercise for the *Yearbook*. I will lay out the current status of armed groups' IHL compliance, what we know (and what we do not know) about armed groups' IHL compliance. This diagnosis of the problem will lead to a comprehensive review of the different policy and legal options, as well as the potential consequences of these options with a view to enhance compliance. This correspondence between problems and solutions—as well as the identification of a research gap in the issue of armed groups' IHL compliance—will be the main contribution of this chapter to the volume. Providing an assessment of the problem and an overview of policies will help chart the way forward for crafting future research. This author will eventually argue that policies for improvement should be chosen depending on the organizational structures of armed groups, their ecology, and the issue-specifics. To build this argument, I start by defining the problem of non-compliance by armed groups in contemporary security to set the contours of this chapter.

3.2 Definitions

Since this chapter's focus is to examine how to improve IHL compliance, I start with the definitions of the three core terms in this chapter's title: (1) "compliance," (2) "international humanitarian law" and (3) "non-state armed groups." The definitions will set the focus and boundary of the subsequent discussion.

3.2.1 Defining Compliance

Compliance is usually defined as behavioral conformity with existing norms and regulations.[2] In the context of armed groups, this means the observed match between behaviors of non-state armed groups and rules of IHL. In this definition, compliance and non-compliance will not be black or white. Rather, compliance will

[1] See Dunoff and Pollack 2013 for interdisciplinary effort between political science and law.

[2] This definition is consistent with other definitions of compliance: See for example the definition of compliance given by Raustiala and Slaughter 2002, p. 539: "a state of conformity or identity between an actor's behavior and a specified rule."

be characterized on a continuum. There will be outright non-compliance or flagrant violations of IHL, but there will also be low levels of compliance that does not amount to egregious violations. In this working definition of compliance, the standard by which compliance is judged will not be legal. This author is not an international lawyer and it is not this author's place to judge whether or not a particular course of action by a non-state actor is legally compliant based on the circumstantial evidence of the act. Rather, the goal here is to set certain standards for compliance hinging on key humanitarian principles, and the deviation from such standards will be labeled as non-compliance. For example, in the case of the principle of distinction between combatants and noncombatants, if many civilians were massacred in a raid to a village, then it would be considered as non-compliance. But a particular case of a civilian killed with an accusation of helping out an enemy cannot be clearly placed as non-compliance because circumstantial evidence is lacking. This loose definition of compliance rather than strict rules of lawful or non-lawful acts for each case may provoke uneasiness for some readers, but this author wants to defend this approach by highlighting that the goal of this chapter is not to judge each act as legal or illegal but to approximate general patterns that are observed in conflict zones. This loose and flexible definition is due to the non-strict nature of IHL rules and the difficulty of applying rules to specific settings. So, the working definition, although imperfect, will facilitate discussion about the laws and politics of non-state actors' IHL compliance without strict judgment on whether a particular action is legally compliant.

3.2.2 *Defining International Humanitarian Law*

International humanitarian law usually entails the principles, rules and regulations that govern the conduct of war, and this chapter focuses on IHL pertaining to non-state armed groups. As for the principles, core humanitarian principles such as the principle of distinction or proportionality are applicable to non-state settings, in addition to customary international law.[3] As for the rules and regulations, applicable IHL includes the Common Article 3 of the Geneva Conventions,[4] and the Additional Protocol II.[5]

It should be emphatically noted that IHL is not the only applicable law in discussing IHL compliance in internal conflicts. IHL overlaps with other areas of international law in the context of armed conflicts, particularly international human rights law (IHRL) and international criminal law (ICL). Internal conflicts, especially

[3] Henckaerts and Doswald-Beck 2005.

[4] Protocol Additional to the Geneva Conventions of 12 August 1949, and relating to the Protection of Victims of Non-International Armed Conflicts, opened for signature 8 June 1977, 1125 UNTS 609 (entered into force 7 December 1978).

[5] Krieger 2013, p. 10; also see Sivakumaran 2012a.

protracted ones characterized by the ebb and flow of violence and non-violence, blur the boundaries of IHL and IHRL.[6] With the advent of the Rome Statute, IHL is even more intertwined with ICL, as the leaders of non-state armed groups can be held accountable within the international criminal legal structure. Given this overlap and norm-embeddedness between IHL, IHRL, and ICL,[7] this chapter will discuss some norms of IHRL and ICL as they are relevant to the IHL discussion.

3.2.3 Defining Non-State Armed Groups

The boundary for armed groups, and what to include and what not to include, is important in discussing legal and policy tools for enhancing IHL compliance. For the purpose of this chapter, I will define non-state armed groups as organized groups that use military means or violence and that operate outside the direct control of states, usually with political aims opposing the established government. This definition requires some organization within a rebel group, thus excluding a ragtag group of individuals; it also requires some sustained level of conflict activity.

The definition includes armed opposition groups, rebel groups, and insurgent organizations in non-international armed conflicts,[8] as well as some terrorist groups.[9] The definition excludes vigilante groups or paramilitaries, as they often do not have political goals to oppose their governments.[10] The definition will also exclude lone-wolf terrorists who act alone because they lack organization.

The definition is a modification of the legal definition in Article 1, para 1 of the Additional Protocol II to the Geneva Conventions (AP II): "dissident armed forces or other organized armed groups which, under responsible command, exercise such

---

[6] Clapham 2015; Alston and Goodman 2012; Clapham 2006.

[7] Scheffer 2012 specifically notes the connection among three bodies of law.

[8] Armed opposition groups are commonly called rebel groups. See Sivakumaran 2012a for the definitional issues of non-international armed conflicts, where hostilities occur between state and non-state actors or between two or more non-state actors.

[9] According to the global terrorism database (GTD) administered by the University of Maryland, about half of the terrorist groups are armed opposition groups. But the present chapter will not include terrorist groups that have global aims (e.g. al-Qaeda) because the wars they wage are not non-international armed conflicts. See Duffy 2005 on the overlap between international law on terror and IHL. I also want to note the difference/similarity between rebel groups and terrorist groups. Rebel groups in civil conflicts are defined based on their goals of opposing existing national governments, while terrorist organizations are identified by their tactics to create fear and intimidation, but there are overlapping in the boundaries of rebel groups and terrorist organizations. See Fortna 2015 for instance. According to this definition, ISIS is a rebel group against the Syrian government but also a terrorist group that employs terror tactics. So, this group will be applicable within the definition given in this chapter.

[10] In fact, some vigilantes or paramilitaries exercise violence on the side of government or work with the government (e.g. "Rangers" within Pakistani army; Autodefensas Unidas de Colombia (AUC) in Colombia).

control over a part of its territory as to enable them to carry out sustained and concerted military operations and to implement this Protocol." My definitional choice comes from the observation that the above legal definition is a very narrow one, considering the wide variety of armed groups operating in the contemporary security scene. Since the AP II definition specifically excludes groups that do not control territory, it also excludes some armed groups that may not have control over territory but are nonetheless organized and militarily influential. Non-territorial armed groups are prevalent in the contemporary security scene; therefore, this chapter purposefully takes a slightly broader definition than that given by AP II to be more applicable and relevant to contemporary security settings.

Beyond these definitional issues, several points are in order before we discuss legal and policy mechanisms to ensure IHL compliance by non-state armed groups.

First, it is necessary to remark on the inquiry itself. The question of compliance by armed groups can be placed within the broad context of compliance literature. Compliance with law is a major question in legal studies as well as in social sciences.[11] Understanding why people obey the law in general is informative, yet this does not directly explain why armed groups obey international law. We must be attentive to the particular contexts in which armed groups are operating within contemporary global conflicts, because this reconfigures our understanding of compliance issues in the specific frame of reference of non-international armed conflicts.

Second, as for the subject at hand, it is important to state the obvious—armed groups resort to arms rather than achieving their political objectives through peaceful political means. These armed groups are groups—with leadership and lower ranking soldiers who opt to advance their goals by the means of political violence. Unless we understand the nature of such groups, it will be difficult to achieve a full understanding of which methods might apply.

Third, I want to clarify our goals in considering "compliance" to be a normative good. We tend to assume that compliance with laws of war is a normatively good thing that warrants promotion, yet this assumption might falter under some circumstances. The primary goal of IHL is to make a war humane by reducing human suffering. Humanity during times of brutality-prone conflicts is what preserves the humanitarian goal. But this second-best aim is distinct from the first-best aim of ending the war. In some cases, we should be prepared to accept unintended consequences of humanitarian policies, since improved compliance might lengthen the duration of war. Providing humanitarian aid in rebel-held areas might have unintended consequences of prolonging the conflict, for example.[12] Acknowledging this, subsequent discussion will focus on the following question: given the continuing occurrence of conflicts, how do we improve armed groups' IHL compliance in order to lessen human suffering?

[11] See Tyler 2006 for the blend of sociology, psychology and political science.

[12] Narang 2015.

3.3 Problem Assessment

How serious is the problem of non-state armed groups' IHL non-compliance? Why does it occur? This section examines the extant knowledge of non-state armed groups and IHL compliance. Empirical patterns as well as recent scholarly and practitioners' understanding of reasons for IHL (non-)compliance by armed groups will be the main themes of this section.

3.3.1 Patterns of Non-Compliance

The baseline expectation for armed groups' international law compliance is generally low. The laws applicable to non-state actors are not always clear, compared to the laws of war applied to states. Also, asymmetric capability vis-à-vis government often makes armed groups resort to terrorism or violence outside of IHL regulations.[13] Given the low initial expectation, we must have a concrete sense of how serious the problem is that we are dealing with. In particular, we seek to identify the areas of egregious and rampant violations since we desire to work on the areas that need improvements. For example, civilian killing continues to be a key concern in conflicts at all levels of intensity, while child soldiering has become less common over time despite some armed groups' persistent violations.[14] According to the One-sided violence project led by Uppsala University, almost all internal conflicts (about 30–40 of them at every point on the global level) document the intentional killing of civilians by non-state armed groups.[15] On the other hand, the use of child soldiering by rebel groups has decreased from about 60 groups in 1990s to 40 groups in 2000s.[16] Even if still suffering from persistent violations by some armed groups and susceptible to resurgence, child soldering has been observed less frequently than the violation of civilian life.

Recent research uncovers a great deal of variation with respect to armed groups' IHL compliance. The author's Rebel Groups and International Law (RGIL) dataset presented in the book, Compliant Rebels: Rebel Groups and International Law, can serve as one picture of the IHL behavior of armed groups.[17] The RGIL dataset quantifies compliance behavior in the issues of civilian killing, child soldiering, and detention visits for armed opposition groups in civil conflicts between 1990 and 2010. On the issue of civilian killing, 50 out of 200 groups have no record of killing civilians in a systematic and widespread fashion. In the case of child soldiering,

[13] Martinovic 2016.

[14] Drumbl 2012; Jo 2015 for the spatial and temporal patterns of IHL violations by armed groups in the issues of child soldiering, civilian killing, as well as in the issue of detention.

[15] Eck and Hultman 2007.

[16] Jo 2015, pp. 156–158.

[17] Ibid.

about 40 groups remain non-compliant and use child soldiers to varying extents. On the issue of detention visits, we cannot directly observe armed groups' treatment of detainees, but the author was able to code whether armed groups in civil conflicts permit the International Committee of the Red Cross (ICRC) to monitor their detention conditions, sourced from the ICRC's annual reports with operation records. Unfortunately, missing data problem looms large. 70% of data pertaining to the acceptance of the ICRC to armed groups' controlled zones are missing due to the difficulty of collecting data or the inability of armed groups to maintain their own detention centers. Despite this data collection difficulty, a study reports that approximately 30% of armed groups in existing records admitted the ICRC.[18]

An evolving conflict scene adds another layer to the problem of IHL non-compliance by armed groups. The patterns of violence are diversified, including self-defense forces (vigilantes), urban gangs, warlords, rebel groups, and terrorist groups. Whether IHL is directly applicable in every case is debatable, but the evolving pattern of global conflicts nudges us toward adaptability in understanding IHL within these contexts. Differing and tailored responses may be required to address the diversity in emerging violence in contemporary global security. This issue is discussed in the "solutions" section.

3.3.2 Why Non-Compliance Occurs

Our understanding of why non-compliance occurs among non-state armed groups will influence how we respond to the problem at hand. Reasons for non-compliance by non-state armed groups are known to be diverse.[19] Some non-compliance might be involuntary. Non-state armed groups might not comply because they are unfamiliar with the law. In other cases, IHL violations could arise due to disjuncture between local norms and global norms. Within armed organizations, lack of internal control can lead to an inability of superior commanders to impose rules among lower-ranking soldiers.[20] Other non-compliance behaviors can be strategic: excessive violence beyond the permissive line of IHL might occur if armed groups purposefully wage violence as a "show of force."[21] Discussion on these reasons will help devise improvements to tackle the problem of armed groups' IHL non-compliance. Below, we will examine the legal and political reasons one by one. The goal is not to give the comprehensive review but to provide stepping stones to the next discussion on what should be done with the problem of non-state armed groups' IHL non-compliance, with the core premise that the understanding of non-compliance reasons should be achieved before solutions are devised.

---

[18] Jo and Thomson 2014.

[19] For the reasons as to why armed groups violate IHL, see Bangerter 2011.

[20] Humphreys and Weinstein 2006.

[21] Cunningham et al. 2012.

3.3.2.1 The Law Is Not Clear

Some find fault in the law itself, suggesting that it is unclear. The clarity of law should usually lead to better compliance if there is a common understanding among the people who exercise the law. But the clarity of international humanitarian law is such that it fails to operate as a useful guideline for actions. For example, the lack of a clear definition of civilians leads some armed groups to craft their own understanding of what constitutes non-combatants in civil conflicts.[22] Some armed groups might have an expansive definition of "direct participation in hostilities"—including those who provide logistics and food. Others might possess a narrow definition to privilege civilian protection. Finding fault in the law, however, does not appear to be a fruitful approach. It is doubtful that clarifying the law will enhance IHL compliance by armed groups. It is not possible for IHL to specify every contingency of conflict situations, and it is not guaranteed that armed group members would know specific rules. Given the inherent uncertainty about the boundaries of IHL and given the lack of legal sophistication of armed groups, minute changes in law are unlikely to sway armed groups' behavior in a dramatic fashion.

3.3.2.2 The Law Is Not Legitimate

Some armed groups would not accept IHL as legitimate. Some Islamic fundamentalist groups also deny western values and reject IHL wholesale. Historically, this rejection also stems from the fact that armed groups have not participated in the making of IHL, and the voices of non-state armed groups have been rendered mute. Their voice has not been heard, except as observers in the Additional Protocol negotiations, and this history of lawmaking might have influenced armed groups' rejection of IHL principles as outside norms. Encouraging participation in IHL lawmaking may be one solution to this, but political hurdles abound, particularly legitimacy concerns of national governments.

3.3.2.3 The Law Does Not Match with Local Norms

Every society accepts fundamental norms regarding the dignity of human life and this universal value is aligned with IHL's core principles, such as the principle of distinction between combatants and non-combatants. Propitious coincidences occur when local norms coincide with IHL norms. The civilian-respecting norms adopted by the Farabundo Martí National Liberation Front (FMLN), for example, organically grew over time, as the group relied on the local population for support and

[22] Crawford 2015.

resources.[23] In other unfortunate circumstances, local norms do not coincide with global norms. Take the issue of child soldiering by non-state armed actors: the "Straight-18" campaign led by global actors set a threshold at age 18 for the ban on child soldiering, but in Islamic cultures, persons of age 13 are already considered to be adults, fully able to function even on the battlefield.[24] This mismatch between local norms and global standards can be a cause for non-compliance.

3.3.2.4 Armed Groups Have Overriding Military Imperatives

In asymmetric warfare where national government forces have a stronger military than non-state armed groups, many might have strategic incentives to violate IHL to gain the tactical advantage. The use of anti-personnel mines by non-state armed groups is cited as a motivation to remedy this situation of military weakness. Also, to attract foreign supporters or in an effort for a "show of force", some armed groups purposefully violate IHL to look militarily strong and to showcase prowess. The Revolutionary United Front in Sierra Leone was said to be in this mind-set when the group engaged in the maiming and killing of civilians.[25]

3.3.2.5 Armed Groups Lack Capacity to Comply

One key reason for non-compliance might simply be that these armed groups lack the capacity to comply. In the case of the anti-personnel mines, for example, some armed groups might have poor equipment available to de-mine the field after using anti-personnel mines. Similarly, regarding the child-soldier issue, non-state armed groups might not have enough capacity to de-mobilize child soldiers and re-integrate them into society. For these types of issues where lack of capacity looms large, the solutions might include having specific assistance to deal with specific non-compliance problems. The Geneva Call's supply of de-mining technologies which come with the Deed of Commitment, or the United Nations' effort for UN action plans that accompany resources for demobilization are such examples.

Organizational control capacity is another enforcement issue that can lower the compliance level of IHL among armed groups. Compared to government military institutions, armed groups generally lack organizational control. Lower ranking soldier violations are common. Citing a prime reason for non-compliance with the United Nations action plans to ban the use of child soldiers, the Moro Islamic Liberation Front (MILF) commander from the Philippines Mindanao region said in

[23] Jo 2015, pp. 59–60.

[24] IRIN news (2011) Moves to end use child soldiers, but problem persists. http://www.irinnews.org/feature/2011/04/08/moves-end-use-child-soldiers-problem-persists. Accessed 28 March 2017.

[25] Salehyan et al. 2014.

an interview that "local commanders sometimes recruit children in their ranks."[26] In these cases, providing training and education to lower-ranking commander levels might be one solution, but the fundamental strategic need to fill the ranks will be difficult to tackle.

Thus far, I have presented five reasons for non-compliance with IHL by non-state armed groups. On the flip side of the same coin, we have to explore reasons for compliance. It logically follows that armed groups are more likely to exhibit compliance when the five previously mentioned conditions are absent: (1) when the law is clear in guidance, (2) when the law carries some representation by non-state armed groups, (3) when the local norms are in broad alignment with global standards, (4) when armed groups do not have overriding military imperatives, (5) when armed groups have capacity and organizational control over rank-and-file behavior. Understanding positive reinforcements is just as important as examining the factors which inhibits armed groups from complying. My recent research suggests that some legitimacy-seeking armed groups comply: those armed groups cultivate political wings, which often become interlocutors with outside actors for humanitarian engagement.[27] Those armed groups get to care about IHL and express commitments in some cases. Also, rebel groups with an established history of civilian relations that build governance (e.g. FMLN in El Salvador)—by providing healthcare or dispute resolution functions—are more amenable to IHL compliance, relative to armed groups that disregard human life relying on external funders (e.g. Revolutionary United Front with the support from Charles Taylor's regime in Liberia). These civilian-rebel social relations will be critical in constructing solutions to the problem of non-compliance, especially if humanitarian engagement can involve the community as a whole. Our knowledge in this matter is currently limited and further theoretical and empirical studies will help clarify the conditions for armed groups' social relations in improving regard for civilian life and other IHL principles.

3.4 Compliance Mechanisms as Solutions

Now that we have covered the patterns of IHL (non-)compliance by non-state armed groups as well as their reasons, this section addresses ways of improving compliance. Existing compliance mechanisms, legal tools, and policy options are discussed to tackle the issue of non-compliance.[28] The primary goal is to examine the policy "tool box" in a comprehensive fashion and to identify research gaps

[26] IRIN news (2011) Moves to end use child soldiers, but problem persists. http://www.irinnews.org/feature/2011/04/08/moves-end-use-child-soldiers-problem-persists. Accessed 28 March 2017.

[27] Jo 2015.

[28] For extant literature, see Gillard 2016; Krieger 2015; Hofmann and Schneckener 2011; Bellal and Casey-Maslen 2011; Ryngaert and Van de Meulebroucke 2011; Sassòli 2010 and Sassòli 2007.

while moving forward to enhance IHL compliance. Currently, extant discussions are mostly focused on compliance mechanisms for states.[29] In a plea to beg to differ, this chapter's core contribution is to synthesize various compliance mechanisms for non-state actor setting in a holistic fashion.

The solutions are devised with the following three considerations.

First, a particular solution will be matched to the problems or reasons for non-compliance. If the cause is lack of capacity in the case of a particular group, we have to deal with the issue of specific capacity building. If the primary issue is a mismatch between local norms and global IHL norms, the solutions must be reconciled to reflect the local norms.

Second, the solutions are to be devised in consideration of the political, economic, and social ecology of armed groups. In particular, policy makers need to identify the locus of power in local settings and understand armed groups' financial dependency (resources or some sponsors) or social networks (community and family networks with diaspora or other nationals within the conflict).

Finally, the issue-specific characteristics will matter. Engagement of armed groups would differ between the problems of preserving cultural properties and the problem of sexual violence. While preservation of cultural properties might require raising awareness and preventing incentives for looting, the issue of sexual violence might require the understanding of organizational structures and cultures of an armed group.

Figure 3.1 sketches the dimensions and variety of available policy options. The two dimensions are the characteristic of measure (diplomatic to military; facilitative to confrontational; soft to hard) as well as the locus of implementation (external or internal, whether armed groups themselves implement the solution or external actors are involved). Soft measures to enhance IHL compliance include legal developments, diplomatic options, as well as humanitarian engagements. Hard options include punishments, sanctions, or military actions. The locus of implementation is also important in understanding agency of the measure and to what extent how the internalization of a solution will be occurring. External solutions refer to the central role of external actors in influencing the outcome; internal solutions mean the centrality of internal structure and autonomous solutions within an armed group unit. This classification is informed by compliance theories and existing studies in other areas of international law.[30] We discuss each option in turn, with the primary focus on the first dimension of soft-and-hard compliance mechanisms. The locus of implementation will be discussed in tandem as needed and as appropriate.

---

[29] The consultative process initiated by the ICRC and the Swiss Government since 2011 is one such effort, to consider the fact-finding commission, periodic reporting, *inter alia*. See International Committee of the Red Cross and Swiss Federal Department of Foreign Affairs 2015.

[30] Particularly, the area of environmental governance and trade governance as well as disarmament treaties. See Dorn and Scott 2000.

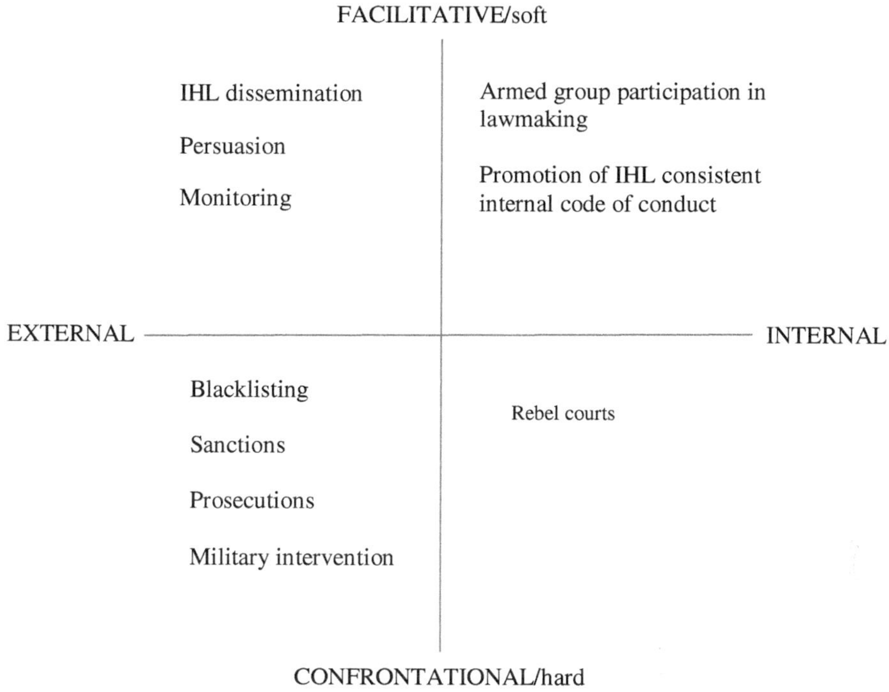

Fig. 3.1 Compliance mechanisms: two dimensions

3.4.1 *Soft Measures*

Soft compliance mechanisms are policy measures short of military actions for enhancing IHL compliance among armed groups. Soft measures include (1) legal developments, (2) humanitarian engagement, and (3) naming and shaming.

3.4.1.1 Legal Developments

One suggested policy option is to rethink the law itself. Some advocate recognizing the role of human rights in IHL.[31] Others suggest an inclusive approach of law-making to increase lawmaking participation by armed groups.[32] The use of soft law instruments, such as unilateral declaration by armed groups, is the center pillar of this approach. The underlying rationale behind this approach is to give ownership to armed groups. The expectation is that this direct participation in lawmaking would

[31] Bellal 2015.

[32] Roberts and Sivakumaran 2012.

promote internalization of norms and strengthen respect for law.[33] The additional basic premise is that legitimacy of law will increase among armed groups via lawmaking participation.[34] However, this solution would have inherent political obstacles. In particular, states, as traditional lawmakers of IHL, would object to the idea of including armed groups for fear of conferring legitimacy to armed groups. Although this lawmaking participation solution has sound rationale, political feasibility is questionable.

3.4.1.2 Humanitarian Engagement

Humanitarian engagement with armed groups refers to the interaction between humanitarian actors and armed groups with the goal of enhancing IHL and facilitating the delivery of humanitarian assistance.[35] Mediation efforts and diplomatic interactions fall into this category of humanitarian engagement. The goal is not to stop the war, but to restrict the violence in an IHL-consistent manner.

Several specific methods of humanitarian engagement exist and many international and non-governmental organizations pour their efforts into this category. Some organizations focus on the methods of persuasion via dialogue, education, or training.[36] The primary goal of education and training is to raise awareness of IHL, and prominent international organizations such as the ICRC and the Geneva Call have this goal as central pillars of their operations. In employing this method of persuasion, the identification of an interlocutor will be critical, as the channels of command and control within armed groups will ensure the implementation of the rules. Also, understanding of local norms and familiarity with local power configurations will be important, as this kind of dialogue might occur by convincing local leaders. Challenges to this persuasion approach include the constricting humanitarian space, as exemplified in *Holder v Humanitarian Law Project*.[37] As humanitarians are restricted or banned from talking to non-state armed groups due to political concerns regarding material support or legitimizing those groups, persuasion methods will be difficult to implement.

An alternative method of humanitarian engagement is to encourage more organic development within armed groups. One example is to aid in the development of internal codes of conduct of armed groups to make them consistent with IHL.[38] This occurred in the case of General Orders by the MILF in the Philippines, for

---

[33] Sivakumaran 2012b.

[34] Recalling Franck's thesis on the connection between legitimacy of law and compliance, see Franck 1990.

[35] MacLeod et al. 2016.

[36] Ratner 2011, p. 459; Bangerter 2015.

[37] Supreme Court of the United States, *Holder v Humanitarian Law Project*, 21 June 2010, 561 U.S. 1 (2010), 130 S.Ct. 2705.

[38] International Council on Human Rights Policy 2000. Organizational discipline is one of the key components for preventing civilian victimization; see Weinstein 2007.

instance.[39] The long-term goal here is to induce "change within"—aiming at internalization and "habitualization",[40] recognizing the importance of rituals and norms within armed organizations. This method might be apt in relation to the issue of sexual violence. Research shows that sexual violence is used for social cohesion purposes during the induction process of new recruits.[41] Uprooting this practice and planting some other rituals, via long-term humanitarian engagement with non-state armed groups, might improve their IHL compliance in the area of sexual violence.

The other more controversial matter is to encourage the use of courts within armed groups, utilizing humanitarian engagement.[42] Rebel courts may confer the benefit of strengthening accountability mechanisms within the ranks of armed groups. To promote rebel courts, however, is a tricky matter, as such mechanisms might conflict with existing states' legal systems and due process might not be given to those tried. Although the presence of due process is usually better than the absence of due process, rebel courts have been criticized due to their instrumental use of courts to advance their political causes and, sometimes, to punish their internal foes. It was recently argued that some warlords have a right to dispute settlement if they sufficiently exhibit good human rights records, and if they have popular approval.[43] According to this logic, under some restricted conditions, armed groups might therefore have political authority and sufficient legitimacy to set up their own courts.

3.4.1.3 Naming and Shaming

Naming and shaming is another soft measure the international community can employ with the aim of ensuring IHL compliance among armed groups. The goal is to use social pressure to alter the behavior of armed groups.[44] This method is used by the United Nations Special Representative for Children and Armed Conflicts as well as by the Watchlist, a non-governmental organization specializing in the child soldiering issue.[45] The blacklists are used for shaming non-state armed groups that

---

[39] The General Order No. 1 is titled "An order promulgating a code of conduct regulating the affairs of the Bangsamoro Islamic Armed Forces prescribing its powers, duties, and functions, and other related purposes" and the General Order No. 2 was titled "An order amending Articles 34 and 36 of the Code of conduct of the Bangsamoro Islamic Armed Forces and for other purposes." See more in Bangerter 2011.

[40] Risse and Sikkink 1999, p. 5.

[41] Cohen 2016.

[42] Sivakumaran 2009.

[43] Blair and Kalamanovitz 2016.

[44] At least among states, these naming and shaming strategies have been shown to be effective. See Krain 2012.

[45] See more in Klostermann 2015.

utilize children in their ranks. Although naming and shaming is classified as a soft approach which does not entail sanctions or punishments, this method includes some confrontational elements.

3.4.2 *Hard Measures*

There are several hard measures with the goal of enhancing IHL compliance by armed groups: (1) sanctions, (2) prosecutions, and (3) military actions.

3.4.2.1 Sanctions

Sanctions—financial restrictions or travel bans—are used with the aim of constraining the ability of non-state armed groups and coercing them to comply with IHL. Targeted sanctions by the United Nations Security Council are an example of such measures to influence the behavior of armed groups.[46] Specific examples of sanctions on rebel groups include the charcoal ban on Al-Shabaab in Somalia or the diamond ban on UNITA in Angola. Although these goals are not explicitly intended for civilian protection, this is increasingly the case.[47] The sanctions are usually imposed when other measures are infeasible, and their effectiveness is often questioned. Recent research finds that sanctions imposed on civil war actors are not effective in saving lives, except in the case of arms embargoes.[48] As a policy tool for enhancing compliance, sanctions appear to have constraining power, but not so much coercive power. Sanctions policies restrict resource flows to non-state armed groups and might bind their hands to reduce IHL violations, though these measures might not coerce them to stop civilian abuses.

3.4.2.2 Prosecutions

Prosecutions—trials at the ad hoc tribunals or at the International Criminal Court—are another hard measure used to ensure IHL compliance by armed groups. This approach of emphasizing individual accountability is a relatively new strategy on the historical scale, with only a couple of decades of experience. The primary logic of employing prosecutions vis-à-vis non-state armed actors is deterrence: by punishing past wrong-doings, prosecutions are meant to deter future IHL violations.

[46] See the work of 1267 Committee for example in sanctioning non-state armed groups.

[47] See Charron 2011.

[48] Hultman and Peksen 2015.

There is some evidence that non-state armed groups feel the pressure of international criminal justice,[49] but how they react to such prosecution pressures requires more research and observation.

3.4.2.3 Military Actions

Military interventions or peacekeeping operations are sometimes used to discipline armed groups towards restraining or stopping violence. Examples include aerial bombing in Syria's ISIS controlled areas, and peacekeeping operations in the Democratic Republic of Congo (DRC). The primary goal of military actions is often geopolitical,[50] but the supplemental effect is such that military actions induce non-state armed groups to comply with IHL and exercise violence with restraint. Recent wisdom on interventions research holds that military interventions are rarely successful.[51] In some cases, military interventions might fuel the violence.[52] Given these mixed findings on the effects of military interventions, the contribution of military actions to enhanced IHL compliance among non-state armed groups is uncertain as well.

3.4.3 Other Measures

Besides soft and hard measures to improve compliance, other measures are possible. The remaining policy options do not target armed groups directly, but target other conflict actors indirectly. Those two actors to be indirectly influenced are states (armed groups' opponents, most of the time) and civilians (victims of non-compliance, in general).

3.4.3.1 Encouraging Compliance by States

It is well known that reciprocity is regarded as the engine of compliance in state-to-state interactions.[53] If reciprocity has its reach in other settings, might IHL compliance by states increase IHL compliance by non-state armed groups? We know that armed groups are often in competition with state actors in fighting for

---

[49] For general systematic evidence related to ICC deterrence, see Jo and Simmons 2016; Jo et al. 2017. For a skeptical view, see Cronin-Furman 2013.

[50] It is well known that the foremost aims of military interventions are geo-political. See Regan 2010.

[51] Lake 2016.

[52] Aslam 2010 finds this pattern in the post-cold war U.S. interventions.

[53] See Morrow 2007 for evidence.

political legitimacy, so state compliance might improve armed groups' behavior. At minimum, we have some grounds to believe this is true in the case of anti-personnel mines and targeting civilians.[54] In the anti-personnel mines issue, non-state armed groups nudged their opposition governments to sign the Ottawa Convention by signing the Deed of Commitment with the Geneva Call. In the civilian targeting issue, high correlation was found in restraining behavior toward civilian targeting between non-state armed groups and their opposition governments. This evidence suggests that encouraging IHL compliance by national governments will also produce ripple effects on the compliance behavior of non-state armed groups.

3.4.3.2 Engaging Communities

Civilians are usually considered only as victims of IHL violations, but recent research finds solutions in engaging civilians so as to improve IHL compliance by non-state armed groups. Researchers and practitioners now think public engagements might be fruitful for enhancing armed groups' IHL compliance. Geneva Call's message via the radio and a smartphone app is one such effort.[55] In fact, there are some instances where civilians have "nudged" armed groups to behave.[56] This community outreach might be useful when local chiefs in clan-based societies perform mediating roles between civilians and armed groups, and when armed groups have close relations with civilians where these civilians, using ethnic and blood ties, can convince armed groups of the utility of exercising restraint. All these efforts are an outgrowth of recognizing that the ecology and social relations of armed groups are important. This solution also stems from an emerging recognition that decentralized methods, such as empowering civilians, might prove to be better in terms of protecting civilians and achieving humanitarian goals. The idea to engage victims to change the behavior of perpetrators has gained ground and is contributing to some innovative solutions, but the extent to which this program would be effective is still unknown.

3.5 Toward a Synthesis

The above review of existing compliance mechanisms helped us identify the areas of success and the gaps in research. Although we know something about each individual compliance mechanism, we still have much to learn. We do not know much about the effectiveness of each mechanism, nor do we know much about the combined effects of some of hard and soft compliance methods that could give us a

[54] Gleditsch et al. 2016. On the civilian killing issue, see Fazal 2013.

[55] Its public awareness campaign is "Fighter Not Killer" (www.fighternotkiller.org).

[56] Kaplan 2013.

more holistic picture of various compliance mechanisms. It is apparent that we do not have a good answer to some basic questions: which policies might work better than others? Which policies should we prioritize in what settings? What are the trade-offs choosing one policy at the expense of the other?[57] How should the available compliance mechanisms cohere? What is the optimal mix or the effective sequence of policies, under what circumstances? How can practitioners unleash innovations in the field?[58] Understanding how various compliance mechanisms interact will be vital as we tackle armed groups' IHL non-compliance in Syria, Yemen, DRC, and beyond. These are questions of critical importance to foreign policy makers and international humanitarian workers, yet we do not have clear answers for those important questions.

With these questions in mind, I conclude this chapter with some conjectures and a research agenda on what I call a "targeted" approach to IHL compliance by non-state armed groups. I specifically argue that devising a tailored and calibrated approach to armed groups is necessary and propose some conjectures, based on the assumptions about the workings of rebel organizations, their political relationships, and my previous research on rebel compliance. These suggestions are grounded in recent research that demonstrates not only variations in compliance behavior, but also differences in organizational structures and social relations within conflict zones. This approach is akin to personalized medicine in medical fields; in recognition of certain features and circumstances, the solutions are customized. What is critical is discerning which armed groups are more vulnerable to social pressures, which armed groups have vested interests in enhancing compliance, and which type of armed groups would be able to carry out the implementation of compliance mechanisms.

3.5.1 Considerations

Three considerations will impact non-state actors' compliance behaviors and give leverage to external actors in influencing their IHL compliance during wartime. The first consideration is within-group organizational characteristics. Most armed groups are politico-military groups, and in the context of humanitarian policy, key determinants to consider are organizational factors such as the command and control structure, the presence of an interlocutor, or the presence of a political wing. The command and control structure of rebel organizations is related to enforceability. Strong command structure strengthens internal control, signaling that the armed group can enforce the rules within the organization effectively although not perfectly. External actors can influence leadership and the internal control will be

[57] One exception is Mills 2015.

[58] Consider the work of mobile gender courts in DRC as explained by Lake 2014. Also, innovations by peacekeeping operations in DRC as described in Tull 2015.

able to reinforce compliance behaviors and IHL values across the ranks. Also, having a clear interlocutor that can be identified by outsiders will make persuasion easier. Having multiple factions and various access points within an armed organization might portend layers of repeated works on the part of humanitarian workers and mediators. Additionally, if armed groups have a political wing, it will make interaction and engagement with international organizations easier. Separated from military wing, a political wing of an armed group can often be a platform for IHL negotiation and dialogue.

The second consideration involves armed groups' economic activities and their resource pool. With regard to a resource base, adaptable armed groups will be less likely to be persuaded or feel prosecutorial pressures. Likewise, groups who are more financially independent are less likely to respond to legal pressure. So, persuasive means or prosecution threats might not work, and ending the conflict via military means might be the only option left to achieve the humanitarian goals.

Third, social relations of armed groups matters in the course of devising policies to improve armed groups' compliance with international law. In particular, relationships with civilians—especially whether or not rebel groups provide governance functions (social service provisions, health systems)—will determine which policy mix would work best in terms of achieving humanitarian goals. Those rebels are more likely to be persuaded and more open to engagement in general, but a protection framework looks promising if interests for protection are aligned between the international community and armed groups controlling the territory.[59]

3.5.2 Conjectures

With the aforementioned considerations, I put forward a set of conjectures. A key undergirding principle is that the choice of policy options will depend on the nature of armed groups. These conjectures can be tested in the future with interviews, field experiments, and policy evaluations.

The first conjecture is about the situation where a policy may not be needed. It states: *some armed groups in local settings where humanitarian principles organically grow may not need any intervention policy.* If norms grow organically that are consistent with international humanitarian law, we might not need to invoke international law. It is when the law and interests are misaligned that we need international law. For example, some Marxist groups like the FMLN built strong relations with civilians, so we might not need IHL-enhancing policies in the case of organically grown norms. The cases where local norms organically grow to match IHL standards will teach us how voluntary compliance can emerge.

[59] Mampilly 2015 records the Naxalites in India who viewed international organizations as competitors to local governance.

The second conjecture concerns the adoption of persuasion methods such as humanitarian engagement. It states: *for an armed group with a clear interlocutor and organizational control, persuasion might work best as the first step of engagement*. If a group has a clear interlocutor (e.g. within the political wing of an armed group) with good organizational control (e.g. within the military wing of an armed group), humanitarian diplomacy might be feasible and work best prior to the implementation of other legal or policy tools. The demand and initiative often comes from armed groups themselves. For example, the willingness of the Peshmerga (Kurds) and the MILF to work with the international community to support their cause facilitated access to training and consultation by international organizations.[60] In the case of the Pershmerga, the persuasion by humanitarian actors led the group to agree in principle with the ban on improvised explosive devices (IEDs). The persuasion cannot guarantee perfect compliance: the Pershmerga commanders think that it is unsafe for refugees to return to war zones and it is okay to use IEDs for these practical reasons. But it can be the first step of engagement before other harder measures can be tried vis-à-vis armed groups with organizational control and humanitarian intent.

The third conjecture is about the conditions for employing hard measures to ensure compliance. It states: *for armed groups with community-based support networks, blacklisting or sanctions may be a feasible and effective approach*. If a group has a support network vulnerable to blacklisting, shaming and political labeling might reduce capacities of a group that might curtail their resources, ultimately inducing compliance, primarily via a coercive mechanisms. The withdrawal of support from a diaspora population, for example, can influence armed groups to behave in a more IHL-consistent fashion. When the Tamil Tigers (LTTE) in Sri Lanka was designated as a terrorist group within the United States, Canada, and Europe, the blacklisting and associated sanctions led the diaspora population to cut back funding toward the group, which affected the LTTE's operation against soft civilian targets.[61]

The fourth conjecture concerns the conditions for employment of military options to enhance IHL compliance by non-state armed actors. It states: *military options are best employed when armed groups embrace norms that are distanced from global norms*. This method relies on the logic of "compellence" (making a threat to force an actor to take some desired action).[62] The humanitarian goal at this point would be to compel compliance by curtailing armed groups' capacity for violence. Although potentially useful when soft measures fail, hard measures are usually expensive to implement with many political obstacles. Drone use or aerial bombing of some armed groups sometimes entail the sacrifice of innocent lives, as recent cases in Syria show.

60 Middle East Research Institute (MERI) 2016; Jo 2015, pp. 160–164.

61 International Crisis Group 2010.

62 See Sechser and Fuhrman 2013, p. 173.

3.5.3 Conclusion

I would like to conclude with three remarks about the conjectures and future direction of the research on non-state armed groups and their IHL compliance.

First, the above conjectures will vary depending on the issue area. Where principal-agent problems loom large (e.g. sexual violence), strong command-control might not work well, so local solutions, such as mobile gender courts in DRC, might be better.[63]

Second, it is important to acknowledge the challenges ahead. Collective action problems likely exist, as evidenced by the effort by the United Nations Office for the Coordination of Humanitarian Affairs. Problems of coordination between the United Nations Security Council, humanitarian non-governmental organizations, host governments, and international policy-makers are likely to pose a challenge.

Third, we need rigorous program evaluations of soft compliance mechanisms short of military actions. Some of the conjectures require creative empirical testing if we want to have empirical backing for these practices. We want to know how soft mechanisms (legal developments, training, or education) occur in the shadow of hard mechanisms (military actions). We also want to know what kind of concerted compliance policies will bear fruits to save lives and preserve humanity. In addition to the rigorous program evaluations, we will need innovations in the field.

More extensive research is required in order to improve our understanding of compliance by armed groups. In particular, how they perceive the legitimacy of international law, how they learn the law, and what incentive schemes help change armed groups' behaviors. We do not know much about how these policies cohere, or why they are combined under certain situations and used separately in others. This, I think, is the research frontier that should be pushed by legal scholars and social scientists in order to make informed policy decisions and further legal developments.

Acknowledgements I would like to thank Professor Heike Krieger for motivating this study and Professor Christophe Paulussen for helpful suggestions. I also wish to thank Yvette Isidori, Margaret McIntyre, and John Niehaus for research assistance. Part of this research effort was supported by the National Science Foundation (SES #1260218). The findings and recommendations in this chapter are those of the author and do not represent the views of the funding agency.

References

Articles, Books and Other Documents

Alston P, Goodman R (2012) International human rights. Oxford University Press, Oxford
Aslam R (2010) U.S. military interventions and the risk of civil conflict. Studies in Conflict and Terrorism 33(3):246–267

[63] Lake 2014.

Bangerter O (2011) Reasons why armed groups choose to respect international humanitarian law or not. International Review of the Red Cross 93(882):353–384

Bangerter O (2015) Comment. Persuading armed groups to better respect international humanitarian law. In: Krieger H (ed) Inducing compliance with international humanitarian law: lessons from the Great Lakes Region. Cambridge University Press, Cambridge, pp 112–124

Bellal A (2015) Challenges of compliance by non-state armed groups. Proceedings on the distinction between international and non-international armed conflicts: Challenges for IHL? XXXVIII Roundtable on Current Issues of International Humanitarian Law, Sanremo, 3–5 September 2015. http://www.iihl.org/wp-content/uploads/2016/01/BELLAL.pdf. Accessed 18 April 2017

Bellal A, Casey-Maslen S (2011) Enhancing compliance with international law by armed non-state actors. Gottingen Journal of International Law 1:175–197

Blair R, Kalamanovitz P (2016) On the rights of the warlords: Legitimate Authority and Basic Protection in Warn-Torn Societies. American Political Science Review 110(3):428–440

Charron A (2011) UN sanctions and conflict: responding to peace and security threats. Routledge, New York

Clapham A (2006) Human rights obligations of non-state actors. Oxford University Press, Oxford

Clapham A (ed) (2015) Human rights and non-state actors. Edward Elgar Publishing, Cheltenham

Cohen D (2016) Rape during civil war. Cornell University Press, Ithaca

Crawford E (2015) Identifying the enemy: civilian participation in armed conflict. Oxford University Press, Oxford

Cronin-Furman K (2013) Managing expectations: international criminal trials and the prospects for deterrence of mass atrocity. International Journal of Transitional Justice 7:434–454

Cunningham K, Bakke K, Seymour L (2012) Shirts today, skins tomorrow: Dual contests and the effects of fragmentation in self-determination disputes. Journal of Conflict Resolution 56 (1):67–93

Dorn W, Scott D (2000) Compliance mechanisms for disarmament treaties. In: Findlay T, Meier O (eds) Verification Yearbook 2000. Vertic, London, pp 229–247

Drumbl M (2012) Reimagining child soldiers in international law and policy. Oxford University Press, Oxford

Duffy H (2005) The "War on Terror" and the framework of international law. Cambridge University Press, Cambridge

Dunoff J, Pollack M (eds) (2013) Interdisciplinary perspectives on international law and international relations: The state of the art. Cambridge University Press, New York

Eck K, Hultman L (2007) One-sided violence against civilians in war: Insights from new fatality data. Journal of Peace Research 44(2):233–246

Fazal T (2013) Secessionism and civilian targeting. APSA 2013 Annual Meeting Paper, American Political Science Association 2013 Annual Meeting. https://ssrn.com/abstract=2300126. Accessed 10 March 2017

Fortna P (2015) Do terrorists win? Rebels' use of terrorism and civil war outcomes. International Organization 69(3):519–556

Franck T (1990) The power of legitimacy among nations. Oxford University Press, Oxford

Gillard EC (2016) Promoting compliance with international humanitarian law. https://www.chathamhouse.org/sites/files/chathamhouse/publications/research/2016-10-05-promoting-compliance-ihl-gillard.pdf. Accessed 20 January 2017

Gleditsch K, Hug S, Schubiger LI, Wucherpfennig J (2016) International conventions and nonstate actors: Selection, signaling, and reputation effects. Journal of Conflict Resolution DOI:10.1177/0022002716650924

Henckaerts JM, Doswald-Beck L (2005) Customary international humanitarian law. International Committee of the Red Cross and Cambridge University Press, Cambridge

Hofmann C, Schneckener U (2011) Engaging non-state armed actors in state- and peace-building: options and strategies. International Review of the Red Cross 93(883):603–622

Hultman L, Peksen D (2015) Successful or counterproductive coercion? The effect of international sanctions on conflict intensity. Journal of Conflict Resolution DOI:10.1177/0022002715603453

Humphreys M, Weinstein J (2006) Handling and manhandling civilians in civil war. American Political Science Review 100(3):429-447

International Committee of the Red Cross and Swiss Federal Department of Foreign Affairs (2015) Strengthening compliance with international humanitarian law, Concluding Report. http://rcrcconference.org/wp-content/uploads/sites/3/2015/04/32IC-Concluding-report-on-Strengthening-Compliance-with-IHL_EN.pdf. Accessed 28 March 2017

International Council on Human Rights Policy (2000) Ends and means: human rights approaches to armed groups. http://www.ichrp.org/files/reports/6/105_report_en.pdf. Accessed 3 October 2016

International Crisis Group (2010) The Sri Lankan Tamil diaspora after the LTTE, Crisis Group Asia Report N°186. https://www.crisisgroup.org/asia/south-asia/sri-lanka/sri-lankan-tamil-diaspora-after-ltte. Accessed 20 October 2016

Jo H (2015) Compliant Rebels: Rebel Groups and International Law in World Politics. Cambridge University Press, Cambridge

Jo H, Simmons B (2016) Can the International Criminal Court Deter Atrocity? International Organization 70(3):443–475

Jo H, Simmons B, Radtke M (2017) Assessing the ICC. In: Squatrito T, Young O, Føllesdal A, Ulfstein G (eds) Performance of International Courts. Cambridge University Press, Cambridge (forthcoming)

Jo H, Thomson C (2014) Legitimacy and compliance with international law: Access to detainees in civil conflict, 1991–2006. British Journal of Political Science 44(2):323–355

Kaplan O (2013) Nudging armed groups: how civilians transmit norms of protection. International Journal of Security and Development 2(3):62

Klostermann R (2015) The UN Security Council's special compliance systems – the regime of children and armed conflict. In: Krieger H (ed) Inducing compliance with international humanitarian law: Lessons from the African Great Lakes Region. Cambridge University Press, Cambridge, pp 313–350

Krain M (2012) *J'accuse*! Does naming and shaming perpetrators reduce the severity of genocides or politicides? International Studies Quarterly 56(3):574–589

Krieger H (2013) A turn to non-state actors: Inducing compliance with international humanitarian law in war-torn areas of limited statehood. SFB-Governance Working Paper Series No. 62. http://www.sfb-governance.de/publikationen/working_papers/wp62/SFB-Governance-Working-Paper-62.pdf. Accessed 20 October 2016

Krieger H (ed) (2015) Inducing compliance with international humanitarian law: Lessons from the African Great Lakes Region. Cambridge University Press, Cambridge

Lake D (2016) The Statebuilder's Dilemma. Cornell University Press, Ithaca

Lake M (2014) Organizing hypocrisy: Providing legal accountability for human rights violations in areas of limited statehood. International Studies Quarterly 58(3):515–526

MacLeod A, Hoffman C, Saul B, Webb J, Hogg CL (2016) Humanitarian engagement with non-state armed groups. https://www.chathamhouse.org/sites/files/chathamhouse/publications/research/2016-04-29-NSAG-macleod-hofmann-saul-webb-hogg.pdf. Accessed 1 November 2016

Mampilly Z (2015) Insurgent governance in the Democratic Republic of Congo. In: Krieger H (ed) Inducing compliance with international humanitarian law: Lessons from the African Great Lakes Region. Cambridge University Press, Cambridge, pp 44–78

Martinovic M (2016) The challenges of asymmetric warfare: Enhancing compliance with international humanitarian law by organized armed groups. Anchor Academic Publishing, Hamburg

Middle East Research Institute (MERI) (2016) Compliance of armed forces with international humanitarian law, Policy Note. http://www.meri-k.org/wp-content/uploads/2016/05/

Compliance-of-Armed-Forces-with-IHL-MERI-Policy-Note-May-2016.pdf. Accessed 10 October 2016

Mills K (2015) International responses to mass atrocities in Africa: Responsibility to protect, prosecute and palliate. University of Pennsylvania Press, Philadelphia

Morrow J (2007) Why do states follow the laws of war? American Political Science Review 101 (3):559–572

Narang N (2015) Assisting uncertainty: How humanitarian aid can inadvertently prolong civil war. International Studies Quarterly 59(1):184–195

Ratner S (2011) Law promotion beyond law talk: The Red Cross, persuasion, and the laws of war. European Journal of International Law 22(2):459–506

Raustiala K, Slaughter A (2002) International law, international relations and compliance. In: Carlsnaes W, Risse T, Simmons B (eds) Handbook of international relations. Sage, London

Regan P (2010) Interventions into civil wars: A retrospective survey with prospective ideas. Civil Wars 12(4):456–476

Risse T, Sikkink K (1999) The socialization of international human rights norms into domestic practices: Introduction. In: Risse T, Ropp S, Sikkink K (eds) The power of human rights: International norms and domestic change. Cambridge University Press, Cambridge, pp 1–38

Roberts A, Sivakumaran S (2012) Lawmaking by non-state actors: Engaging armed groups in the creation of international humanitarian law. Yale Journal of International Law 37(1):107–152

Ryngaert C, Van de Meulebroucke A (2011) Enhancing and enforcing compliance with international humanitarian law by non-state armed groups: An inquiry into some mechanisms. Journal of Conflict and Security Law 16(3):443–272

Salehyan I, Wood R, Siroky D (2014) External rebel sponsorship and civilian abuse: A principal-agent analysis of wartime atrocities. International Organization 98(3):633–661

Sassòli M (2007) The implementation of international humanitarian law: Current and inherent challenges. Yearbook of International Humanitarian Law 10:45–73

Sassòli M (2010) Taking armed groups seriously: Ways to improve their compliance with international humanitarian law. International Humanitarian Legal Studies 1:5–51

Scheffer D (2012) All the missing souls: A personal history of the war crimes tribunals. Princeton University Press, Princeton

Sechser T, Fuhrman M (2013) Crisis bargaining and nuclear blackmail. International Organization 67(1):173–95

Sivakumaran S (2009) Courts of armed opposition groups: Fair trials or summary justice? Journal of International Criminal Justice 7(3):489–513

Sivakumaran S (2012) The law of non-international armed conflict. Oxford University Press, Oxford

Sivakumaran S (2012) The ownership of international humanitarian law: Non-state armed groups and the formation of enforcement of IHL rules. In: Perrin B (ed) Modern warfare: Armed groups, private militaries, humanitarian organizations, and the law. UBC Press, Vancouver

Tull D (2015) UN peacekeeping in the Democratic Republic of the Congo: The travails of civilian protection. In: Krieger H (ed) Inducing compliance with international humanitarian law: Lessons from the Great Lakes Region. Cambridge University Press, Cambridge, pp 399–416

Tyler T (2006) Why people obey the law. Princeton University Press, Princeton

Weinstein J (2007) Inside rebellion: The politics of insurgent violence. Cambridge University Press, New York

Case Law

Supreme Court of the United States, *Holder v Humanitarian Law Project*, 21 June 2010, 561 U.S. 1 (2010), 130 S.Ct. 2705

Treaties

Protocol Additional to the Geneva Conventions of 12 August 1949, and relating to the Protection of Victims of Non-International Armed Conflicts, opened for signature 8 June 1977, 1125 UNTS 609 (entered into force 7 December 1978)

Chapter 4
Crime-Based Targeted Sanctions: Promoting Respect for International Humanitarian Law by the Security Council

Hilde D. Roskam

Abstract The UN Security Council (Security Council) has the task to maintain and restore the international peace and security. As a part of this task, it has the competence to impose targeted sanctions against individuals and entities that commit violations of international humanitarian law, when this poses a threat to the international peace. In recent years—since 2004—the Security Council expressly created the possibility to actually make use of this competence by adopting listing criteria towards that end in eight different sanctions regimes. Indeed, many individuals and substantially less entities have been listed by the Security Council or a sanctions committee (partly) because they committed violations of international humanitarian law. This tool has also been used against armed groups and their leaders in the Central African Republic (CAR) and the Democratic Republic of Congo (DRC) that violated international humanitarian law (IHL), e.g. by recruiting and using children. The studies into the two cases showed that these measures have not been implemented effectively and that it is not clear what exactly armed groups should do in order to have the measures against them lifted. More generally, it is questionable whether the Security Council is the best organ to deal with violations of IHL and whether targeted sanctions are useful in ensuring respect for IHL. Because the practice of imposing sanctions in response to violations of IHL is quite new, it is possible that relevant concerns, especially practical problems, can and will be addressed in the future. However, even then, it is problematic to leave the enforcement of IHL to the Security Council.

Hilde D. Roskam is a Ph.D.-candidate at the Grotius Centre for Public International Law of the Leiden University. She would like to thank Prof. Dr. N.J. Schrijver and Dr. D.A. Dam for commenting on a previous version of this chapter.

H.D. Roskam (✉)
Facultyof Law, Department of Public International Law, Leiden University, Postbus 9520, 2300 LA Leiden, The Netherlands
e-mail: h.d.roskam@law.leidenuniv.nl

T.D. Gill et al. (eds.), *Yearbook of International Humanitarian Law 2016*,
Yearbook of International Humanitarian Law 19,
https://doi.org/10.1007/978-94-6265-213-2_4

Keywords Targeted sanctions · Security Council · International humanitarian law – Armed groups · Crime-based sanctions · Democratic Republic of the Congo · Central African Republic

Contents

4.1 Introduction

Non-state armed groups play an increasingly important role in intrastate and interstate armed conflicts. This poses the problem of enforcing compliance by those groups with rules of international humanitarian law (IHL). The UN Security Council (Security Council) has identified enhancing compliance of non-state armed groups with their obligations under international law as a core challenge to effectively protecting civilians.[1] In a later resolution on the Protection of Civilians in Armed Conflict, the Security Council reiterated "its primary responsibility for the maintenance of international peace and security and, in this context, the need to promote and ensure respect for the principles and rules of international humanitarian law".[2] One of the tools available to the Security Council is the imposition of targeted sanctions against those violating international humanitarian law. The imposition of targeted sanctions against individuals and groups that committed violations of international law, more specifically international humanitarian law,

[1] UN Security Council 2009b, preamble.

[2] UN Security Council 2014d, preamble.

can be labeled as crime-based targeted sanctions, according to the categorization of different types of targeted sanctions as developed by Moiseienko and Hufnagel. Crime-based targeted sanctions are targeted measures that are imposed in response to a wrong-doing that is normally treated as criminal offence.[3] The idea of imposing such crime-based targeted sanctions was already recommended by the Secretary-General in 1999 in a report that contained recommendations "aimed at identifying ways in which the Security Council can promote full respect for international humanitarian, human rights and refugee law, by States and non-state actors, and particularly by parties to conflicts."[4] Recommendation 22 of this report reads:

> I recommend that the Security Council:
> 22. Make greater use of targeted sanctions to deter and contain those who commit egregious violations of international humanitarian law and human rights law, as well as those parties to conflicts which continually defy the resolutions of the Security Council, thereby flouting its authority.[5]

The idea to impose sanctions against those violating international humanitarian law also came up in relation to the more specific item of Children and Armed Conflict. In Resolution 1539 the Security Council stresses its "determination to ensure respect for its resolutions and other international norms and standards for the protection of children affected by armed conflict"[6] and "takes note with deep concern of the continued recruitment and use of children by parties mentioned in the Secretary-General's report in situations of armed conflict which are on its agenda, in violation of applicable international law relating to the rights and protection of children".[7] It then "expresses its intention to consider imposing targeted and graduated measures, through country-specific resolutions […] against these parties if they refuse to enter into dialogue, fail to develop an action plan or fail to meet the commitments included in their action plan".[8] The intention to impose targeted measures against parties to situations that are on the Council's agenda and in violation of applicable international law relating to the rights and protection of children in armed conflict is repeated in Resolution 1612.[9]

Also in relation to the Security Council's thematic issue of Women, Peace and Security, the Council expressed the intention to "take into consideration the appropriateness of targeted and graduated measures against parties to situations of

[3] Moiseienko and Hufnagel 2015, pp. 357–358.

[4] UN Security Council 1999, para 35.

[5] Ibid., Recommendation 22.

[6] UN Security Council 2004, preamble.

[7] Ibid., para 5.

[8] Ibid., para 5(c).

[9] UN Security Council 2005c, para 8.

armed conflict who commit rape and other forms of sexual violence against women and girls in situations of armed conflict".[10] The same intention was expressed in subsequent resolutions.[11]

Parallel to the adoption of resolutions that expressed the intention to adopt targeted sanctions against entities and individuals violating the rights of children and women in armed conflict, the Security Council also adopted listing criteria that rendered possible the imposition of these sanctions. It did so in eight cases since 2004, namely Côte d'Ivoire, the Democratic Republic of the Congo (DRC), Sudan, Somalia, Libya, the Central African Republic (CAR), Yemen and South Sudan. In two of these situations, the DRC and the CAR, the Security Council has adopted targeted sanctions against armed groups and their leaders that violated rules of international humanitarian law.

This chapter will analyze the imposition of targeted sanctions as a means to promote respect of armed groups and their leaders for IHL. Section 4.2 will first discuss the competence of the Security Council to impose targeted sanctions against those violating IHL, and secondly the way the Security Council made the imposition of sanctions towards this end possible by adopting relevant listing criteria. Section 4.3 will then contain more detailed studies of the two situations in which the Security Council adopted targeted sanctions against armed groups and their leaders who violated rules of international humanitarian law. As a conclusion, Sect. 4.4 will critically analyze this recent practice. It will first deal with the question whether the Security Council would be an appropriate organ to promote respect for IHL. Secondly, it will discuss whether targeted sanctions are the appropriate tool to enhance compliance with IHL.

4.2 Crime-Based Targeted Sanctions: Competence and First Practice

This section will discuss the competence of the Security Council to impose sanctions against groups and individuals violating rules of international humanitarian law. First, the competences and tasks of the Security Council under the Charter of the United Nations (UN Charter) are discussed. Subsequently, this section will show how the Security Council in practice started to use this competence, by adopting listing criteria that target perpetrators of violations of IHL. A short evaluation concludes the section.

[10] UN Security Council 2008b, para 5.

[11] UN Security Council 2009a, para 10; and UN Security Council 2010, para 7.

4.2.1 The Competence of the Security Council to Impose Sanctions Against Those Violating IHL

The Security Council is the United Nations organ entrusted with the primary responsibility for the maintenance of the international peace and security.[12] To fulfil its tasks, the Security Council is competent to take measures under Chapter VII of the UN Charter that are binding on the member states of the United Nations.[13] However, before the Security Council can take binding decisions on the use of forcible or non-forcible measures, it has to determine that a threat to the peace exists.[14] The concept of threat to the peace functions thus as the threshold for any Security Council enforcement action, since the concepts of "breach of the peace" and "act of aggression" are hardly used.[15] The definition of the concept of "threat to the peace" is not clear from the UN Charter and it can be concluded that the Security Council has a considerable margin of appreciation to decide on the existence of a threat to the peace.[16] And while the power of the Security Council is not unlimited,[17] the Council may decide that violations of international humanitarian law could pose a threat to the international peace and security, even when taking place within a single state. In fact, the Security Council has made this decision in an increasing number of situations.

When the Security Council has determined that a situation that involves violations of IHL constitutes a threat to the international peace and security, it consequently may take measures under Chapter VII of the UN Charter, including the imposition of sanctions against "violators" based on Article 41. This finding might seem somewhat counterintuitive, as it is generally accepted that the Council's task is to maintain international peace, which is not the same as enforcing international law.[18] However, it cannot be overlooked that many cases in which a threat to the peace was determined to exist involve (massive) violations of international law, especially human rights law or international humanitarian law. A prior finding of illegality thus often forms the basis for determining the existence of a threat to the

[12] Charter of the United Nations, opened for signature 26 June 1945, 1 UNTS XVI (entered into force 24 October 1945) (UN Charter), Article 24.

[13] Ibid., Article 25 and Chapter VII.

[14] Ibid., Article 39. This consecutive order cannot solely be based on the wording of Articles 41 or 42, but follows from the entirety of Chapter VII. See Farral 2007, pp. 64–65.

[15] Lamb 1999, pp. 361–388.

[16] See e.g. United Nations Conference on International Organization 1945; Brichambaut 2001, pp. 269–276; López-Jacoiste 2010, p. 279; Orakhelashvili 2011, p. 156.

[17] See e.g. Orakhelashvili 2006, pp. 68–70; Schweigman 2001, p. 163 and following; Krisch 2012, p. 1258; De Wet 2004, p. 193; Vradenburgh 1991. See also UN Charter, above n 12, Articles 27–32.

[18] Kelsen 1950, p. 294.

peace and for taking enforcement measures.[19] The relationship between violations of law and threats to the peace is logical as Orakhelashvili explains:

> The argument that an Article 39 determination of a 'threat to the peace' can be made in relation to state conduct in accordance with international law projects a systemic inconsistency on the international legal system. For, if a conduct of a state is lawful yet threatens international peace, then the conclusion is that the pertinent rules of international law authorize that state to act in a way threatening international peace.[20]

Since the adoption of the UN Charter, many rules of international law have developed or have been codified or crystallized, also specifically in the field of international humanitarian law. In addition to states, as Orakhelashvili argues, it would be increasingly difficult to conceive how individuals or armed groups could pose a threat to the peace without violating any rule of international law. As a result, the Security Council's task to maintain peace will increasingly cohere with ensuring respect for international law.

A second argument could be made here. It is not only logical that the Security Council will play a role in enforcing respect for IHL, it is also what the international community expects from the Council. Indeed, several legal developments after the adoption of the UN Charter indicate that the international community sees a role for the United Nations and the Security Council in enforcing international norms deemed of fundamental importance, and more specifically in enforcing IHL. For example, Article VIII of the Convention on the Prevention and Punishment of the Crime of Genocide (Genocide Convention) provides that competent organs of the United Nations can take action upon the request of the members to the Convention in order to prevent or suppress acts of genocide.[21] Article 89 of Additional Protocol I to the Geneva Conventions provides that in case of serious violations of IHL Contracting Parties undertake to act jointly or individually, in co-operation with the United Nations and in conformity with the UN Charter.[22] In addition, the concept of the Responsibility to Protect, as adopted in the 2005 World Summit Outcome Document reads:

> we are prepared to take collective action, in a timely and decisive manner, through the Security Council, in accordance with the Charter, including Chapter VII, on a case-by-case basis and in cooperation with relevant regional organizations as appropriate, should peaceful means be inadequate and national authorities are manifestly failing to protect their populations from genocide, war crimes, ethnic cleansing and crimes against humanity.[23]

---

[19] Schweigman 2001, p. 156; Gowlland-Debbas 2011, p. 42; Gowlland-Debbas 2001, p. 288; Shraga 2011, p. 12–13.

[20] Orakhelashvili 2011, p. 172.

[21] Convention on the Prevention and Punishment of the Crime of Genocide, opened for signature 9 December 1948, 78 UNTS 277 (entered into force 12 January 1951), Article VIII.

[22] Protocol Additional to the Geneva Contentions of 12 August 1949, and relating to the Protection of Victims of International Armed Conflicts, opened for signature 12 December 1977, 1125 UNTS 3 (entered into force 7 December 1979) (Additional Protocol I), Article 89; Bourloyannis 1991–1992, p. 339 and 342.

[23] UN General Assembly 2005, para 139.

Although none of these legal instruments grants additional competences to the Security Council, nor explicitly confers upon the Council the task of enforcing international humanitarian law, they do create expectations about the way the Security Council interprets its competences and responsibilities.[24] They show that the international community envisages some task for the Security Council when it comes to ensuring respect for international humanitarian law. This view is even further supported by the fact that the Rome Statute of the International Criminal Court foresees a role for the Security Council in enforcing international legal norms and holding individuals accountable for such violations.[25]

4.2.2 The Security Council's Use of the Competence to Impose Crime-Based Sanctions

The Security Council thus may take action to ensure respect for IHL when it has determined that a threat to the peace exists, and is increasingly expected to do so. One of the measures it could take is imposing sanctions, including against individuals and groups, based on Article 41 of the UN Charter. Article 41 provides the Security Council with a considerable freedom of appreciation to take measures not involving the use of armed force. Since the article does not provide for a closed list of possible measures, the Security Council is free in deciding the type of measures and their binding nature.[26] This margin of discretion extends to the selection of targets against whom the measures will be applied.[27]

Since 2004, the Security Council started to make use of crime-based targeted sanctions. It has adopted listing criteria directed at individuals or entities responsible for violations of international humanitarian law and/or international human rights law in eight different sanctions regimes since 2004. These sanction regimes concern Somalia, the Democratic Republic of the Congo, Côte d'Ivoire, Sudan, Libya, the Central African Republic, Yemen and South Sudan. The exact formulation of the listing criteria differs per sanction regime. For example, relevant listing criteria adopted in relation to the Central African Republic read as follows:

> (b) [individuals and entities] involved in planning, directing, or committing acts that violate international human rights law or international humanitarian law, as applicable, or that constitute human rights abuses or violations in the Central African Republic, including acts involving sexual violence, targeting of civilians, ethnic- or religious-based attacks, attacks on schools and hospitals, and abduction and forced displacement;

---

[24] See e.g. Lopez 2013, p. 781; Roscini 2010.

[25] Rome Statute of the International Criminal Court, opened for signature 17 July 1998, 2187 UNTS 90 (entered into force 1 July 2002), e.g. Articles 13(b) and 16.

[26] López-Jacoiste 2010, p. 284; Al-Anbari 2001, p. 372; Schrijver 1994, p. 155; Krisch 2012, p. 1260.

[27] Martenczuk 1999, p. 545.

(c) [individuals and entities] recruiting or using children in armed conflict, in violation of applicable international law;[28]

These criteria are quite precisely formulated. They refer to the specific conflict in the Central African Republic, they give examples of conduct that would be in violation of international law and that thus would fall under the designation criteria, and they specify that not only those who commit violations of international law might be subjected to sanctions, but also those that are involved in the planning or direction of the objectionable conduct.

In other sanction regimes the Security Council has adopted less concrete criteria, for example in the case of Sudan:

> those individuals, as designated by the committee [...], based on the information provided by Member States, the Secretary-General, the High Commissioner for Human Rights or the Panel of Experts [...], and other relevant sources, who [...] commit violations of international humanitarian or human rights law or other atrocities.[29]

Here it is only mentioned that individuals who commit violations of international law or atrocities can be subjected to targeted sanctions. The criterion is not explicitly limited to the conflict in Sudan, and the objectionable conduct potentially is quite broad ("atrocities"). Interestingly, the resolution provides for a list of authorities that may provide the information on which the listing is based. Other sanction regimes only express that targeted measures can be imposed on individuals "designated by the Committee". In the case of Sudan only individuals could be listed, whereas other sanction regimes allow for the listing of entities. Some of the eight sanctions regimes explicitly mention leaders of armed groups as possible subject of sanctions. In some cases, specific designation criteria only aim at leaders of (armed) groups. For example, in the case of South Sudan, only "leaders of any entity, including any South Sudanese government, opposition, militia, or other group",[30] that have engaged in sanctionable activities can be subjected to sanctions.

In any case, the relevant designation criteria focus on individuals and sometimes also entities directly responsible for violations of international law. They do not refer to those that *might* be involved in the commission of serious violations of international law nor to individuals that are *in the eyes of the Sanction Committee* deemed responsible for violations of international humanitarian law. Based on the wording of the designation criteria, the Security Council envisages to target individuals and entities with direct responsibility for violations of international humanitarian law. The sanctions that consequently are imposed based on these listing criteria thus indeed fall under the definition of crime-based targeted sanctions, as these individuals could potentially also be criminally prosecuted for the acts for which they have been listed. Yet, the primary task of the Security Council and the primary aim of these sanctions still would be the maintenance of international peace, and not the

[28] UN Security Council 2014a, para 37(b) and (c).

[29] UN Security Council 2005a, para 3(c).

[30] UN Security Council 2015c, para 8.

enforcement of international humanitarian law. In recent resolutions that provide for designation criteria relating to violations of international humanitarian law, this is made expressly clear by providing the link between violations of IHL and a threat to the peace. For example, Resolution 2206 concerning the situation in South Sudan imposes an asset freeze and travel ban on individuals and entities

> designated as responsible for or complicit in, or having engaged in, directly or indirectly, actions or policies that threaten the peace, security or stability of South Sudan.[31]

The Security Council in the next paragraph of the Resolution:

> [u]nderscores that such actions or policies may include, but are not limited to:
>
> (c) Planning, directing, or committing acts that violate applicable international human rights law or international humanitarian law, or acts that constitute human rights abuses in South Sudan;
>
> (d) The targeting of civilians, including women and children, through the commission of acts of violence (including killing, maiming, torture, or rape or other sexual violence), abduction, enforced disappearance, forced displacement, or attacks on schools, hospitals, religious sites, or locations where civilians are seeking refuge, or through conduct that would constitute a serious abuse or violation of human rights or a violation of international humanitarian law;
>
> (e) The use or recruitment of children by armed groups or armed forces in the context of the armed conflict in South Sudan;
>
> […][32]

Individuals and entities are thus primarily listed because they threaten the peace, security or stability of South Sudan. The threat to the peace and security can consist of actions that are in violation of international humanitarian law. The same method of sanctioning those responsible for violations of IHL because these violations are regarded a threat to the international peace and security is adopted in relation to the situation in Yemen, and in the reformulated listing criteria concerning Libya and the Democratic Republic of the Congo.[33] This is an important indication that the Security Council imposes sanctions mainly for the maintenance of peace, rather than with the purpose of enforcing international law.

4.2.3 Evaluation

The Security Council is thus competent to impose sanctions in response to violations of international humanitarian law, if the situation constitutes a threat to the international peace. In the more recent sanctions regimes, the Security Council made this link between a threat to the peace and violations of IHL expressly clear,

---

[31] Ibid., para 6.

[32] Ibid., para 7(c), (d) and (e).

[33] UN Security Council 2014b, paras 17 and 18 (Yemen); UN Security Council 2014c, para 4 (Libya); UN Security Council 2015b, para 5.

by stating that individuals could be listed when they pose a threat to the international peace, and that such a threat could consist of committing violations of IHL.

In recent years, the Security Council adopted listing criteria referring to violations of IHL as the basis for the imposition of sanctions in eight cases. The exact wording of these designation criteria differs per situation. As illustrated above, some listing criteria spell out specific violations of IHL, whereas criteria in other sanctions regimes refer to "violations of IHL" generally. Arguments in favor of both approaches have been made. For instance, Schotten and Biehler argue that the focus of the Security Council on selected norms of IHL in some sanctions regimes (mainly related to children and armed conflict and sexual violence) could lead to the belief that other violations of IHL are regarded to be less grave in the eyes of the Security Council.[34] The Group of Experts for the DRC acknowledges the problem of a selective approach to violations of IHL and stated:

> The Group interprets subparagraph 4(e) [of Resolution 1857] as encompassing all violations of international human rights and international humanitarian law, not limited to the specific abuses listed in the subparagraph, and especially in consideration of the context of indiscriminate attacks on the civilian population perpetrated by armed groups and FARDC. A comprehensive and independent approach to monitoring and addressing human rights abuses, versus a selective focus on specific violations or on a particular category of victims, becomes all the more needed in the current security context in eastern Democratic Republic of Congo.[35]

On the other hand, research shows that when there is only a general listing criteria for violations of IHL, it is less likely that specific information about violations committed against children is brought to the attention of the Committee and that perpetrators of these violations are added to the sanctions list.[36]

In any case, the adoption of listing criteria with the aim to impose sanctions against individuals and entities that commit violations of IHL, indicates the importance the Security Council attaches to ensuring respect for IHL. The many individuals and some entities listed under these regimes are a further expression of the Security Council's willingness to promote compliance with IHL.

4.3 The Imposition of Targeted Sanctions Against Armed Groups: Two Case Studies

This section will examine in more detail two cases in which the Security Council imposed targeted sanctions on armed groups and their leaders that committed violations of international humanitarian law. The first case concerns the Democratic

[34] Schotten and Biehler 2008, p. 323.

[35] Security Council Committee Established Pursuant to Resolution 1533 (2004) Concerning the Democratic Republic of the Congo 2009, para 310.

[36] Kandiah Thompson 2014, p. 116.

Republic of the Congo, where three armed groups are listed, the second concerns the Central African Republic where one armed group has been subjected to targeted sanctions.[37] Both case studies will address the criteria under which the groups are listed, the leaders that have been listed in connection with the groups, the goals the Security Council aims to pursue by the imposition of targeted sanctions and the implementation of the measures.

4.3.1 Case 1: The Democratic Republic of the Congo

Already in 2003 the Security Council determined that the situation in the Democratic Republic of the Congo constituted a threat to the peace.[38] Since then, it has adopted numerous resolutions on the situation, mainly relating to the threat posed by the presence of Congolese and foreign armed groups in the Eastern part of the DRC.[39]

Of the many armed groups that are or have been active in the DRC, three have been subjected to an asset freeze. These are the Allied Democratic Forces (ADF), the Forces Démocratiques de Libération du Rwanda (FDLR) and the Mouvement du 23 Mars (M23).

On 30 June 2014, the ADF has been listed as CDe.001 under the sanctions regime concerning the DRC. The ADF was created in 1995 and is located in the DRC near the border with Uganda. It has an estimated strength of about 1500 fighters.[40] The narrative summary refers to the following basis for the listing:

- Recruited and used child soldiers in violation of applicable international law (S/RES/2078, para 4(d))
- Committed numerous violations of international human rights and international humanitarian law against women and children, including killing, maiming, and sexual violence (S/RES/2078, para 4(e))

[37] The only other sanctions regime of the eight mentioned in this Chapter that imposed sanctions against an armed group is the regime concerning Somalia. However, Al-Shabaab in Somalia has been excluded here, as it can be argued that this organization mostly would qualify as a terrorist organization. Al-Shabaab has publicly announced that it is cooperating with Al-Qaeda. It is mainly listed for engaging in acts that threaten the peace, security and stability of Somalia and obstructing the delivery of humanitarian assistance. The narrative summary refers to the actions of Al-Shabaab as coercing and intimidating the Somali population. A campaign of bombings and targeted killings was intended to disrupt the elections. No specific mention is made to the violation of international humanitarian law generally, whereas this clearly is the case in relation to the other four groups elaborated on in this section.

[38] UN Security Council 2003, preamble.

[39] See e.g. UN Security Council 2008a, preamble.

[40] Security Council Committee Established Pursuant to Resolution 1533 (2004) Concerning the Democratic Republic of the Congo (2014) Narrative Summaries of Reasons for Listing, CDe.001, Allied Democratic Forces (ADF). https://www.un.org/sc/suborg/en/sanctions/1533/materials/summaries/entity/allied-democratic-forces-%28adf%29. Accessed 4 July 2017.

- Participated in attacks against the United Nations Organization Stabilization Mission in the Democratic Republic of the Congo (MONUSCO) peacekeepers (S/RES/2078, para 4(i))[41]

The narrative summary refers to reports of the Group of Experts on the DRC, the Africa Director for Human Rights Watch, Africa Report, a Uganda People's Defence Force (UPDF) spokesperson, Global Horizontal Note, MONUSCO and a report of the Secretary-General on conflict-related sexual violence which indicates several violations of IHL and human rights law. The narrative summary provides several examples of these violations, e.g. "[a]ccording to the GoE's [Group of Experts] 2012 final report, the ADF recruits include children, as exemplified by the case of an ADF recruiter who was captured by Ugandan authorities in Kasese with six young boys on his way to the DRC in July 2012."[42]

The only individual designated with special reference to the leadership of ADF is Jamil Mukulu,[43] who has been listed on 13 October 2011, well before the imposition of sanctions against ADF itself. This is despite the fact that the narrative summary for ADF indicates that Hood Lukwago is ADF's military commander. In addition, ADF according to the 1533 (2004) sanctions list was split into several small groups as of December 2014, with Mukulu leading one main group, and Seka Baluku leading the other.[44] Baluku and Lukwago thus far have not been subjected to sanctions.

The FDLR is listed as CDe.005 on 31 December 2012. It is one of the largest foreign armed groups operating in the DRC and it was formed in 2000.[45] The narrative summary refers to the following basis for the listing:

- Committed serious violations of international law involving the targeting of women and children in armed conflict, including killing and maiming, sexual violence and forced displacement (S/RES/2078, para 4(e))[46]

---

[41] Ibid.

[42] Ibid.

[43] Security Council Committee Established Pursuant to Resolution 1533 (2004) Concerning the Democratic Republic of the Congo (2015) Narrative Summaries of Reasons for Listing, CDi.015, Jamil Mukulu. https://www.un.org/sc/suborg/en/sanctions/1533/materials/summaries/individual/jamil-mukulu. Accessed 4 July 2017.

[44] Security Council Committee Established Pursuant to Resolution 1533 (2004) Concerning the Democratic Republic of the Congo (2014) Narrative Summaries of Reasons for Listing, CDe.001, Allied Democratic Forces (ADF). https://www.un.org/sc/suborg/en/sanctions/1533/materials/summaries/entity/allied-democratic-forces-%28adf%29. Accessed 4 July 2017.

[45] Security Council Committee Established Pursuant to Resolution 1533 (2004) Concerning the Democratic Republic of the Congo (2014) Narrative Summaries of Reasons for Listing, CDe.005, Forces Democratiques de Liberation du Rwanda (FDLR). https://www.un.org/sc/suborg/en/sanctions/1533/materials/summaries/entity/forces-democratiques-de-liberation-du-rwanda-%28fdlr%29. Accessed 4 July 2017.

[46] Ibid.

The narrative summary refers to Amnesty International, Human Rights Watch, the Group of Experts on the DRC, "United Nations investigation" and the UN in general as sources of information regarding violations of IHL committed by the FDLR. These violations include the raping of women and girls, the decapitation and burning alive of civilians and recruitment of children below the age of 18.[47]

Ten individuals with a leading position in the FDLR have been listed under the same sanction regime. All these individuals were listed before the armed group itself was listed.[48]

The M23 has been listed as CDe.006 on 31 December 2012. The narrative summary reveals the following basis for its listing:

- Complicit in and responsible for committing serious violations of international law involving the targeting of women and children in situations of armed conflict in the DRC including killing and maiming, sexual violence, abduction, and forced displacement (S/RES/2078, para 4(e)).[49]

The narrative summary refers to eyewitness testimonies and "numerous reports, investigations and testimonies" to substantiate the justification of the listing of M23. The narrative summary reveals violations including mass killings of civilians, extensive forced recruitment of children, and raping of women and girls.[50]

Five individuals have been listed in relation to M23.[51] It is relevant to note that their official positions are not always clear. For example, Eric Badege and Sultani

---

[47] Ibid.

[48] The following persons have been listed in relation to the FDLR: Gaston Iyamuremye, CDi.003, FDLR President and FDLR-FOCA 2nd Vice-President (1 December 2010); Callixte Mbarushimana, CDi.010, Executive Secretary of the FDLR and Vice-President of the FDLR military high command (3 March 2009); Sylvestre Mudacumura, CDi.012, Military Commander of FDLR-FOCA (1 November 2005); Leodomir Mugaragu, CDi.013, Chief of Staff of the FDLR-FOCA (1 December 2010); Leopold Mujyambere, CDi.014, Commander of the Second Division of FDLR-FOCA (3 March 2009); Ignace Murwanashyaka, CDi.016, President of the FDLR and supreme commander of the FDLR-FOCA (1 November 2005); Straton Musoni, CDi.017, 1st Vice-President of the FDLR (29 March 2007); Felicien Nsanzubukire, CDi.023, 1st battalion leader of the FDLR-FOCA (1 December 2010); Pacifique Ntawunguka, CDi.024, Commander of the First Division of FDLR-FOCA (3 March 2009); Stanislas Nzeyimana, CDi.026, Deputy Commander of the FDLR-FOCA (3 March 2009).

[49] Security Council Committee Established Pursuant to Resolution 1533 (2004) Concerning the Democratic Republic of the Congo (2014) Narrative Summaries of Reasons for Listing, CDe.006, M23. https://www.un.org/sc/suborg/en/sanctions/1533/materials/summaries/entity/m23. Accessed 4 July 2017.

[50] Ibid.

[51] The following persons have been listed in relation to M23: Eric Badege, CDi.001, "a military commander of the M23" (31 December 2012); Innocent Kaina, CDi.004, Sector Commander in the M23 (30 November 2012); Sultani Makenga, CDi.008, "a military leader" of the M23 (13 November 2012); Boudoin Ngaruye Wa Myamuro, CDi.019, Third highest ranking military commander within the M23 (30 November 2012); Jean-Marie Lugerero, CDi.028, Coordinator of the political wing of M23 (31 December 2012). In addition, Taganda (or Ntaganda) has been referred to as leader of the M23 by the Group of Experts (UN Security Council, Group of Experts

Makenga are just referred to as “a military commander” or “a military leader”.[52] Two of the individuals have been listed together with M23. The three others have been listed before M23 itself was listed.

4.3.1.1 The Goals

The Security Council in the resolution establishing the travel ban and asset freeze in relation to the DRC determined that “it shall review the measures […] in the light of progress accomplished in the peace and transition process in the Democratic Republic of the Congo, in particular with regard to the integration of the Armed Forces and of the National Police”.[53] In subsequent resolutions this phrase has been modified several times, until it reads

> decides that […] it shall review the measures set forth in this resolution, with a view to adjusting them, as appropriate, in light of the security situation in the DRC, in particular progress in security sector reform and in disarming, demobilizing, repatriating, resettling and reintegrating, as appropriate, Congolese and foreign armed groups, with a particular focus on children among them, and compliance with this resolution.[54]

In addition, the resolutions refer to a set of demands, that needs to be fulfilled. The failure to comply with these demands has led to the continuous renewal of the targeted measures and other measures taken by the Security Council. These demands, however, mainly refer to obligations on the side of the government of the DRC and the governments of neighbouring countries.[55] Other repeatedly highlighted demands refer to the obligation to cooperate with the Group of Experts and the United Nations Organization Mission in the Democratic Republic of the Congo (MONUC) and to ensure their safety and that of UN personnel generally.[56] Finally, para 5 of Resolution 1596 “demands that all parties […] help the Government of

on the Democratic Republic of the Congo 2013). He is being subjected to sanctions, but his narrative summary only refers to leadership of UPC/L, an armed group preceding M23.

[52] Security Council Committee Established Pursuant to Resolution 1533 (2004) Concerning the Democratic Republic of the Congo (2014) Narrative Summaries of Reasons for Listing, CDi.001, Eric Badege. https://www.un.org/sc/suborg/en/sanctions/1533/materials/summaries/individual/eric-badege. Accessed 4 July 2017; and Security Council Committee Established Pursuant to Resolution 1533 (2004) Concerning the Democratic Republic of the Congo (2014) Narrative Summaries of Reasons for Listing, CDi.008, Sultani Makenga. https://www.un.org/sc/suborg/en/sanctions/1533/materials/summaries/individual/sultani-makenga. Accessed 4 July 2017.

[53] UN Security Council 2005b, para 17.

[54] UN Security Council 2016b, para 37.

[55] See e.g. UN Security Council 2005d, paras 15 and 16 which demand of those governments to take measures to prevent the use of their territories in support of violations of the arms embargo and impede support to the illegal exploitation of natural resources; See also UN Security Council 2003, para 18.

[56] UN Security Council 2003, paras 15 and 19; UN Security Council 2005b, para 19.

National Unity and Transition implement its commitments regarding disarmament, demobilization and reintegration of foreign and Congolese combatants, and regarding security sector reform".[57] The goals the Security Council aims to pursue are thus quite clear, although it is much less clear what armed groups should do themselves in order to have the measures against them lifted, and how the asset freeze might help in achieving the goals pursued.

The Group of Experts on the DRC sheds more light on the specific aim of the targeted measures when it writes:

> The Ituri armed groups benefit from the commercial and logistical networks they have developed in neighbouring States as well as in countries further afield. The Group reiterates the need to limit the cross-border freedom of movement of these armed groups and strongly encourages that measures be taken to deny them access to funds that are used to sustain their military apparatus, in violation of the arms embargo. To this end, the Group recommends that the Security Council consider imposing a travel ban on and freezing the assets of representatives of the Ituri armed groups, in particular their high-ranking leaders.[58]

Over a year later, the Group of Experts indicated that listing armed groups in addition to their leaders could prove useful:

> The Group observes that although some individual members of FDLR have been listed by the Security Council as subject to financial and travel sanctions, FDLR organizations have not. It would be advantageous to peace and security in the region if FDLR organizations were listed as sanctionable entities and if membership in those organizations were to lead to automatic financial sanctions and travel bans.[59]

Limiting access to funds that could be used for weapons is thus one goal of targeted measures. Another, according to the Group of Experts, is that sanctions could act as a deterrent and can assist in "establishing a conducive environment for the extension of State control and the dismantling of networks that are not compliant with United Nations resolutions."[60]

4.3.1.2 Implementation

The targeted measures have not been well implemented. The Group of Experts in relation to the DRC in 2007 noted that it was not aware of any enforcement actions relating to the sanctions and that all sanctioned individuals and entities continue their activities with impunity.[61] The same criticism is repeated in subsequent years.

---

[57] UN Security Council 2005b, para 5.

[58] UN Security Council, Group of Experts on the Democratic Republic of the Congo 2005a, para 241.

[59] UN Security Council, Group of Experts on the Democratic Republic of the Congo 2006, para 56.

[60] UN Security Council, Group of Experts on the Democratic Republic of the Congo 2005b, para 19.

[61] UN Security Council, Group of Experts on the Democratic Republic of the Congo 2007, paras 139 and 23.

The Group of Experts warned that its work will have little impact if member states do not enforce compliance with the sanctions regime[62] and stated that the limited implementation seriously undermined the credibility of the sanctions regime.[63] Later reports mention several violations of the sanctions, supported by the DRC's neighbouring countries.[64]

4.3.2 Case 2: The Central African Republic

Since 24 January 2013, when the Security Council expressed "concern at the lack of State authority outside the capital, which has led to a serious security vacuum in many parts of the Central African Republic, and has allowed the emergence and development of national and foreign armed groups, including the Lord's Resistance Army (LRA) to operate in the CAR",[65] the Security Council has adopted many resolutions dealing with the situation in the CAR, eventually resulting in the imposition of targeted measures.

One armed group has been listed under the CAR sanctions regime, which is the Lord's Resistance Army.

On 7 March 2016 the Lord's Resistance Army (LRA) was listed as CFe.002. The LRA emerged in the 1980s in Uganda and has operated in the CAR, the DRC, South Sudan and Sudan.[66] The basis of its listing is explained as follows in the narrative summary:

- engaging in or providing support for acts that undermine the peace, stability or security of the CAR (S/RES/2262, para 12)
- providing support for armed groups or criminal networks through the illicit exploitation or trade of natural resources, including diamonds, gold and wildlife products in or from the CAR (S/RES/2262, para 13(d))
- involved in planning, directing, or committing acts that violate international human rights law or international humanitarian law, as applicable, or acts that constitute human rights abuses or violations, in the CAR, including acts involving sexual violence, targeting of civilians, ethnic- or religious-based

---

[62] UN Security Council, Group of Experts on the Democratic Republic of the Congo 2008, paras 195–196.

[63] UN Security Council, Group of Experts on the Democratic Republic of the Congo 2009, para 378(28).

[64] UN Security Council, Group of Experts on the Democratic Republic of the Congo 2013, para 205.

[65] UN Security Council 2013a, preamble.

[66] Security Council Committee Established Pursuant to Resolution 2127 (2013) Concerning the Central African Republic (2016) Narrative Summaries of Reasons for Listing, CFe.002, Lord's Resistance Army. https://www.un.org/sc/suborg/en/sanctions/2127/materials/summaries/entity/lord's-resistance-army. Accessed 4 July 2017.

attacks, attacks on schools and hospitals, and abduction and forced displacement (S/RES/2262, para 13(b))
- recruiting or using children in armed conflict in the CAR, in violation of applicable international law (S/RES/2262, para 13(c))[67]

The narrative summary only refers to the words "reported" and "reportedly" when it lists the violations of IHL that the LRA has committed. No specific sources are mentioned. Those violations include numerous abductions, rape, killing, looting and destruction of property.[68]

Resolution 2262 concerning the CAR provides a listing criterion aimed at leaders of armed groups: "being leaders of an entity that the Committee has designated pursuant to paras 36 or 37 of resolution 2134 (2014) or this resolution […]."[69] Joseph Kony, described as founder, religious leader, chairman and commander in chief of LRA has been listed on 7 March 2016, together with the LRA, but without reference to this specific basis for listing.[70] Two others, Ali and Salim Kony, have been listed with reference to this criterion, even while their official position within the LRA is not very clear. Ali is referred to as potential successor of Joseph Kony and involved in the operational planning of the LRA.[71] Salim is so-called head commander of the LRA's field headquarters and responsible for the management of financial and logistical networks.[72] Both are also responsible for enforcing discipline and are held to be "members of Joseph Kony's leadership inner-circle, who are responsible for executing Joseph Kony's orders" and were listed on 23 August 2016.[73]

4.3.2.1 The Goals

In relation to the situation in the Central African Republic, the Security Council in general terms stated that

---

[67] Ibid.

[68] Ibid.

[69] UN Security Council 2016a, para 13(g).

[70] Security Council Committee Established Pursuant to Resolution 2127 (2013) Concerning the Central African Republic (2016) Narrative Summaries of Reasons for Listing, CFi.009, Joseph Kony. https://www.un.org/sc/suborg/en/sanctions/2127/materials/summaries/individual/joseph-kony. Accessed 4 July 2017.

[71] Security Council Committee Established Pursuant to Resolution 2127 (2013) Concerning the Central African Republic (2016) Narrative Summaries of Reasons for Listing, CFi.010, Ali Kony. https://www.un.org/sc/suborg/en/sanctions/2127/materials/summaries/individual/ali-kony. Accessed 4 July 2017.

[72] Security Council Committee Established Pursuant to Resolution 2127 (2013) Concerning the Central African Republic (2016) Narrative Summaries of Reasons for Listing, CFi.011, Salim Kony. https://www.un.org/sc/suborg/en/sanctions/2127/materials/summaries/individual/salim-kony. Accessed 4 July 2017.

[73] Ibid.

> it shall be prepared to review the appropriateness of the measures contained in this resolution, including the strengthening through additional measures, in particular the freezing of assets, modification, suspension or lifting of the measures, as may be needed at any time in light of the progress achieved in the stabilization of the country and compliance with this resolution.[74]

Several times the Security Council points to the critical importance of the effective implementation of the sanctions regime[75] and it states that violations of the travel ban can undermine the peace, stability or security of the Central African Republic.[76] Again, it is not immediately clear what the Security Council expects from the groups and individuals targeted. The Sanctions Committee concerning the Central African Republic sheds a bit more light on the purpose of the targeted measures in its press releases.[77] In a press release concerning a meeting with the special representatives of the Secretary-General on Children and Armed Conflict and on Sexual Violence in Conflict, it is stated that:

> [c]ommittee members expressed the view that the designation of certain individuals for financial and travel sanctions would send a strong message that the international community would no longer tolerate the serious atrocities being committed by all sides in the Central African Republic, and that perpetrators of such acts would be held accountable.[78]

Members of the Committee have stressed that the sanctions measures are in place to protect the Central African Republic and help it consolidate peace and security.[79] Another press release seems to suggest that the sanctions contribute to reducing impunity in the CAR.[80] Although this is helpful in identifying the purpose of the sanctions, it is still not clear what groups and individuals should do to have the sanctions against them lifted.

---

[74] UN Security Council 2013b, para 61; See also subsequent Resolutions, e.g. UN Security Council 2015a, para 25; UN security Council 2016a, para 32.

[75] E.g. UN Security Council 2015a, preamble.

[76] Ibid., para 6; UN Security Council 2016a, para 7.

[77] Although these press releases indicate that they are "for information media. Not an official record", they often prove to be a valuable source of information.

[78] UN Security Council (2014) Security Council Sanctions Committee Concerning Central African Republic Meets with Special Representatives of Secretary-General, Press Release SC/1138. https://www.un.org/press/en/2014/sc11388.doc.htm. Accessed 15 June 2017.

[79] UN Security Council (2015) Security Council Sanctions Committee on Central African Republic Meets with CAR Government, MINUSCA and Panel of Experts to Discuss Arms Embargo, Press Release SC/11999. https://www.un.org/press/en/2015/sc11999.doc.htm. Accessed 15 June 2017.

[80] UN Security Council (2015) Security Council Sanctions Committee Concerning Central African Republic Convenes Meeting with Regional States on Arms Embargo, Press Release SC/12024. https://www.un.org/press/en/2015/sc12024.doc.htm. Accessed 15 June 2017.

4.3.2.2 Implementation

The Panel of Experts is not positive about the implementation of the sanctions in relation to the CAR. It notes that the lack of cooperation with the panel reduces the ability of member states to implement the travel ban. It points to security links related to the trivialisation of the sanctions regime by member states and concludes that the credibility of sanctions and the threat of sanctions will be undermined.[81]

4.3.3 Evaluation

When analysing the case studies in detail, a number of relevant conclusions can be made.

First of all, all four armed groups were clearly listed—as the narrative summaries reveal—because they committed violations of international humanitarian law. For all groups, the violations committed constitute an important basis for the imposition of sanctions. Those sanctions are thus truly crime-based targeted sanctions in accordance with the definition of Moiseienko and Hufnagel. Interestingly, this cannot so easily be concluded for the sanctions that are imposed against the leaders of the armed groups. 19 individuals have been listed as a leader of one of these four armed groups. Only five out of the 19 narrative summaries refer to personal responsibility for violations of international humanitarian law.[82] Individuals are

[81] UN Security Council, Panel of Experts on the Central African Republic 2015, Annex 14, paras 14–15.

[82] These are: Joseph Kony of the LRA, who is listed as involved in planning, directing, or committing acts that violate international human rights law, or international humanitarian law (Security Council Committee Established Pursuant to Resolution 2127 (2013) Concerning the Central African Republic (2016) Narrative Summaries of Reasons for Listing, CFi.009, Joseph Kony. https://www.un.org/sc/suborg/en/sanctions/2127/materials/summaries/individual/joseph-kony. Accessed 4 July 2017); Eric Badege and Sultani Makenga, who as leaders of M23 are "responsible for serious violations involving the targeting of children or women" (Security Council Committee Established Pursuant to Resolution 1533 (2004) Concerning the Democratic Republic of the Congo (2014) Narrative Summaries of Reasons for Listing, CDi.001, Eric Badege. https://www.un.org/sc/suborg/en/sanctions/1533/materials/summaries/individual/eric-badege. Accessed 4 July 2017; and Security Council Committee Established Pursuant to Resolution 1533 (2004) Concerning the Democratic Republic of the Congo (2014) Narrative Summaries of Reasons for Listing, CDi.008, Sultani Makenga. https://www.un.org/sc/suborg/en/sanctions/1533/materials/summaries/individual/sultani-makenga. Accessed 4 July 2017); and Innocent Kaina and Baudoin Ngaruye Wa Myamuro (both leaders of M23) who are responsible for and have committed severe violations of human rights law and international humanitarian law, according to their narrative summaries (Security Council Committee Established Pursuant to Resolution 1533 (2004) Concerning the Democratic Republic of the Congo (2014) Narrative Summaries of Reasons for Listing, CDi.004, Innocent Kaina. https://www.un.org/sc/suborg/en/sanctions/1533/materials/summaries/individual/innocent-kaina. Accessed 4 July 2017; and Security Council Committee Established Pursuant to Resolution 1533 (2004) Concerning the Democratic Republic of the Congo (2014) Narrative Summaries of Reasons for Listing, CDi.019, Baudoin Ngaruye Wa

thus primarily targeted as being a leader of an armed group that commits violations of IHL. In most cases, the sanctions against leaders are thus not imposed because of direct responsibility for violations of IHL and are not truly crime-based. The personal criminal responsibility in these cases is not expressly clear.

Secondly, although many similarities can be discovered in the imposition of sanctions against the four groups, there is clearly not a standard or automatic approach of the Security Council. In two of the cases, the narrative summaries quite clearly reveal the sources on which the listing is based. In the other two cases, the underlying evidence is not clear. In addition, the imposition of sanctions against the leaders of the armed groups is different in every case, with respect to the date the sanctions are adopted (prior to the armed groups, at the same time, or after the listing of the armed group itself) and the number of leaders sanctioned (only the main leader(s) or a wider circle of influential persons).

Thirdly, in the case of the DRC as well as in the case of the CAR, the overall purpose of the Security Council action is quite clear. Also, in both cases there are some explicit views on the purpose of crime-based sanctions, e.g. deterrence or signalling disapproval. However, a clear view on what is expected from the armed group or their leaders is lacking in all cases. It is thus not clear when exactly the sanctions against a particular group or individual should be lifted.

Finally, it is clear that the implementation of the sanctions in both situations is far from perfect. This is noted by the Group and Panel of Experts, and is also clear from the fact that in both situations none of the neighbouring countries submitted an implementation report to the relevant sanctions committee.[83]

4.4 An Evaluation of Crime-Based Targeted Sanctions as a Tool to Ensure Respect for IHL

This section will evaluate the imposition of targeted measures against those responsible for violations of IHL, in particular armed groups and their leaders. First of all, it will be discussed whether the Security Council would be the right organ to deal with violations of IHL. Secondly, the specific tool of targeted measures as a means to ensure respect for IHL is discussed. This section aims to highlight some challenges to the imposition of crime-based targeted sanctions by the Security Council, as well as to elaborate on the potential of this tool. It should, however, be

Myamuro. https://www.un.org/sc/suborg/en/sanctions/1533/materials/summaries/individual/baudoin-ngaruye-wa-myamuro. Accessed 4 July 2017).

[83] See the list of implementation reports submitted so far: https://www.un.org/sc/suborg/en/sanctions/1533/implementation-reports (for the DRC) and https://www.un.org/sc/suborg/en/sanctions/2127/implementation-reports (for the CAR). Accessed 31 October 2016.

noted that this section does not aim to be exhaustive and that it may be too early for a conclusive evaluation of these sanctions.

4.4.1 The Security Council and Ensuring Respect for IHL

Is the Security Council the best, or at least an appropriate organ to ensure respect for international humanitarian law, e.g. by way of imposing sanctions on armed groups? If you look at the competences of the Security Council and its powers as well as the expectations from the international community about the role the Security Council should play in dealing with violations of IHL, the answer can be affirmative. However, there are some indications that the Security Council might not be the best organ to deal with violations of IHL. First of all, the Security Council is a political organ composed of fifteen members of whom five have the right to veto any decision. The composition of this organ and its rules of procedure necessarily lead to selectivity, both with regard to the situations the Security Council will deal with, as well as the individual violations the Security Council will take action on. The Security Council does not deal with all conflicts and it does not deal with them in the same manner.[84] One could argue that responding to violations of international law, or more specifically international humanitarian law, requires a more automatic and consistent approach.[85] Indeed, the Security Council is criticized for imposing sanctions against armed groups that recruited children in the DRC, while not against the Congolese army who was listed by the Secretary-General as committing grave violations against children every year since 2005.[86]

A second concern could be that specifically international humanitarian law should not be dealt with by a political organ, since the branch of IHL is perceived as neutral and impartial and therefore should be enforced in a neutral and impartial manner.[87] The International Committee of the Red Cross (ICRC) in 1993 stated that: "the measures decided upon and recommendations made by the Security Council under Chapter VII of the Charter cannot be considered neutral within the meaning of international humanitarian law, even though their ultimate objective may in some cases include the aim of putting an end to violations of that law."[88] As a result, the ICRC holds that humanitarian organizations cannot have a role in the execution of these measures. It concludes that "it is important to mark a clear distinction between action taken to facilitate the application of international

[84] Cryer 2006, p. 248.

[85] See e.g. Roscini 2010, pp. 352–354.

[86] Koller and Eckenfels-Garcia 2015, p. 9.

[87] Van Baarda 1994, p. 147.

[88] International Committee of the Red Cross 1993, p. 428; see also Van Baarda 1994, p. 145.

humanitarian law (which is primarily based on the consent of the Parties to conflict), and action (which does not exclude coercion) to maintain or restore peace."[89]

Thirdly, the Security Council was originally envisaged to deal with interstate conflicts and have states as its principal addressee. While it might not be too controversial for the Security Council to address non-state actors and even impose sanctions against individuals,[90] it is questionable whether the Security Council and its sub-organs have adequate competences and procedural possibilities to deal with more intrastate concerns, such as individual violations of IHL. While the Security Council is capable to identify *in abstracto* the persons whom it holds to be a threat to the peace, the identification of specific individuals who pose such a threat through the commission of violations of IHL requires specific investigation methodologies that the sanctions committees and groups or panels of experts do not always have.[91] This is crucial, because very detailed knowledge is necessary about the situation and the possible targets, in order to be able to effectively implement sanctions.[92]

Finally, the UN Charter does not foresee a procedure to challenge the decisions of the Security Council. There is no Court or other reviewing mechanism available for persons who are subjected to targeted measures. While every sanctions regime has a delisting procedure and individuals could request their de-listing through the Focal Point or the state of its nationality, for an individual this procedure could hardly be labeled fair or easily accessible. An individual has to provide the information why it does no longer meet the designation criteria. With the limited justification provided for their listing in the first place and the lack of transparency in the decision-making process, it is difficult for an individual to adequately address the concerns of the Sanctions Committee, who—as a final barrier—usually decides by consensus, so that individual member states could block any delisting. Crime-based targeted sanctions have not (yet) lead to a great number of judicial procedures, in the same way as happened after the adoption of anti-terrorism sanctions. The reason for this is not clear, but it might be due to the fact that crime-based sanctions are not always well known by states or even the individuals subjected to the sanctions. In addition, they are not well implemented. Furthermore, the targeted individuals and armed groups might not have significant amounts of assets that can be found and frozen, whereas this might be different for terrorist organizations or suspected terrorists. In a similar way, individuals involved in an intrastate conflict might hardly ever travel abroad, so that the sanctions do not bother them in a significant way. It might even be the case that crime-based targeted sanctions are more accurately imposed because it might be easier to identify

[89] International Committee of the Red Cross 1993, p. 429.

[90] Krisch 2012, p. 1270; Bolani 2003, p. 430; Sassòli 2001, pp. 247–248.

[91] Fassbender 2012, p. 60 and 61.

[92] Hufbauer et al. 2007, p. 141; See also Ward 2005, p. 167.

perpetrators of violations of IHL than to identify potential terrorists. Of course, indeed judicial proceedings in the future might hamper national or regional implementation of sanctions, but at the same time could lead to better institutional guarantees.

4.4.2 Targeted Sanctions as a Tool to Ensure Respect for IHL

In addition to the question whether the Security Council is an appropriate organ to deal with violations of IHL, it is questionable whether targeted measures are an appropriate tool to ensure respect for IHL. In theory, sanctions could be employed for three generally accepted purposes: to coerce behavioural change, to constrain a target from carrying out certain activities and to signal that a certain action is in violation to an international norm.[93] Contrary to so-called comprehensive sanctions, targeted sanctions are regarded flexible. They can be adapted to changing circumstances or to behavioural changes.[94] Targeted sanctions might thus be an ideal or at least practical tool to ensure respect for IHL and to respond to violations of IHL in a timely and adequate manner.

However, in practice crime-based targeted sanctions might be not that ideal. First of all, the successful imposition of targeted sanctions is dependent on the implementation of these measures by the member states of the Security Council. Although they are obliged to carry out the decisions of the Security Council,[95] targeted measures often are not completely implemented in the way envisaged by the Security Council and its sub-organs. Especially the cooperation of the state against whose nationals the sanctions are imposed and its neighbouring states is essential for the effective implementation of travel bans and asset freezes on individuals and non-state entities. In this respect it is notable that none of the neighbouring states of both the CAR and the DRC have submitted an implementation report pointing out how and to what extent they have implemented the sanctions.[96] And indeed, in both cases the implementation of the targeted measures is not well evaluated by the competent sub-organs. The criticism of the Groups of Experts for the DRC and the Panel of Experts on the CAR, reveals that the sanctions regime as designed by the Security Council can be quite different from the measures eventually implemented. This makes it difficult to achieve the aims the Security Council envisages to achieve. In addition, it seems questionable whether sanctions could

---

93 Biersteker et al. 2016, p. 21.

94 Ibid., p. 14; Giumelli 2015, p. 1356.

95 UN Charter, above n 12, Article 25.

96 See the list of implementation reports submitted so far: https://www.un.org/sc/suborg/en/sanctions/1533/implementation-reports (for the DRC) and https://www.un.org/sc/suborg/en/sanctions/2127/implementation-reports (for the CAR). Accessed 31 October 2016.

contribute to the enforcement of IHL given the difficulties relating to their implementation.

In addition to the fact that member states are not always willing to implement and enforce sanctions regimes,[97] targeted measures will only work when the circumstances are right. When borders are porous, border control is weak and when individuals lack assets, travel bans and asset freezes could hardly be implemented and will likely not have the intended effect.[98]

Furthermore, implementation of the sanctions is also dependent on practicalities such as budget and adequate staff. Panels of Experts in relation to all the sanction regimes dealing with individuals and entities responsible for violations of international humanitarian law, point to lack of time, lack of cooperation, lack of staff, methodological concerns, security constraints, and other factors implicating their work. They indicate that it is difficult to carry out all the necessary investigations in order to fulfil their mandate and continuously point to insufficient implementation of sanction regimes because of these constraints.

A final concern might be that it is not clear how exactly the imposition of asset freezes and travel ban will help ending or preventing violations of international humanitarian law, even when well implemented. As Forsythe argues, sanctions might have an impact on their targets, but they might not compel any change in their behaviour. When armed groups experience that banking is more difficult, they will not necessarily stop using child soldiers.[99] More research into the rationale behind imposing crime-based targeted sanctions is necessary.

4.4.3 Evaluation

From the above it follows that the imposition of targeted sanctions by the Security Council as a means to ensure respect for norms of international humanitarian law by armed groups, is not beyond concern. It is questionable whether the Security Council would be the most appropriate organ to deal with violations of IHL. In addition, because of the many difficulties related to the effective implementation of the sanctions regime, it is hard to see how targeted sanctions can be an effective tool to ensure respect for IHL. Of course, a number of the above raised issues could be solved. When a Panel or Group of Experts does not have the required knowledge about a particular situation and possible targets, it might rely—and in practice these

[97] Alting von Geusau 1999, p. 10.

[98] See e.g. Elliot 2005, p. 12; see also UN Security Council, Group of Experts on the Democratic Republic of the Congo 2006, where the Group of Experts for the DRC refers to the absence of border control and ever-porous borders, and consequently of the failure to implement the sanctions, paras 32, 185 and 216.

[99] Forsythe 2014, p. 133.

Experts do rely—on the expertise and knowledge of the special representatives of the Secretary-General on Children and Armed Conflict and on Sexual Violence in Conflict and of the Security Council's Working Group on Children and Armed Conflict. In several cases, including in the cases of the DRC and the CAR, these bodies have provided the expert groups with relevant information and with names of individuals and entities that in their eyes should be listed for targeted measures.[100] Other important improvements can be made and different proposals thereto already have been made. For example, important suggestions have been provided by Koller and Eckenfels-Garcia who, among else, propose the establishment of a thematic sanction regime dealing with violations of IHL committed against children, for which the Security Council Working Group on Children and Armed Conflict could act as a permanent sanctions committee.[101] In this way, sanctions regimes can draw upon the knowledge, experience and investigative techniques of existing UN mechanisms, even more than they already do.

While the practical concerns relating to the implementation of sanctions might be solved in the future—although this will not be easy—it is unlikely that anything will change with regard to the political nature of the Security Council and the possibilities to protest against any decision of the Security Council and its sub-organs. When looking at the shortcomings of the Security Council entirely from an IHL-perspective, these shortcomings might be impossible to overcome. However, it is important to keep in mind that the Security Council's primary responsibility is the maintenance of the international peace and security. The targeted sanctions analysed in this chapter have been imposed as a result of this responsibility and are not purely law enforcement measures. This is reiterated by the fact that the Security Council in recent resolutions stresses that violations of international humanitarian law can pose a threat to the international peace, and that individuals and entities are indeed listed because they pose a threat to the peace, not primarily because they committed violations of IHL. Important procedural guarantees, impartiality and neutrality are possibly essential for an organ solely equipped to deal with law enforcement, but might be relativized a little in relation to the Security Council.

---

[100] See e.g. UN Security Council (2014) Security Council Sanctions Committee Concerning Democratic Republic of Congo Meets with Special Representatives of Secretary-General, Press Release SC/11577. http://www.un.org/press/en/2014/sc11577.doc.htm. Accessed 15 June 2017; UN Security Council (2015) Security Council Sanctions Committee Concerning Democratic Republic of Congo Meets with Special Representative for Children and Armed Conflict, Press Release SC/12140. https://www.un.org/press/en/2015/sc12140.doc.htm. Accessed 15 June 2017; UN Security Council (2015) Secretary-General's Special Representative Briefs Security Council Committees on Plight of Children in Central African Republic, Press Release SC/12157. https://www.un.org/press/en/2015/sc12157.doc.htm. Accessed 15 June 2017.

[101] Koller and Eckenfels-Garcia 2015, pp. 30–32.

4.5 Conclusion

The Security Council has the task to maintain and restore the international peace and security. As a part of this task, it has the competence to impose targeted sanctions against individuals and entities that commit violations of international humanitarian law, when this poses a threat to the international peace. In recent years —since 2004—the Security Council expressly created the possibility to actually make use of this competence by adopting listing criteria towards that end in eight different sanctions regimes. Indeed many individuals and substantially less entities have been listed by the Security Council or a sanctions committee (partly) because they committed violations of international humanitarian law. This tool has also been used against armed groups and their leaders in the CAR and the DRC that violated IHL, e.g. by recruiting and using children. The studies into the two cases showed that these measures have not been implemented effectively and that it is not clear what exactly armed groups should do in order to have the measures against them lifted. More generally, it is questionable whether the Security Council is the best organ to deal with violations of IHL and whether targeted sanctions are useful or effective in ensuring respect for IHL. Because the practice of imposing sanctions in response to violations of IHL is quite new, it is possible that relevant concerns, especially practical problems, can and will be addressed in the future. However, even then, it is problematic to leave the enforcement of IHL to the Security Council. If sanctions are implemented more effectively in the future, it might be very welcome that the Security Council's actions to maintain the international peace as a side effect might increase the respect for IHL. Much more should not be expected from crime-based targeted sanctions. The need to search for other mechanisms to enforce rules of IHL on armed groups is once again clear.

References

Articles, Books and Other Documents

Al-Anbari AA (2001) The Impact of United Nations Sanctions on Economic Development, Human Rights and Civil Society. In: Gowlland-Debbas V (ed) United Nations Sanctions and International Law. Kluwer Law International, The Hague, pp 371–380.

Alting von Geusau FAM (1999) Recent and Problematic: The Imposition of Sanctions by the UN Security Council. In: Van Genugten WJM, de Groot GA (eds) United Nations Sanctions: Effectiveness and Effects, Especially in the Field of Human Rights: A Multi-Disciplinary Approach. Intersentia, Antwerp, pp 1–18.

Biersteker TJ, Tourinho M, Eckert SE (2016) Thinking about United Nations targeted sanctions. In: Biersteker T, Eckert SE, Tourinho M (eds) Targeted Sanctions: The Impact and Effectiveness of United Nations Action. Cambridge University Press, Cambridge, pp 11–37.

Bolani ML (2003) Security Council Sanctions on Non-State Entities and Individuals. Revue d'Histoire du Droit International 56:401–439.

Bourloyannis C (1991–1992) The Security Council of the United Nations and the Implementation of International Humanitarian Law. Denver Journal of International Law and Policy 20:335–355.

Cryer R (2006) The Security Council and International Humanitarian Law. In: Breau SC, Jachec-Neale A (eds) Testing the Boundaries of International Humanitarian Law. British Institute of International and Comparative Law, London, pp 245–275.

de Brichambaut MP (2001) The Role of the United Nations Security Council in the International Legal System. In: Michael Byers (ed) The Role of Law in International Politics. Essays in International Relations and International Law. Oxford University Press, Oxford, pp 269–276.

de Wet E (2004) The Chapter VII Powers of the United Nations Security Council. Hart Publishing, Oxford/Portland.

Elliot KA (2005) Trends in Economic Sanctions Policy: Challenges to conventional wisdom. In: Wallensteen P, Staibano C (eds) International Sanctions: Between Words and Wars in the Global System. Routledge, New York, pp 3–14.

Farral JM (2007) United Nations Sanctions and the Rule of Law. Cambridge University Press, Cambridge.

Fassbender B (2012) The Security Council: Progress is Possible but Unlikely. In: Cassese A (ed) Realizing Utopia: The Future of International Law. Oxford University Press, Oxford, pp 53–61.

Forsythe DP (2014) The UN Security Council and Human Rights: Promising Developments, Persistent Problems. Journal of Human Rights 13:121–145.

Giumelli F (2015) Understanding United Nations targeted sanctions: An empirical analysis. International Affairs 91:1351–1368.

Gowlland-Debbas V (2001) The Functions of the United Nations Security Council in the International Legal System. In: Byers M (ed) The Role of Law in International Politics. Essays in International Relations and International Law. Oxford University Press, Oxford, pp 277–314.

Gowlland-Debbas V (2011) The Security Council as Enforcer of Human Rights. In: Fassbender B (ed) Securing Human Rights? Achievements and Challenges of the UN Security Council. Oxford University Press, Oxford, pp 36–74.

Hufbauer GC, Schott JJ, Elliott KA, Oegg B (2007) Economic Sanctions Reconsidered, 3rd edn. Peterson Institute for International Economics, Washington DC.

International Committee of the Red Cross (1993) Report on the Protection of War Victims, International Review of the Red Cross 33:391–445.

Kandiah Thompson S (2014) Children and Armed Conflict. In: Genser J, Stagno Ugarte B (eds) The United Nations Security Council in the Age of Human Rights. Cambridge University Press, Cambridge, pp 98–120.

Kelsen H (1950) The Law of the United Nations. A Critical Analysis of Its Fundamental Problems. Frederick A. Praeger, New York.

Koller DS, Eckenfels-Garcia M (2015) Using Targeted Sanctions to End Violations Against Children in Armed Conflict. Boston University of International Law Journal 33:1–35.

Krisch N (2012) Chapter VII Action with Respect to Threats to the Peace, Breaches of the Peace, and Acts of Aggression. Introduction to Chapter VII: The General Framework. In: Simma B, Khan DE, Nolte G, Paulus A (eds) The Charter of the United Nations. A Commentary, 3rd edn, vol II. Oxford University Press, Oxford, pp 1237–1271.

Lamb S (199) Legal Limits to United Nations Security Council Powers. In: Goodwin-Gill GS, Talmon S (eds) The Reality of International Law: Essays in Honour of Ian Brownlie. Oxford University Press, Oxford, pp 361–388.

Lopez GA (2013) Enforcing Human Rights Through Economic Sanctions. In: Shelton D (ed) The Oxford Handbook of International Human Rights Law. Oxford University Press, Oxford, pp 772–794.

López-Jacoiste E (2010) The UN Collective Security System and its Relationship with Economic Sanctions and Human Rights. In: Van Bogdandy A, Wolfrum R (eds) Max Planck Yearbook of United Nations Law 14:273–335.
Martenczuk B (1999) The Security Council, the International Court and Judicial Review: What Lessons from Lockerbie? European Journal of International Law 10(3):517–547.
Moiseienko A, Hufnagel S (2015) Targeted Sanctions, Crimes and State Sovereignty. New Journal of European Criminal Law 6:351–371.
Orakhelashvili A (2006) The Power of the UN Security Council to Determine the Existence of a "Threat to the Peace". Irish Yearbook of International Law 1:61–99.
Orakhelashvili A (2011) Collective Security. Oxford University Press, Oxford.
Roscini M (2010) The United Nations Security Council and the Enforcement of International Humanitarian Law. Israel Law Review 43:330–359.
Sassòli M (2001) Sanctions and International Humanitarian Law – Commentary. In: Gowlland-Debbas V (ed) United Nations Sanctions and International Law. Kluwer Law International, The Hague, pp 241–248.
Schotten G, Biehler A (2008) The Role of the UN Security Council in Implementing International Humanitarian Law and Human Rights Law. In: Arnold R, Quénivet N (eds) International Humanitarian Law and Human Rights Law: Towards a new merger in international law. Martinus Nijhoff Publishers, Leiden, pp 309–327.
Schrijver N (1994) The Use of Economic Sanctions by the UN Security Council: An International Law Perspective. In: Post HHG (ed) International Economic Law and Armed Conflict. Martinus Nijhoff Publishers, Dordrecht, pp 123–161.
Schweigman D (2001) The Authority of the Security Council under Chapter VII of the UN Charter. Legal limits and the Role of the International Court of Justice. Kluwer Law International, The Hague.
Security Council Committee Established Pursuant to Resolution 1533 (2004) Concerning the Democratic Republic of the Congo (2009) Final report of the Group of Experts on the DRC submitted in accordance with paragraph 8 of Security Council resolution 1857 (2008), UN Doc. S/2009/603.
Shraga D (2011) The Security Council and Human Rights – From Discretion to Promote to Obligation to Protect. In: Bardo Fassbender (ed) Securing Human Rights? Achievements and Challenges of the UN Security Council. Oxford University Press, Oxford, pp 8–36.
United Nations Conference on International Organization (1945) Statement of the Rapporteur of Committee III/3. Doc. 134, III/3/3, 11 U.N.C.I.O. Docs. 785 (1945).
UN General Assembly (2005) Resolution 60/1, 2005 World Summit Outcome. UN Doc. A/RES/60/1.
UN Security Council (1999) Report of the Secretary-General to the Security Council on the Protection of Civilians in Armed Conflict. UN Doc. S/1999/957.
UN Security Council (2003) Resolution 1493 (2003). UN Doc. S/RES/1493.
UN Security Council (2004) Resolution 1539 (2004). UN Doc. S/RES/1539.
UN Security Council (2005a) Resolution 1591 (2005). UN Doc. S/RES/1591.
UN Security Council (2005b) Resolution 1596 (2005). UN Doc. S/RES/1596.
UN Security Council (2005c) Resolution 1612 (2005). UN Doc. S/RES/1612.
UN Security Council (2005d) Resolution 1649 (2005). UN Doc. S/RES/1649.
UN Security Council (2008a) Resolution 1807 (2008). UN Doc. S/RES/1807.
UN Security Council (2008b) Resolution 1820 (2008). UN Doc. S/RES/1820.
UN Security Council (2009a) Resolution 1888 (2009). UN Doc. S/RES/1888.
UN Security Council (2009b) Resolution 1894 (2009). UN Doc. S/RES/1894.
UN Security Council (2010) Resolution 1960 (2010). UN Doc. S/RES/1960.
UN Security Council (2013a) Resolution 2088 (2013). UN Doc. S/RES/2088.
UN Security Council (2013b) Resolution 2127 (2013). UN Doc. S/RES/2127.
UN Security Council (2014a) Resolution 2134 (2014). UN Doc. S/RES/2134.
UN Security Council (2014b) Resolution 2140 (2014). UN Doc. S/RES/2140.
UN Security Council (2014c) Resolution 2174 (2014). UN Doc. S/RES/2174.

UN Security Council (2014d) Resolution 2175 (2014). UN Doc. S/RES/2175.
UN Security Council (2015a) Resolution 2196 (2015). UN Doc. S/RES/2196.
UN Security Council (2015b) Resolution 2198 (2015). UN Doc. S/RES/2198.
UN Security Council (2015c) Resolution 2206 (2015). UN Doc. S/RES/2206.
UN Security Council (2016a) Resolution 2262 (2016). UN Doc. S/RES/2262.
UN Security Council (2016b) Resolution 2293 (2016). UN Doc. S/RES/2293.
UN Security Council, Group of Experts on the Democratic Republic of the Congo (2005a) Report of the Group of experts submitted pursuant to resolution 1552 (2004). UN Doc. S/2005/30.
UN Security Council, Group of Experts on the Democratic Republic of the Congo (2005b) Report of the Group of experts submitted pursuant to resolution 1596 (2005). UN Doc. S/2005/436.
UN Security Council, Group of Experts on the Democratic Republic of the Congo (2006) Report of the Group of experts submitted pursuant to resolution 1654 (2006). UN Doc. S/2006/525.
UN Security Council, Group of Experts on the Democratic Republic of the Congo (2007) Final report of the Group of Experts on the Democratic Republic of the Congo, pursuant to Security Council resolution 1698 (2006). UN Doc. S/2007/423.
UN Security Council, Group of Experts on the Democratic Republic of the Congo (2008) Final report of the Group of Experts on the DRC submitted in accordance with paragraph 18(d) of Security Council resolution 1807 (2008). UN Doc. S/2008/773.
UN Security Council, Group of Experts on the Democratic Republic of the Congo (2009) Final report of the Group of Experts on the DRC submitted in accordance with paragraph 8 of Security Council resolution 1857 (2008). UN Doc. S/2009/603.
UN Security Council, Group of Experts on the Democratic Republic of the Congo (2013) Midterm report of the Group of Experts on the DRC submitted in accordance with paragraph 5 of Security Council resolution 2078 (2012). UN Doc. S/2013/433.
UN Security Council, Panel of Experts on the Central African Republic (2015) Final report of the Panel of Experts on the Central African Republic extended pursuant to Security Council resolution 2196 (2015). UN Doc. S/2015/936.
Van Baarda TA (1994) The Involvement of the Security Council in Maintaining International Humanitarian Law. Netherlands Quarterly of Human Rights 12:137–152.
Vradenburgh AM (1991) The Chapter VII Powers of the United Nations Charter: Do They Trump Human Rights Law? Loyola of Los Angeles International and Comparative Law Review 14:175–205.
Ward CA (2005) The Counter-Terrorism Committee: Its relevance for implementing targeted sanctions. In: Wallensteen P, Staibano C (eds) International Sanctions: Between Words and Wars in the Global System. Routledge, New York, pp 167–180.

Treaties

Charter of the United Nations, opened for signature 26 June 1945, 1 UNTS XVI (entered into force 24 October 1945).
Convention on the Prevention and Punishment of the Crime of Genocide, opened for signature 9 December 1948, 78 UNTS 277 (entered into force 12 January 1951).
Protocol Additional to the Geneva Contentions of 12 August 1949, and relating to the Protection of Victims of International Armed Conflicts, opened for signature 12 December 1977, 1125 UNTS 3 (entered into force 7 December 1979).
Rome Statute of the International Criminal Court, opened for signature 17 July 1998, 2187.
UNTS 90 (entered into force 1 July 2002).

Chapter 5
Engaging Armed Groups Through the Development of Human Rights Obligations: Incorporating Practice, Motivation and Ideology to Promote Compliance with International Law

Daragh Murray

Abstract Non-State armed groups exert extensive influence on populations around the world. However, international law does not effectively regulate the relationship between armed groups and populations subject to their authority or influence and so much of this interaction occurs in a legal vacuum. This chapter proposes international human rights law as a solution. The application of international human rights law obligations to armed groups is increasingly accepted, but the precise content of the resultant obligations is unclear. Significantly, the development of the law in this regard presents a unique opportunity to actively engage armed groups, and to encourage their compliance with human rights law, and international law more broadly. It is suggested that if the practice of armed groups and their motivations are incorporated into the development of human rights obligations, then the resultant obligations can be used not only to regulate armed group activity but also to guide it. Human rights law can be used to demonstrate to armed groups *how* they can govern in the best interests of the affected population—thereby promoting human rights protection—and *why* it is in their interest that they do so—thereby promoting compliance. This chapter examines armed groups' practice, motivations, and ideology and discusses armed group governance activities related to the administration of justice and service provision in order to illustrate how the proposed approach could proceed. Although the focus is on international human rights law, where international humanitarian law is applicable it must also inform the development of any obligations.

Daragh Murray is a Lecturer in International Human Rights Law at the School of Law & Human Rights Centre, University of Essex, Wivenhoe Park, CO4 3SQ, United Kingdom. Email: d.murray@essex.ac.uk. Phone: 00(44)1 206 872661.

D. Murray (✉)
International Human Rights Law, School of Law & Human Rights Centre, University of Essex, Wivenhoe Park, Colchester CO4 3SQ, UK
e-mail: d.murray@essex.ac.uk

T.D. Gill et al. (eds.), *Yearbook of International Humanitarian Law 2016*,
Yearbook of International Humanitarian Law 19,
https://doi.org/10.1007/978-94-6265-213-2_5

Keywords Armed groups · Governance · Compliance · Human rights · Humanitarian law · Engagement

Contents

5.1 Introduction

Non-State armed groups exert significant influence over the lives of millions of individuals across the world.[1] For example, the Mai Mai, the Democratic Forces for the Liberation of Rwanda (FDLR), and other armed groups exert influence over large parts of the eastern Democratic Republic of Congo,[2] at its peak the Islamic State exercised governmental authority over up to 10 million people in Iraq and Syria,[3] while in Afghanistan, Nepal, and Sri Lanka, armed groups established governance systems parallel to those of the State.[4] Yet, despite the reality of armed

[1] For the purposes of this chapter, non-State armed groups are those armed groups that (a) exist independently of the State and (b) are sufficiently organised to impose internal discipline.

[2] Hoffmann 2015, pp. 165–66; Buchanan E (2015) Battle for control of the DRC: Who are the Democratic Forces for the Liberation of Rwanda (FDLR)? http://www.ibtimes.co.uk/battle-control-drc-who-are-democratic-forces-liberation-rwanda-fdlr-1526271. Accessed 30 April 2017; Mampilly 2015, pp. 65–67.

[3] Nebehay S (2015) Islamic State-controlled parts of Syria, Iraq largely out of reach: Red Cross. http://www.reuters.com/article/us-mideast-crisis-syria-icrc-idUSKBN0M921N20150313. Accessed 10 April 2017.

[4] UN Assistance Mission in Afghanistan (UNAMA) 2013, p. 24; Bangerter 2012, p. 51; TamilNet (2003) Thamil Eelam judiciary said a basis for rebuilding northeast. http://www.tamilnet.com/art.html?catid=79&artid=10277. Accessed 10 April 2017.

group influence and governance, the relationship between armed groups and individuals subject to their authority is not subject to any effective international regulation. This chapter proposes that the development of armed groups' human rights obligations can be used to fill this gap. Specifically, it suggests that if the practice of armed groups and their motivations are incorporated into the development of human rights obligations then the resultant obligations can be used not only to regulate armed group activity but also to guide it: human rights law can be used to demonstrate to armed groups *how* they can govern in the best interests of the affected population, and *why* it is in their interest to do so.

In situations of non-international armed conflict, the law of armed conflict does establish important safeguards to regulate the behaviour of non-State armed groups.[5] However, at least three issues arise. First, these obligations are restricted to armed groups party to an armed conflict, and are therefore not applicable with respect to certain (often influential) armed groups.[6] Second, the relevant law of armed conflict primarily consist of rules relevant to the conduct of hostilities and "negative" rules regulating the treatment of individuals. They do not describe *how* an armed group should treat individuals subject to their control or what their obligations are in this regard. Third, the law of armed conflict does not clarify the scope and content of an armed group's authority. For example, it is unclear whether armed groups can take legislative or judicial measures to maintain public order in the interests of the affected population. As such, although it establishes essential protections, the law of armed conflict does not provide guidance as to how armed groups should regulate life in areas subject to their influence or control.

This absence of international regulation results in both a legal and practical vacuum. The fact that armed groups are not subject to effective international regulation means that, from the perspective of international law, armed groups are free to act as they choose. In effect, they are granted a form of supreme sovereignty, superior even to that of States who remain constrained by the requirements of international law.[7] At the same time, individuals subject to armed group authority and influence are denied the protection of their fundamental rights: the State is incapable of exerting control, while international law does not address armed groups (the *de facto* authority) and does not therefore provide a means of regulating armed group behaviour and preventing arbitrary rule. This absence of regulation also gives rise to a practical deficit: armed groups are given no indication as to how they should act in the best interests of the affected population. This precludes the development of any form of best practice, lessons-learned, or guidance, frustrating

5 The law of armed conflict is also referred to as international humanitarian law (IHL).

6 Examples of armed groups operating outside armed conflict include the Urabeños in Colombia, and—prior to May 2013—Boko Haram in Nigeria. See International Criminal Court, The Office of the Prosecutor (2013), para 129; International Criminal Court, Office of the Prosecutor (2012), para 89.

7 PCIJ, *Customs Regime between Germany and Austria (Protocol of March 19th, 1931)*, Advisory Opinion, 5 September 1931, PCIJ Rep Series A/B, No. 41, Individual Opinion of Judge Anzilotti, 5 September 1931, p. 57.

efforts to ensure consistent minimum levels of protection in armed group affected areas.

International human rights law offers a potential solution. This body of law was designed to regulate the relationship between an authority and the individuals subject to that authority. Importantly, international human rights law contains in-built flexibility, ensuring that its application can be adapted in light of the exigencies of the situation.[8] As such, international human rights law can provide a regulatory framework that is capable of ensuring that armed groups act in the best interests of the affected population, to the extent possible under the circumstances. Of course, in situations of armed conflict, the relevant law of armed conflict must necessarily inform the content of any obligations. However, as the focus of this chapter is on the overall approach to the development of armed group obligations, and how international human rights law can be used to overcome gaps in the law of armed conflict, the law of armed conflict is not explicitly addressed.[9]

As a starting point, this chapter accepts that certain armed groups can be bound by international human rights law.[10] Indeed, various UN bodies and mechanisms—including the UN Security Council—increasingly assert that armed groups must comply with human rights obligations.[11] However, the question remains as to *how* specific obligations under international human rights law should be applied to armed groups. Two factors are relevant in this regard. First, it is clear that armed groups are not States, and it is therefore not appropriate that they be subject to the same obligations as States.[12] Second, it is equally apparent that all armed groups are not alike. Significant differences in capacity, resources, and control/influence exist among armed groups, and it is not appropriate that all armed groups be subject to equivalent obligations. To address these factors, a context-dependent approach is adopted, whereby obligations are divided between the armed group and the State, and applied in a gradated manner; this is discussed briefly below.[13] Yet, although useful, this framework only regulates the general application of human rights obligations. The specific content of the human rights obligations imposed on armed groups at each stage of gradation remains uncertain. Accordingly, while it may now be tentatively accepted that international human rights law applies to armed groups, the specific content of the obligations imposed are unclear.

This is an unsatisfactory situation. If armed groups are to be subject to obligations under international human rights law they must know the content of those

[8] Relevant in this regard are prohibitions of "arbitrary" treatment, limitations built in to certain rights, and derogation regimes.

[9] It is noted that law of armed conflict provisions relating to detention, trial, humane treatment, and humanitarian assistance are of particular relevance to the issues discussed herein.

[10] See, generally, Murray 2016.

[11] Although the extent, or content, of these obligations typically remains unspecified. See, generally, Clapham 2014.

[12] At least not initially, certain advanced armed groups may be subject to obligations broadly equivalent to those of States, although the issue of sovereignty will remain a distinguishing factor.

[13] See Sect. 5.2.

obligations, and what they must do to comply. Equally, if the international community in general, and bodies such as the Human Rights Council in particular, are to evaluate armed groups' compliance with international human rights law, the standards by which armed groups are held to account must be known. The law must be developed in this regard.

This chapter suggests that the development and elaboration of armed groups' human rights obligations offers an opportunity to engage with armed groups. This engagement serves three purposes. First, assessing armed groups' needs and motivations facilitates the development of obligations that are relevant and capable of being implemented in practice. This approach is reflective of the manner in which the law of armed conflict is developed. Within the law of armed conflict, States' armed forces are directly engaged in order to ensure that the law is capable of striking an appropriate balance between the requirements of military necessity and the interests of humanity. It stands to reason that, if the development of the obligations imposed on armed groups is to be effective, a similar approach should be adopted. This has been noted by Sassòli: "[t]he main reason for involving armed groups in the development of IHL is that this would constitute the best way to ensure that compliance with IHL is realistic for them […] Their contribution is […] needed to make sure that the law is realistic".[14] Although this statement was made in relation to the development of international humanitarian law, the reasoning applies equally to international human rights law: the law must be developed in a manner capable of ensuring that it can be implemented in practice.

Second, engaging with armed groups' motivations and their military reality facilitates an understanding of why they act. This can be used to encourage compliance by demonstrating how the law corresponds to armed groups' interests. As noted by Bangerter: "telling decision-makers and commanders about legal standards is essential but one must back this up with persuasive arguments that show such standards to be relevant to the persons able to take decisions and give orders."[15] The development of such arguments requires that, *inter alia*, the practice of diverse armed groups, and the thinking of key guerrilla strategists, be taken into account. Addressing the needs, practice, and motivations of armed groups and incorporating these factors into the development of the law offers an opportunity to promote compliance and to encourage the acceptance of human rights obligations by the armed groups themselves, a factor essential to implementation. The UN Secretary-General has underlined the importance of this approach, stating that "[t]he incentives for armed groups to comply with the law should be emphasized".[16]

Third, the process of engagement, and the resultant increased understanding of armed groups' reality, will facilitate the development of practical human rights-compliant guidance addressing *how* armed groups can fulfil their obligations. By demonstrating how activities that serve the best interests of the affected

---

[14] Sassòli 2010, p. 21.

[15] Bangerter 2011b, p. 8.

[16] UN Security Council 2009, para 41.

population may also serve the best interests of armed groups, and by demonstrating how these activities can be implemented, this approach to the development of armed groups' human rights obligations offers an opportunity to engage with armed groups with the goal of ensuring protection of the affected populations' human rights. This corresponds with the ICRC's approach to engagement:

> The law should be presented and discussed "strategically" in a manner that is relevant and adapted to the context, and as part of a deliberate plan of engagement with the parties. [...] The law should be discussed in terms that are concrete and operational. [...] It is especially important to bear in mind the motivation and the perceptions of the parties to the conflict.[17]

Necessarily, the attribution of human rights obligations to armed groups may result in the attribution of certain related rights. For example, if an armed group is bound by the human rights law obligation to protect—which requires that the armed group protect individuals from the acts of third party actors—this in turn requires that the armed group be granted a degree of legislative authority. In such situations the armed group must be able to either apply or enact rules that regulate the behaviour of the population in a non-arbitrary manner, and they must be able to enforce these rules by means of detention and prosecution as appropriate.[18]

The approach presented in this chapter may be problematic from the perspective of certain States. States may oppose efforts to engage armed groups, and to encourage armed groups to engage in human rights-compliant governance activities, on legitimacy and sovereignty grounds.[19] States frequently express the concern that the legitimisation of armed groups may imply, *inter alia*, the illegitimacy of the State, the erosion of State authority, or the legitimacy of using force against the State. Equally, recognition of armed group authority to engage in certain activities may be regarded as a threat to, or undermining of, State sovereignty. These concerns are not baseless. It is beyond question that the attribution of human rights obligations to armed groups—and the related recognition of armed groups' "right" to engage in certain activities—denotes a limitation of the territorial State's authority. However, it is important to recall that State authority is not limited consequent to the attribution of legal obligations to armed groups. Rather, it is limited by the acts of the armed groups themselves, and by the associated inability of the State to impose its authority. It is only because the armed group has displaced the authority of the State—thereby forcing itself onto the international plane—that human rights obligations are attributed to it.[20] As such, the extent of the obligations imposed are directly limited by the extent to which the armed group has displaced the State. This attribution does not undermine the State's sovereign claim to its

[17] International Committee of the Red Cross 2008, p. 13.

[18] See Murray 2016, pp. 195–197.

[19] This issue is discussed further in Murray 2016, pp. 170–171.

[20] Similarly, the law of armed conflict only applies to armed groups that have satisfied certain organisational requirements in situations of "sustained and concerted violence". This threshold of intensity denotes the limitation of State authority.

territory,[21] and the State remains subject to rights and obligations with respect to the entirety of the population and the territory, although the content of these obligations is altered.

It is worth noting that the acknowledgement of armed groups' human rights obligations may be in States' interests. In Sri Lanka, for example, the State continued to provide healthcare and other services in Liberation Tigers of Tamil Eelam (LTTE)-controlled areas. The Government reportedly consider that this served a strategic interest, as it maintained a link with the Tamil population, and served as a means of weaning "the population away from the insurgents by providing public goods."[22] The continued provision of State services in armed group controlled areas is a common—if surprising—feature of armed conflict. A human rights-based approach can facilitate this interaction between the State and its citizens in armed group affected areas. This has the potential to demonstrate the State's continuing relationship with the population and to highlight the State's central role with respect to the provision of essential services.

Of course, this is not to dismiss States' concerns. This chapter focuses on encouraging armed group compliance. Further work is necessary to understand how to effectively engage States on armed group related issues.

Section 5.2 will briefly discuss a framework for the application of human rights obligations to armed groups. Section 5.3 will discuss the scope of armed group governance activities, in order to demonstrate the importance of this issue, while Sect. 5.4 discusses individuals' interest in stable governance. Section 5.5 examines why armed groups engage in governance activities and the means by which armed groups can be encouraged to comply with international law. Section 5.6 then examines what international human rights law has to offer armed groups, focusing on issues related to the administration of justice and service provision. This final section is illustrative, and is intended to demonstrate the role that international human rights law *could* play. The process of engagement and development of armed groups' human rights obligations is not yet sufficiently developed and so this illustrative discussion is necessarily dependent on the existing, State-centric understanding of international human rights law.

5.2 A Framework for the Application of Human Rights Law Obligations to Armed Groups

As a starting point this chapter accepts that certain armed groups—including groups party to a non-international armed conflict, and groups that have established an independent existence, are bound by international human rights law.[23] In order to

---

[21] See, ECtHR, *Ilascu and Others v Moldova and Russia*, Grand Chamber Judgment, 8 July 2004, Application No. 48787/99 (*Ilascu*), para 313.

[22] Mampilly 2011, p. 114.

[23] Murray 2016, Chapter 5(III).

regulate the application of human rights obligations, an adapted form of the "respect, protect, fulfil" framework may be utilised.[24] This adapted framework acknowledges the significant difference in capacity between States and armed groups, and between armed groups themselves. Accordingly, obligations are applied in a gradated, context-dependent manner, based on the extent to which the armed group has displaced State authority.

Under this framework armed groups are initially subject to the obligation to respect, then the obligation to fulfil—broken down into its facilitate, provide and promote components—and finally the obligation to protect. Armed groups that have effectively displaced State authority and who exercise exclusive control over a territory and population, such as the LTTE or the Islamic State, are therefore subject to significantly greater human rights obligations than a guerrilla group at a less advanced state of insurgency, such as the Barisan Revolusi Nasional-Coordinate (BRN-C) in Thailand.

At the initial stage of obligation all armed groups bound by international human rights law are subject to the obligation to respect. As a primarily, although not exclusively, negative obligation, the obligation to respect can be satisfied by all armed groups possessing international legal personality;[25] indeed, the human rights obligations imposed on armed groups at this stage of gradation are similar to those imposed on armed groups party to a non-international armed conflict.[26] As the group develops and displaces the State to an increasing extent, it is subject to the obligation to fulfil, comprised of the obligation to fulfil (provide),[27] fulfil (facilitate)[28] and fulfil (promote).[29] Initially, it is likely that the obligation to facilitate will be most directly relevant to armed groups, given the reduced resources required to satisfy this obligation when compared to the obligation to provide.[30] For example, if there is a medical emergency or epidemic in an area subject to the control of the armed group, and the group does not have the resources to provide direct medical assistance (satisfying the obligation to provide), then the obligation to facilitate requires that the group ensure affected individuals' rights by facilitating the

[24] Ibid., pp. 181–183.

[25] The ability to exert control over group members is a requirement for international legal personality.

[26] See, for example, Article 3 common to the four Geneva Conventions of 1949.

[27] This obligation requires the authority to directly provide for the fulfilment of a right, "when individuals or a group are unable, for reasons beyond their control, to realize that right themselves by the means at their disposal". Committee on Economic, Social and Cultural Rights 2000, para 37.

[28] This obligation requires "positive measures to *assist* individuals and communities to enjoy the right" in question. Committee on Economic, Social and Cultural Rights 2002, para 25 (emphasis added).

[29] This obligation requires the provision of, *inter alia,* appropriate education with respect to the right in question. Ibid.

[30] Armed groups do, however, engage in direct service provision in accordance with the obligation to provide. For instance, the LTTE provided primary health care in areas under their control in Sri Lanka. Stokke 2006, p. 1031.

provision of medical care by the State or third party organisations, such as the ICRC, MSF, or the WHO.[31] In this instance, merely satisfying the obligation to respect would be insufficient as it would be incapable of securing the affected populations' rights.

Satisfaction of the obligation to fulfil requires a balancing of the underlying provide, facilitate and promote components. The means by which the right is fulfilled is left to the discretion of the armed group. In certain situations it may be permissible for the armed group to fulfil a right solely by means of the obligation to facilitate, thereby reducing the overall resource constraints imposed on the group.[32] This is not problematic: it is the protection of individuals' rights that is important, and not the specific means by which they are secured. However, if at any point the armed group can better ensure the right by a combination of the obligations to provide and facilitate, or though the obligation to provide alone, then not doing so may violate the group's human rights obligations. The obligations to provide and facilitate are interdependent means of securing the overall obligation to fulfil. They cannot be abused in order to abdicate responsibility: "if an armed group does not, or cannot, satisfy the obligation to provide, it must satisfy the obligation to facilitate, and vice versa."[33]

The obligation to protect requires that the armed group protect individuals from threats to their rights posed by third parties. As such, the obligation to protect relates to issues of public order and the rule of law, and therefore to the regulation of the life of the affected population. Both the preventive and remedial components of the obligation to protect require some form of legislative authority. The armed group must either apply or promulgate rules so that individuals can regulate their behaviour, and detention and prosecution may be necessary if these rules are violated. The requirement of a certain degree of legislative authority necessitates that "the application of the obligation to protect to armed groups be restricted to those groups who have displaced state authority and exercise exclusive control over a territory and population."[34]

This gradated approach is facilitated by the territorial State's continuing obligations with respect to the entirety of its national territory, including those areas where its authority has been effectively displaced.[35] Accordingly, while armed groups may be subject to a limited number of human rights obligations in a given

---

[31] For instance, in Senegal "state health teams, accompanied by ICRC staff, vaccinated people in areas controlled by armed groups": International Committee of the Red Cross 2015, p. 107. In Syria, the State and armed groups have negotiated humanitarian access in certain situations: BBC News (2014) Syria crisis: Evacuation operation in Homs begins. http://www.bbc.co.uk/news/world-middle-east-26078328. Accessed 10 April 2017.

[32] For instance, in certain SPLM controlled areas of Southern Sudan, the armed group facilitated the provision of education by allowing Jesuit Relief Services to establish and operate the education system. Mampilly 2011, pp. 160–161.

[33] Murray 2016, p. 195.

[34] Ibid., p. 197.

[35] See, for example, *Ilascu*, above n 21, para 313.

context, the State's continuing obligations avoids a vacuum in protection vis-à-vis the remaining rights. The result is a "division" of obligations between the State and the armed group. Although the concept of subjecting States to continuing obligations in armed group territory may appear disingenuous at first glance, such activity is actually relatively routine. For instance, both the Indian and Sri Lankan State continued to provide services in areas controlled by the Naxalites and the LTTE respectively,[36] while the Iraq and Syrian Governments continued to pay the salaries of oil and gas workers in Islamic State-controlled areas.[37] Of course, the obligations imposed on the State must correspond to the reality of the situation: if the State attempts to provide services, but the armed group refuses, then the State cannot be said to have violated its obligations.

The governance activities discussed below take place across the full spectrum of gradation. For example, armed groups existing at minimum levels of capacity and influence frequently engage in detention operations and some form of policing functions, while the most sophisticated groups oversee a State-like apparatus. The obligations to respect, fulfil and protect are all engaged. However, the adapted "respect, fulfil, protect" framework only addresses the overall attribution of rights; the actual content of the rights imposed at each stage of gradation remains to be determined. Determining the specific content of these obligations is not the purpose of this chapter. Rather, this chapter suggests *how* the development of the content of obligations can be approached.

5.3 Armed Group Governance in Practice

This section will briefly discuss the scope of armed group governance activities in order to gain a better understanding of armed group practice. It is not suggested that the practice discussed herein is ideal, or human rights-compliant, instead it is merely intended to reflect the governance activities carried out by armed groups.

A large number of armed groups engage in some form of governance activity, even at the early stages of their capacity/development. As noted by Arjona, Kasfir and Mampilly:

> When rebels secure territory, they must decide how they will interact with local residents. [...] A surprisingly large number of rebel groups engage in some sort of governance, ranging from creating minimal regulation and informal taxation to forming popular assemblies, elaborate bureaucracies, schools, courts, and health clinics [...][38]

---

[36] Suykens 2015, p. 152; Mampilly 2011, p. 112.

[37] Solomon E (2015) The Isis economy: Meet the new boss. https://www.ft.com/content/b2c6b5ca-9427-11e4-82c7-00144feabdc0. Accessed 26 April 2017.

[38] Arjona et al. 2015, p. 1.

This section will look at armed group governance activity in relation to two broad areas: stability, security and the administration of justice; and the provision of services.

5.3.1 Stability, Security and the Administration of Justice

The establishment of stability and security in areas subject to their control or influence is a key concern of armed groups, and typically constitutes one of the first activities that armed groups engage in.[39] This is most frequently achieved by the establishment of some form of policing system, in a manner broadly similar to that adopted by States. Dependent upon the capacity of the armed group, and the extent of the control exercised, the specific policing measures adopted can vary considerably. For example, armed groups at less developed capacity levels, such as the BRN-C or the Mai Mai, have established rudimentary policing functions, consisting primarily of patrols and a form of "force projection".[40] At somewhat more advanced levels, the Democratic Union Party (PYD) provides policing through its armed wing in Kurdish controlled areas of Syria. The group controls access to towns, and ensures stability and security in areas subject to its control.[41] Similarly, in 2013 the Al Nusrah Front established the "Sharia Committee for the Eastern Region" which included the creation of a local police force.[42] At more advanced levels, the Islamic State has established two police forces with distinct jurisdictions. The religious police are responsible for enforcing Shari'a law, while the local police force is responsible for ensuring internal security and implementing court orders.[43] In Sri Lanka, the LTTE established an advanced policing infrastructure. Local police stations were established throughout LTTE-controlled areas, "with assigned duties of preventing and detecting crime, regulating traffic and disseminating information about crime prevention to the civilian population."[44] Both LTTE-supporters and opponents are reported as acknowledging that a high degree of rule of law was maintained in LTTE areas.[45]

Interestingly, stability and security measures implemented by armed groups may be a direct response to the conflict, and the resultant absence of the rule of law. For example, following the 2003 invasion of Iraq and the collapse of the Iraqi

[39] Mampilly 2015, p. 48.

[40] See Human Rights Watch 2007a, p. 21; Hoffmann 2015, p. 165.

[41] International Crisis Group 2013, p. 21.

[42] Roggio B (2013) Al Nusrah Front poised to take over last major city on Euphrates River. http://www.longwarjournal.org/archives/2013/03/al_nusrah_front_pois.php. Accessed 30 April 2017.

[43] Caris and Reynolds 2014, pp. 15–17 and 19.

[44] Stokke 2006, p. 1028.

[45] Ibid.

Government, the Mahdi Army led by Muqtada Al-Sadr moved to fill the ensuing power vacuum by deploying its members "to impose law and order, protect hospitals and public buildings".[46] In Greece, the communist Greek People's Liberation Army (ELAS) played a similar role following the capitulation of the Italian Army in 1943. The ELAS moved to suppress the ensuing wave of criminality, "thereby becoming the supplier of public order in areas with no or limited state presence."[47] In the Central African Republic the absence of the rule of law, and the failure of the State to protect the local population from banditry, was itself an important element in the emergence of the People's Army for the Restoration of Democracy (APRD). The group sought to restore stability and as it developed the APRD incorporated local armed self-defence forces.[48]

The administration of justice is another element relevant to the establishment and maintenance of stability and security. It involves active engagement in the lives of the affected population, and may include measures ranging from mediation or dispute settlement to the judicial enforcement of religious, customary, State, or armed group-promulgated laws. As with policing measures, the development of justice mechanisms may arise as a result of necessity. For instance, Marwan Gayed, a former State judge who defected to the opposition in Aleppo, said of the creation of the United Courts Council: "we created this temporary judicial council as an emergency solution, like when a doctor removes a bullet from a patient without using an anaesthetic."[49]

Armed groups may enforce the law through a number of different mechanisms, such as people's courts, religious courts, or courts established by the armed groups themselves. People's courts are commonly adopted by communist-inspired armed groups. For example, in India the Naxalites established people's courts where representatives of the local population are responsible for overseeing the judicial process, and reaching a verdict.[50] Similarly, in Nepal the Communist Party of Nepal-Maoist (CPN-M) regarded peoples' courts as central to their governance activities. These courts applied the CPN-M public legal code which provided that:

> Investigations shall be carried out by the security organ, prosecutions by the People's Prosecutor and decisions by the People's Court. The organs of the state shall rely on the people, based on evidence and criterion of law.[51]

[46] International Crisis Group 2008, p. 7.

[47] Kalyvas 2015, pp. 126–127.

[48] Human Rights Watch 2007b, p. 5.

[49] Watson I, Razek R (2013) Rebel court fills void amid Syrian civil war. http://edition.cnn.com/2013/01/25/world/meast/syria-rebel-court/index.html. Accessed 21 April 2017.

[50] International Crisis Group 2008, p. 20; Roy A (2010) Walking with the comrades. http://www.outlookindia.com/magazine/story/walking-with-the-comrades/264738. Accessed 21 April 2017.

[51] Sivakumaran 2009, p. 493.

People's courts were also established by the Communist Party of the Philippines (CPP) in the Philippines, although they were strongly criticized by the Special Rapporteur on extrajudicial, summary or arbitrary executions.[52]

Armed groups may also draw on existing or historical mechanisms for the administration of justice. In Sudan, for example, the Sudan People's Liberation Army (SPLA) utilised courts that applied "the customary law which was in force before the establishment of SPLA authority."[53] Similarly, in Indonesia the Free Aceh Movement (GAM) re-activated traditional village level courts and councils presided over by an Islamic judge. These courts formed part of a hierarchical system, at village, sub-district, and district levels. Lower level courts dealt with petty theft and local disputes, while more serious complaints were addressed at higher levels.[54] In Iraq, the Mahdi Army established a rule of law system with arbitration committees composed of tribal chiefs,[55] while religious courts have also been used by armed groups to settle disputes in Syria and Lebanon.[56]

Armed groups may also develop their own court systems. In Syria and Iraq the Islamic State established an advanced system of courts operating within a hierarchical structure.[57] Interestingly, the Islamic State also established a "Court of Grievances" where members of the local population may bring complaints against Islamic State fighters or commanders, with reports indicating that Islamic State members are punished for transgressions.[58] For example, the Islamic State "executed one of its leaders in Deir Ezzor after it accused him of embezzlement and robbery."[59] In Sri Lanka the LTTE operated what is perhaps the most advanced judicial system established by an armed group. The LTTE court system consisted of 17 courts operating in a hierarchical structure, including six district courts, two high courts, a court of appeal, and the equivalent of a Supreme Court. The courts enforced the Tamil Eelam Civil and Penal Codes, developed by the LTTE.[60]

It is important to note, however, that armed groups do not require exclusive territorial control in order to engage in the administration of justice. In Northern Ireland the Provisional IRA operated an underground court system and engaged in "community policing",[61] while in Afghanistan the prevalence of Taliban courts have been reported as "rendering official government courts all but inoperable".[62] Due to the Taliban's lack of stable and exclusive territorial control these courts do

---

[52] UN General Assembly 2008, para 32.

[53] Kuol 1997, p. 12.

[54] Human Rights Watch 2001, p. 10 and 22.

[55] International Crisis Group 2006a, p. 20.

[56] See Human Rights Watch 2012, p. 133.

[57] Caris and Reynolds 2014, pp. 18–19.

[58] Weiss and Hassan 2015, p. 224 and 228.

[59] Weiss and Hassan 2015, pp. 227–228.

[60] Sivakumaran 2009, p. 494.

[61] Murray 2015; Toolis 1991.

[62] International Crisis Group 2011, p. 17.

not operate from fixed locations but rather move around, "using mosques as bases from which to deliver their rulings".[63]

5.3.2 Service Provision

The provision of services is another key component of both State and armed group governance. In practice, armed groups engage in a wide variety of service provision.[64] However, in order to provide an initial illustration of armed group activity, this section will focus on health and education.

As with other armed group activities, health care is provided at various levels of sophistication. For example, in Ethiopia (now Eritrea) the Eritrean People's Liberation Front (EPLF) established a network of "barefoot doctors" who traversed EPLF territory providing health services to the population,[65] while in India the Naxalites established basic mobile health care provision in areas subject to their control.[66] At a somewhat more advanced level, the FARC established mobile health clinics in rural areas of Colombia which provided health care, including dental care and minor surgery.[67] At a significant step up in terms of the extent of services provided, the Islamic State is reported as having taken over the operation of State health care facilities and hospitals in areas subject to their control in Iraq and Syria.[68] At perhaps the most advanced level of armed group health care provision, Hezbollah in Lebanon established a health infrastructure to rival that of the State. Indeed, it has been reported that:

> the competence and capability of Hezbollah's services have become an embarrassment to the central Lebanese government who cannot provide services throughout the region with the efficiency of Hezbollah. The group has even assumed control of medical facilities in the south and it is estimated to treat over 400,000 patients a year.[69]

Armed groups also engage in the provision of education-related services, again at varying levels of effectiveness. In southern Sudan, for example, the Sudan

---

[63] Babak Q (2010) Afghanistan: Taliban justice "fairer" than state's. http://www.infosud.org/Afghanistan-Taliban-justice-fairer,8710. Accessed 10 April 2017.

[64] See generally Arjona et al. 2015.

[65] Pool 2001, p. 100.

[66] Shah 2013, p. 489.

[67] Al Jazeera English (2011) Colombia rebel army brings healthcare to the jungle. https://www.youtube.com/watch?v=1hxkoiZVJRQ. Accessed 10 April 2017.

[68] Cunningham E (2014) Islamic State imposes a reign of fear in Iraqi hospitals. https://www.washingtonpost.com/world/middle_east/islamic-state-imposes-a-reign-of-fear-in-iraqi-hospitals/2014/11/25/94476f3e-6382-11e4-ab86-46000e1d0035_story.html?utm_term=.f6d6eb24a6c7. Accessed 21 April 2017; Caris and Reynolds 2014, p. 22.

[69] Kindt 2009, p. 132.

People's Liberation Movement-North (SPLM-N) administer schools in their territory on the basis of neighbouring States' curriculum, and report difficulties in recruiting qualified teachers.[70] In Rojava, Syria, the PYD runs approximately 2,500 schools, including a university, although facilities have been damaged in fighting,[71] while in Lebanon students attending Hezbollah-runs schools consistently score top marks on the national high school exam.[72] As with healthcare, States and armed groups often interact to ensure the delivery of education in armed group controlled areas. For example, in Afghanistan the government continues to run schools in Taliban controlled areas, although these schools operate in accordance with Taliban imposed rules.[73]

The above examples of armed group governance activity are not intended to be exhaustive. Rather, they are intended to illustrate the fact that armed groups do actively engage in a wide variety of governance activities. Two factors are worth highlighting in this regard. First, armed groups operating at all levels of capacity and sophistication engage in these activities, providing services that range from underground "community policing" to advanced hierarchical court systems applying laws developed by the armed groups themselves. Second, and importantly for present purposes, all armed groups engage in these activities. Although the specific identity of the armed group may influence *how* services are provided—for instance, Maoist style insurgencies may utilise people's courts, while groups such as the Islamic State or the Mahdi Army may utilise religious courts—armed groups engage in governance activities irrespective of their motivation or ideological foundation.

5.4 Affected Individuals' Interest in Armed Group Governance

Affected populations have a particular interest in armed group governance activities. Beyond political considerations, this interest is related to individuals' desire to live as normal a life as possible, including in difficult or extreme circumstances. In this regard it has been argued that:

> order provided through "good" governance has a value in itself because it satisfies a basic need of the population – that is, a certain predictability of social life. A particular social order may be unjust or outright oppressive, but as long as it answers such general demands,

[70] Somer 2015, pp. 17–18.

[71] Ibid.

[72] Cambanis T (2013) Hizbollah Mahdi schools mix math with doctrine. https://www.ft.com/content/e0be1122-2695-11e3-9dc0-00144feab7de. Accessed 10 April 2017.

[73] Khaja N (2014) Afghanistan Conflict: Life inside a Taliban stronghold. http://www.bbc.co.uk/news/world-south-asia-29658839. Accessed 10 April 2017.

> in particular the demand for security and the possibility to make a living, it is often acceptable to the majority.[74]

Importantly from the perspective of potential international regulation, this interest in, and potential acceptance of, armed group activity is not dependent upon identification with, or acceptance of, the armed group as such. Rather, it is a pragmatic decision derived from the need for stability and predictability in order that an element of normalcy be maintained: "[t]o put it crudely, [the armed group] may not be liked but it will be tolerated as long as people can continue to live in comparative peace."[75]

These observations are supported by reference to the experiences of individuals living in areas subject to armed group governance activities. In Pakistan, for example, it was reported that:

> Military actions and policy have contributed to the anarchical situation that pro-Taliban militants are more than happy to fill. Their demonstrated ability to restore order, prosecute criminals and dispense speedy justice was welcomed by many civilians fed up with violence and insecurity.[76]

Indeed, it is reported that in certain areas of Afghanistan the general population have demonstrated a preference for Taliban courts due to the perception that they are fairer and less corrupt than Government courts.[77] The situation in Iraq provides a similar example. In 2006 it was reported that people would rather lodge complaints at arbitration committees established by the Mahdi Army "than the police station, which does nothing. The Arbitration Committee is well organised. It summons the relevant people, and the matter is adjudicated after the various parties have been heard."[78] Similar experiences have been reported in relation to governance activities conducted by the Islamic State, reinforcing the conclusion that affected populations value a degree of stability and security in extreme circumstances, irrespective of the nature of the armed group. It is reported that:

> So far as the local population is concerned, the project of the Islamic State as a functioning body capable of providing services and maintaining order has great impact. Beforehand, in the Sunni areas of Syria and Iraq, state officials were all too often associated with corruption and misgovernment.[79]

---

[74] Förster 2015, p. 208.

[75] Bangerter 2011a, p. 11.

[76] International Crisis Group 2006b, p. 22.

[77] "In recent months, the Taliban opened a northern front in Kunduz, Baghlan and Badakshan provinces, with a strong contingent of al-Qaeda foreigners among them, according to senior Afghan officials. In all these areas, a new saying prevails: 'Government courts for the rich (because the judges are bribable), Taliban justice for the poor.' And Taliban justice, they say, is usually more swift and fair." McGirk T (2009) Behind the Taliban's Resurgence in Afghanistan. http://content.time.com/time/world/article/0,8599,1923303,00.html. Accessed 10 April 2017.

[78] International Crisis Group 2006a, p. 20.

[79] Barrett 2014, p. 43.

A trader from Mosul, interviewed by the *Financial Times* stated that: "[c]ompared to past rules, Isis is a lot easier to deal with. Just don't piss them off and they leave you alone."[80] The trader further stated that, "[i]f they could only maintain services – then people would support them until the last second."[81] Other reports have positively commented on the fact that both Islamic State members and the local population are subject to the same judicial system, and that measures to eradicate corruption and bribes (reportedly a feature of the previous regimes) have resulted in an improvement in daily life and business activities.[82]

Affected populations' support is dependent upon the quality of governance or service provision, and bad governance may undermine support. For example, a report including an interview with a local resident reported that Al Nusrah in Syria:

> quickly alienated many locals under its rules because of its incompetence. "Their services were bad," he said. "They took large amounts of taxes and didn't offer a lot. They started making a lot of bad decision in their rule. They tried to be good rulers but they really failed, that's why the people are alienated from them."[83]

Ultimately it must be concluded—even from these brief examples—that affected populations have a real and pressing interest in stability, security and the maintenance of service provision. As such, they have a pragmatic interest in governance activities conducted by armed groups, irrespective of any affinity for the group, or the nature of the group itself.[84]

5.5 Why Do Armed Groups Engage in Governance Activities?

Having confirmed that armed groups routinely engage in a wide variety of governance activities, and that "good" governance activities conducted by armed groups may be received positively by affected populations, armed groups' motivations for engaging in such activities must be ascertained. Understanding armed groups' motivation is essential in relation to both the development of appropriate human rights obligations, and the development of effective strategies to engage with armed groups in relation to human rights compliance.

The fact that a large number of armed groups—operating at significantly different capacity levels and on the basis of distinct motivations—engage in governance activities suggests that they perceive it as in their interests to do so. This

---

[80] Solomon 2015, above n 37.

[81] Ibid.

[82] Weiss and Hassan 2015, p. 226; Barrett 2014, p. 43.

[83] Daragahi B (2016) Syria's Al-Qaeda Branch Now Wants To Rule Like ISIS. https://www.buzzfeed.com/borzoudaragahi/syrias-al-qaeda-branch-now-wants-to-rule-like-isis?utm_term=.klM6lxVJK#.tmWNdn3JW. Accessed 10 April 2017.

[84] See in this regard, Bangerter 2011a, p. 11; Förster 2015, p. 210.

interest in governance may be explained on the basis of two key factors, relating to (a) armed groups' interest in a compliant population, and (b) armed groups' claim to represent a particular population (representational legitimacy).[85] An armed group may act on the basis of either one, or a combination of these factors. For instance, a for-profit armed group such as a drug cartel may benefit from a compliant population but may not wish to pursue representational legitimacy, while both factors may be relevant for a group such as the FARC.

Armed groups' interest in a compliant population is explained by the fact that individuals are "strategic actors", with the capacity to provide or withhold support.[86] In particular, affected populations can assist armed groups through the provision of resources, recruits, information and shelter, or they can undermine the armed group by withholding or attempting to withhold resources, by protesting against armed group rule, or by providing information on armed group activities to the enemy.[87] As such, it has been concluded that for armed groups to win, it is not enough for them to dominate areas subject to their control, they must also gain the support of the population.[88] In purely military terms, this is a pragmatic conclusion. Armed groups possess limited resources: it is in the group's interest that their human and military resources be directed towards defeating the enemy, rather than controlling the population.[89] The Special Tribunal for Sierra Leone commented on the Revolutionary United Front (RUF)'s interest in a compliant population in *Prosecutor v Sesay, Kallon and Gbao*:

> It is noteworthy that these instances of systematic discipline of fighters for crimes committed against civilians occurred in locations where the RUF had a relatively stable control over that territory and we find that the objective of such actions was [to] secure the loyalty of civilians for the success of their operations.[90]

Armed groups may also claim to represent a particular population, and may have an interest in ensuring good governance on this basis. For example, communist-inspired insurgencies frequently engage in "people's war", in which ensuring legitimacy among the population—and particularly within a certain "class"—plays a key role. Examples in this regard include the Naxalites in India, the CPN-M in Nepal, and the FARC in Colombia.[91] Other armed groups claim to represent either a nation, or a particular community. Examples in this regard include the PYD in Syria, the Popular Front for the Liberation of Saguia el-Hamra and Río de Oro (POLISARIO) in Western Sahara, and the Mai Mai in the Democratic

---

[85] See generally Bangerter 2011a. These issues are discussed further below.

[86] Weinstein 2007, p. 163.

[87] Arjona et al. 2015, p. 3.

[88] Hoffmann 2015, p. 185.

[89] Coggins 2015, p. 113.

[90] SCSL, *Prosecutor v Sesay, Kallon and Gbao,* Judgment, 2 March 2009, Case No. SCSL-04-15-T, para 707.

[91] It is not suggested that all of these groups adhered to the phases of revolution developed by Mao.

Republic of the Congo. Equally, the Islamic State claims to represent a particular Sunni Muslim community, while other groups—such as the Free Libya Army or the Free Syria Army—claim to represent "the people" in the face of government oppression.

The compliant population and representational legitimacy factors are reflected in guerrilla doctrine. For example, Mao Tse-tung stated that: "[b]ecause guerrilla warfare basically derives from the masses and is supported by them, it can neither exist nor flourish if it separates itself from their sympathies and cooperation."[92] In this regard, and reflective of the compliant population factor, Mao noted that, "[t]he people must be inspired to cooperate voluntarily. We must not force them, for if we do, it will be ineffectual".[93] Vo Nguyen Giap reached a similar conclusion, stating that "victory is only possible by uniting the whole people within the bosom of a firm and wide national united front based on the worker-peasant alliance."[94] Giap discussed governance in more detail elsewhere:

> During the years of war, various erroneous tendencies appeared. Either we devoted our attention only to the organization and growth of the armed forces while neglecting the mobilization and organization of large strata of the people; or we mobilized the people for the war without heeding seriously their immediate everyday interests; or we thought of satisfying the immediate interests of the people as a whole, without giving due attention to those of the peasants. […] To lead the resistance to victory, we had to look after the strengthening of the army, while giving thought to mobilizing and educating the people, broadening and consolidating the National United Front. We had to mobilize the masses for the resistance while trying to satisfy their immediate interest in improving their living conditions.[95]

The insights discussed above have in turn been translated into rules, codes of conduct, and guidance promulgated by armed groups.[96] For example, during the communist insurgency in China, the Eighth Route Army adopted the "Three Rules and Eight Remarks":

Rules

1. All actions are subject to command.
2. Do not steal from the people.
3. Be neither selfish nor unjust.

Remarks

1. Replace the door when you leave the house.
2. Roll up the bedding on which you have slept.
3. Be courteous.

---

[92] Tse-tung 1989, p. 44.

[93] Quoted in Shah 2013, p. 488.

[94] Stetler 1970, p. 98.

[95] Ibid., p. 103. In relation to the experiences of the NRA in Uganda, see also Weinstein 2007, p. 175.

[96] For a compilation of relevant practice see http://www.theirwords.org run by Geneva Call.

4. Be honest in your transactions.
5. Return what you borrow.
6. Replace what you break.
7. Do not bathe in the presence of women.
8. Do not without authority search the pocketbooks of those you arrest.[97]

These rules and remarks highlight the need for discipline, but also the essential importance of ensuring that the population are not mistreated. They have been hugely influential, and have been adopted (or adapted) by a large number of armed groups around the world, including the RUF, the CPP/NPA (Communist Party of the Philippines/New People's Army), the Naxalites, the SPLA, and the Conseil National de Libération (CNL).[98] Other armed group codes reflect similar sentiments. For example, in Colombia, the National Liberation Army (ELN) Principles of Military Doctrine state simply that: "[w]ithin our ranks, we will not permit or tolerate abuses against the population; they are our reason for being and our relationship with them should be above reproach."[99] Reflective of this motivation, Che Guevara has stated that "[t]he fundamental principle that ought to prevail is that of paying always for all merchandise taken from a friend."[100] The code of conduct (*lahiya*) adopted by the Afghan Taliban also stresses the need to ensure good relations with the population:

> Taking care of public property and the lives and property of the people is considered one of the main responsibilities of the mujahed; you must try very hard to carry out this responsibility and not allow those opportunists and materials, those armed people who are interested in material gain, to harm or bother the people or destroy their assets.[101]

Armed groups attempt to ensure good relations with their constituent population through governance activities. As stated by Guevara:

> The council – or central department of justice, revolutionary laws, and administration – is one of the vital features of a guerrilla army fully constituted and with territory of its own. The council should be under the charge of an individual who knows the laws of the country; if he understands the necessities of the zone from a judicial point of view, this is better yet; he can prepare a series of decrees and regulations that help the peasant to normalize and institutionalize his life within the rebel zone.[102]

---

[97] Tse-tung 1989, p. 92.

[98] Bangerter 2012, p. 70.

[99] Quoted in Human Rights Watch 1998.

[100] Guevara 2007, p. 61.

[101] Bangerter 2012, p. 95. From the same document, see similarly: ELN/FARC principle 1, "our daily behaviour, and the purpose underlying our activities, should be borne in the people's interests"; KLA "Improper behaviour with respect to the civilian population is to be prevented in all KLA units"; EGP Guatemala, "I will respect our people, their property, and their customs".

[102] Guevara 2007, p. 67.

5.5.1 Armed Group Governance and Compliance with International Law

The fact that armed groups recognise "good governance" as being in their interest presents an opportunity to encourage armed groups' compliance with international law generally, and with a human rights-based approach to armed group governance in particular. For example, Olivier Bangerter, former ICRC Advisor for Dialogue with Armed Groups, has stated that "the fact that IHL serves an objective in line with that of many armed groups is, for them, a convincing argument."[103] Accordingly, if international human rights law can be demonstrated to serve an objective in line with that of armed groups, this too should be a convincing argument.

A number of the identified bases for armed group compliance correspond to armed groups' identified interests in governance activities. Two relevant bases for compliance are the convictions of the armed group—these "may be of traditional, moral, cultural, political, and/or religious origin"[104]—and their military interest.[105] An armed group's convictions may be linked to the concept of reputational legitimacy discussed above, while in the context of governance activities, the military interest of an armed group may be tied to the compliant population factor. Bangerter also notes that an armed group's interest in ensuring a positive public image may be a factor driving compliance, as a result of the strategic possibilities it may open up.[106] Compliance with human rights is widely regarded as a key factor either preventing or facilitating international support, and armed group governance may be an emerging factor in this regard. For example, Mampilly notes that in the current international climate, and as a result of focused media attention, there may be increased pressure on armed groups to establish a governance system. He cites the pressure placed on the nascent National Transitional Council in Libya as an example in this regard.[107]

5.6 What Can International Human Rights Law Offer Armed Groups and Affected Populations?

This section intends to illustrate how international human rights law could play a role with respect to the regulation of armed group governance activities. It necessarily focuses on existing State-centric understandings of international human rights

---

[103] Bangerter 2011a, p. 6.
[104] Ibid., p. 7.
[105] Ibid., p. 9.
[106] Ibid., p. 8.
[107] Mampilly 2015, p. 48.

law, and is intended as a "demonstration of concept". Work to examine and incorporate armed group activity, motivation, and so on, is not sufficiently advanced to offer concrete armed group specific guidance. The approach presented is not intended to focus exclusively on limiting, or restricting, armed group activity, although activities that are not compatible with international human rights law will necessarily be prohibited. Instead, this approach is based on the understanding that international human rights law has the potential to assist armed groups, by providing guidance as to how they can engage in governance activities in a human rights-compliant manner. The provision of "guidance" is regarded as central to both encouraging armed group compliance, and facilitating armed group governance in the best interests of the affected population.

In examining its potential role it is important to note that international human rights law was designed to regulate the exercise of authority in the best interests of the population, while taking into account the needs of the authority as they relate, for example, to the maintenance of public order, national security, the protection of others, or the protection of the life of the nation.[108] It is equally important to note that international human rights law is not composed of exclusively negative obligations, designed solely to restrict or limit the scope of acceptable activity. It also requires that authorities develop and implement measures designed to ensure that rights are protected in practice, and provides (at least initial) guidance in this regard.[109] As such, it is suggested that if the content of the international human rights law obligations imposed on armed groups are developed in an appropriate manner, then the law can be used to provide guidance to armed groups and in this way to shape their governance activities. As discussed above, this is in the interests of armed groups, as it will facilitate good relations with the populations subject to their authority. It is also in the interests of the affected populations themselves as it is a means of ensuring that their fundamental rights continue to be respected and protected to the extent possible, while facilitating an element of stability in public affairs, thereby allowing them to live as normal a life as possible under the circumstances.

In order to demonstrate how international human rights law obligations can be used to guide armed group governance activities, this section will first look at issues relating to stability, security and the administration of justice before addressing service provision. Discussion in this regard is intended to illustrate how international human rights law could be used to engage armed groups in the interests of affected populations; it is not intended to be exhaustive. As noted at the outset of this chapter, the content of the specific human rights obligations discussed below have not yet been developed (as applied to armed groups) and this is not the

[108] As demonstrated, for example, by the derogation clauses in treaties such as the European Convention on Human Rights and the International Covenant on Civil and Political Rights, and the limitations built into certain rights, such as the rights to freedom of expression or freedom of assembly.

[109] See for example, Committee on Economic, Social and Cultural Rights 2000; Human Rights Committee 2014.

purpose of this chapter. Rather, it is hoped that a fuller understanding as to the potential impact of international human rights law vis-à-vis armed group activity will facilitate the development of these obligations in a manner relevant to the reality of armed groups, and in a form that is capable of being applied on the ground.

5.6.1 Stability, Security and the Administration of Justice

Issues relating to stability, security and the administration of justice are intrinsically related to the predictability—and quality—of life in areas subject to armed group influence or control. In order to ensure a semblance of normality, the affected population must know how to regulate their behaviour, and they should know that if they abide by the rules in place, then they will not be subject to sanction. As discussed above, a certain predictability in social life is a basic need of the population, and if an armed group can satisfy this requirement, "it is often acceptable to the majority".[110]

The development of a non-arbitrary system of governance is essential to ensuring predictability in armed group affected areas. Rules should be clear, and applied consistently and equally. In this regard it is essential that rules also be applied to members of the armed group themselves.[111] Arbitrary rule is characterised by armed group members' ability to act "above the law", and to treat the affected population as they please. In such circumstances, predictability of life is undermined if not negated. Weinstein notes the importance of predictability and the equal application of relevant rules in the context of armed group governance:

> The credibility of formal institutions is […] strengthened over time through repeated interactions in which members of both parties live up to one another's expectations. Accordingly, the rebel group's internal system of monitoring and control plays a critical role in reinforcing the formal institutions of governments. When violations of either the formal arrangements or the unstated codes of behaviour are committed by rebel leaders or their members, civilians expect that these violations will be punished. In order to preserve a precedent of responsible behaviour, the punishment must be consistently applied, and civilians must have knowledge of its application.[112]

[110] Förster 2015, p. 208. See also above, Sect. 5.4.

[111] An example in this regard is the importance attributed to the Islamic State's equal application of the law to both affected individuals and the group's own members. See the comment of Ghazwan Abdul Rahman in Mahmood M (2015) Life in Mosul one year on: "ISIS with all its brutality is more honest than the Shia government". https://www.theguardian.com/world/2015/jun/10/mosul-residents-one-year-on-isis-brutality. Accessed 10 April 2017.

[112] Weinstein 2007, p. 171.

Conversely, when an armed group fails to secure stability, and acts in an arbitrary manner, it undermines stability in areas subject to its control or influence, and risks alienating the affected population.[113] For example, the former Head of the LTTE Judicial Division in Killnochchi noted that the LTTE initially used mediation boards to regulate life in territory subject to their control, but that these suffered from problems arising from arbitrary rulings: "the mediation board system was a failure because many of those who sat on the mediation boards weren't educated and trained in law. It created a lot of problems for the Liberation Movement and led to frictions with society."[114]

The prohibition of arbitrary interference with individuals' rights is a core component of international human rights law, and human rights law can therefore offer guidance to armed groups regarding how to govern in a non-arbitrary manner.

The promulgation of rules by armed groups is a case on point. In order to facilitate stability, predictability, and good relations with the population, rules promulgated by armed groups should be accessible, understandable, and clear in their content. International human rights law requirements relating to the "quality" of a law are therefore relevant. For example, the Human Rights Committee has stated that "laws authorizing the application of restrictions should use precise criteria and may not confer unfettered discretion on those charged with their execution."[115] In order to protect against arbitrary application, the formulation of a rule should also protect against "inappropriateness, injustice, lack of predictability and [ensure] due process of law."[116] As such, the Inter-American Court of Human Rights has stated that:

> crimes must be classified and described in precise and unambiguous language that narrowly defines the punishable offense [...] this means a clear definition of the criminalized conduct, establishing its elements and the factors that distinguish it from behaviors that are either not punishable offences or are punishable but not with imprisonment. Ambiguity in describing crimes creates doubts and the opportunity for the abuse of power [...][117]

Accordingly, in relation to armed group rule or law making, international human rights law requires, *inter alia*, that:

- A rule or law created or enforced by an armed group be accessible to the concerned population. This requires that an affected individual must be aware of the rules established to regulate their behaviour; they must "have an indication that is adequate in the circumstances of the legal rules applicable to a given case."[118]

[113] See above, Sect. 5.4.

[114] TamilNet, above n 4. See further, Stokke 2006, p. 1027.

[115] Human Rights Committee 1999, para 13.

[116] Human Rights Committee, *Albert Womah Mukong v Cameroon*, Views, 21 July 1994, Communication No. 458/19 91, UN Doc. CCPR/C/51/D/458/1991, para 9.8.

[117] IACtHR, *Castillo Petruzzi et al. v Peru*, Judgment, 20 May 1999, Series C No. 59, para 121.

[118] ECtHR, *Sunday Times v the United Kingdom*, Judgment, 16 April 1979, Application No. 6538/74, para 49.

- The rule or law must be formulated with sufficient precision so as to enable an individual to effectively regulate their behaviour. This is central to the protection against arbitrary rule, and requires that an individual must be able "to foresee, to a degree that is reasonable in the circumstances the consequences which a given action may entail".[119]
- Within the framework for the administration of justice there must also be protection against arbitrary interference by the authorities.

Adherence to these requirements should assist armed group efforts to govern in a non-arbitrary manner, thereby facilitating stability and predictability in their interactions with the population. Armed groups may potentially satisfy these requirements in a number of ways. In order to ensure accessibility—and to conform with the *nullem crimen sine lege* requirement—an armed group may apply the laws in place. In Syria, for example, the FSA applied the existing Syrian penal code,[120] while the Libyan Criminal Code was used by the National Transitional Council.[121] Existing alternatives to State law, such as local customary or religious law may also be used, as discussed above in relation to groups such as the SPLA and GAM.[122] Of course, an armed group may promulgate their own laws, and the LTTE and CPN-M are prominent examples in this regard.[123] A combination of these possibilities may also be applied, and this may be a means of ensuring regulation of the population, while reducing the legislative burden imposed on armed groups. In Somaliland, for example, the authorities primarily applied the former State law, but augmented this with a new juvenile code, and applied traditional law in rural areas.[124]

The development of international human rights law has an important role to play in determining the extent to which armed groups can enforce or develop rules, and the activity that these rules may regulate.[125] In this regard a model penal and civil code could be developed that builds on armed groups' experiences and the main requirements of armed group rule, and adheres to international human rights law. With respect to public knowledge of the rules in place, a number of possibilities exist. The Islamic State reportedly read out the applicable rules in public a number of times each week,[126] while posters, radio broadcasts, or even social media all provide alternative and accessible means of reaching the population.

---

[119] Ibid.

[120] Human Rights Watch 2012, p. 3.

[121] National Transitional Council/ Free Libyan Army 2011.

[122] See above Sect. 5.3.1.

[123] See respectively Stokke 2006, p. 1027; Sivakumaran 2009, p. 493.

[124] "Somaliland" in Geneva Call 2010, p. 30.

[125] See Murray 2016, pp. 240–247.

[126] Cockburn P (2015) Isis, a year of the caliphate: Day-to-day life in the "Islamic State"—where any breach of restrictive, divinely inspired rules is savagely punished. http://www.independent.co.uk/news/world/middle-east/isis-a-year-of-the-caliphate-day-to-day-life-in-the-islamic-state-where-any-breach-of-restrictive-10348151.html. Accessed 21 April 2017.

It is not suggested that these examples represent ideal behaviour. However, international human rights law does establish rules that correlate to armed group's motivations for engaging in governance activity. For instance, by clearly detailing individuals' rights, and the scope of an authority's legitimate activity—with respect to both the promotion and limitation of individuals' rights—international human rights law can establish clear protection against arbitrary interference by armed groups. As such, the content of the human rights obligations applied to armed groups should be developed in light of armed group practice and their motivations. Examples of armed group governance activities should be examined and explored in order to determine both how any imposed obligations can be implemented, and to identify any best practice in this regard. This section only touched briefly on issues relating to the administration of justice for illustrative purposes. Further issues relating to detention and trials by armed groups, including potential satisfaction of the requirement that judicial review be independent, are discussed in greater detail elsewhere.[127]

5.6.2 Service Provision

As discussed above, a large number of armed groups engage in some form of service provision, including during the early stages of insurgency when the armed group does not exercise significant territorial control or possess an advanced organisational structure. Armed groups regard service provision as a means of facilitating good relations with the population and developing legitimacy, while from the populations' perspective continued service provision is evidently in their best interest. Indeed, service provision and stability/predictability are arguably the two most important elements of armed group rule from the perspective of the population, given their role in ensuring or maintaining a semblance of normalcy.

International human rights law, and particularly economic, social and cultural rights, are directly relevant to the provision of public services. These rules are intended to ensure that the population has access to those services essential to the fulfilment of their human rights, and they regulate the State's (or the authority's) distribution of resources by, *inter alia*: identifying a minimum core of economic, social and cultural rights that must be implemented immediately; providing guidance as to how the progressive realisation of rights should occur; and establishing safeguards intended to overcome discrimination and ensure the equal enjoyment of rights.

Applied to armed group service provision, economic, social and cultural rights are relevant in at least two key respects. First, they provide guidance as to *how* services should be provided. For instance, by specifying the minimum permissible levels of service provision, and by identifying how human rights-compliant access

[127] See Murray 2016, Chapter 8(I).

to those services can be ensured.[128] Second, economic, social and cultural rights can be used to ensure the delivery of essential services in armed group controlled areas, by facilitating armed group cooperation with third party entities, such as the territorial State or international organisations, in relation to service delivery.[129] The social justice imperative underpinning economic, social and cultural rights also directly relates to armed groups' desire to ensure good relations with populations subject to their influence or control.[130]

5.6.2.1 How Armed Groups Engage in Service Provision

With respect to *how* armed groups should engage in service provision, international human rights law establishes the underpinning principles of equality and non-discrimination which should inform all activity, and provides specific guidance in relation to how services are provided, the allocation of resources, and the scope of permissible activity that an armed group can engage in.

In relation to non-discrimination, the Committee on Economic, Social and Cultural Rights has stated that: "[n]on-discrimination and equality are fundamental components of international human rights law and essential to the exercise and engagement of economic, social and cultural rights."[131] Discrimination is defined as: "any distinction, exclusion, restriction or preference or other differential treatment that is directly or indirectly based on the prohibited grounds of discrimination and which has the intention or effect of nullifying or impairing the recognition, enjoyment or exercise, on an equal footing, of Covenant rights."[132] The Committee has developed guidance as to how discrimination can be overcome,[133] and taking efforts to address discrimination can clearly assist armed groups in developing good relations with the population subject to their control or influence. Undertaking specific measures in this regard may be particularly appealing to armed groups that claim to represent a people or a community, such as the People's Protection Units (YPG) in Syria, or communist-inspired insurgencies which frequently adopt social justice-based language.

Of course, it must be acknowledged that discrimination is central to the organisational identity of certain groups, and progress in eradicating discriminatory structures may be difficult to achieve. An example in this regard is the Islamic State. This group narrowly defines its community as a subset of the Sunni Muslim faith and actively discriminates against those external to this community, as evidenced

---

[128] This is discussed in Sect. 5.6.2.1.

[129] This is discussed in Sect. 5.6.2.2.

[130] In relation to the social justice underpinning, see Committee on Economic, Social and Cultural Rights 1999a, para 4.

[131] Committee on Economic, Social and Cultural Rights 2009, para 2.

[132] Ibid., para 7.

[133] See generally, ibid.

by the group's high profile oppression of the Yazidi population.[134] Such conduct is clearly inconsistent with the requirements of international human rights law and in such circumstances there may be little that the law can do to modify the Islamic State's discriminatory behaviour.

International human rights law also offers specific guidance in relation to how services may be provided by armed groups, establishing guidelines in relation to "access", "quality", "availability" and "accessibility".[135] In order to illustrate their potential utility, this section will focus on access and quality.

The "access" requirement is intended to ensure that all individuals have access to specific resources and goods. As such, it consists of a number of components, including physical access and economic access. The physical access requirement is intended to ensure that the full population have access to a specific resource. For instance, this requirement can provide guidance to armed groups should they develop primary health care facilities, or education institutions, noting that such resources should be within safe physical reach of the population. A human rights-based approach may assist in overcoming inequality arising from urban-rural divides. Returning to the examples discussed above, this could have informed the EPLF's deployment of barefoot doctors, or the FARC or Naxalite's deployment of mobile health clinics.

Equally, the economic accessibility requirement is intended to ensure that essential services or goods are not financially inaccessible. For example, in relation to the right to food, the Committee on Economic, Social and Cultural Rights has stated that:

> Economic accessibility implies that personal or household financial costs associated with the acquisition of food for an adequate diet should be at a level such that the attainment and satisfaction of basic needs are not threatened or compromised. Economic accessibility applies to any acquisition pattern or entitlement through which people procure their food and is a measure of the extent to which it is satisfactory for the enjoyment of the right to adequate food.[136]

In order to ensure this objective armed groups may be required, for example, to impose price controls on certain goods, or to develop food aid schemes, and armed groups frequently engage in this type of activity in practice. For example, the Islamic State reportedly fixed grain prices, and delivered humanitarian aid; the FARC provided free-of-charge health services; while even drug gangs in Rio de Janeiro are reported as providing food and social programmes. International human rights law can regulate this activity, providing guidance as to what goods or services should be subject to price controls, or provided either free-of-charge or with appropriate subsidies.

---

[134] See, for example, BBC News (2016) Islamic State committing genocide against Yazidis, says UN. http://www.bbc.co.uk/news/world-middle-east-36547467. Accessed 10 April 2017.

[135] Committee on Economic, Social and Cultural Rights 2000, para 12.

[136] Committee on Economic, Social and Cultural Rights 1999a, para 13.

The "quality" requirement is intended to ensure that services are provided at an appropriate level. For example, individuals should have access to food of a sufficient quality to satisfy their dietary needs.[137] Specific guidance is also given in relation to health care. The Committee on Economic, Social and Cultural Rights states that: "health facilities, goods and services must also be scientifically and medically appropriate and of good quality. This requires, *inter alia*, skilled medical personnel, scientifically approved and unexpired drugs and hospital equipment, safe and potable water, and adequate sanitation."[138] This guidance can assist armed groups in identifying the factors necessary to ensure that health care facilities are adequately supplied and staffed, and may also assist in the prioritisation of resource allocation.

International human rights law can also assist armed groups with respect to the allocation of resources. Of course, the means by which human rights are best fulfilled is necessarily context-dependent, but international human rights law can offer guidance in relation to what services or goods should be prioritised. For example, the minimum core content of specific rights should be realised immediately. If this is not the case, then resources should be directed in order to remedy this situation. For example, the minimum core of the right to health establishes an obligation:

(a) To ensure the right of access to health facilities, goods and services on a non-discriminatory basis, especially for vulnerable or marginalized groups;
(b) To ensure access to the minimum essential food which is nutritionally adequate and safe, to ensure freedom from hunger for everyone;
(c) To ensure access to basic shelter, housing and sanitation, and an adequate supply of safe and potable water;
(d) To provide essential drugs, as from time to time defined under the WHO Action Programme on Essential Drugs;
(e) To ensure equitable distribution of all health facilities, goods and services;
(f) To adopt and implement a national public health strategy and plan of action, on the basis of epidemiological evidence, addressing the health concerns of the whole population; the strategy and plan of action shall be devised, and periodically reviewed, on the basis of a participatory and transparent process; they shall include methods, such as right to health indicators and benchmarks, by which progress can be closely monitored; the process by which the strategy and plan of action are devised, as well as their content, shall give particular attention to all vulnerable or marginalized groups.[139]

Accordingly, if, for example, the minimum core of the right to education is satisfied,[140] but the minimum core of the right to health is not, resources should be

[137] Ibid., para 8.
[138] Committee on Economic, Social and Cultural Rights 2000, para 12(d).
[139] Ibid., para 43.
[140] See, Committee on Economic, Social and Cultural Rights 1999b, para 57.

directed towards the health sector ahead of education.[141] Other deficits with respect to the satisfaction of minimum core obligations may give rise to the armed group's obligation to fulfil (facilitate) requiring them to engage with the State or international organisations. The requirement that a national health plan be adopted and implemented is a case on point. This obligation is arguably beyond the capacity of most, if not all, armed groups acting alone, but it may be satisfied by facilitating either the continued operation of State health services, or by requiring that armed groups engage with international organisations such as MSF or the ICRC.[142] Of course, it must be acknowledged that the effective human rights-compliant allocation of resources is a hugely complicated issue, to which there is no accepted approach. Nevertheless, existing understandings of international human rights law do offer initial guidance, while ongoing efforts to develop understanding in this regard, and to operationalise economic, social and cultural rights, can be applied to armed groups.

International human rights law can also assist in establishing an armed group's scope of permissible activity. For example, a core principle of all economic, social and cultural rights is the principle of non-retrogression, which prohibits a reduction in the level of rights protection. The Committee on Economic, Social and Cultural Rights has clearly stated that there is a "strong presumption" that retrogressive measures are not permissible. Accordingly, when an armed group takes over the provision of services as a result of the displacement of State authority, it should not engage in measures that result in a reduction in the level of rights protection. A certain service level degradation may be an inevitable result of the conflict: this would not constitute a prohibited retrogressive measure. At issue are measures deliberately undertaken by an armed group. For example, education is a particularly sensitive issue in non-international armed conflict on the basis of, *inter alia*, the influence of education on understandings of the historical narrative, root causes of the conflict, and so on. As a result, armed groups may wish to take over or to control the provision of education, by replacing State teachers with teachers appointed by the armed group. If this qualifies as a retrogressive measure—if, for example, the armed group appoints teachers who are not sufficiently qualified—then it would be inconsistent with international human rights law, and therefore impermissible. In this situation the armed group has three possible options: to allow State teachers to continue, perhaps operating under certain constraints imposed by the armed group;[143] to find an alternative to State teachers, perhaps with the assistance of a non-governmental organisation;[144] or to adopt a compromise,

[141] Situations in which obligations cannot be satisfied on the basis of the armed group's resources alone are discussed in the next section.

[142] These issues are discussed further below in Sect. 5.6.2.2.

[143] Khaja N (2014) Afghanistan Conflict: Life inside a Taliban stronghold. http://www.bbc.co.uk/news/world-south-asia-29658839. Accessed 10 April 2017.

[144] For example, Jesuit Relief Services assisted the SPLA in the establishment of an education system in southern Sudan. The establishment of parallel services is not ideal, however, given the additional resource constraints imposed.

whereby the State teachers remain in place, but armed group appointed teachers take certain classes appropriate to their interest, such as civic education. In this situation international human rights law will have actively prevented an armed group from taking a specific, desired course of action. However, adopting one of the identified course of action will result in a solution capable of ensuring human rights protection. This is in the interests of the affected population, and should also assist in the development of relations between the armed group and the population, as it demonstrates that the armed group is capable of altering their conduct in the population's interests.

Clearly, the economic, social and cultural rights provisions discussed in this section were developed to apply to States and as such they are not straightforwardly applicable to armed groups. For instance, armed groups are unlikely to have the resources or information required in order to prioritise service provision on the basis of statistical indicators, or through the use of disaggregated data. Necessarily, the content of imposed obligations must be adapted to the reality of armed groups. However, armed groups do not exist in a complete vacuum and it is possible that assistance may be sought from other actors. For example, assistance in relation to the identification of health care needs or priorities may be sought from the ICRC, MSF or other international or non-governmental organisations. In certain circumstances, WHO country teams may also be able to assist.[145] Again, the reality of the situations in which armed groups provide services must be borne in mind. In such exceptional situations simply maintaining the provision of even basic services is often an important starting point, and guidance provided by international human rights law can assist armed groups in ensuring that the affected population's rights are respected and protected, to the extent possible.

5.6.2.2 Ensuring Resource Provision in Armed Group Controlled Areas

The application of international human rights law obligations to armed groups, and compliance with these obligations by armed groups, may also facilitate access to resources, and the third party provision of essential services in areas subject to armed group control or influence. As noted above, international human rights law establishes minimum core obligations in relation to economic, social and cultural rights. Failure to satisfy minimum core obligations constitutes a *prima facie* violation of international human rights law. However, in exceptional circumstances—triggered, for example, by a lack of resources—it is possible that minimum core obligations cannot be ensured immediately. Necessarily, such exceptions are strictly regulated and the responsible authority "must demonstrate that every effort has been made to use all resources that are at its disposition in an effort to satisfy, as a matter

[145] See, for example, Committee on Economic, Social and Cultural Rights 2000, para 63.

of priority, those minimum obligations".[146] Applied to armed groups, the available resources include those of the group itself, those of the territorial State (recalling its continuing obligations), and those of the international community more generally.[147]

Applying a human rights-based approach to governance will assist an armed group in identifying instances where minimum core obligations are not fulfilled, and where the armed group is either required to provide the necessary resources directly or to engage with either the territorial State or third party entities. Importantly, a group's adoption of a human rights-based approach may also assist these entities in their efforts to engage with the armed group as (broad) human rights compliance may overcome certain political obstacles. Although it may seem surprising, this form of cooperation in service delivery is actually routine in practice. For example, territorial States routinely allow international organisations or NGOs—such as the ICRC, MSF, or other agencies—to operate from, or transit through, their territory in order to deliver services in areas controlled by opposition armed groups.[148] Necessarily, these organisations must engage, and coordinate with, armed groups in order to operate in areas subject to armed group control.[149] Interestingly, the territorial State may also itself deliver services in armed group controlled areas. As discussed above, the Sri Lankan Government continued to provide health and other services in LTTE controlled territory, the Afghan Government continued to supply teachers and run schools in Taliban controlled areas, while in Senegal the State cooperated with the ICRC to deliver an immunisation programme in armed group controlled areas.

This cooperation is in the armed group's interest, as it demonstrates an ability to provide services and to govern. For example, MSF engaged with a Somali commander who controlled parts of Mogadishu, including the area within which one of their hospitals was located. They concluded that, "[f]rom the rebels' point of view, it was in their interest to support assistance for their wounded and displaced populations and to encourage the aid organisations to attest to the crimes committed by the Ethiopian army with the support of the government militias."[150] Equally, in 2008 the ICRC in Afghanistan reportedly concluded that the Taliban "was now seeing more potential benefits in securing access to medical aid for themselves and their social base than in preventing it",[151] and the provision of medical services was regarded as a means of demonstrating "able and legitimate government".[152] Interestingly, it has been found that although the armed groups do not typically supply aid or assistance themselves, they "often receive the credit on the

---

[146] Committee on Economic, Social and Cultural Rights 1990, para 10.

[147] Murray 2016, pp. 193–194.

[148] This is the case, for example, in Syria, Israel, and Libya today.

[149] See generally Magone et al. 2011.

[150] Neuman 2011, p. 85.

[151] Crombé 2011, p. 57.

[152] Ibid., 2011 p. 62.

ground".[153] In India, for example, the Naxalites were regarded as "masters in using State services to advance their agenda."[154] Such cooperation is evidently also in the population's interest, as it ensures that services are provided, and their rights protected. Interestingly, and perhaps less obviously, it may also be in the territorial State's interest—in addition, of course, to being a binding obligation under international human rights law. For example, the Sri Lankan Government reportedly provided services in LTTE controlled areas as a way of maintaining a connection to the Tamil people, and "official government strategy across multiple administrations was to wean the population away from the insurgents by providing public goods."[155]

5.7 Conclusion

The application of human rights obligations to armed groups is by no means universally accepted. However, tentative steps are being taken in this regard, and it seems likely that such measures—particularly in the context of the Human Rights Council—will continue. As such, it is essential that the content of any human rights obligations imposed on armed groups be clarified. The international community in general, and entities that engage with armed groups in particular, must know the content of armed groups' obligations if engagement, or even just monitoring and documentation, is to be effective. Equally, if human rights law is to be relevant to armed groups, armed groups must know what human rights law requires of them.

This chapter suggests that the absence of detailed human rights law presents a unique opportunity. In developing armed groups' human rights obligations, efforts should be made to engage with armed groups, and to incorporate their practice and motivation. Such engagement serves three principal purposes. First, assessing and incorporating armed groups' needs and motivations will facilitate the development of obligations that are relevant to armed groups, and capable of being implemented in practice. Second, understanding armed groups' motivations and practice can be used to engage armed groups around why it is in their interest to comply with international human rights law. Third, this process provides an opportunity to develop guidance as to how armed groups can comply with international human rights law, and to identify any existing best practice in this regard. If human rights law is to be used to guide armed group behaviour, it seems appropriate that examples of armed group behaviour populate any guidance. Of course, in situations of armed conflict relevant law of armed conflict rules must necessarily be incorporated into the development of any obligations.

---

[153] Coggins 2015, p. 113.

[154] Suykens 2015, p. 152.

[155] Mampilly 2011, p. 114.

Taking the example of armed group governance, this chapter discussed how human rights-compliant government may be in the interests of both affected populations, and the armed groups themselves. The administration of justice and service provision were used to illustrate international human rights law's potential role in engaging and guiding armed groups. Evidently this discussion is only the starting point. Significantly more work needs to be done to understand what armed groups do and why they do it, and to translate this understanding into effective, practicable human rights obligations. However, this initial discussion does clearly highlight the correlation between international human rights law and armed groups' interests, and indicates the utility—and potential impact—of the suggested approach to the development of armed groups' human rights obligations.

References

Articles, Books and Other Documents

Arjona A, Kasfir N, Mampilly Z (2015) Introduction. In: Arjona A, Kasfir N, Mampilly Z (eds) Rebel Governance in Civil War. Cambridge University Press, New York, pp 1–20

Bangerter O (2011a) Reasons why armed groups choose to respect international humanitarian law or not. International Review of the Red Cross 93(882):353–384

Bangerter O (2011b) Talking to Armed Groups. Forced Migration Review 37:7–9

Bangerter O (2012) Internal Control: Codes of Conduct within Insurgent Armed Groups – Small Arms Survey Occasional Paper No. 31. Small Arms Survey, Graduate Institute of International and Development Studies, Geneva

Barrett R (2014) The Islamic State. http://soufangroup.com/wp-content/uploads/2014/10/TSG-The-Islamic-State-Nov14.pdf. Accessed 10 April 2017

Caris CC, Reynolds S (2014) ISIS Governance in Syria, Middle East Security Report 22. Institute for the Study of War, http://www.understandingwar.org/sites/default/files/ISIS_Governance.pdf. Accessed 10 April 2017

Clapham A (2014) Focusing on Armed Non-State Actors. In: Clapham A, Gaeta P (eds) The Oxford Handbook of International Law in Armed Conflict. Oxford University Press, Oxford, pp 766–810

Coggins BL (2015) Rebel Diplomacy: Theorizing Violent Non-State Actors' Strategic Use of Talk. In: Arjona A, Kasfir N, Mampilly Z (eds) Rebel Governance in Civil War. Cambridge University Press, New York, pp 98–118

Committee on Economic, Social and Cultural Rights (1990) General Comment 3: The nature of States parties obligations, UN Doc. E/1991/23

Committee on Economic, Social and Cultural Rights (1999a) General Comment 12: The right to adequate food, UN Doc. E/C.12/1999/5

Committee on Economic, Social and Cultural Rights (1999b) General Comment 13: The right to education, UN Doc. E/C.12/1999/10

Committee on Economic, Social and Cultural Rights (2000) General Comment 14: The right to the highest attainable standard of health, UN Doc. E/C.12/2000/4

Committee on Economic, Social and Cultural Rights (2002) General Comment 15: The right to water, UN Doc. E/C.12/2002/11

Committee on Economic, Social and Cultural Rights (2009) General Comment 20: Non-Discrimination in Economic, Social and Cultural Rights, UN Doc. E/C.12/GC/20
Crombé X (2011) Afghanistan: Regaining Leverage. In: Magone C, Neuman M, Weissman F (eds) Humanitarian Negotiations Revealed: The MSF Experience. Hurst & Company, London, pp 49–68
Förster T (2015) Dialogue Direct: Rebel Governance and Civil Order in Northern Côte d'Ivoire. In: Arjona A, Kasfir N, Mampilly Z (eds) Rebel Governance in Civil War. Cambridge University Press, New York, pp 203–225
Geneva Call (2010) In Their Words: Perspectives of Armed Non-State Actors on the Protection of Children from the Effects of Armed Conflict. https://www.genevacall.org/wp-content/uploads/dlm_uploads/2014/01/2010_GC_CANSA_InTheirWords. Accessed 10 April 2017
Guevara EC (2007) Guerrilla Warfare. BN Publishing, Thousand Oaks
Hoffmann K (2015) Myths Set in Motion: The Moral Economy of Mai Mai Governance. In: Arjona A, Kasfir N, Mampilly Z (eds) Rebel Governance in Civil War. Cambridge University Press, New York, pp 158–179
Human Rights Committee (1999) General Comment 27: Freedom of Movement, UN Doc. CCPR/C/21/Rev.1/Add.9
Human Rights Committee (2014) General Comment 35: Liberty and security of person, UN Doc. CCPR/C/GC/35
Human Rights Watch (1998) War Without Quarter: Colombia and International Humanitarian Law. https://www.hrw.org/legacy/reports98/colombia/. Accessed 10 April 2017
Human Rights Watch (2001) Indonesia: The War in Aceh. https://www.hrw.org/reports/2001/aceh/indacheh0801.pdf. Accessed 10 April 2017
Human Rights Watch (2007a) Central African Republic, State of Anarchy: Rebellion and Abuses Against Civilians. https://www.hrw.org/report/2007/09/14/state-anarchy/rebellion-and-abuses-against-civilians/. Accessed 10 April 2017
Human Rights Watch (2007b) No One is Safe: Insurgent Attacks on Civilians in Thailand's Southern Border Provinces. https://www.hrw.org/reports/2007/thailand0807/. Accessed 10 April 2017
Human Rights Watch (2012) Syria: End Opposition Use of Torture, Executions. https://www.hrw.org/news/2012/09/17/syria-end-opposition-use-torture-executions. Accessed 10 April 2017
International Committee of the Red Cross (2008) Increasing Respect for International Humanitarian Law in Non-International Armed Conflicts. https://www.icrc.org/sites/default/files/topic/file_plus_list/0923-increasing_respect_for_international_humanitarian_law_in_non-international_armed_conflicts.pdf. Accessed 10 April 2017
International Committee of the Red Cross (2015) Annual Report 2014. https://www.icrc.org/en/document/ICRC-annual-report-2014. Accessed 10 April 2017
International Criminal Court, The Office of the Prosecutor (2012) Report on Preliminary Examination Activities. http://iccforum.com/media/background/africa/2012-11-22_ICC_OTP_Report_on_Preliminary_Examination_Activities.pdf. Accessed 10 April 2017
International Criminal Court, The Office of the Prosecutor (2013) Report on Preliminary Examination Activities. https://www.icc-cpi.int/OTP%20Reports/otp-report-2013.aspx. Accessed 10 April 2017
International Crisis Group (2006a) Iraq's Muqtada Al-Sadr: Spoiler or Stabiliser? https://d2071andvip0wj.cloudfront.net/55-iraq-s-muqtada-al-sadr-spoiler-or-stabiliser.pdf. Accessed 10 April 2017
International Crisis Group (2006b) Pakistan's Tribal Areas: Appeasing the Militants. https://d2071andvip0wj.cloudfront.net/125-pakistan-s-tribal-areas-appeasing-the-militants.pdf. Accessed 10 April 2017
International Crisis Group (2008) Iraq's Civil War, the Sadrists and the Surge. https://d2071andvip0wj.cloudfront.net/72-iraq-s-civil-war-the-sadrists-and-the-surge.pdf. Accessed 10 April 2017

International Crisis Group (2011) The Insurgency in Afghanistan's Heartland. https://d2071andvip0wj.cloudfront.net/207-the-insurgency-in-afghanistan-s-heartland.pdf. Accessed 10 April 2017

International Crisis Group (2013) Syria's Kurds: A Struggle Within a Struggle. https://d2071andvip0wj.cloudfront.net/syrias-kurds-a-struggle-within-a-struggle.pdf. Accessed 10 April 2017

Kalyvas SN (2015) Rebel Governance During the Greek Civil War, 1942–1949. In: Arjona A, Kasfir N, Mampilly Z (eds) Rebel Governance in Civil War. Cambridge University Press, New York, pp 119–137

Kindt MT (2009) Hezbollah: A State within a State. In: Kindt M, Post J, Schneider B (eds) The World's Most Threatening Terrorist Networks and Criminal Gangs. Palgrave Macmillan, New York, pp 123–144

Kuol MA (1997) Administration of Justice in the (SPLA/M) Liberated Areas: Court Cases in War-Torn Southern Sudan. Refugee Studies Programme, University of Oxford, Oxford

Magone C, Neuman M, Weissman F (eds) (2011) Humanitarian Negotiations Revealed: The MSF Experience. Hurst & Company, London

Mampilly Z (2011) Rebel Rulers: Insurgent Governance and Civilian Life during War. Cornell University Press, Ithaca

Mampilly Z (2015) Insurgent Governance in the Democratic Republic of the Congo. In: Krieger H (ed) Inducing Compliance with International Humanitarian Law: Lessons from the African Great Lakes Region. Cambridge University Press, Cambridge, pp 56–67

Murray A (2015) Wilson held power over life and death of IRA volunteers if they transgressed. http://www.independent.ie/irish-news/wilson-held-power-over-life-and-death-of-ira-volunteers-if-they-transgressed-31067402.html. Accessed 19 September 2017

Murray D (2016) Human Rights Obligations of Non-State Armed Groups. Hart Publishing, Oxford and Portland

National Transitional Council/ Free Libyan Army (2011) Procedure on detaining or capturing people, Frontline Manual. http://www.ejiltalk.org/wp-content/uploads/2011/08/Final-Libyan-LOAC-Guidelines-17-May-2011.ppt. Accessed 10 April 2017

Neuman M (2011) Somalia: Everything is Open to Negotiation. In: Magone C, Neuman M, Weissman F (eds) Humanitarian Negotiations Revealed: The MSF Experience. Hurst & Company, London, pp 77–94

Pool D (2001) From Guerrillas to Government: The Eritrean People's Liberation Front. Ohio University Press, Athens OH

Sassòli M (2010) Taking Armed Groups Seriously: Ways to Improve their Compliance with International Humanitarian Law. International Humanitarian Legal Studies 1:5–51

Shah A (2013) The intimacy of insurgency: beyond coercion, greed or grievance in Maoist India. Economy and Society 42(3):480–506

Sivakumaran S (2009) Courts of Armed Opposition Groups: Fair Trials or Summary Justice. Journal of International Criminal Justice 7:489–513

Solomon E (2015) The Isis economy: Meet the new boss. https://www.ft.com/content/b2c6b5ca-9427-11e4-82c7-00144feabdc0. Accessed 19 September 2017

Somer J (2015) Education and Armed Non-State Actors: Towards a comprehensive agenda. Background Paper for the PEIC/Geneva Call Workshop, 23–25 June 2015, Geneva. http://www.protectingeducation.org/sites/default/files/documents/background_paper_for_the_peic_geneva_call_workshop.pdf. Accessed 10 April 2017

Stetler R (ed) (1970) The Military Art of People's War: Selected Writings of General Vo Nguyen Giap. Monthly Review Press, New York and London

Stokke K (2006) Building the Tamil Eelam State: Emerging state institutions and forms of governance in LTTE-controlled areas in Sri Lanka. Third World Quarterly 27(6):1021–1040

Suykens B (2015) Comparing Rebel Rule Through Revolution and Naturalization: Ideologies of Governance in Naxalite and Naga India. In: Arjona A, Kasfir N, Mampilly Z (eds) Rebel Governance in Civil War. Cambridge University Press, New York, pp 138–157

Toolis K (1991) Informer: The Life and Death of an I.R.A. Man. http://www.nytimes.com/1991/02/03/magazine/informer-the-life-and-death-of-an-ira-man.html?pagewanted=all. Accessed 19 September 2017

Tse-tung M (1989) Mao Tse-tung on Guerrilla Warfare. U.S. Marine Corps, Washington D.C.

UN Assistance Mission in Afghanistan (UNAMA) (2013) Afghanistan Annual Report 2012: Protection of Civilians in Armed Conflict. http://www.refworld.org/docid/512b26a92.html. Accessed 10 April 2017

UN General Assembly (2008) Human Rights Council: Report of the Special Rapporteur on extrajudicial, summary or arbitrary executions, Philip Alston. Addendum – Mission to Philippines, UN Doc. A/HRC/8/3/Add.2

UN Security Council (2009) Report of the Secretary-General on the protection of civilians in armed conflict, UN Doc. S/2009/277

Weinstein JM (2007) Inside Rebellion: The Politics of Insurgent Violence. Cambridge University Press, New York

Weiss M, Hassan H (2015) ISIS: Inside the Army of Terror. Regan Arts, New York

Case Law

ECtHR, *Ilascu and Others v Moldova and Russia,* Grand Chamber Judgment, 8 July 2004, Application No. 48787/99

ECtHR, *Sunday Times v the United Kingdom*, Judgment, 16 April 1979, Application No. 6538/74

Human Rights Committee, *Albert Womah Mukong v Cameroon*, Views, 21 July 1994, Communication No. 458/19 91, UN Doc. CCPR/C/51/D/458/1991

IACtHR, *Castillo Petruzzi et al v Peru*, Judgment, 20 May 1999, Series C. No. 59

PCIJ, *Customs Regime between Germany and Austria (Protocol of March 19th, 1931)*, Advisory Opinion, 5 September 1931, PCIJ Rep Series A/B, No. 41, Individual Opinion of Judge Anzilotti

SCSL, *Prosecutor v Sesay, Kallon and Gbao,* Judgment, 2 March 2009, Case No. SCSL-04-15-T

Chapter 6
Armed Groups and Procedural Accountability: A Roadmap for Further Thought

Katharine Fortin

Abstract This chapter investigates the meaning of the term "accountability", as it is used in policy discussions surrounding armed groups. It takes a detailed look at literature from public administration on the concept of procedural accountability and applies it to the various accountability mechanisms that evaluate the conduct of armed groups against international norms. In doing so, the chapter points out some of the shortcomings of some of these accountability mechanisms. It ends by examining some of the more innovative accountability models, such as the process created by Geneva Call and the ad hoc processes created by the UNAMA field office in Afghanistan vis-à-vis the Taliban.

Keywords Accountability · Armed groups · Compliance · International humanitarian law · Human rights law

Contents

Katharine Fortin (k.m.a.fortin@uu.nl) is a lecturer in public international law at the Netherlands Institute of Human Rights, Utrecht University and a member of the Utrecht Centre of Accountability and Liability Law.

K. Fortin (✉)
Utrecht Centre of Accountability and Liability Law, Netherlands Institute of Human Rights, Utrecht University, Utrecht, The Netherlands
e-mail: k.m.a.fortin@uu.nl

T.D. Gill et al. (eds.), *Yearbook of International Humanitarian Law 2016*,
Yearbook of International Humanitarian Law 19,
https://doi.org/10.1007/978-94-6265-213-2_6

6.1 Introduction

The purpose of this chapter is to seek a better understanding of how to achieve the accountability of armed groups under international law. The chapter applies insights from public administration literature on the concept of procedural accountability, to monitoring mechanisms which evaluate the conduct of armed groups against international norms. In doing so, the chapter considers whether, and to what extent, State orientated systems of accountability are able successfully to hold non-State actors, such as armed groups, accountable. Showing that it is problematic simply to include armed groups in procedures which were designed by States, for States, the chapter examines some innovative alternative accountability models. These include the process created by Geneva Call and the ad hoc practices of the United Nations Assistance Mission in Afghanistan (UNAMA)'s office in vis-à-vis the Taliban. The chapter thereby shows that accountability mechanisms which are tailor-made for armed groups may be able to produce a better model of accountability that not only holds armed groups to account but simultaneously reinforces efforts to persuade armed groups to take ownership of humanitarian norms and comply with them.

6.2 Accountability Context

The background to this chapter's focus on accountability lies in the changed context of modern armed conflicts. While formerly armed conflicts used to be international, nowadays they are mainly non-international and therefore involve one or more armed groups.[1] They also involve high numbers of civilian casualties.[2] As a result, today's conflict landscape creates a pressing need to *inter alia* understand how armed groups fit, and should be treated, within the system of international law which is primarily created and enforced by States. It is against this context that an increasing number of studies have been undertaken that seek to shed light on the source and scope of armed groups' obligations under international humanitarian law and international human rights law.[3] The new conflict landscape has also prompted research on how better to secure the compliance of armed groups with these norms, through *inter alia* humanitarian engagement, special agreements and undertakings.[4] In response to the high civilian casualties of modern armed conflict, there has been a consistent emphasis put on the importance of the accountability of both State actors

---

[1] On the lack of inter-state conflict, see Pettersson and Wallensteen 2015; and Crawford 2014.

[2] See for example the joint statement by the Secretary-General of the United Nations and the President of the ICRC of 31 October 2015: ICRC (2015) World at a turning point: Heads of UN and Red Cross issue joint warning. https://www.icrc.org/en/document/conflict-disaster-crisis-UN-red-cross-issue-warning. Accessed 29 June 2017; see also UN Security Council (2016a), paras 3, 4 and 9.

[3] See for example Zegveld 2002; Sivakumaran 2012; Murray 2016; Fortin 2017.

[4] See for example Bangerter 2011, 2015; Bellal and Casey-Maslen 2011; Bongard and Somer 2011, Heffes and Kotlik 2014; Sassòli 2010; Saul 2017; Sivakumaran 2015.

and armed groups.[5] It is this latter issue that this chapter seeks to examine more carefully, focusing specifically on the accountability of armed groups.

Within most discussions about the need to secure the accountability of armed groups, the term "accountability" is employed narrowly to refer to the need to secure criminal prosecutions of an armed group's individual members.[6] While acknowledging that criminal prosecutions are a fundamentally important way of securing justice for victims of violations of international humanitarian law, this chapter focuses instead on the accountability of the armed groups themselves. The rationale behind this approach is the view that the current focus on criminal prosecutions is insufficient because it fails to address in numerous ways the full scale of harm committed by those armed groups as entities in their own right.[7] Firstly, individual criminal prosecutions pay very little attention to the role played by the *organisation* behind the perpetrators (i.e. the armed group) and its ability to amplify the powers of the group's constituent individual members.[8] Secondly, not all violations of international humanitarian law or international human rights law amount to war crimes.[9] As a result, international criminal law on its own is not capable of providing legal redress for all violations of international humanitarian law or international human rights law perpetrated by armed groups. Thirdly, and in a similar vein, criminal tribunals are only able to order reparations for individuals and communities that match the individual perpetrator's contribution to the crimes charged.[10] As a result, prosecutions are unable to secure redress for the full spectrum of collective violations committed by a particular party to an armed conflict.[11]

The structural inability of international criminal law to address the total harm caused by armed groups is evident by comparing the evolution of the accountability framework for armed groups with the evolution of that for States. The accountability framework for States initially comprised of judicial fora where the responsibility of the organisation (i.e. the State) could be found. It only later included

---

[5] Since 2009, the United Nations Secretary-General has identified "accountability" for violations of international law as one of the "core challenges" of the international community. See UN Security Council 2009.

[6] See a general review of the Reports of the Secretary-General on the protection of civilians in armed conflict, 2009–2016 which focus systematically on accountability; see Brunée 2005, p. 47.

[7] For a rare acknowledgment of the need for measures beyond the prosecution of individual perpetrators, see UN Security Council 2009, paras 68–73.

[8] Kleffner 2009, p. 245; and Moffett 2015, p. 325.

[9] UN Security Council 2009, para 69.

[10] Although the International Criminal Court (ICC) Appeals Chamber has confirmed that collective reparations are possible, it has also confirmed that a convicted person's liability for reparations must be proportionate to the harm caused and, *inter alia*, his or her participation in the commission of the crimes for which he or she was found guilty, in the specific circumstances of the case. See *Prosecutor v Thomas Lubanga Dyilo*, Judgment on the appeals against the "Decision establishing the principles and procedures to be applied to reparations" of 7 August 2012 with AMENDED order for reparations (ANNEX A) and public annexes 1, 2, 3 March 2015, Case No ICC-01/04-01/06-3129, para 118.

[11] Moffett 2015, p. 325.

judicial fora which could make findings about the individual criminal responsibility of State agents. The ability to prosecute individuals for international crimes was developed post-World War II in reaction to a view that a sole recourse to State responsibility was not a sufficient remedy for international crimes, because international crimes are committed by *individuals* and not only by *abstract entities.*[12] Paradoxically when it comes to armed groups, the pattern of development has developed in a converse manner. The accountability framework started by securing the criminal responsibility of armed group members, and there are, as yet, very few judicial fora in which armed groups can be held to account, as legal entities.[13] This anomaly confirms the sense in investing further effort in securing the accountability of armed groups themselves, alongside efforts to advance the individual criminal responsibility of armed groups' members.[14]

It is common nowadays for a multiplicity of UN accountability mechanisms to make statements identifying violations by armed groups of particular humanitarian norms. For many years special rapporteurs acting under mandates created by the Human Rights Council (HRC) (and its predecessor the Commission on Human Rights) have examined the acts of armed groups when they visit States embroiled in non-international armed conflicts.[15] Equally, the UN Security Council and the HRC now consistently address the acts of armed groups as well as States, in situations of non-international armed conflicts.[16] Likewise, the acts of armed groups are also regularly scrutinised by UN field offices and commissions of inquiry, alongside States.[17] While human rights treaty bodies have been traditionally reluctant to address armed groups in their findings, in 2013 the Committee on the Elimination of Discrimination against Women (CEDAW) indicated a willingness to assess the acts of armed groups in instances where they have an identifiable political structure and exercise significant control over population or territory.[18] It is these kinds of

[12] Nuremberg International Military Tribunal, *United States of America, French Republic, United Kingdom and the USSR v Hess, Goring et al.*, Judgment, 1 October 1946, para 447.

[13] For examples of instances in which armed groups have been held responsible in domestic jurisdictions, see Moffett 2015, pp. 335–345.

[14] UN Security Council 2009, para 68; see also Bellal 2015, pp. 305–306 and Moffett 2015, pp. 325–330.

[15] One of the earliest examples of a Special Rapporteur examining the acts of armed groups was in 2001. See UN General Assembly 2000, para 27; for a more recent example see UN General Assembly 2016c.

[16] UN Security Council 2016b, c, d, e, f; UN General Assembly 2016a, b.

[17] See for example MONUSCO and OHCHR 2014.

[18] See the CEDAW Committee's General Recommendation No. 30 on women in conflict prevention, conflict and post-conflict situations of 18 October 2013 which states that "although non-State actors cannot become parties to the Convention [...] under certain circumstance, in particular where an armed groups with an identifiable political structure exercises significant control over territory and population, non-State actors are obliged to respect international human rights". Committee on the Elimination of Discrimination against Women (CEDAW) 2013; on the willingness of human rights treaty bodies to monitor the acts of armed groups, see also Sassòli 2010, p. 39.

non-judicial accountability mechanisms that are the subject of this chapter. For while these kinds of accountability mechanisms are an important positive step in securing the accountability of armed groups, the attention that they give to armed groups has occurred out of necessity, rather than planning or design.[19] As a result, little consideration has been given to the question studied by this chapter, namely whether, and to what extent, a State orientated procedural system can effectively deliver the accountability of armed groups.[20]

6.3 Definitions of Accountability

In legal literature, little differentiation is made between the term "accountability" and the term "responsibility". Both terms are used interchangeably to refer to judicial processes whereby actors are held responsible for wrongful acts. Yet when it comes to armed groups, there are significant advantages in understanding the term accountability more broadly than responsibility. Indeed, interpreting accountability more broadly allows an enquiry into the "answerability" of armed groups to go forward, despite the current lack of rules on the circumstances in which armed groups can be held responsible for the legal acts of their members and the lack of judicial fora for formally establishing their responsibility.[21] Menno Kamminga, who conducted a notable study into accountability, found that responsibility was a "limited subcategory" of the "wider concept" of accountability.[22] In doing so, he drew upon one of the observations made by the International Court of Justice in the *Corfu Channel* case where the Court found that "a State on whose territory an act contrary to international law has occurred, may be called upon to give an explanation".[23] Interestingly, the court found that the State's duty to give an explanation for its actions existed independently from any finding that the State had *prima facie* responsibility for such an act.

The identification of the distinction between accountability and responsibility goes to the heart of what has been termed the *procedural side* of accountability. Indeed, it is argued that a better understanding of the procedural dimension of accountability provides valuable insights into how the accountability of armed groups can better be achieved, in a rich variety of non-judicial contexts. It is furthermore argued that in order to gain a better understanding of the concept,

---

[19] See the account by Philip Alston, Special Rapporteur on Extrajudicial, Summary or Arbitrary Killings, in which he explains *how* and *why* the mandate was forced to find a means to respond to extrajudicial killings by armed groups, UN General Assembly 2007, paras 40–44.

[20] See Brunée 2005 for an evaluation of this question.

[21] There is a growing body of literature considering the responsibility of armed groups for wrongful acts. See for example Moffett 2015; Bílková 2015; Verhoeven 2015, but the idea is still nascent.

[22] Kamminga 1992, pp. 45.

[23] ICJ, *Corfu Channel case*, Judgment, 9 April 1949, [1949] I.C.J. Reports 4, p. 4 and 18.

public administration literature is the best place to start. Here the term accountability has long been used to refer to procedures which ensure that public power is held in check. However, for many years within this field the term accountability was also over-used, without any attention given to its meaning. In a bid to "save the concept"[24] from nebulousness, a number of authors embarked on a series of analytical studies designed to identify the core sense of the term. In doing so, they developed an important body of writing defining the concept of accountability as a procedural mechanism. This literature is helpful when looking at procedural mechanisms currently holding armed groups to account as it helps identify what accountability is and how it can be achieved.

Mulgan, a key author within this movement to clarify the concept of accountability, finds that there are at least four key requirements/components for defining accountability as a mechanism: (i) the accountability forum must be a third party; (ii) the accountability forum should have "rights of authority" over the entity under scrutiny (iii) the person being held accountable must have the opportunity to explain his conduct; and (iv) the accountability forum must have the possibility of imposing sanctions.[25] Bovens, another key author in this movement, identified the same key features in his writing. He asserts that there needs to be a "relationship" between an actor and an accountability forum, in which the actor has an "obligation to explain and to justify his or her conduct" and the forum can ask questions and "pass judgment", such that the actor will face "consequences".[26] It is significant that Curtin and Nollkaemper, some of the few legal scholars to have explored the term, adopt a similar definition of accountability. Perhaps not surprisingly considering their legal focus, they include the further requirement that the behaviour of the actor being held to account must be scrutinised against "prior established rules or principles".[27] Before seeing how the main constituent components of these definitions apply to accountability mechanisms that address the acts of armed groups, their features are examined in more detail below.

It is clear from the literature on accountability referred to above, that one of its most important requirements is the need for account to be given to a third party. According to Mulgan's definition above, accountability must be external, in that the account is given to an entity "outside" the person or body being held to account.[28] Indeed, it is this need for "a significant other" that distinguishes the concept of accountability from other concepts that fall outside the term's core scope, for example, personal culpability, morality and professional ethnics.[29] Accountability has a key external dimension in that it involves a relationship between an actor

[24] Bovens 2007, p. 449.
[25] Mulgan 2000, p. 555.
[26] Bovens 2010, p. 951.
[27] Curtin and Nollkaemper 2005, p. 8.
[28] Mulgan 2000, p. 555.
[29] Bovens 2007, p. 450.

—"the accountor"—and a forum "the accountee".[30] According to public administration literature, the external forum can have many manifestations. It can be a particular individual or agency, but it may also be a more virtual entity, such as the general public.[31] In other words, an accountability process, and the relationship upon which it is based, can be of varying degrees of formality and institutionalisation. At its most formal, it will be created and managed by a judicial institution, such as a tribunal or court.[32] At its most informal, the relationship may be created by an ad hoc interaction between a politician and the media or between a public body and a civil society organisation.[33] The observation that accountability can be achieved by less formal structures is helpful when considering the accountability of armed groups. It demonstrates that the lack of judicial fora able to hold armed groups to account—and the lack of secondary rules on how to attribute wrongful acts to armed groups—need not *per se* be a bar to achieving their accountability. Indeed, it has been asserted that it is precisely these types of formal obstacles that have created the rich variety of alternative non-judicial modes of accountability for non-State actors, on the international plane.[34]

Irrespective of the type of forum, public administration literature consistently emphasises that the forum must have "rights of authority" over those it is calling to account. By this it is meant that the accountability mechanism is able to assert rights of "superior authority" over those being held to account, including "the right to demand answers and impose sanctions".[35] Significantly, authors writing on accountability have indicated that these "rights of authority" can have a different character in every forum. For example, if the entity is a court, the forum will have "legal authority"; if the forum is an employer it will have "professional authority;" if the forum is a journalist, it will have "moral authority". Yet no matter what the character of the "authority", it has been recognised that it is "crucial that the actor *is, or feels, obliged to inform the forum about his or her conduct*".[36] This sense of obligation may stem from formal rules obliging the actor to subject its behaviour to scrutiny by the forum in question but it could also stem from a feeling of moral obligation. In that sense, it can be seen to be inherently connected to the requirement articulated by Curtin and Nollkaemper that the behaviour of the actor is held to account against "prior established rules or principles".[37]

---

[30] Ibid.; see also Grant and Keohane 2005, p. 29.

[31] Bovens 2007, p. 450 and 460. It is noteworthy that Bovens calls this a 'horizontal accountability' relationship. See also Curtin and Nollkaemper 2005, p. 10 for a discussion of different persons or institutions to which account can be rendered.

[32] Bovens 2007, p. 460; and Bovens 2010, p. 951.

[33] Mulgan 2000, p. 565; and Bovens 2007, p. 455.

[34] Brunée 2005, p. 24.

[35] Mulgan 2000, p. 555.

[36] Bovens 2010, p. 952.

[37] Curtin and Nollkaemper 2005, p. 8.

When looking at existing accountability mechanisms for armed groups, it is interesting to note that literature exploring the idea of accountability indicates that it needs to include a "*social interaction and exchange*, in that one side, that calling for the account, seeks answers and rectification while the other side, that being held accountable, responds and accepts sanctions".[38] In other words, public administration literature asserts that a mechanism will not achieve accountability if it simply metes out censure, judgment or punishment upon a wrongdoer. Accountability can only be achieved if there is a truth-seeking process that gives the accountee an opportunity to ask questions and the accountor an opportunity to render "an account" of his or her conduct. In other words, the process needs to comprise of a "back-and-forth conversation" or an "ongoing process of account-giving and account-taking".[39] This requirement tallies with Kamminga's observation that unlike "responsibility", the term "accountability" indicates that the entity being held to account has a duty to provide an "explanation".[40] This requirement fits with the fact that courts and tribunals, fora that lawyers would most instantly identify as accountability mechanisms, tend to give the respondent—be it an individual or organisation—the opportunity to give an account of his or her behaviour.[41]

Whether or not the term "accountability" includes "sanctions" is a subject of debate among public administration scholars.[42] Some authors consider that the process of "'*calling* to account' [...] [is] incomplete without a process of rectification".[43] Despite disagreement on this question, many writers acknowledge that most accountability mechanisms have the power to impose "sanctions", when the term is interpreted widely.[44] For example, it has been pointed out that in many circumstances the issuance of public criticism, shaming, stigmatisation or even simple exposure will constitute a sanction of sorts, for many actors.[45] It has also been pointed out that an accountability mechanism may also judge an actor's

---

[38] Mulgan 2000, p. 555.

[39] Rached 2016, p. 4.

[40] Kamminga 1992, p. 5.

[41] It is noteworthy in this respect that the right to defend oneself and thereby render an "account" of one's behaviour is enshrined in Article 6 of the European Convention for the Protection of Human Rights and Fundamental Freedoms, opened for signature 4 November 1950, 213 UNTS 221 (entered into force 3 September 1953); Article 14 of the International Covenant of Civil and Political Rights, opened for signature 16 December 1966, 999 UNTS 171 (entered into force 23 March 1976) (ICCPR); and Article 8 of the American Convention on Human Rights, opened for signature 22 November 1969, 1144 UNTS 123 (entered into force 18 July 1978); It is also found in Article 21 and 20 of the Statutes of the International Criminal Tribunal for the former Yugoslavia and Rwanda, respectively, UN Security Council 1993 and UN Security Council 1994; and Article 67 of the Rome Statute of the International Criminal Court, opened for signature 17 July 1998, 2187 UNTS 90 (entered into force 1 July 2002).

[42] Bovens 2007, p. 451; and Mulgan 2000, p. 556.

[43] Mulgan 2000, p. 556. See also Rached 2016, p. 9.

[44] Bovens 2007, p. 452.

[45] Rached 2016, p. 9.

behaviour positively, rather than negatively.[46] For although the word "sanction" has a heavy connotation of penalty to most people, formally it encompasses both positive and negative meanings i.e. penalties or rewards.[47] As a result, the sanctions requirement will also be satisfied when a mechanism finds that an entity being held to account is not guilty of any wrongdoing.

6.4 Towards an Accountability of Armed Groups?

Having reviewed the various elements of the definition of accountability, it can be seen that many of the non-judicial accountability mechanisms mentioned above (e.g. the UN Security Council, etc.) are capable of achieving accountability when they scrutinise State action. Mechanisms that are created by States to review State action against State-created norms have normative and procedural "rights of authority" over the States that they scrutinise. Likewise, State-made accountability mechanisms incorporate procedural rights for States to refute the allegations against them. Examples of these procedural rights can be seen in the fact that human rights treaty bodies request States to submit their own report, before they make their own findings on the State's compliance with the treaty obligations.[48] Similarly, it is customary for the President of the UN Security Council to invite representatives of States which are on the agenda of the Council to participate in any session examining that State.[49] In a similar manner, States scrutinised by the HRC via its Universal Periodic Review procedure or special sessions are given the opportunity to provide an account of their position to the Council.[50] However, when the same mechanisms turn their attention to the acts of armed groups, the situation is quite different. The following section considers how the bodies which are currently holding armed groups to account—in the wider sense of the word—compare to the definition of "accountability" set out above. The only part of the definition which is

---

[46] Bovens 2007, p. 452.

[47] See Oxford English Dictionary, Online edition, http://www.oed.com. Accessed 10 July 2017.

[48] See for example Article 40 ICCPR, above n 41, which invites States parties to submit reports on the measures they have adopted to give effect to the rights in the Covenant and on the progress made in the enjoyment of those rights.

[49] Rule 37 of the Provisional Rules of Procedure of the Security Council allows any member of the United Nations which is not a member of the United Nations Security Council to be invited, as a result of the decision of the Security Council, to participate without a vote in the discussion of any question brought before the Security Council when *inter alia* the Security Council considers that the interests of the member are specially affected. UN Security Council 1983.

[50] For the Universal Periodic Review, see the UN General Assembly Resolution 60/251, which created the Human Rights Council and described how the new universal periodic review process would be a "cooperative mechanism, based on an interactive dialogue, with the full involvement of the country concerned". UN General Assembly 2006, para 5(e); see the special sessions of the Human Rights Council, for example UN General Assembly 2017a; and UN General Assembly 2017b.

not scrutinised explicitly in this latter section is that of "sanctions". It has been seen that this requirement will in most instances be fulfilled when a monitoring mechanism produces a report or public statement, detailing an armed group's behaviour.

When the above components of accountability are compared with the accountability mechanisms that are scrutinising the acts of armed groups, it can be seen that the externality requirement is generally the easiest to satisfy. For despite their other arguable shortcomings, the United Nations accountability mechanisms that evaluate the acts of armed groups against international law standards are clearly external to the armed groups in question. Indeed, the requirement of externality is more likely to be an issue for accountability processes set up by the armed groups themselves. This can be seen by looking at an example involving the Taliban in Afghanistan. In 2013, the Taliban announced that it had taken steps to address civilian casualties by establishing "a special commission under the supervision of the military commission for the avoidance of civilian losses".[51] Although the Taliban has not made the commission's *modus operandi* public, it has indicated that its mandate is to "get information" and "evaluate [...] civilian losses" attributed to Taliban members.[52] In September 2014, the Taliban openly encouraged Afghans to report any information about civilian casualties to the commission, regardless of the perpetrator. The group promised that it would conduct "comprehensive investigation[s]", impart justice according to *Sharia* law, "pave the way for mutual conciliation" and "create proper condition[s] to offer compensation and extend condolence to the victim party."[53]

So far, the Taliban has refused to make the details of individual investigations public. However, in 2016, they published four reports that contained the findings of its newly created "special organ", detailing civilian casualties for 2016.[54] In its annual 2016 report, the Taliban claimed to have documented 5 232 civilian casualties between January–December 2016, of which 71% were caused by the "Americans and the stooge administration" and 12% were caused by the Taliban. These figures starkly contradict with UNAMA's findings for the same period, which found 11 418 civilian casualties, 61% of which it attributed to Anti-Government elements. Historically, UNAMA has welcomed the Taliban's reports on the basis that it "welcomes public reporting by all sides of the conflict, including the Taliban".[55] However, it has also repeatedly made clear that it will not accept the Taliban findings without extensively corroborating their veracity. As a result, UNAMA takes pains to diligently check the many "war crimes" reports produced by the Taliban, and publish a record of its verification efforts.[56] UNAMA has also emphasised on more than one occasion that such reports from the Taliban are only valuable if their findings are communicated to those responsible for battlefield

[51] UNAMA and OHCHR 2013, p. 5.

[52] Ibid.

[53] UNAMA and OHCHR 2014, p. 73.

[54] UNAMA and OHCHR 2016b, p. 76.

[55] UNAMA and OHCHR 2016a, p. 73.

[56] See for example UNAMA and OHCHR 2012a, p. 17; and UNAMA and OHCHR 2013, p. 36.

actions i.e. its fighters.[57] In a similar vein, UNAMA has warned that the Taliban should not issue these reports, simply as part of a public relations exercise.[58]

UNAMA has also asked for more details, on how the Taliban's new fact-finding commission defines the term "civilian". It has furthermore asked about the Taliban's code of conduct regarding civilian casualty protection, its mechanisms to ensure accountability and any cases against its members.[59] Yet as far as this author is aware, the UNAMA has not yet explicitly commented on the organ's independence. Yet, the definition of accountability above highlights the importance of this aspect. For it is unlikely that a "special organ" under the supervision of the Taliban's "military commission" can satisfy the requirement of "externality" that is needed to deliver effective accountability. When examining this question, it would be relevant to find out whether the Taliban's "special organ" is operationally independent from its military chain of command.[60] It would also be relevant to determine whether the Taliban's military chain of command retains discretion on the opening and closing of investigations against particular members of the group.[61]

Although it is relatively straightforward for United Nations mechanisms to satisfy the externality requirement, it will be shown below that some of the other requirements are more challenging. In particular, the idea that an accountability forum must have "rights of authority" over an armed group is more difficult. Indeed, it has been shown above that it requires attention to two distinct but connected ideas: the authority of the norms and the authority of the forum. The former requirement stems from Curtin and Nollkaemper's observation that any judgment or assessment needs to be rendered on the basis of "prior established rules or principles".[62] Indeed, it seems obvious that where it is doubtful whether a particular entity is bound by a particular norm, the persuasive force of any statement finding that entity to have violated that norm will be inevitably diminished. This highlights the acute need for clarity on the question about which norms of international law are binding upon armed groups. While it has been long accepted that armed groups are bound by Article 3 Common to the Geneva Conventions and Additional Protocol II of the Geneva Conventions, the application of human rights law to armed groups remains controversial.[63] The "rights of authority" argument set out above explains why it is essential to find clarity on these questions, for the accountability of armed

[57] UNAMA and OHCHR 2011b, p. 4; UNAMA and OHCHR 2012b, p. 5; and UNAMA and OHCHR 2015b, p. 56; UNAMA and OHCHR 2016b, p. 78.

[58] UNAMA and OHCHR 2015b, p. 55; UNAMA and OHCHR 2016a, p. 73; and UNAMA and OHCHR 2016b, p. 78.

[59] UNAMA and OHCHR 2016a, p. 73.

[60] See ECtHR, *Al-Skeini and Others v UK*, Grand Chamber Judgment, 7 July 2011, Application No. 55721/07, paras 167 and 172–175 for judicial guidance on the requirement of externality or independence.

[61] Ibid.

[62] Curtin and Nollkaemper 2005, p. 8.

[63] Saul 2017, p. 3; for recent studies of the obligations of armed groups under human rights law, see Fortin 2017; Murray 2016.

groups to be achieved. For so long as there is doubt and debate about the legal legitimacy of applying particular norms to armed groups, the force of any pronouncements by mechanisms seeking to achieve the accountability of armed groups under human rights law will be compromised and restricted.[64]

According to the accountability literature, it is also important to give attention to the question of whether armed groups *feel bound* by particular norms. For while as a matter of positive law, it is widely agreed that armed groups do not need to consent to be bound by humanitarian norms, the value and effectiveness of procedural accountability will clearly be heightened in instances where an armed group expresses its consent to a norm. [65] In instances where an armed group feels an affinity with the content of humanitarian norms, the "rights of authority" of the mechanism will be greater.[66] This observation demonstrates that contemporary efforts to promote the "ownership" of the humanitarian norms by armed groups are not only useful to increase armed groups' compliance with international humanitarian law, but also useful to achieve their accountability.[67] Current studies have shown that armed groups can take ownership of humanitarian norms in different ways, a few of which will be mentioned here. First it has been demonstrated that there is an important value in consulting armed groups about the *need* for new norms, even though they are not formal actors in the norm creation process.[68] Such efforts can help ensure that any resultant norms are realistic and capable of implementation.[69] The ownership of norms by armed groups may also be achieved by their being consulted in the drafting process of new treaty norms.[70] Ownership of norms may also be achieved by armed groups signing special agreements that go beyond their treaty obligations under international humanitarian law.[71]

As part of efforts to promote compliance, armed groups are also regularly encouraged to sign deeds of commitment setting out their commitment to certain existing humanitarian norms.[72] The efforts of Geneva Call have been pioneering in this regard. Over the last seventeen years, the organisation has created an original "inclusive" approach under which armed groups can express their adherence to international humanitarian norms by means of deeds of commitment, thereby taking ownership of these rules.[73] If individuals in the higher ranks of an armed group

[64] This idea is explored in more detail in Fortin 2017, pp. 4–5 and 15–18.

[65] For the role of State consent in the creation of obligations for armed groups, see Murray 2016; Sivakumaran 2006; Kleffner 2011; Fortin 2017. For the view that consent of an armed group is relevant in the context of human rights obligations, see Ryngaert 2008, p. 308.

[66] There is scope for further research on the 'authority' of international law as applied by armed groups, but this is left for further studies.

[67] Bellal and Casey-Maslen 2011, p. 191; see also Sassòli 2010, p. 6 and 25–26.

[68] Sassòli 2010, pp. 15–20 and 22; Rondeau 2011, p. 658.

[69] Rondeau 2011, p. 659.

[70] Ibid., p. 658.

[71] Heffes and Kotlik 2014.

[72] Sassòli 2010, p. 25; Sivakumaran 2015, p. 130; Ryngaert and Van de Meulebroucke 2011.

[73] See Bongard and Somer 2011 for an overview of Geneva Call's work.

agree to particular norms, there is a greater likelihood that these norms will be respected and implemented.[74] While there is no guarantee that deeds of commitment will be complied with, it is notable that Geneva Call has rarely encountered non-compliance in its work.[75] Armed groups are also being encouraged to create internal regulations in the form of codes of conduct defining the type of behaviour that the leadership expects from its members.[76] Although these efforts have borne fruit, sometimes when an armed group adopts humanitarian norms, the integrity of the norms are lost during the internalisation process.[77] For example, armed groups may deviate from standard interpretations of key international humanitarian law terms.[78] For instance, the SPLM in Sudan passed penal laws that took a problematically wide approach to the issue of which individuals they could target.[79] It will be shown below that similar problems have arisen in relation to the Taliban's approach to the notion of civilian.

The application of the "rights of authority" requirement at a normative level additionally highlights the need for accountability mechanisms to make sure that there is a solid connection between the conduct they are scrutinising and the entity that is being held to account. This is crucial for the mechanism to have rights of authority over the entity, and not just over its individual members. It has been pointed out already that accepted rules of attribution, when it comes to armed groups, are not yet in existence. Yet the "rights of authority" requirement reminds us that when an accountability mechanism makes conclusive pronouncements about the behaviour of an armed group violating a particular norm, it needs to pay attention to the issue of attribution. Thus it must demonstrate how it has ascribed the individual conduct that it has scrutinised, to the armed group. Scholars working in this area have noted that accountability mechanisms scrutinising the acts of armed groups often only give minimal attention to the issue of attribution.[80] This may be because of the aforementioned lack of rules providing guidance on *how* and *when* attribution can be ascertained, as a matter of law. It may also be because entities such as commissions of inquiry see their role to be primarily aimed at the gathering evidence for the establishment of criminal courts in the future. As a result, commissioners may feel that their priority is to identify individual crimes, rather than establish the responsibility of the group. However, on the basis that many accountability mechanisms make findings that armed groups are violating international norms, a consideration of attribution remains important, in order for the mechanism's findings vis-à-vis the group to also have validity.

---

[74] Saul 2017, p. 13; Bangerter 2015, pp. 123–124; Schneckener and Hofmann 2015, pp. 96–97. See also ICRC 2008, p. 22.

[75] Bongard and Somer 2011, p. 696.

[76] Bangerter 2012. See in particular p. 12 on the definition of codes of conduct.

[77] Sivakamaran calls this "translation". Sivakumaran 2015, p. 133.

[78] See Saul 2017, p. 14.

[79] Sivakumaran 2015, p. 137.

[80] Bellal 2015.

The other important limb of the right of authority argument pertains to the "right of authority" of the accountability mechanism itself, over the armed group. The existence of this criterion reminds us that it is important to give consideration not only for the armed group's acceptance of the underlying norm, but also its relationship with the forum itself. Indeed, it is argued that this is an aspect of the accountability definition that needs more consideration, particularly at UN level. For it is noteworthy that in most instances, accountability mechanisms applying international law have traditionally held States to account, rather than armed groups. Having created the United Nations system, States have the opportunity to participate within its procedures, and provide an account of their behaviour in instances where they are held to account.[81] As a result, when the UN General Assembly, UN Security Council, Human Rights Council, a special rapporteur or a human rights treaty body calls out a State for violating a provision of international law, there are many procedural avenues—formal and informal—through which States can provide their own account of their behaviour.[82] The accountability frameworks monitoring States' compliance with humanitarian norms contain procedural channels through which States can enter into "social interaction and exchange" with the monitoring mechanism, and refute the factual allegations against them.[83]

However, when these fora turn their attention to armed groups, the relationship between addressee and accountability forum is completely different. Armed groups have not been involved in the process of designing these accountability mechanisms and nor do they have formal procedural rights within them. As a result, within many of these accountability systems, armed groups have no recourse to procedural channels, enabling them to refute the allegations against them. This not only causes a tension but also compromises the ability of these mechanisms to deliver "accountability". For although armed groups are the subject of the mechanisms' findings, they have little "relationship" with them in a procedural sense, and no opportunity to participate in a dialogue about their behaviour. This observation is illustrated by the fact that in some instances where armed groups are the subject of the substantive findings of such a mechanism, they are excluded from the report's recommendations. For example, in the 2014 final report of the International Commission of Inquiry on the Central African Republic, the Séléka and Anti-balaka groups were identified as parties to the armed conflict, but not addressed in the recommendations section. The recommendations were addressed only to the Transitional Government, the United Nations Multidimensional Integrated Stabilization Mission in the Central African Republic (MINUSCA), the UN Security Council, the UN Secretary-General, the Office of the UN High Commissioner for Human Rights (OHCHR), the HRC and relevant regional organisations, such as the African Union (AU) and the European Union (EU).[84]

[81] See n 49 and n 50 of this chapter.

[82] Ibid.

[83] Mulgan 2000, p. 355.

[84] UN Security Council 2014.

Likewise, in the Report of the OHCHR on the situation of human rights in Mali in 2012, 28 paragraphs were devoted to documenting the violations in the north of the country under the control of *inter alia* the National Movement for the Liberation of Azawad (MNLA), Al Qaeda in the Islamic Maghreb (AQIM), Ansar Dine and the Movement for Oneness and Jihad in West Africa (MUJAO), but the report's conclusions only made recommendations to the government of Mali and the international community, but did not address the armed groups.[85]

It is unclear whether omissions of this kind are the result of a political sensitivity on the part of the reports' drafters or oversight. Certainly practice on this issue is inconsistent. For example, the Commission of Inquiry for Syria has consistently addressed its recommendations to the armed groups involved in the conflict in Syria, since its inception.[86] Yet the fact that some reports do not address armed groups in their recommendations at all creates pause for thought. For according to the literature surveyed above, accountability needs to involve a "social interaction and exchange".[87] Perhaps most pertinently, it has been shown that it is important that accountability mechanisms give an actor the opportunity to explain its conduct to others.[88] It is clear from the definitions of accountability explored in this chapter, that accountability mechanisms that censure armed groups, without any attempt to communicate that censure to the armed groups themselves, are compromising their ability to deliver "accountability". Their statements remain important, in that they constitute international condemnation of particular actions and contribute to subsequent prosecutions, but they are unlikely to affect the behaviour of the entity whose conduct is subject to scrutiny. While it would be unrealistic to expect all accountability mechanisms to feed into armed groups' behaviour on the ground, it is notable that small changes seem to have been achieved through the existence of a social interaction and exchange between the monitoring mechanism in question and the armed group. The two examples that are explored below relate to the UNAMA office in Afghanistan and the work of Geneva Call.

6.4.1 UNAMA

Perhaps the most interesting example to highlight in this respect can be found in a further review of the practice of the UNAMA office in Afghanistan, which has already been mentioned above. UNAMA was established in March 2002 by UN Security Council Resolution 1401 at the request of the government of Afghanistan, with a mandate to monitor and promote human rights and the protection of civilians in armed conflict. Twice annually, UNAMA produces a report on the Protection of

---

[85] UN General Assembly 2012b, paras 18–46 and 66–70.

[86] See for example, UN General Assembly 2011, para 113; UN General Assembly 2012a, para 133. See also UN Human Rights Council 2009, p. 427.

[87] Mulgan 2000, p. 555.

[88] Curtin and Nollkaemper 2005, p. 8.

Civilians in Armed Conflict. Comparing the reporting process with the definition of accountability above, it can be seen that the UNAMA field office is capable of delivering a wide-sense of accountability, albeit not judicial in character. It is applying international norms to the parties to the armed conflict, and it is producing a documentation of its findings. Most fascinatingly, a study of UNAMA's reports demonstrates that they have produced a conversation between the UNAMA office and the Taliban. The reports evidence an "evolving dialogue" between the Taliban and UNAMA on humanitarian issues over the last five years.[89] Most notably, in 2011, the Taliban started responding to the UNAMA reports, in many cases disputing the casualties that had been attributed to it and providing its own list of incidents that UNAMA had not taken account of. In response, UNAMA diligently reviewed the status of each listed incident provided by the Taliban, preparing a detailed response which was later shared with the Taliban source.[90] While sharing its reaction, UNAMA regularly commented that the Taliban's definition of civilian was inconsistent with international humanitarian law.[91] Even though over the last years, the Taliban has started its own investigative unit, it continues to respond to UNAMA's reports.[92]

It is clear from the UNAMA reports that there is a social interaction and exchange between the UNAMA and the Taliban, both inside and outside of the reporting process. In many instances, this is clearly mutually critical. The Taliban regularly denies the allegations made by UNAMA against it and has accused UNAMA of producing propaganda.[93] It has also seemingly rejected UNAMA's 2016 report on the Protection of Civilians in Armed Conflict entirely saying that its own civilian casualty unit is better placed to gather figures on civilian casualties.[94] In turn, the UNAMA has regularly criticised the Taliban for causing high civilian casualties and chided it for not following through its commitments on the ground.[95] Yet over the years, the dialogue between the two entities seems to have contributed to the Taliban devoting more attention to humanitarian norms, at least on paper.[96]

[89] UNAMA and OHCHR 2011a, p. 11.

[90] See UNAMA and OHCHR 2012a, p. 17; see also UNAMA and OHCHR 2014, p. 76; and UNAMA and OHCHR 2016b, p. 78 where it indicates that it monitors "public reporting" by all parties to the conflict.

[91] See for example UNAMA and OHCHR 2011b, p. 15; UNAMA and OHCHR 2012b, pp. 5–6, 14, 17 and 28–29; UNAMA and OHCHR 2013, p. 33; UNAMA and OHCHR 2014, p. 74; UNAMA and OHCHR 2015b, p. 54.

[92] See the analysis of the special unit above. See also for example UNAMA and OHCHR 2014, p. 76; and UNAMA and OHCHR 2016b, p. 77, detailing the Taliban refutation of the UNAMA and OHCHR Midyear Report 2016 (UNAMA and OHCHR 2016a).

[93] UNAMA and OHCHR 2014, p. 75.

[94] See the full Taliban response to the UNAMA and OHCHR Final Report 2016 in UNAMA and OHCHR 2016b, Annex 6, pp. 122–123.

[95] UNAMA and OHCHR 2016b, p. 78.

[96] UNAMA has often expressed frustration that the Taliban's statements that it plans to take measures to protect civilians do not translate into better protection for civilians on the ground.

Perhaps most importantly, it is notable that the Taliban's definition of civilians—although still not consistent with international humanitarian law—has become wider over the course of the years, so that it now provides greater protection for non-military government workers.[97] It is likely that this change can be credited at least partly to UNAMA's regular and consistent response to the Taliban's reports and engagement on the content of international humanitarian law norms. UNAMA has made a habit of reminding the Taliban that its deliberate targeting and killing of civilian members of the Government administration is a violation of international humanitarian law.[98] It also has regularly instructed the Taliban that only military objects may be the lawful objects of attack and that civilians may not be targeted unless, and only for such time as they take a direct part in hostilities. Perhaps most importantly, the dialogue between the two entities ensures that UNAMA's comments are reaching the Taliban's leaders. For it appears that the Taliban has developed an internal practice of reading UNAMA's reports and responding to them. For example, in a public statement in 2013, the Taliban acknowledged receipt of UNAMA's 2013 Mid-Year Report on the Protection of Civilians, which had been provided to it several hours prior to its public launch. Interestingly, it chastised UNAMA that it had not been given enough time to analyse its contents or discuss its conclusions.[99] In some ways, this chastisement may be seen as a success for UNAMA as it confirms that the Taliban is prepared to devote time and effort to considering its statements.

The UNAMA example shows the benefits of such a dialogue with armed groups, where it is possible, on the content of humanitarian norms. While the Taliban's compliance with international humanitarian law in Afghanistan remains highly unsatisfactory, it can be seen how the existence of such a dialogue can have the effect of ensuring that international humanitarian law is discussed within armed groups—a necessary first step towards its internalisation.[100] Secondly, it increases

---

See UNAMA and OHCHR 2011b, p. 15; UNAMA and OHCHR 2014, p. 77; UNAMA and OHCHR 2015b, p. 54; and UNAMA and OHCHR 2016b, p. 78.

[97] For the Taliban's unlawful targeting of government officials and workers, see UNAMA and OHCHR 2012b, p. 17. For the Taliban's evolving attitude to the definition of "civilian", see UNAMA and OHCHR 2013, p. 32. Here UNAMA expressed concern about the Taliban's definition of "civilian" as "those who are in no way involved in fighting: the white bearded people, women, children and common people who live an ordinary life". In January 2015, the Taliban broadened this definition to "any person who is not engaged in activities against the Taliban: "those people who do not stand shoulder to shoulder with the enemy forces and are not considered to be carrying out actions against Jihad". UNAMA and OHCHR 2014, p. 74. In April 2015, the Taliban issued a statement that seemed to recognise that government workers have civilian status. See UNAMA and OHCHR 2015a, p. 66.

[98] UNAMA and OHCHR 2012b, p. 17; UNAMA and OHCHR 2013, p. 14 and 33; UNAMA and OHCHR 2015b, pp. 44–45; and UNAMA and OHCHR 2016b, p. 61.

[99] UNAMA and OHCHR 2013, pp. 32–33.

[100] See Bangerter 2011, p. 355; see also Bangerter 2015 on the importance of dialogue with armed groups to promote the acceptance of humanitarian norms.

the prospect of an armed group taking ownership of key definitions, such as the definition of "civilian" and ensuring that they are in line with international humanitarian law. Thirdly, it provides armed groups with the opportunity to provide an account of their behaviour in a manner that brings them "in from the cold" procedurally. It was seen in the public administration definitions above that a true accountability process must allow the actor being held to account, with an opportunity to provide an account of its own behaviour. On a deeper level, dialogue between an armed group and an accountability mechanism such as UNAMA, may be seen as the first step toward achieving a level of acceptance of the accountability mechanism by the group. It prevents the pronouncements of the accountability mechanism being *merely* directed at the international community. Instead, it allows the statements to play a role in efforts designed to persuade armed groups to comply with humanitarian norms. This allows the process of accountability to go beyond mere chastisement and carry with it a "promise of performance".[101] In other words, it achieves a model of accountability that is not only backward looking but also forward looking.[102] Such a model, which may be particularly suited to UN field offices reporting on local actors, not only holds armed groups to account but simultaneously contributes to efforts taken to persuade armed groups to take ownership of humanitarian norms and comply with them.

6.4.2 Geneva Call

Before ending, it is also significant to note how closely the *modus operandi* of Geneva Call matches the definitions of accountability explored in this chapter. While the organisation does not hold itself out as pursuing accountability *per se*, it can be seen that this is what it achieves in its work. In encouraging armed groups to sign deeds of commitments on humanitarian norms, the organisation fulfils the requirement that an assessment of the armed group's conduct is on the basis of "prior established rules or principles". It also ensures that Geneva Call has normative rights of authority over the group, as there is no room for the armed group to reject the norm on the basis that it is "State-made" and the group's ownership of the norm thereby is secured. After an armed group signs a deed of commitment, Geneva Call provides support and monitoring to ensure that its commitments are honoured. Under the deed of commitment, the armed group agrees to allow and cooperate with the monitoring of its compliance by Geneva Call and even provides self-reporting on its compliance.[103] This ensures that Geneva Call also has procedural "rights of authority" over the armed groups. In instances of non-compliance,

---

[101] Rached 2016, p. 11; Dubnick questions whether there is a correlation between accountability and future performance in Dubnick 2005.

[102] Curtin and Nollkaemper 2005, p. 8.

[103] Sassòli 2010, p. 36.

Geneva Call may choose to conduct an onsite verification mission, as it did in Central Mindanao in the Philippines in 2009. Geneva Call also reserves the right to publicise the group's compliance or non-compliance. As a result, non-compliance is met with consequences that range from private censure to public condemnation. It is seen from this description that Geneva Call works in a manner that is able to deliver accountability. In that sense, it is a clear demonstration that mechanisms which are tailor-made for non-State actors are much more easily able to achieve their accountability, than mechanisms which were designed for States.

6.5 Conclusions

This chapter calls for reflection on what "accountability" means in the context of policy discussions relating to armed groups. Indeed, when looking at issues relating to armed groups, it has been shown that the term "accountability" is more helpful that the concept of "responsibility" because it separates the concept of "answerability" from "responsibility". Indeed, it has been shown that a wider approach to "accountability" allows an enquiry into the answerability of armed groups to go forward, despite the fact that the rules on responsibility of armed groups have not yet been fully worked out. Moreover, the chapter has demonstrated that an inquiry into the accountability of armed groups requires not only an inquiry into how the rules apply to armed groups but also an inquiry into the legitimacy of these rules and the authority of the various institutions monitoring their compliance. As a result, it is a particularly appropriate lens through which the accountability mechanisms currently scrutinising the acts of armed groups can be assessed. Indeed, in a world where a sole focus on legal arguments is regularly proving inadequate to solve the problem of increasing violence by armed groups, the concept of "accountability" provides a useful roadmap for further research on other ways to engage with armed groups on humanitarian norms. It also provides an indication of the directions in which the procedural framework of international law might have to develop in order to accommodate armed groups in the legal framework.

Importantly, this chapter shows that when State-based accountability mechanisms make changes in their normative mandate to accommodate new actors, without accompanying shifts in procedure, their ability to attain "accountability" over these new actors is compromised. It aims therefore to prompt reflection on the value of UN bodies turning their attention to armed groups, without an accompanying shift in procedure. Recognising that there is value in a State-orientated system and understanding that States will likely object to giving armed groups' procedural rights within it, the chapter's recommendations in this respect are modest. Rather than calling for an overhaul of the State-based system, the chapter argues that parallel tailor-made mechanisms may be the best way to achieve the accountability of armed groups. Indeed, it shows that accountability frameworks which are tailor-made for non-State actors—such as the process created by Geneva Call—can more easily achieve the accountability of armed groups, than mechanisms which were designed for States. This is partly because such mechanisms can more easily secure normative and institutional authority over armed groups, because they are dependent upon the consent and participation of the armed groups. Yet, the chapter argues that understanding accountability as a "social interaction" may facilitate small changes to be made by certain State-based accountability mechanisms, to bring armed groups in from the procedural cold.

Perhaps most importantly, this chapter shows that accountability is not an on/off property, but a graduated concept. As a result, it shows that small changes to State-based systems of accountability may, if the circumstances of the armed conflict allow them, contribute to increasing their effectiveness in relation to armed groups. For example, the chapter shows that it may make a difference whether an armed group is addressed in a body's recommendations, whether the report is sent to the group prior to publication and whether the armed group has a procedural channel through which it can refute or reply to the allegations against it. The chapter shows that small adjustments, particularly by field offices, may help create a relationship and dialogue between the mechanism and the armed group. While in some instances the creation of such a relationship will not be possible due to the nature of the conflict or the nature of the armed group, this chapter shows how dialogues and interactions—when they are possible—can also bring humanitarian benefits. Indeed, it has shown that giving armed groups the opportunity to provide an account of their actions not only contributes to the authority of the forum but also strengthens armed groups' ownership of norms. In that respect, the chapter has demonstrated that non-judicial accountability mechanisms hold the potential to be more than just a means to facilitate the prosecution of individuals or express condemnation of a particular group. They may also have prospective value, in that they can feed into efforts designed to improve an armed group's compliance with international humanitarian law.

References

Articles, Books and Other Documents

Bangerter O (2011) Reasons why armed groups choose to respect international humanitarian law or not. International Review of the Red Cross 93(882):353–384

Bangerter O (2012) Internal Control: Codes of Conduct within Insurgent Armed Groups, Small Arms Survey Occasional Paper No. 31. Small Arms Survey, Graduate Institute of International and Development Studies, Geneva

Bangerter O (2015) Comment – Persuading armed groups to better respect international humanitarian law. In: Krieger H (ed) Inducing compliance with international humanitarian law. Cambridge University Press, Cambridge, pp 112–124

Bellal A (2015) Establishing the direct responsibility of non-state armed groups for violations of international norms: Issues of attribution. In: Gal-Or N, Ryngaert C, Noortmann M (eds) Responsibilities of the non-state actor in armed conflict and the market place. Brill Nijhoff, Leiden, pp 304–321

Bellal A, Casey-Maslen S (2011) Enhancing compliance with international law by armed non-state actors. Goettingen Journal of International Law 3(1):175–197
Bílková V (2015) Establishing direct responsibility of armed opposition groups for violations of international humanitarian law. In: Gal-Or N, Ryngaert C, Noortmann M (eds) Responsibilities of the non-state actor in armed conflict and the market place. Brill Nijhoff, Leiden, pp 263–284
Bongard P, Somer J (2011) Monitoring armed non-state actor compliance with humanitarian norms: A look at international mechanisms and the Geneva Call deed of commitment. International Review of the Red Cross 93(883):673–706
Bovens M (2007) Analysing and assessing public accountability, a conceptual framework. European Law Journal 13(4):447–468
Bovens M (2010) Two concepts of accountability: Accountability as a virtue and as a mechanism. West European Politics 33(5):946–967
Brunée J (2005) International legal accountability through the lens of the law of state responsibility. Netherlands Yearbook of International Law 36:21–56
Committee on the Elimination of Discrimination against Women (CEDAW) (2013) General Recommendation No. 30 on women in conflict prevention, conflict and post-conflict situations. UN Doc. CEDAW/C/GC/30
Crawford E (2014) From inter-state and symmetric to intra-state and asymmetric: Changing methods of warfare and the law of armed conflict in the 100 years since World War One. Yearbook of International Humanitarian Law 17:95–118
Curtin D, Nollkaemper A (2005) Conceptualizing accountability in international and European law. Netherlands Yearbook of International Law 36:3–20
Dubnick M (2005) Accountability and the promise of performance: in search of the mechanisms. Public Performance and Management Review 28(3):376–417
Fortin K (2017) The accountability of armed groups under human rights law. Oxford University Press, Oxford
Grant RW, Keohane RO (2005) Accountability and abuses of power in world politics. American Political Science Review 99(1):29–43
Heffes E, Kotlik M (2014) Special agreements as a means of enhancing compliance with international humanitarian law in non-international armed conflicts: An inquiry into the governing legal regime. International Review of the Red Cross 96(895/896):1195–1224
ICRC (2008) Increasing Respect for International Humanitarian Law in Non-International Armed Conflicts. ICRC, Geneva
Kamminga M (1992) Inter-state accountability for violations of human rights. University of Pennsylvania Press, Philadelphia
Kleffner J (2009) The collective accountability of organized armed groups for system crimes. In: Van der Wilt H, Nollkaemper A (eds) System Criminality in International Law. Cambridge University Press, Cambridge, pp 238–269
Kleffner J (2011) The applicability of international humanitarian law to organized armed groups. International Committee of the Red Cross 93(882):443–461
Moffett L (2015) Beyond attribution: Responsibility of armed non-state actors for reparations in Northern Ireland, Colombia and Uganda. In: Gal-Or N, Ryngaert C, Noortmann M (eds) Responsibilities of the non-state actor in armed conflict and the market place. Brill Nijhoff, Leiden, pp 323–344
MONUSCO, OHCHR (2014) Report of the United Nations Joint Human Rights Office on Human Rights Violations Committed by the Mouvement du 23 Mars (M23) in North Kivu Province, April 2012–November 2013. http://www.ohchr.org/Documents/Countries/CD/UNJHROOctober2014_en.pdf. Accessed 19 May 2017
Mulgan R (2000) "Accountability": An ever-expanding concept? Public Administration 78 (3):555–573
Murray D (2016) Human rights obligations of non-state armed groups. Bloomsbury, Oxford/Portland
Pettersson T, Wallensteen P (2015) Armed conflicts 1946–2014. Journal of Peace Research 52 (4):535–550

Rached DH (2016) The concept(s) of accountability: Form in search of substance. Leiden Journal of International Law 29(2):317–342

Rondeau S (2011) Participation of Armed Groups in the Development of the Law Applicable to Armed Conflicts. International Review of the Red Cross 92(883):649–672

Ryngaert C (2008) Human rights obligations of armed groups. Revue Belge de Droit International 1(2):355–381

Ryngaert C, Van de Meulebroucke A (2011) Enhancing and enforcing compliance with international humanitarian law by non-state armed groups: An inquiry into some mechanisms. Journal of Conflict and Security Law 16(3):443–472

Sassòli M (2010) Taking armed groups seriously: Ways to improve their compliance with international humanitarian law. Journal of International Humanitarian Legal Studies 1(1):5–51

Saul B (2017) Enhancing civilian protection by engaging non-state armed groups under international humanitarian law. Journal of Conflict & Security Law 22(1):39–66

Schneckener U, Hofmann C (2015) The power of persuasion: The role of international non-governmental organisations. In: Krieger H (ed) Inducing compliance with international humanitarian law. Cambridge University Press, Cambridge, pp 79–111

Sivakumaran S (2006) Binding armed opposition groups. International and Comparative Law Quarterly 55:369–394

Sivakumaran S (2012) The law of non-international armed conflict. Oxford University Press, Oxford

Sivakumaran S (2015) Implementing humanitarian norms through non-state armed groups. In: Krieger H (ed) Inducing Compliance with International Humanitarian Law. Cambridge University Press, Cambridge, pp 125–146

UNAMA, OHCHR (2011a) Afghanistan, Midyear Report 2011, Protection of Civilians in Armed Conflict. https://unama.unmissions.org/sites/default/files/2011_midyear_poc.pdf. Accessed 19 May 2017

UNAMA, OHCHR (2011b) Afghanistan, Final Report 2011, Protection of Civilians in Armed Conflict. https://unama.unmissions.org/sites/default/files/unama_poc_report_final_feb_2012.pdf. Accessed 19 May 2017

UNAMA, OHCHR (2012a) Afghanistan, Midyear Report 2012, Protection of Civilians in Armed Conflict. https://unama.unmissions.org/sites/default/files/2012_mid-year_report.pdf. Accessed 19 May 2017

UNAMA, OHCHR (2012b) Afghanistan, Final Report 2012, Protection of Civilians in Armed Conflict. https://unama.unmissions.org/sites/default/files/2012_annual_report_eng_0.pdf. Accessed 19 May 2017

UNAMA, OHCHR (2013) Afghanistan, Final Report 2013, Protection of Civilians in Armed Conflict. https://unama.unmissions.org/sites/default/files/feb_8_2014_poc-report_2013-full-report-eng.pdf. Accessed 19 May 2017

UNAMA, OHCHR (2014) Afghanistan, Final Report 2014, Protection of Civilians in Armed Conflict. https://unama.unmissions.org/sites/default/files/2014-annual-report-on-protection-of-civilians-final.pdf. Accessed 19 May 2017

UNAMA, OHCHR (2015a) Afghanistan, Midyear Report 2015, Protection of Civilians in Armed Conflict. https://unama.unmissions.org/sites/default/files/unama_protection_of_civilians_armed_conflict_midyear_report_2015_final_august.pdf. Accessed 19 May 2017

UNAMA, OHCHR (2015b) Afghanistan, Final Report 2015, Protection of Civilians in Armed Conflict. https://unama.unmissions.org/sites/default/files/poc_annual_report_2015_final_14_feb_2016.pdf. Accessed 19 May 2017

UNAMA, OHCHR (2016a) Afghanistan, Midyear Report 2016, Protection of Civilians in Armed Conflict. https://unama.unmissions.org/sites/default/files/protection_of_civilians_in_armed_conflict_midyear_report_2016_final_rev.1-9sept.pdf. Accessed 19 May 2017

UNAMA, OHCHR (2016b) Afghanistan, Final Report 2016, Protection of Civilians in Armed Conflict. https://unama.unmissions.org/sites/default/files/protection_of_civilians_in_armed_conflict_annual_report_2016_final280317.pdf. Accessed 19 May 2017

UN General Assembly (2006) Resolution 60/251. Human Rights Council. UN Doc. A/RES/60/251
UN General Assembly (2007) Report of the Special Rapporteur on extrajudicial, summary or arbitrary executions. UN Doc. A/62/265
UN General Assembly (2011) Human Rights Council: Report of the Independent International Commission of Inquiry on the Syrian Arab Republic. UN Doc. A/HRC/S-17/2/Add.1
UN General Assembly (2012a) Human Rights Council: Report of the Independent International Commission of Inquiry on the Syrian Arab Republic. UN Doc. A/HRC/19/69
UN General Assembly (2012b) Human Rights Council: Report of the United Nations High Commissioner for Human Rights on the situation of human rights in Mali. UN Doc. A/HRC/22/33
UN General Assembly (2016a) Human Rights Council: Resolution S-25/1. The deteriorating situation of human rights in the Syrian Arab Republic, and the recent situation in Aleppo. UN Doc. A/HRC/RES/S-25/1
UN General Assembly (2016b) Human Rights Council: Resolution S-26/1. Situations of human rights in South Sudan. UN Doc. A/HRC/RES/S-26/1
UN General Assembly (2016c) Human Rights Council: Report of the Special Rapporteur on extrajudicial, summary or arbitrary executions on his Mission to Ukraine. UN Doc. A/HRC/32/39/Add.1
UN General Assembly (2017a) Human Rights Council: Report of the Human Rights Council on its twenty-sixth special session (on the human rights situation in South Sudan). UN Doc. A/HRC/S-26/2
UN General Assembly (2017b) Human Rights Council: Report of the Human Rights Council on its twenty-fifth special session (on the deteriorating situation in the Syrian Arab Republic). UN Doc. A/HRC/S-25/2
UN Security Council (1983) Provisional Rules of Procedure of the Security Council. UN Doc. S/96/Rev.7
UN Security Council (1993) Report of the Secretary-General pursuant to paragraph 2 of Security Council Resolution 808 (1993). UN Doc. S/25704
UN Security Council (1994) Resolution 955 (1994). UN Doc. S/RES/955
UN Security Council (2009) Report of the Secretary-General on the protection of civilians in armed conflict. UN Doc. S/2009/277
UN Security Council (2014) Final Report of the International Commission of Inquiry on the Central African Republic. UN Doc. S/2014/928
UN Security Council (2016a) Report of the Secretary-General on the protection of civilians in armed conflict. UN Doc. S/2016/447
UN Security Council (2016b) Resolution 2295 (2016). UN Doc. S/RES/2295
UN Security Council (2016c) Resolution 2293 (2016). UN Doc. S/RES/2293
UN Security Council (2016d) Resolution 2274 (2016). UN Doc. S/RES/2274
UN Security Council (2016e) Resolution 2301 (2016). UN Doc. S/RES/2301
UN Security Council (2016f) Resolution 2299 (2016). UN Doc. S/RES/2299
Verhoeven S (2015) International responsibility of armed opposition groups. In: Gal-Or N, Ryngaert C, Noortmann M (eds) Responsibilities of the non-state actor in armed conflict and the market place. Brill Nijhoff, Leiden, pp 285–303
Zegveld L (2002) The accountability of armed opposition groups in international law. Cambridge University Press, Cambridge

Case Law

ECtHR, *Al-Skeini and Others v UK*, Grand Chamber Judgment, 7 July 2011, Application No. 55721/07

ICC, *Prosecutor v Thomas Lubanga Dyilo*, Judgment on the appeals against the "Decision establishing the principles and procedures to be applied to reparations" of 7 August 2012 with AMENDED order for reparations (Annex A) and public annexes 1 and 2, 3 March 2015, Case No. ICC-01/04-01/06-3129

ICJ, *Corfu Channel case*, Judgment, 9 April 1949, [1949] ICJ Reports 4

Nuremberg International Military Tribunal, *United States of America, French Republic, United Kingdom and the USSR v Hess, Goring et al.*, Judgment, 1 October 1946

Treaties

American Convention on Human Rights, opened for signature 22 November 1969, 1144 UNTS 123 (entered into force 18 July 1978)

European Convention for the Protection of Human Rights and Fundamental Freedoms, opened for signature 4 November 1950, 213 UNTS 221 (entered into force 3 September 1953)

International Covenant of Civil and Political Rights, opened for signature 16 December 1966, 999 UNTS 171 (entered into force 23 March 1976)

Rome Statute of the International Criminal Court, opened for signature 17 July 1998, 2187 UNTS 90 (entered into force 1 July 2002)

Part II
Other Articles

Chapter 7
Knock on the Roof: Legitimate Warning or Method of Warfare?

Jeroen C. van den Boogaard

Abstract This chapter aims to address the practice of using a "knock on the roof" as a warning before air strikes are launched in order to mitigate civilian casualties during armed conflict. It involves the dropping of non-explosive or low-impact type of munitions on the intended target. This "knock" is reportedly accompanied by other specific warnings, such as telephone calls and text-messages, indicating that the attack on the building is imminent. The knock is intended to be used on a legitimate military objective, leaving no doubt that the attack is in fact about to happen, and urging civilians to relocate to a safer place. This chapter aims to analyse whether, and if so, under which circumstances, the knock on the roof practice may be used within the boundaries of international humanitarian law (IHL), both as a warning and as a method of warfare.

Keywords Conduct of hostilities · Targeting · Precautionary measures · Methods of warfare · Warning

Contents

Jeroen C. van den Boogaard works as an assistant professor of military law at the Netherlands Defence Academy and as a lecturer and researcher at the University of Amsterdam. The author wishes to thank Arjen Vermeer, Sandra Krähenmann, Rogier Bartels and Sigrid Redse Johansen as well as the anonymous reviewers for their valuable comments on an earlier draft. Further comments are welcome via j.c.vandenboogaard@uva.nl. All usual caveats apply.

J.C. van den Boogaard (✉)
Netherlands Defence Academy, University of Amsterdam, Amsterdam, The Netherlands
e-mail: j.c.vandenboogaard@uva.nl

T.D. Gill et al. (eds.), *Yearbook of International Humanitarian Law 2016*,
Yearbook of International Humanitarian Law 19,
https://doi.org/10.1007/978-94-6265-213-2_7

7.1 Introduction

Warfare in densely populated areas is difficult and dangerous, especially when waged against a non-state armed group hiding among the civilian population in order to gain a tactical advantage against a military superior opponent. Commanders are obliged to take feasible precautionary measures in order to mitigate damage to civilian objects, and minimise civilian casualties.[1] One of these precautions is the obligation to warn the civilian population, as required by Article 57(2)(c) of Additional Protocol I to the Geneva Conventions (AP I).

In recent years, the practice of the knock on the roof has been used as a warning with the purpose of mitigating civilian casualties. It consists of using so-called knock on the roof munitions before air strikes are launched. This involves the dropping of non-explosive or low-impact types of munitions on the intended target to provide notice to civilians of the imminence of a subsequent attack and thereby encourage them to evacuate the area.[2] The practice has been used by the Israeli

[1] Article 57 of the Protocol Additional to the Geneva Conventions of 12 August 1949, and relating to the Protection of Victims of International Armed Conflicts, opened for signature 12 December 1977, 1125 UNTS 3 (entered into force 7 December 1979) (AP I). The duty to take precautionary measures applies for the most part equally to both international and non-international armed conflicts as a matter of customary international humanitarian law. See Henckaerts and Doswald-Beck 2005, pp. 55–67, Rules 15–21. Note however that according to the ICRC, Rule 21, which is the equivalent to Article 57(3) AP I, only *arguably* applies to non-international armed conflicts ("When a choice is possible between several military objectives for obtaining a similar military advantage, the objective to be selected must be that the attack on which may be expected to cause the least danger to civilian lives and to civilian objects"). ICRC Customary IHL Database (2016) Rule 21. Target Selection. https://ihl-databases.icrc.org/customary-ihl/eng/docs/v1_rul_rule21. Accessed 3 July 2017 (emphasis added).

[2] See for example IDF (2014) How is the IDF Minimizing Harm to Civilians in Gaza. http://www.idfblog.com/blog/2014/07/16/idf-done-minimize-harm-civilians-gaza/. Accessed 23 December 2016. According to US Air Force major General Peter Gersten, a hellfire missile was used by US forces in an attack against Daesh in a manner that "it wouldn't destroy the building, simply knock on the roof to ensure that [civilians] were out of the building". See also Torbati Y and Ali I (2016) U.S. military used "roof knock" tactic in Iraq to try to warn civilians before bombing. www.reuters.com/article/us-mideast-crisis-usa-airstrike-idUSKCN0XN2NK. Accessed 23 December 2016.

Defense Forces (IDF) during the armed conflicts in Gaza in 2008, 2012 and 2014[3] and by the United States Air Force during an aerial attack on a Daesh target in Mosul in Iraq in April 2016.[4] The knock is reportedly often accompanied by specific warnings, such as telephone calls and text-messages, indicating that the attack on the building is imminent. The knock is intended to be used on a legitimate military objective, leaving no doubt that the attack is in fact about to happen, and "to signal the impending danger and give civilians in or near the target a last opportunity to seek safety before an attack".[5]

At least one State[6] and a number of authors have accepted the legality of the knock on the roof practice,[7] but the practice of the knock on the roof has not been welcomed without criticism. The first type of criticism is that a warning using the knock on the roof practice is not effective, because civilians have no means to distinguish the knock from an actual attack[8] and an attack using projectiles, even when only a small explosive charge is used, can not reasonably be understood as a warning.[9] Secondly, the practice has been criticised because it would be contrary to the prohibition against launching an attack for the primary purpose of spreading

[3] See for example IDF (2014) How is the IDF Minimizing Harm to Civilians in Gaza. http://www.idfblog.com/blog/2014/07/16/idf-done-minimize-harm-civilians-gaza/. Accessed 23 December 2016. See also Independent (2014) Israel-Gaza conflict: Israeli "knock on roof" missile warning revealed in remarkable video. http://www.independent.co.uk/news/world/middle-east/israel-gaza-conflict-israeli-knock-on-roof-missile-warning-technique-revealed-in-stunning-video-9603179.html. Accessed 23 December 2016.

[4] See for example Reuters (2016) U.S. military used "roof knock" tactic in Iraq to try to warn civilians before bombing. www.reuters.com/article/us-mideast-crisis-usa-airstrike-idUSKCN0XN2NK. Accessed 23 December 2016.

[5] State of Israel 2015 (Israeli Report on the 2014 Gaza War).

[6] The Netherlands does not use the knock on the roof procedure, but the Minister of Foreign Affairs of the Kingdom of the Netherlands wrote to the Parliament of the Netherlands on 4 July 2016 that "the 'knock on the roof' method is in accordance with IHL when it complies with the requirements of precautionary measures and its use poses no danger to the civilian population. Whether a specific use of the method complies with IHL needs to be determined on the basis of the specific circumstances ruling at the time and the way it is used. It is therefore impossible to provide a definite assessment of the legality of the use of this method." See Minister of Foreign Affairs of the Kingdom of the Netherlands (2016) Letter to the Parliament, no. DVB/CV-106/16.

[7] Schmitt 2010, p. 829, arguing that any type of attacks, including the knock, on military objectives is permitted under IHL. In their elaborate analysis of the warning obligations during armed conflict, Baruch and Neuman conclude that the knock on the roof warnings are legitimate as warning shots and "it is incorrect to view them as an attack 'against civilians', because they are not fired at civilians, since the objective of their use is to avoid harm to civilians." See Baruch and Neuman 2011, p. 388.

[8] See for example Mahmoud Abu Rahma of the Gaza based Al Mezan Center for Human Rights: "Imagine you are in Gaza and there are airstrikes everywhere, and many families are in the bottom floor of their home [...] Families miss the sound of the 'warning' missile because it sounds like just another explosion." Lister T and Abdelaziz S (2014) Israeli military's "knock on roof" warnings criticized by rights groups. http://edition.cnn.com/2014/07/15/world/meast/mideast-israel-strike-warnings/. Accessed 23 December 2016.

[9] United Nations General Assembly 2009 (The Goldstone Report).

terror among the civilian population.[10] A third type of criticism is the claim that the knock is prohibited because it is in essence a direct attack on civilians or, as far as objects are concerned, an attack on a civilian object.[11]

Armed forces that wish to start, or continue to use the knock on the roof need to know whether, and if so, under which circumstances, the knock on the roof practice may be used within the boundaries of IHL, both as a warning and as a method of warfare. This chapter therefore first provides an analysis of the rules with regard to warnings under IHL in Sect. 7.2. Subsequently, Sect. 7.3 deals with the question of whether the knock on the roof may qualify as a legitimate warning under IHL and will address the three types of criticism. In Sect. 7.4, a further analysis will follow to assess the legality of the practice as a method of warfare, analysing the definition of an attack under IHL in relation to the knock on the roof practice. Section 7.4 will furthermore analyse the collision of norms that presents itself when the knock on the roof practice is used against a civilian object, which are immune from direct attack and explore a number of avenues to solve this collision. This chapter will conclude by proposing circumstances that would presumptively justify the knock on the roof as a legitimate precautionary measure to enhance the protection of the civilian population during armed conflict.

7.2 Warnings Under IHL

The conduct of hostilities is governed by IHL treaty and customary rules, among which the rules of distinction, precautionary measures and proportionality are crucial. These rules apply both in situations where an armed group uses deadly force in a chaotic gunfight in an urban area as in situations where a deliberate airstrike is preceded by an elaborate and detailed targeting procedure.[12] Military commanders will need to assess the possibility of collateral damage resulting from a planned attack. In case collateral damage is anticipated, the commander is obliged to take feasible precautionary measures in order to mitigate, or in any event minimise the expected collateral civilian casualties and damage to civilian objects.[13]

---

[10] United Nations General Assembly 2009 (The Goldstone Report), para 533; see also Dill J (2014) Guest Post: Israel's Use of Law and Warnings in Gaza. http://opiniojuris.org/2014/07/30/guest-post-israels-use-law-warnings-gaza/. Accessed 23 December 2016.

[11] Amnesty International stated that it has "documented cases of civilians killed or injured by such missiles [used for knocking on the roof] in previous Israeli military operations on the Gaza Strip". Amnesty International UK (2014) Israel/Gaza: UN must impose arms embargo as civilian death toll rises. https://www.amnesty.org.uk/press-releases/israelgaza-un-must-impose-arms-embargo-civilian-death-toll-rises. Accessed 23 December 2016.

[12] See for example Pratzner 2016 for a description of a targeting procedure, pp. 77–97.

[13] See generally Quéguiner 2006; Baruch and Neuman 2011; Corn 2015; Sassòli and Quintin 2014; and Henderson 2009, pp. 157–196.

The rules pertaining to warnings are part of these precautionary measures. The precautionary measures implement the more general obligations of parties to any armed conflict to, first, distinguish between the civilian population and military objectives[14] and, second, to take constant care to spare the civilian population, civilians and civilian objects in conducting their military operations.[15] This includes the obligation for the specific situation of an attack, to take all feasible precautions to avoid, and in any event to minimise incidental loss of civilian life, injury to civilians and damage to civilian objects. The IHL proportionality rule applies both as a precautionary measure in itself and as a specific rule prohibiting as a final check those attacks which may be expected to cause incidental loss of civilian life, injury to civilians, damage to civilian objects, or a combination thereof, which would be excessive in relation to the concrete and direct military advantage anticipated.[16]

The obligation to warn the civilian population is one of the precautionary measures that need to be taken by those who plan or decide upon an attack. Article 57(2)(c) AP I states that "effective advance warning shall be given of attacks which may affect the civilian population, unless circumstances do not permit."[17] The last part of the provision indicates that it is highly situational whether the circumstances permit the parties to the conflict to give an advance warning in case an attack is expected to affect the civilian population. However, attackers can choose from a wide range of different options to convey the warning. These options include general messages to the civil or military authorities of the opponent, radio broadcasts, messages conveyed through loudspeakers, general or specific warning leaflets,[18] "fly-by" manoeuvres, telephone calls or text messages, warning shots or even simple hand gestures to signal civilians in a certain safe direction.

It is imperative for any discussion on precautionary obligations of the attacking side to recall that the opponent has its own obligation to take feasible precautions against the effects of attacks, also known as "passive precautions".[19] These include the obligation to protect the civilian population under the control of the defending

---

[14] Article 48 AP I, above n 1; and Customary IHL Rule 1, Henckaerts and Doswald-Beck 2005, pp. 3–8.

[15] Article 57(1) AP I, above n 1; and Customary IHL Rule 15, Henckaerts and Doswald-Beck 2005, pp. 51–55.

[16] Articles 51(5)(b), 57(2)(a)(iii) and 57(2)(b) AP I, above n 1; and Customary IHL Rule 14, Henckaerts and Doswald-Beck 2005, pp. 46–50; see also generally Watkin 2005. A thorough analysis of the IHL proportionality rule is outside the scope of this chapter.

[17] Customary IHL Rule 20 similarly states that "Each party to the conflict must give effective advance warning of attacks which may affect the civilian population, unless circumstances do not permit." See Henckaerts and Doswald-Beck 2005, pp. 62–65.

[18] Gaughan 2015 notes: "Prior to D-Day, Allied planes dropped leaflets to warn French civilians to move at least two kilometres away from the railway centers that the American and British bombers targeted. One leaflet specifically advised: 'Move away as much as possible from ironworks, railway stations, junctions, train depots, repair shops.'" See Gaughan 2015, p. 269 (footnotes omitted).

[19] Article 58 AP I, above n 1; and Customary IHL Rules 22–24, Henckaerts and Doswald-Beck 2005, pp. 68–76; see also Sassòli and Quintin 2014, pp. 112–122; and Jensen 2016, pp. 147–175.

party against the effects of attacks by, to the extent feasible, avoiding locating military objectives within or near densely populated areas and by removing civilians and civilian objects from the vicinity of military objectives. The passive precautionary obligations are however worded less absolute, and as a result, "these obligations are weaker than those of an attacker".[20] Furthermore, there is a number of other specific provisions found in IHL where providing warnings needs to be considered, but these warnings concern specifically protected objects and persons, not the general protection of the civilian population.[21]

The objective of warning the civilian population is "to give civilians the chance to protect themselves"[22] in situations where an impending attack may put them in danger. Therefore, the obligation extends to situations where it is uncertain whether civilians will be affected by the attack and where the attack is expected to result in more than "mere inconveniences to civilians".[23] To achieve that objective, it is essential that the duty to give warning is taken into account throughout the different stages of a targeting process, even in situations where there is only little time for taking precautionary measures before an attack is launched. The options for warning civilians must thus continuously be addressed as an inherently relevant factor in the process of choosing between the available options of attack. Warnings are potentially most effective during operations against targets that are situated in populated areas. This however does not relieve attackers from their duty to warn before attacking a military objective where a small number of civilians is expected to be present, nor does giving a warning relieve an attacker of the obligation of taking other feasible precautionary measures.

Effectiveness of the warning is the crucial constituent element of the duty to warn civilians. "Effective means that it enables 'civilians to take shelter or leave the area and [...] civil defence authorities to take appropriate measures.'"[24] The situation on the location where the attack is planned is decisive to evaluate the effectiveness of the warning, and thus its legality. In some cases general warnings will be sufficient to fulfil the obligation to warn effectively, whereas in other situations general warnings may not to be sufficient if these may not be expected to be effective. In those latter situations, the warning must be more specific, as far as

[20] Sassòli and Quintin 2014, p. 117.

[21] For example: military (Article 21 of Geneva Convention (I) for the Amelioration of the Condition of the Wounded and Sick in Armed Forces in the Field, opened for signature 12 August 1949, 75 UNTS 31 (entered into force 21 October 1950) (GC I); and civilian (Article 19 of Geneva Convention (IV) relative to the Protection of Civilian Persons in Time of War, opened for signature 12 August 1949, 75 UNTS 287 (entered into force 21 October 1950) (GC IV) and 13(1) AP I, above n 1) medical establishments and units if these are used to commit, outside their humanitarian duties, acts harmful to the enemy and civil defence facilities and personnel (Article 65(1) AP I, above n 1).

[22] Sandoz et al. 1987, para 2225 (p. 687).

[23] HPCR 2013, p. 133 (Commentary); see also Baruch and Neuman 2011, pp. 374–375; and State of Israel 2015, p. 170.

[24] UK Ministry of Defence 2004, p. 84.

circumstances permit. The difference between a general warning and a specific warning is the extent to which the instructions to the civilian population indicate clearly and timely in which way the civilian population can avoid the danger the impending attack will pose to them. In some cases, this may mean that a previous warning must be updated, possibly including the instruction that the attack has been postponed or called off and indications of the areas where the civilian population may seek refuge. The warning is ineffective if its meaning is unclear from the perspective of the civilian population and no indication is provided how they may take action in order to enhance their safety against the danger of a planned attack.[25] Some States maintain that as soon as an effective warning has been given, no further warnings are required by the rules of IHL.[26] However, if it becomes clear to an attacker that additional warnings would further increase the protection of the civilian population and the circumstances ruling at the time permit, it would seem that the obligation to avoid or in any event minimise civilian damage would compel that further warnings are given.[27]

To issue a warning to the civilian population is a legal obligation for military commanders, although it may also, for good reasons, be motivated by policy, political, operational or ethical considerations. Depending on the circumstances, whenever civilians may be affected by an attack and the attackers are in a position to warn the civilian population, the obligation to warn is "unequivocal".[28]However, in a situation in which the accomplishment of the mission depends on the element of surprise, circumstances "do not permit" the attacker to warn the civilian population. An example is the attack on a military commander of the enemy who is located in a populated area: if a warning is given, this may be expected to also reach the targeted commander and thus issuing a warning would nullify the possibility to successfully accomplish the mission. As a result, the duty to warn is more likely to present itself in situations where objects that qualify as military objectives are targeted, as opposed to situations where individuals are the target of an attack, because objects are generally less easily relocated.

A second situation in which a warning is not required by law is when the warning would bring the safety of the attacking forces into a more dangerous position. An example in point is the operation "Linebacker II" that consisted of

[25] Ibid.: "[t]o be effective the warning must be in time and sufficiently specific and comprehensible".

[26] See for example the Israel 2014 Gaza War Report, in which it is maintained that "[o]nce an effective warning has been given, international law does not require additional warnings." State of Israel 2015.

[27] This follows from the general obligation of Article 57(1) AP I, above n 1, to take constant care, that continues to apply.

[28] Dill states that "[t]he law recognizes that sometimes it may not be possible to warn. Crucially the provision does not say 'warn if possible', but 'warn unless impossible'. It is open to interpretation when that is the case and reasonable people may disagree, but the default is to issue a warning and it is a failure to do so that requires explanation. Warnings are not acts of charity." See Dill J (2014) Guest Post: Israel's Use of Law and Warnings in Gaza. http://opiniojuris.org/2014/07/30/guest-post-israels-use-law-warnings-gaza/. Accessed 23 December 2016.

extensive air attacks by the US Air and Naval air assets against targets in North Vietnam in 1972. Carnahan notes that "[g]iven the extremely heavy air defenses surrounding Hanoi during the campaign, circumstances obviously did not permit warning the Vietnamese civilians before each raid."[29] Of course, there is a limit to exposing the civilian population to danger when compared to measures to enhance the safety of the attacking forces. It may be assumed that given the extensive legal obligation with regard to the protection of the civilian population, their safety must in principle prevail over preventing the destruction of military equipment. Thus, the use of some types of weapons can under no circumstances lead to the invocation of this rationale to refrain from warning. For example, in the case of long-range cruise missiles or unmanned armed drones, only the element of surprise to accomplish the mission can be invoked to justify refraining from warning the civilian population, but not the safety of the attacking forces.

The accomplishment of the mission may thus provide a legitimate reason to refrain from issuing a warning. This could be the case for military objectives that are easily relocated, thus making the element of surprise a crucial part of the operation. Furthermore, in the case of an extremely time-sensitive target, no time may be available for the attacker to issue a warning to the civilian population. This may include situations in which the window of opportunity to attack is simply too short, or when the attacking force is under attack itself. In these situations, further protection is provided to the civilian population by the other precautionary measures, and particularly the IHL proportionality rule, which serves as the safety net for situations in which the anticipated civilian damage would be excessive compared to the direct and concrete military advantage anticipated from the planned attack.[30] A further exception to the duty to effectively warn is the situation in which warning the civilian populations or their authorities is simply impossible. In cases where no lines of communications are reasonably available, issuing an effective warning may be practically impossible and unrealistic. The inherent balance between humanity and military necessity omnipresent in the rules of IHL recognises this possibility.

Military commanders may generally be expected to be willing to consider the options to warn, because warnings improve a military commanders' options to attack, because with a decreased civilian presence, it become less likely an attack will result in excessive civilian harm and therefore qualify as unlawfully indiscriminate.[31] Issuing a warning is thus an important factor in the planning and execution of any attack anticipated to place civilians or civilian property at risk. Of course, it may not always be exactly clear where and how the opposing side plans to fight the next battle. Therefore, a certain factor of reasonableness is inherent in the obligation to warn. This is true because the obligation only applies "unless

[29] Carnahan 1982, p. 866.

[30] Articles 51(5)(b), 57(2)(a)(iii) and 57(2)(b) AP I, above n 1.

[31] Baruch and Neuman therefore see a warning as a "useful tool in the hands of commanders for gaining more freedom of action." See Baruch and Neuman 2011, p. 373.

circumstances do not permit", but can also be derived from practical obstacles. In the example of distributing warnings on air-dropped leaflets, for example, one needs to take into account that it takes a certain period to print and distribute leaflets. The obligation to warn can however only be meaningfully adhered to when military commanders and their planning staff consider different possible warning options in the planning phases of a future military operation.[32] One of these options is the knock on the roof practice. The issue of whether the knock on the roof may qualify as a legitimate warning under IHL will be the subject of the next section.

7.3 Knock on the Roof as a Warning

So far, the knock on the roof procedure has been used by the IDF and the US, although it seems that the US' use of the practice is limited to one instance. Perhaps since in that attack the knock did not cause the desired effect,[33] it seems that US forces have currently not (yet) adopted the practice as part of the standard targeting procedure. The IDF regards the knock on the roof practice as a method to warn that exceeds its obligations under IHL[34] and claims that it is a very effective method to warn the civilian population.[35] With regard to the claim that the practice is not

[32] See also Corn 2014, p. 16: "The feasibility for issuing warnings prior to attack, to include when, how, and to whom, should be factored into all courses of action, and not just raised as a consideration after they have been developed.".

[33] See Torbati Y and Ali I (2016) U.S. military used "rock knock" tactic in Iraq to try to warn civilians before bombing. www.reuters.com/article/us-mideast-crisis-usa-airstrike-idUSKCN0XN2NK. Accessed 23 December 2016.

[34] Major General Dan Efroni, the IDF Military Advocate General, states with regard to the knock on the roof procedure that "our colleagues overseas have criticized [the IDF] for implementing precautionary measures that exceed the requirements of international law, and risk forming opinions that such practices are customary law or accepted practice, thereby raising the threshold of the required precautionary measures by others states." See Efroni 2014, p. 82; see also State of Israel 2015, p. 180: "In certain instances where warnings were unheeded or unfeasible, the IDF, as a progressive precaution that went beyond the requirements of international law, fired a low-explosive at the target's roof."

[35] Dill claims that the practice is consistently ineffective, even counter-productive, referring to Amnesty International, Human Rights Watch and the United Nations. Dill J (2014) Guest Post: Israel's Use of Law and Warnings in Gaza. http://opiniojuris.org/2014/07/30/guest-post-israels-use-law-warnings-gaza/. Accessed 23 December 2016. However, according to a former head of the Legal Service of the IDF, the knock on the roof method was used more than 200 times during operation Cast Lead in 2008–2009 in Gaza, and he claimed that the method was effective every time it was used. See Van den Boogaard 2011, p. 265. In addition, Israel stated in the 2014 Gaza War Report that "the employment of 'roof-knocking' was highly effective, preventing many civilian injuries and deaths". See State of Israel 2015, p. 180; see also the Report of the High Level Military Group: "the IDF has further developed a unique tactical innovation aimed at the preservation of innocent life, which to our knowledge is unprecedented in warfare, the 'knock on the roof' procedure. Given the extensive nature of the IDF's warning protocol, the clear evidence that it has saved lives, and the tactical innovation brought to bear in doing so - which exceeds our

legally required, but is done on the basis of policy considerations, it is submitted that this statement fails to acknowledge that the obligation to warn must be judged on the basis of its effectiveness, not on the question whether earlier general or even specific warnings have been issued. Dill points out that if the warned population does not leave after the warning, this does not change their status and protection, nor does it relieve the attacker of the duty to implement other feasible measures to further mitigate the risk of collateral civilian damage. In its 2014 report, the IDF acknowledges that civilians must not be discounted in the proportionality calculation just because they have been warned.[36]

7.3.1 Understanding the Knock as a Warning

An obvious first issue that needs to be addressed is the question whether it is reasonable to expect that the knock generates the desired effect in the sense that civilians understand the firing of projectiles as a warning. The IDF has been criticised for using the knock on the roof on the basis that civilians have no means to distinguish the knock from an actual attack.[37] Assuming that the intention of the attacking side is to avoid or minimise civilian damage, it would be to the benefit of the attacking side that the intention of the knock is clear. Therefore in order to ascertain that the civilian population responds to the knock by leaving the intended target of the main attack effort, additional measures may be required. The effectiveness of such a warning can be enhanced by requiring the knock to be accompanied by other specific modes of warning, such as telephone calls, or publicly explaining the practice of knocking on the roof. Furthermore, when the use of the knock on the roof practice as a warning is announced by the attacking side, and has been used regularly, the civilian population may be expected to better understand the knock as a mode of warning. In cases where there is no additional clarification and announcement of the practice, it may at first be unreasonable to expect the civilian population to respond to the knock by leaving their house, instead of

---

own armies' current practices - we are concerned about recent attempts on the basis of incorrect legal interpretations to discredit Israel's practices in this regard." See High Level Military Group (HLMG) 2015.

[36] The Israel 2014 Gaza War Report notes that "the IDF did not regard civilians who heeded [warnings] as voluntary human shields and thus legitimate targets for attack. Nor did the IDF discount such civilians for purposes of its proportionality analyses." See State of Israel 2015, p. 177.

[37] See for example Mahmoud Abu Rahma of the Gaza-based Al Mezan Center for Human Rights: "Imagine you are in Gaza and there are airstrikes everywhere, and many families are in the bottom floor of their home [...] Families miss the sound of the 'warning' missile because it sounds like just another explosion." Lister T and Abdelaziz S (2014) Israeli military's "knock on roof" warnings criticized by rights groups. http://edition.cnn.com/2014/07/15/world/meast/mideast-israel-strike-warnings/. Accessed 23 December 2016.

remaining in their houses in order to take cover against hostilities taking place outside.[38] It seems therefore necessary for armed forces planning to use the knock on the roof practice, or other innovative ways of warning the civilian population, to put effort into announcing the intended effect of the warning method.

As a result, the unannounced use of a knock employed in isolation without further warnings, would in many situations not comply with the requirements of IHL, since the warning would lack effectiveness. However, when the use of the knock is announced and is accompanied by other modes of warning explaining the message, there is no reason why the practice of the knock on the roof would not be understood as an effective warning. In these circumstances, especially for civilians who are aware that they are located in or close to a military objective, the knock will unequivocally be understood as a last warning before the actual attack, and the civilians may be expected to understand that their immediate safety is at stake. In particular, if the authorities of the defending party to the conflict fail to communicate warnings to the civilian population, the use of the knock on the roof may be the best way to unambiguously convey the message that an attack is imminent. States using the knock on the roof as well as States planning to use the technique in the future, thus need to communicate to the civilian population and their authorities in a timely and clear manner that, and how, the knock on the roof will be used as a means to warn civilians of an impending attack.

7.3.2 The Prohibition of Acts the Primary Purpose of Which Is to Spread Terror Among the Civilian Population

A second type of criticism regards the claim[39] that the practice is in fact an act or threat of violence the primary purpose of which is to spread terror among the civilian population.[40] Dill voices her concern that in circumstances in which the civilian population has in fact no means to leave, the practice may induce terror in violation of the second sentence of Article 51(2) AP I.[41] Clearly, the knock on the roof practice cannot be dismissed in its totality on this ground, provided the intention of the practice is to warn the civilian population.[42] First, that intention is in

[38] "'In some but not all cases, families receive telephone calls from the Israeli military in advance,' said Philip Luther, Middle East and North Africa Director at Amnesty International." Ibid.

[39] The Goldstone report notes in para 533: "The technique of using small explosives to frighten civilians into evacuation, even if the intent is to warn, may cause terror and confuse the affected civilians." United Nations General Assembly 2009, para 533; see also Dill J (2014) Guest Post: Israel's Use of Law and Warnings in Gaza. http://opiniojuris.org/2014/07/30/guest-post-israels-use-law-warnings-gaza/. Accessed 23 December 2016.

[40] Article 51(2) AP I, above n 1, second sentence reads: "Acts or threats of violence the primary purpose of which is to spread terror among the civilian population are prohibited.".

[41] See Dill J (2014) Guest Post: Israel's Use of Law and Warnings in Gaza. http://opiniojuris.org/2014/07/30/guest-post-israels-use-law-warnings-gaza/. Accessed 23 December 2016.

[42] See also Baruch and Neuman 2011, pp. 375–377.

contradiction with the prohibition of attacks the *primary purpose* of which is to spread terror. Second, the level of fear instilled by a terror attack must surpass the level of fear and anxiety that the civilian population may generally be expected to experience during hostilities in populated areas.[43] Furthermore, in situations where a warning using the knock on the roof practice is not followed by a major attack, this does not necessarily change the legality of the warning, because there may have been very different reasons not to proceed with the attack.[44] One obvious motivation to cancel a planned attack is the aspiration of the attacker to limit collateral harm to the civilian population as required by IHL. Other reasons may be that the asset that was tasked with attacking the target was redirected to another, more important target, or the weapon that was employed for the major attack simply malfunctioned. The difficulty is obviously that in hindsight, the exact intention of the attacking forces does not become clear when the knock is not followed by an actual attack. But it seems that this does not qualify as a terror attack under IHL. In addition, there is a difference between a warning and a threat which may amount to inducing terror. The latter may be understood as announcing "an attack directed at the civilian population",[45] whereas the former announces an attack on a military objective that may affect the civilian population. Only when an announcement is intentionally vague, in terms of places where the civilians may seek hiding or when an attack may take place, it may in some circumstances be labelled as a threat, instead of a warning.

In sum, it is simply not credible to condemn a knock type of warning, the purpose of which is to mitigate risk to civilians, as a violation of the prohibition against launching an attack for the purpose of spreading terror among the civilian population. Ultimately, an incidental consequence is not synonymous with illicit intent.

7.3.3 *Warning or Attack on Civilians?*

The third point is the issue of whether the knock is a warning or an attack on civilians, or, as far as objects are concerned, an attack on a civilian object.[46] The

---

[43] As the ICRC Commentary on AP I notes: "there is no doubt that acts of violence related to a state of war almost always give rise to some degree of terror among the population and sometimes also among the armed forces. It also happens that attacks on armed forces are purposely conducted brutally in order to intimidate the enemy soldiers and persuade them to surrender. This is not the sort of terror envisaged here." See Sandoz et al. 1987, para 1940 (p. 618). This is confirmed by the International Criminal Tribunal for the former Yugoslavia (ICTY); see ICTY, *Prosecutor v Dragomir Milosevic*, Judgment, 12 December 2007, Case No. IT-98-29/1, para 888: "to constitute terror, an intent to instil fear beyond this level is required."

[44] Baruch and Neuman 2011, p. 377: "there are cases where decisions change for different reasons, including operational, policy and humanitarian considerations."

[45] Sassòli and Quintin 2014, p. 108.

[46] Article 49(1) AP I, above n 1, defines "attacks" as "acts of violence against the adversary, whether in offence or in defence." See Sect. 7.4 below for a more thorough analysis of the term 'attack' within the framework of IHL.

Goldstone Report states that the knock "in essence constitutes a form of attack rather than a warning."[47] Furthermore, according to a spokesman of the Gaza based Al Mezan Center for Human Rights: "[t]he sending of a missile cannot be considered a warning. It is the targeting of civilians with a weapon, regardless of how small, and it is a violation of the Geneva conventions".[48]

Accordingly, a fundamental question related to the legality of using the knock on the roof procedure is whether launching a munition can be considered a warning, or is automatically and always considered an attack. It is submitted that as long as no other IHL obligations are violated, there is no reason to consider it impossible to launch an attack as a warning, as may also be done by firing a warning shot in a safe direction. That kinetic force may be used as a method to warn is confirmed by the Commentary to the HPCR Air and Missile Warfare Manual, which gives the example of the firing of tracer ammunition as a method of warning civilians to take cover for an impending attack.[49] It is thus submitted that the terms "attack" and "warning" are not necessarily mutually exclusive.[50] However, when the knock does violate other IHL obligations, its legality must not only be addressed in view of its function as a warning, but also as an attack and thus as a method of warfare.

To further clarify in Sect. 7.4 how this must be understood, it needs to be noted first that different scenarios may lead to different outcomes. As mentioned above, the knock on the roof practice has mostly been used in areas with a high civilian presence. It then matters what type of object the attack plans to target: whether the target is a building that in its entirety qualifies as a military objective, or whether the situation is such that military objectives are located in an otherwise civilian object. Obviously, only military objectives may be attacked under IHL.

Two different categories of potential targets may be distinguished: an example of target category A is a weapons cache for medium-large rockets located in a residential building, where a civilian family still lives, and which is surrounded by other civilian residences.[51] It seems that it is highly probable that on the basis of the circumstances ruling at the time, the entire building is a military objective, particularly because the rockets are not easily removed. A similar situation may arise when a civilian residence conceals the entrance of a tunnel used for military

---

[47] United Nations General Assembly 2009 (The Goldstone Report), para 541.

[48] Mahmoud Abu Rahma, in Lister T and Abdelaziz S (2014) Israeli military's "knock on roof" warnings criticized by rights groups. http://edition.cnn.com/2014/07/15/world/meast/mideast-israel-strike-warnings/. Accessed 23 December 2016.

[49] HPCR 2013, p. 133 (Commentary). The Commentary however states that this may be done in some situations where this is the only feasible method of warning.

[50] For a view that "warnings are not attacks", see Sassòli and Quintin 2014, p. 109.

[51] See for example the Allegation Concerning the Deaths of Members of the Abu Itta Family in Tel Al-Za'atar: "a warning strike was executed on the roof of the building in which the weapons cache was located [...] as part of the 'knock on the roof' procedure." IDF MAG Corps (2014) Operation Protective Edge: Examinations and Investigation, Update no. 3. http://www.law.idf.il/1007-en/Patzar.aspx. Accessed 23 December 2016.

purposes.[52] Furthermore, if sufficient information is available on the actual continued military use of a civilian residence,[53] the entire object may qualify as a military objective in accordance with Article 52(2) AP I and the civilian house loses its protection against direct attack and becomes a military objective as long as it makes an effective contribution to military action and its total or partial destruction, offers a definite military advantage in the circumstances ruling at the time.[54] It is submitted that in these examples, the civilians present in the house must be warned unless circumstances do not permit and there is no reason not to use the knock on the roof practice to do this, provided it is established that this will be an effective advance warning.

However, another situation arises when the target (target category B) is principally a civilian object. An example is a residential house that belongs to the family of a commander of the opposing forces. The house itself cannot be attacked because it does not qualify as a military objective, however the commander may be targeted directly. If the commander is the target of a planned attack, a warning would not be required when he is present in the house because it would nullify the chances of a successful attack. Whether the attack may proceed, killing the family members and destroying the civilian structure, depends on the outcome of the assessment required by the IHL proportionality rule, taking into account the circumstances ruling at the time. In situations where the commander uses his residence only on occasion to communicate or meet with other members of the opposing force, it is submitted that this use alone is insufficient to conclude that the residential house is now continuously used as a "command and control centre" and thus a military objective because of that use. A similar situation exists when the knock on the roof is directed to another civilian house than the actual military objective, for example because the knock cannot be directed to the military objective since civilians have gathered on its roof or because the house is adjacent to the military objective.[55]

---

[52] Lister T and Abdelaziz S (2014) Israeli military's 'knock on roof' warnings criticized by rights groups. http://edition.cnn.com/2014/07/15/world/meast/mideast-israel-strike-warnings/. Accessed 23 December 2016.

[53] The Israel 2014 Gaza War Report refers on p. 158 to "a residential home regularly being used as an operational planning site" as a military objective, and cites the house of Yehya Sinwar as an example (p. 161). State of Israel 2015, p. 158 and 161.

[54] See possibly the "Allegation Concerning the Death of Kaware Family Members in Khan Yunis (8 July 2014)". The IDF has identified the Kaware house as a military objective, although it is not clear on which grounds. IDF MAG Corps (2014) Operation Protective Edge: Examinations and Investigation, Update no. 2 & 3. http://www.law.idf.il/1007-en/Patzar.aspx. Accessed 23 December 2016. See also the discussion by Schmitt and Merriam of the attacks on the homes of Hamas leaders, Schmitt and Merriam 2015, p. 212.

[55] See for example the Allegation Concerning the Deaths of Members of the Abu Itta Family in Tel Al-Za'atar: "a warning strike was executed on the roof of the building in which the weapons cache was located, *as well as on the roof of the adjoining building which was expected to be significantly impacted as a result of the strike*, as part of the 'knock on the roof' procedure." IDF MAG Corps (2014) Operation Protective Edge: Examinations and Investigation, Update no. 3. http://www.law.idf.il/1007-en/Patzar.aspx. Accessed 23 December 2016 (emphasis added).

In all situations as described for target category B, the knock would possibly violate IHL's fundamental prohibition to launch direct attacks on civilian objects.[56] As a result, the knock in these circumstances cannot be understood as a warning in the sense of Article 57 AP I, but as a method of warfare. The IDF admits that the knock on the roof method, "like other kinetic means, may be imperfect"[57] and it may be telling that in the 2014 Gaza War Report, Israel discusses the knock on the roof method not under the heading of the "provision of effective advance warnings" (Section VI.D.2.b), but under the heading of "Means and Methods of Attack" (Section VI.D.2.c). In situations where there is no military objective to which the knock can be directed, its use seems therefore problematic. Even when it would be established that this situation only occurs in a very limited number of instances, it may still be an impediment to take measures to save civilian lives. Therefore, the issue of whether under these circumstances the knock on the roof may nonetheless qualify as a legitimate method of warfare under IHL needs to be addressed.

7.4 Knock on the Roof as a Method of Warfare

The precautionary measures obligations require parties to an armed conflict to choose their means and methods of attack with a view to avoiding, and in any event in minimising, incidental loss of civilian life, injury to civilians, and damage to civilian objects, in addition to the provision of warnings and other precautions.[58] Like any new method of warfare, a legal assessment of the knock on the roof practice is required to establish whether the practice complies with the rules on the conduct of hostilities under IHL, because the right of the parties to an armed conflict to choose methods or means of warfare is not unlimited.[59] More in particular, when adopting a new method of warfare, parties to an armed conflict need to determine whether its employment would be prohibited by IHL in some or all circumstances.[60]

If the target is a civilian object, such as in the situation of target category B, IHL provides a very clear rule. As long as the structure retains its civilian status, attacking

---

[56] Assuming the knock qualifies as an attack as defined under IHL, see Sect. 7.4.

[57] See State of Israel 2015, p. 180.

[58] Article 57(2)(a)(ii) AP I, above n 1; and Customary IHL Rule 17, Henckaerts and Doswald-Beck 2005, pp. 56–58.

[59] Article 35(1) AP I, above n 1.

[60] Article 36 AP I, above n 1. Although it is unclear whether this rule constitutes customary IHL, the principle that both new weapons and methods of warfare must adhere to the existing IHL obligations and restrictions of the parties to an armed conflict is undisputed. It results from the "general application of good-faith treaty adherence". See Parks 2005, p. 57. Furthermore, the ICRC is of the opinion that "[p]arties to an armed conflict are limited in their choice of weapons, and in the means and methods of warfare they use, by the rules of international humanitarian law […] and] [a]t the 28th International Conference of the Red Cross and Red Crescent, States party to the Geneva Conventions declared that 'in light of the rapid development of weapons technology and in order to protect civilians from the indiscriminate effects of weapons and combatants from unnecessary suffering and prohibited weapons, all new weapons, means and methods of warfare should be subject to rigorous and multidisciplinary review.'" See ICRC (2011) Review of new weapons. https://www.icrc.org/en/document/review-new-weapons. Accessed 23 December 2016.

it would violate the prohibition to directly attack civilian objects. As a result, the knock itself is *prima facie* prohibited in this situation as a method of warfare if it qualifies as an attack as defined under IHL, even if this knock would save lives as a precautionary measure. Furthermore, IHL proscribes that no precautionary measure "may be construed as authorizing any attacks against the civilian population, civilians or civilian objects."[61] This means that the knock is illegal under this article when it is considered a precautionary measure that is aimed at the civilian population, unless it is argued that it is not a precautionary measure, but an attack.[62]

An important issue to clarify is therefore whether the launch of the inert explosive, or non-explosive knock is an attack as defined in Article 49 AP I. If the knock would not qualify as an attack under that definition, one could argue that as a result, the prohibition to attack civilians is inapplicable to launching the knock, as well as the rules on the precautions in attack, including the proportionality rule. If the knock would not qualify as an attack under that definition, one could argue that as a result, the prohibition to attack civilians is inapplicable to launching the knock, as well as the rules on the precautions in attack, including the proportionality rule, except for the obligation to take constant care to spare the civilian population, which applies to all military operations. Attacks are defined by Article 49 AP I as "acts of violence against the adversary, whether offence or in defence." Since the knock consists of the launch of a projectile against a target, the proposal not to regard the knock as an attack seems counter-intuitive, also because the term "attack" must be understood in a broad sense.[63] Furthermore, using a kinetic explosive munition seems emblematic of "an act of violence". Nonetheless, it may be argued that the knock is not aimed "against the adversary" and thus it would fail to meet this particular component of the definition of an attack. This assertion remains problematic, however, because if the knock is not directed to the adversary, as a consequence, it must inevitably be directed to the civilian population.[64] As a result, the knock violates the ground rule

[61] See Article 57(5) AP I, above n 1. According to the ICRC Commentary to this provision, it is "possibly self-evident [and] [...] a confirmation. The law relating to the conduct of hostilities is primarily a law of prohibition: it does not authorize, but prohibits certain things. However, in view of the wording of some of the provisions of this article which take into account military necessity, it is understandable that the Diplomatic Conference wished to stress that these provisions may not be construed so as to a justify attacks against the civilian population." See Sandoz et al. 1987, para 2238 (p. 689).

[62] According to Sassòli and Quintin: "as warnings are not attacks, they may be directed at the morale of the civilian population." See Sassòli and Quintin 2014, p. 109.

[63] Sandoz et al. 1987, p. 1880.

[64] One could argue that the knock is directed to a safe direction, but it is submitted that the launch of a projectile on a civilian object, such as the knock on the roof, can under no circumstances be understood as a safe direction. This is confirmed by the finding of a spokesman of Amnesty International that the munitions used for the knock have caused civilian casualties; Amnesty International stated that it has "documented cases of civilians killed or injured by such missiles [used for knocking on the roof] in previous Israeli military operations on the Gaza Strip". Amnesty International UK (2014) Israel/Gaza: UN must impose arms embargo as civilian death toll rises. https://www.amnesty.org.uk/press-releases/israelgaza-un-must-impose-arms-embargo-civilian-death-toll-rises. Accessed 23 December 2016.

that parties to a conflict "shall direct their operations only against military objectives."[65] Also, it seems undesirable and even dangerous to argue that the legal restrictions that protect the civilian population are inapplicable to a military operation that includes the deployment of kinetic weapons. Furthermore, the view that the words "directed against the adversary" are a crucial component of the definition of an attack seems debatable at best. Taking that view to the extreme would even mean that any use of armed force against the own civilian population would not qualify as an attack as defined in Article 49 AP I, since also in that case, the attack is not directed against the adversary. It must therefore be concluded that the interpretation that a knock is something else than an attack, must be dismissed. Since the knock consists of the use of a projectile, it clearly qualifies as an attack as defined under IHL within the ordinary meaning to be given to the term. Therefore, all targeting rules must be applied to the firing of the knock, including the prohibition to directly attack civilian objects.

In essence, thus, some of the critique on the knock on the roof practice seems justified, because in the situations described as target category B, where the roof of the house that is used for the knock is not a military objective, it seems that launching a projectile on the house would constitute a direct attack on a civilian object. This also applies to the civilian house that is adjacent to a military objective.[66] Assuming the good-faith effort of the attacker to minimise civilian casualties by employing the knock on the roof technique, this would lead to the undesirable outcome that a legally required effective warning method is available which would prevent killing civilians, but that this method cannot be used as a result of another obligation that also aims to save civilian lives. The result is a situation of two contradicting legal obligations that share a common object and purpose.

When two treaty norms collide, a first response for their interpretation must be to refer to Article 31 of the Vienna Convention on the Law of Treaties. The first step is to analyse whether the collision can be solved by interpreting the two norms in "good faith in accordance with the ordinary meaning to be given to the terms of the treaty in their context and in the light of its object and purpose."[67]

It is submitted that the interpretation in the context and in the light of the object and purpose of the two colliding norms point in the same direction, which is the protection of the civilian population, but that the ordinary meaning of the

[65] Article 48 AP I, above n 1.

[66] The IDF report notes that knocks would be directed "at the target's roof", see State of Israel 2015, p. 180. However, knocks have also been launched at civilian houses located next to military objectives. See the Allegation Concerning the Deaths of Members of the Abu Itta Family in Tel Al-Za'atar: "a warning strike was executed on the roof of the building in which the weapons cache was located, *as well as on the roof of the adjoining building which was expected to be significantly impacted as a result of the strike*, as part of the 'knock on the roof' procedure." IDF MAG Corps, Operation Protective Edge: Examinations and Investigation, Update no. 3. http://www.law.idf.il/1007-en/Patzar.aspx. Accessed 23 December 2016 (emphasis added).

[67] Article 31(1) of the Vienna Convention on the Law of Treaties, opened for signature 23 May 1969, 1155 UNTS 331 (entered into force 27 January 1980) (VCLT).

prohibition of directly attacking civilians in this situation precludes solving the norm collision through a standard interpretation. Therefore, recourse must be sought to other means of conflict of norms resolution. One solution in situations of norm conflict is to assess whether a hierarchy exists between the two conflicting rules of international law.[68] Although both rules are found in similar treaty provisions and are both similarly accepted as customary IHL, it is generally accepted that the principle of distinction, that prohibits attacking civilians, is a norm of *jus cogens*.[69] This would solve the norm collision in the sense that the prohibition to attack civilian objects by using the knock on the rule prevails over the obligation of effective warning. However, this solution would also mean that the protection of civilian objects would take priority over the protection of civilian lives, whereas IHL is generally understood to place an emphasis on avoiding human suffering over preventing the destruction of objects.[70] This solution is therefore diametrically opposed to the object and purpose of the *jus cogens* rule, which is to save civilian lives rather than to allow civilian deaths, as a result of a strict prohibition on using the knock on the roof on a civilian object in order to save civilian lives. Furthermore, prohibiting the knock on civilian objects is also contrary to other important rules of IHL pertaining to the protection of the civilian population, such as the obligation to take all feasible precautions in the choice of means and methods of attack with a view to avoiding, and in any event to minimizing, incidental loss of civilian life, injury to civilians and damage to civilian objects.[71] As a result, this solution poses additional legal difficulties.

There are a number of other options to address this conflict of norms, which will be addressed in the following sections. The first is to interpret the two colliding rules in order to circumvent the apparent collision between two legal obligations.[72] This could be done by broadening the interpretation of the concept of military objectives to include the objects on which the knock may be launched; by re-interpreting the knock as something different than an attack, or by treating the knock as part of the larger operation that does aim to attack a military objective. The second venue to resolve the inherent collision between the two obligations of IHL is

---

[68] See generally Shelton 2003, pp. 145–172; see also International Law Commission 2006.

[69] See for example the Constitutional Court of Columbia in 2007 (Constitutional Case No. C-291/07) as presented by the ICRC in the online ICRC database of State practice of the ICRC customary IHL study: "parties to a conflict are bound to make every effort to distinguish between military objectives and […] civilian property. This rule is found in international treaties applicable in internal armed conflicts and is binding on Colombia. It forms part of customary international humanitarian law and has attained *ius cogens* status". ICRC Customary IHL Database (2016) Colombia – Practice relating to Rule 7. The principle of Distinction between Objects and Military Objectives. https://ihl-databases.icrc.org/customary-ihl/eng/docs/v2_cou_co_rule7. Accessed 23 December 2016 (italics in original).

[70] Watkin 2005, p. 13: "[IHL] can be interpreted to place a higher premium on life than on the damage or destruction to 'objects'."

[71] Article 57(2)(a)(ii) AP I, above n 1.

[72] Milanovic 2009, p. 73: "An apparent conflict is one where the content of the two norms is at first glance contradictory, yet the conflict can be avoided, most often by interpretative means."

to use other suitable legal techniques of resolving norm collisions, such as to prioritise one rule over the other temporarily,[73] in light of the underlying principles that may allow one of the two obligations to be set aside.[74]

7.4.1 *Interpreting IHL Norms to Solve the Norm Collision*

Interpretation of IHL norms requires taking into account the object and purpose of the field of IHL. As Kleffner notes:

> [...] [IHL] treaties need to be interpreted not in isolation but in the broader context of the actual application and interpretation of the respective treaty and the legal obligations of the parties to it. The reference to the interpretation of a treaty 'in light of its object and purpose' also invites us to consider that object and purpose of LOAC treaties. While the specifics may be confined to the individual treaty [...], [IHL] treaties have in common the broader object and purpose of striking a reasonable balance between humanitarian considerations, on the one hand, and considerations of military necessity, on the other hand. Accordingly, the interpretation of [IHL] treaties needs to be guided by a balanced and nuanced approach, rather than by the dominance of one of the two considerations.[75]

One option to dissolve the collision between the two competing IHL norms of warning civilians and the prohibition to attack civilian objects is to allow a more expansive interpretation of the notion of military objectives for the purpose of enabling the knocks on the roof.[76] Military objectives are defined as "those objects which by their nature, location, purpose or use make an effective contribution to military action *and* whose total or partial destruction, capture or neutralization, in the circumstances ruling at the time, offers a definite military advantage."[77] The intention of the knock on the roof is obviously *not* to destroy the military objective. Therefore, it may be argued that the category of military objectives for the purpose of launching a knock on the roof may be expanded by deleting the second prong from its definition. As a result, the knock on the roof does not have to satisfy the condition that it must be expected to offer a definitive military advantage. In essence, the advantage sought by the knock is primarily of a humanitarian nature, although it is clearly also militarily advantageous when the civilian population has left an area where hostilities take place. This limited definition of military objectives would lead to a larger set of objects that can be attacked, but not destroyed, to include civilian objects containing only a very limited military use or purpose.

---

[73] The ILC Fragmentation Report calls this to attach relative priority to one rule (the duty to warn) over the other (the prohibition to attack civilian objects), allowing the former to be "set aside only temporarily [allowing it] to influence [the latter] 'from the background'", see International Law Commission 2006, p. 16.

[74] Van den Boogaard 2013, pp. 25–26.

[75] Kleffner 2016, p. 75.

[76] For a discussion of the notion of military objectives, see generally Jachec-Neale 2015.

[77] Article 52(2) AP I, above n 1 (emphasis added).

Interpreting the concept of a military objective such that *any* military use would qualify the target of the knock as a military objective for the purpose of launching the knock, would thus arguably provide a solution for those objects that serve some limited military purpose. However, the examples of target category B show that the knock on the roof practice has also been used against civilian objects without any military use or purpose. Thus, this expansive interpretation of the concept of military objectives for the purpose of the knock would not lead to an all-encompassing solution, because it would still provide no solution for launching knocks on civilian objects adjacent to military objectives. Furthermore, any overly broad interpretation of the concept of military objectives seems unadvisable in more general terms, because it would certainly result in an embarkation on a slippery slope. It seems difficult, if not impossible, to justify that an entire structure may qualify as a military objective for the purpose of launching a knock on the roof, but as a civilian object when the complete destruction of the military objective contained therein is assessed (such as the example in which only a small portion of a larger residential building is used for military purposes in situations where the capability to attack only the military objective is available). Therefore, it is submitted that the interpretation of a military objective through the two-pronged test contained in Article 52(1) AP I must be left untouched also for the purpose of dissolving the collision between the two competing IHL norms of warning civilians and the prohibition to attack civilian objects.

A second possible solution is to interpret the knock as a "warning shot", and thus as a "signal" instead of an attack.[78] In the context of the law of naval warfare, warning shots are a long and established practice.[79] By analogy, under US national regulations, warning shots used in order to board a vessel in a law enforcement situation, are "considered a 'signal' to a vessel to stop, not a use of force"[80] and may be used if all other measures to signal a ship to stop have failed.[81] However, it seems that with regard to the use of warning shots, the situation on land is incomparable to the situation at sea, because there is no danger of hitting civilians or civilian objects at sea when a shot is fired across the bows. Naval warning shots and the knock on the roof method are therefore incomparable.

[78] See Baruch and Neuman 2011, p. 387.

[79] For example, Article 2 of the Hague Convention (IX) concerning Bombardment by Naval Forces in Time of War, opened for signature 18 October 1907, 36 Stat. 2351 (entered into force 26 January 1910), already obliged the commander of a warship to "take all due measures in order that the town may suffer as little harm as possible". Schindler and Toman 2004, p. 1079. See also Article 34(1) of Geneva Convention (II) for the Amelioration of the Condition of Wounded, Sick and Shipwrecked Members of Armed Forces at Sea, opened for signature 12 August 1949, 75 UNTS 85 (entered into force 21 October 1950) (GCII): "The protection to which hospital ships and sick-bays are entitled shall not cease unless they are used to commit, outside their humanitarian duties, acts harmful to the enemy. Protection may, however, cease only after due warning has been given [...]".

[80] Allen 2005, p. 133.

[81] Ibid.

Of course, the IHL rules on the conduct of hostilities on land do not require to first fire a warning shot to the opponent before an actual attack is launched, although there is neither a prohibition to do so. It is imaginable that during armed conflict, military forces use warning shots, for example to warn civilians that they are approaching a military roadblock and they need to slow down in order to allow the forces at the roadblock to check civilian vehicles. These are routine operations during armed conflict that in most cases are closer to law enforcement than to combat. Baruch and Neuman argue that "the widespread use of warning shots in law enforcement situations reinforces the lawfulness of using warning shots from the air [...] as a method of warning civilians prior to attack."[82] It is submitted that although it is possible that the practice of warning shots during law enforcement operations may increase the awareness of the purpose of the knock on the roof method, this does not impact the question of its legality as an attack. At best it may be said that it may increase its effectiveness. The knock on the roof however differs from such warning shots in the sense that it is meant as a signal during combat and that it is directed to the civilian population, not to the opponent. The question therefore remains whether the knock during armed conflict is equivalent to a warning shot as it is used in law enforcement practice. It must be noted that warning shots fired in law enforcement operations on land, like naval warning shots, must be aimed at a safe direction. The knock on the roof is however not aimed at a safe direction, but at the construction from which the civilians are meant to distance themselves. Thus, even if warning shots are meant only as a signal to the civilian population, warning shots still qualify as attacks under Article 49 AP I when they are launched in the direction of civilians or civilian objects. It is thus concluded that interpreting the knock as a warning shot, or signal, does not solve the collision of the two norms.

A third alternative interpretation to effectively solve the conflict between the legal obligation to spare civilian lives as much as possible over the prohibition to aim the knock on a civilian object, is to understand the knock as part of the larger attack on the military objective. This is an analogy to the declaration of a number of States that in the assessment of the expected military advantage in the context of the proportionality calculation, the military advantage expected from that attack must be viewed "as a whole". In this interpretation, it is acknowledged that the knock is in fact also an attack, and that it must be directed to a military objective, but its objective is to scare the civilian population away, before the subsequent attack destroys the military objective. If the totality of the collateral damage of the total attack (thus of both the knock and the actual attack) is not excessive in relation to the military objective of the attack as a whole, the knock is not illegal, provided it has as its objective that it minimises the collateral damage resulting from the total attack.[83] Therefore, this interpretation may be of use when the knock is used against

[82] See Baruch and Neuman 2011, p. 387.

[83] Conducting a *prima facie* illegal, minor initial attack like the knock may however not be used with a different purpose, such as a ruse of war. See for example Baruch and Neuman 2011, pp. 376–377.

a civilian object adjacent to a military objective, in the knowledge that the main attack effort will likely lead to severe damage to that civilian object as permitted collateral damage of the main attack. Nonetheless, this approach does not change the fact that the knock still violates the prohibition to attack civilian objects and does as such thus not solve the conflict of norms. After all, it is unacceptable under any interpretation of IHL to directly attack the civilian population or civilian objects as part of a larger military operation that aims to achieve a certain military advantage, unless the civilian objects and civilians may be regarded as legitimate incidental damage under the IHL proportionality rule.

To sum up, interpreting the existing legal obligations fails to dissolve the norm collision that exists when the knock on the roof technique is used against a civilian object. Therefore, the next section will search for a different approach to solve the conflict of norms.

7.4.2 Prioritising the Protection of Civilian Life

Since interpretation of the norm conflict seems insufficient to solve the conflict between the two colliding norms of IHL, other avenues need to be sought in order to solve the collision.[84] Hence, other suitable legal techniques of resolving the conflict of norms must be employed to prioritise one rule over the other temporarily.[85] The priority of different norms may be concluded from using techniques such as *lex specialis derogat lex generali*,[86] in light of the underlying principles that reinforce setting one of the two obligations aside temporarily.

The International Law Commission has defined the *lex specialis* rule as follows:

> Sometimes *lex specialis* is [...] understood more narrowly to cover the case where two legal provisions that are both valid and applicable, are in no express hierarchical relationship, and provide incompatible direction on how to deal with the same set of facts. In such case, *lex specialis* appears as a conflict-solution technique. It suggests that instead of the (general) rule, one should apply the (specific) exception. In both cases, however, priority falls on the provision which is 'special', that is, the rule with a more precisely delimited scope of application.[87]

---

[84] Milanovic 2009, p. 73: "resolution requires one conflicting norm to prevail or have priority over another".

[85] International Law Commission 2006, p. 16.

[86] Pouw 2013, p. 130: "The maxim *lex specialis derogat lex generali* is a historically deeply rooted and nowadays commonly accepted mechanism to regulate normative relationships of two norms being simultaneously valid and applicable to the same subject matter. In its traditional meaning, the *lex specialis* principle entails that in situations of simultaneous applicability of two norms to a similar factual situation, the more specific norm is awarded priority over the norm that is more general.".

[87] International Law Commission 2006, p. 35.

In the current situation, the prohibition to attack civilians and civilian objects in all circumstances, including through the knock on the roof, is a general rule, applying to all situations. The obligation to issue an effective advance warning to save civilian lives is a much more specific rule, applying only to the specific situation where circumstances permit. As such, arguably, it should be the more specific rule on effective warning that should be prioritised temporarily in order to enable the use of the knock on the roof technique as a warning on civilian objects. Nonetheless, when a norm of IHL is prioritised over another, it needs to be ensured that the reasonable balance between considerations of humanity and military necessity remains intact.[88]

It is submitted therefore that the priority of the obligations to provide effective advance warning and to take all feasible precautions in the choice of means and methods of warfare over the prohibition to use the knock on a civilian objective must be supported by assessing the underlying principles of IHL. The most important of these principles are those of humanity and military necessity.[89] These principles of IHL, "guide and bind armed members of the parties to the conflict"[90] and represent the object and purpose of the specific conventional and customary rules of IHL. Of course, the result of solving the current norm collision must preserve the "delicate" balance between the IHL principles of military necessity and humanity.[91] Setting aside a legal rule by reference to the underlying principles of the applicable legal framework can only be done in exceptional cases[92] and never to such an extent that it allows considerations of military necessity to evade the restrictions posed by IHL on the conduct of hostilities.[93] It is submitted that prioritising the obligation to warn over the strict prohibition for the purpose of launching a knock on a civilian object is in accordance with both the principle of military necessity as with that of humanity. Although much more could be said about the exact content and effect of these principles, a short check suffices for the current discussion. With regard to the principle of military necessity, launching the knock is an enabler for military forces using the technique to attack military objectives "in the knowledge that less civilian collateral damage is expected".[94]

---

[88] Kleffner 2016, p. 75.

[89] According to Schmitt: "Although carte blanche deviation from established legal norms based on military necessity is impermissible, the balancing of necessity and humanity pervades contemporary international law in both a general and a specific sense. See Schmitt 2010, p. 798.

[90] Van den Boogaard 2013, p. 26.

[91] Schmitt 2010.

[92] Van den Boogaard 2013, pp. 25–26.

[93] Schmitt 2010, p. 798. See Hayashi 2016, p. 105, who notes that based on the character of the underlying notion of humanity, that "affirmative aspects of humanity and chivalry may survive the process of [IHL] norm-creation and operate as additional layers of lawfulness determination over positive [IHL rules]." And that this is not the case for military necessity.

[94] Baruch and Neuman 2011, p. 395: "successful warnings that lead to most civilians leaving a combat area do allow military forces more freedom of action in the knowledge that less civilian collateral damage is expected.".

Simultaneously, protecting those not taking part in hostilities by minimizing collateral civilian casualties is in accordance with the IHL principle of humanity. The balance between these principles thus seems preserved, and thus the core principles are no obstacle to allowing the knock on the roof to be used on civilian objects with the intention to save civilian lives.

It seems that prioritising the obligation to warn the civilian population, supported by a balance of IHL's two core principles, as suggested in this section, may be the only possible way to harmonise the two conflicting norms. Even when the intention and purpose of the knock is to save civilian lives, launching the knock on a civilian object will usually lead to some minor material damage to that object. However, this minor material damage is generally more acceptable than attacking a military objective that is expected to cause civilian casualties without a warning, where such warning would have been possible. This is in line with the generally accepted notion that more value needs to be attached to loss of civilian life than damage to civilian objects in IHL proportionality assessments.[95] Great caution however needs to be exercised, for allowing a civilian object to be affected by a knock on the roof can arguably only be excused in cases where the intention of the knock is to save civilian lives in accordance with the object and purpose of IHL in general and as a last resort to achieve that objective. In the end, if it is not accepted that the argument that the knock on the roof is a legitimate method of warfare on the basis of the application of the *lex specialis* method in order to prioritise the rules on precautions over the general prohibition to attack civilian objects, this would open up the door for criminal prosecutions of military personnel. It deserves mentioning however that in the enforcement phase of the rules of IHL, the intention to warn the civilian population in order to minimise possible civilian casualties may absolve criminal responsibility for the violation of the prohibition to attack civilian objects[96] during a prosecution under (international) criminal law.[97]

7.5 Conclusion

IHL provides a legal framework that provides attackers with a certain margin of appreciation, but its application is complicated if the opponent operates contrary to its obligations with regard to precautionary measures against the effects of hostilities.[98] The knock on the roof is a legitimate method to warn the civilian population against an impending attack against a military objective. It rather effectively warns

---

[95] Watkin 2005, p. 13.

[96] See Rome Statute of the International Criminal Court, opened for signature 17 July 1998, 2187 UNTS 90 (entered into force 1 July 2002) (Rome Statute); the relevant crimes are codified in Articles 8(2)(b)(ii) for IACs and 8(2)(e)(ii) for NIACs.

[97] Ibid., Articles 30 and 32.

[98] See for example the Goldstone Report, United Nations General Assembly 2009, paras 439–498 (pp. 111–124). Furthermore, Jensen points to the possibilities modern technologies provide to

civilians to evacuate urgently from the location where an airstrike is imminent. The practice of the knock on the roof thus complies with the objective of warnings, which is to give civilians the chance to protect themselves.[99] The critique that the civilian population cannot reasonably be expected to understand the knock as a warning, as well as the critique that the knock constitutes a terror attack, must be dismissed. There are many scenarios in which the knock may be used without the result occurring that civilians or civilian objects are directly attacked.

The knock on the roof practice may however pose legal difficulties in situations where there is no military objective to which the knock can be directed. The knock is thus not only a warning, but it may also be an attack as defined under IHL. A strict reading of the IHL rules on the conduct of hostilities would give priority to the absolute prohibition to attack civilian objects and prohibit, as a method of warfare, the launch of the knock at a civilian object. However, in a very limited number of cases, and under strict conditions, the illegality of the use of the knock on the roof against a civilian object may arguably temporarily be set aside by the obligation to provide effective warning. Of course, any conduct that may amount to setting aside the prohibition to attack civilians, must be treated with suspicion. It is submitted that the practice, that complies with the basic principle of precautions in attack, may be reconciled under strict conditions with the other rules of IHL, more in particular the prohibition to attack civilian objects. These conditions are, first, that the warning must be expected to be effective because it is accompanied by other modes of warning and second, that the knock on the civilian object reasonably must be expected to save civilian lives and be in accordance with the core principles of IHL. When these conditions are met, the knock on the roof practice may be regarded as a legitimate method of warfare.

References

Books, Articles and Other Documents

Allen G (2005) Limits on the use of force in maritime operations in support of WMD counter-proliferation initiatives. Israel Yearbook on Human Rights 35:115–180.

Baruch PS, Neuman N (2011) Warning civilians prior to attack under international law: Theory and practice. In: Pedrozo RA, Wollschlaeger DP (eds) International Law and the Changing Character of War. Naval War College International Law Studies 87:359–412.

Carnahan BM (1982) "Linebacker II" and protocol I: The convergence of law and professionalism. The American University Law Review 31:861–870.

defenders in order to comply with their part of the "shared" responsibility to protect civilians during armed conflict. See Jensen, p. 174.

[99] The only armed forces that have used the knock on the roof procedure on a substantial number of occasions, the IDF, have reported that a large number of different precautions were taken during the armed conflicts in Gaza and that the knock on the roof procedure was effective in saving civilian lives. See State of Israel 2015, p. 178.

Corn GS (2015) War, law, and the oft overlooked value of process as a precautionary measure. Pepperdine Law Review 42:419–466.
Efroni D (2014) Challenges posed by international law in the context of urban warfare – Insights from the Operation Pillar of Defense. Military and Strategic Affairs Special Issue April 2014:81–87.
Gaughan AJ (2015) Collateral damage and the laws of war: D-Day as a case study. The American Journal of Legal History 55:229–285.
Hayashi N (2016) Basic principles. In: Liivoja R, McCormack T (eds) Routledge Handbook of the Law of Armed Conflict. Routledge, London and New York, pp 89–105.
Henckaerts J-M, Doswald-Beck L (2005) Customary International Humanitarian Law, Volume I: Rules. Cambridge University Press, Cambridge.
Henderson I (2009) The contemporary law of targeting. Brill Nijhoff, Leiden.
High Level Military Group (HLMG) (2015) An Assessment of the 2014 Gaza Conflict. http://www.high-level-military-group.org/pdf/hlmg-assessment-2014-gaza-conflict.pdf. Accessed 23 December 2016.
HPCR (2013) Manual on International Law Applicable to Air and Missile Warfare. Cambridge University Press, Cambridge.
International Law Commission (2006) Fragmentation of International Law: Difficulties Arising from the Diversification and Expansion of International Law. Report of the Study Group of the International Law Commission, UN Doc. A/CN.4/L.682.
Jachec-Neale A (2015) The concept of military objectives in international law and practice. Routledge, London and New York.
Jensen ET (2016) Precautions against the effects of attacks in urban areas. International Review of the Red Cross 98:147–175.
Kleffner JK (2016) Sources of the Law of Armed Conflict. In: Liivoja R, McCormack T (eds) Routledge Handbook of the Law of Armed Conflict. Routledge, London/New York, pp 71–88.
Milanovic M (2009) Norm conflict in international law: Whither human rights? Duke Journal of Comparative & International Law 20:69–131.
Parks WH (2005) Conventional weapons and weapon reviews. Yearbook of International Humanitarian Law 8:55–142.
Pouw EH (2013) International human rights law and the law of armed conflict in the context of counterinsurgency: With a particular focus on targeting and operational detention. PhD thesis, University of Amsterdam. http://hdl.handle.net/11245/1.399596. Accessed 6 June 2017.
Pratzner PR (2016) The current targeting process. In: Ducheine PAL, Schmitt MN, Osinga FPB (eds) Targeting: The challenges of modern warfare. TMC Asser Press, The Hague, pp 77–97.
Quéguiner JF (2006) Precautions under the law governing the conduct of hostilities. International Review of the Red Cross 88:793–821.
Sandoz Y, Swinarski C, Zimmermann B (eds) (1987) Commentary on the additional protocols of 8 June 1977 to the Geneva Conventions of 12 August 1949. Martinus Nijhoff Publishers and International Committee of the Red Cross, Geneva.
Sassòli M, Quintin A (2014) Active and passive precautions in air and missile warfare. Israel Yearbook on Human Rights 44:69–123.
Schindler D, Toman J (2004) The laws of armed conflicts: A collection of conventions, resolutions, and other documents, 4th edn. Brill Nijhoff, Leiden.
Schmitt MN (2010) Military necessity and humanity in international humanitarian law: Preserving the delicate balance. Virginia Journal of International Law 50:796–839.
Schmitt MN, Merriam JJ (2015) The tyranny of context: Israeli targeting practices in legal perspective. University of Pennsylvania Journal of International Law 37:53–138.
Shelton D (2003) International Law and "Relative Normativity". In: Evans MD (ed) International Law. Oxford University Press, Oxford, pp 145–172.
State of Israel (2015) The 2014 Gaza Conflict, 7 July–26 August 2014. Factual and Legal Aspects. http://mfa.gov.il/ProtectiveEdge/Documents/2014GazaConflictFullReport. Accessed 23 December 2016.

United Kingdom Ministry of Defence (2004) The Manual of the Law of Armed Conflict. Oxford University Press, Oxford.
United Nations General Assembly (2009) Report of the United Nations Fact-Finding Mission on the Gaza Conflict. UN Doc. A/HRC/12/48.
Van den Boogaard JC (2011) Voorzorgsmaatregelen bij aanvallen en de legaliteit van de knock on the roof methode (Precautions in attack and the legality of the "knock on the roof" method). Militair Rechtelijk Tijdschrift (Military Law Review) 104(3):262–275.
Van den Boogaard JC (2013) Fighting by the principles: Principles as a source of international humanitarian law. In: Matthee M, Toebes B, Brus M (eds) Armed conflict and international law: In search of the human face. Liber amicorum in memory of Avril McDonald. TMC Asser Press, The Hague, pp 3–31.
Watkin K (2005) Assessing proportionality: Moral complexity and legal rules. Yearbook of International Humanitarian Law 8:3–53.

Case Law

ICTY, *Prosecutor v Dragomir Milosevic*, Judgment, 12 December 2007, Case No IT-98-29/1.

Treaties

Geneva Convention (I) for the Amelioration of the Condition of the Wounded and Sick in Armed Forces in the Field, opened for signature 12 August 1949, 75 UNTS 31 (entered into force 21 October 1950).
Geneva Convention (II) for the Amelioration of the Condition of Wounded, Sick and Shipwrecked Members of Armed Forces at Sea, opened for signature 12 August 1949, 75 UNTS 85 (entered into force 21 October 1950).
Geneva Convention (IV) relative to the Protection of Civilian Persons in Time of War, opened for signature 12 August 1949, 75 UNTS 287 (entered into force 21 October 1950).
Hague Convention (IX) concerning Bombardment by Naval Forces in Time of War, opened for signature 18 October 1907, 36 Stat. 2351 (entered into force 26 January 1910).
Protocol Additional to the Geneva Conventions of 12 August 1949, and relating to the Protection of Victims of International Armed Conflicts, opened for signature 12 December 1977, 1125 UNTS 3 (entered into force 7 December 1979).
Rome Statute of the International Criminal Court, opened for signature 17 July 1998, 2187 UNTS 90 (entered into force 1 July 2002).
Vienna Convention on the Law of Treaties, opened for signature 23 May 1969, 1155 UNTS 331 (entered into force 27 January 1980).

Chapter 8
Year in Review 2016

Kate Pitcher, Sophie van der Valk and Geneviève Girard

Abstract The year 2016 was marked by several noteworthy events with particular relevance to international humanitarian law, such as: the continuance of the conflict in Syria, the prolongation of violence in Libya, the intensification of hostilities in Yemen, the proliferation of armed groups in Mali, the decline of the Islamic State (IS)'s territorial control in Iraq, Libya and Syria and the conclusion of a peace agreement in Colombia; the release of four reports on the use of chemical weapons in Syria by the Joint Investigative Mechanism (JIT) established last year by the United Nations (UN) and the Organisation for the Prohibition of Chemical Weapons (OPCW); the publication of a new Commentary on the First Geneva Convention by the International Committee of the Red Cross (ICRC); and several key decisions by international, hybrid, and national courts related to the adjudication of war crimes, crimes against humanity, and genocide, including landmark judgments in the *Bemba* and *Al Madhi* cases at the International Criminal Court (ICC) and in the case of Hissène Habré at the Extraordinary African Chambers (EAC). This chapter addresses a number of these issues amongst other events of note. The Year in Review is not intended to be a comprehensive summary of all events that occurred in 2016, but rather a sampling of events of note with particular relevance to international humanitarian law.

Kate Pitcher is a former research assistant for the T.M.C. Asser Instituut who contributed to this chapter between 24 March 2016 and 26 February 2017. Sophie van der Valk is PhD candidate at Trinity College Dublin. Geneviève Girard was the Editorial Assistant of the Yearbook of International Humanitarian Law 2016 (vol. 19).

K.M. Pitcher (✉)
The Hague, The Netherlands
e-mail: km.pitcher@gmail.com

S. van der Valk
Dublin, Ireland
e-mail: sophievandv@gmail.com

G. Girard
T.M.C. Asser Instituut, The Hague, The Netherlands
e-mail: g.girard@asser.nl

T.D. Gill et al. (eds.), *Yearbook of International Humanitarian Law 2016*,
Yearbook of International Humanitarian Law 19,
https://doi.org/10.1007/978-94-6265-213-2_8

Keywords International humanitarian law · International criminal law · Armed conflict · War crimes · Prosecutions · Arms control · Terrorism · Armed groups

Contents

8.1 Ongoing Conflicts and Other Developments

8.1.1 Afghanistan

The Afghan National Security Forces continued to combat Taliban and Islamic State (IS)[1] affiliated insurgencies in 2016. According to the United Nations (UN), the number of civilian casualties hit a half year high, since counting began in 2009, with 5 166 civilians killed or injured between January and July 2016.[2] Attacks targeting

[1] Islamic State (IS) is used throughout this chapter to refer to the Islamic State, ISIS, ISIL and Daesh.

[2] UN News Centre (2016) Afghan civilian casualties hit half-year record, with 5,166 dead or maimed – UN. http://www.un.org/apps/news/story.asp?NewsID=54543#.WJnZ3lMrLIU. Accessed 13 February 2017.

civilians continued in 2016, with a number of deadly attacks in Kabul, with the Taliban and IS affiliated groups claiming responsibility.[3] These include: a suicide attack involving a truck in Kabul on 16 April carried out by the Taliban;[4] an attack involving multiple suicide bombers belonging to IS who targeted a large protest march on 23 July;[5] and an attack, which was carried out against the American University in Kabul on 24 August.[6] The UN has condemned these attacks and called for anti-government groups to cease targeting civilians.[7] Attacks have targeted all actors in society, such as media workers,[8] mine clearance staff,[9] judicial officials,[10] police,[11] worshippers,[12] and local elders.[13] Moreover, there has been an increase in the recruitment of child soldiers by the Taliban from late 2015 through to early 2016.[14] This practice was also continued by other forces involved in the conflict, despite the criminalisation of the practice by the Afghan government. Schools have

[3] Human Rights Watch (2017) World Report 2017 – Events of 2016, p. 65. https://www.hrw.org/world-report/2017. Accessed 9 July 2017.

[4] UN News Centre (2016) Afghanistan: UN condemns Taliban attack in Kabul. http://www.un.org/apps/news/story.asp?NewsID=53718&Kw1=Afghanistan+&Kw2=&Kw3=#.V_9FCo997cs. Accessed 20 February 2017.

[5] UN News Centre (2016) Afghanistan: UN condemns terrorist attack that leaves scores dead in Kabul. http://www.un.org/apps/news/story.asp?NewsID=54542&Kw1=Afghanistan+&Kw2=&Kw3=#.V_9GMY997cs. Accessed 20 February 2017.

[6] UN News Centre (2016) Afghanistan: UN mission condemns attack on American University in Kabul. http://www.un.org/apps/news/story.asp?NewsID=54756&Kw1=Afghanistan+&Kw2=&Kw3=#.V_9Gio997cs. Accessed 20 February 2017.

[7] UN News Centre (2016) UN strongly condemns series of attacks in Afghanistan. http://www.un.org/apps/news/story.asp?NewsID=54271&Kw1=Afghanistan+&Kw2=&Kw3=#.V_9F04997cs. Accessed 20 February 2017.

[8] UN News Centre (2016) UN condemns suicide attack targeting media in Kabul. http://www.un.org/apps/news/story.asp?NewsID=53059&Kw1=Afghanistan+&Kw2=&Kw3=#.V_9EI4997cs. Accessed 20 February 2017.

[9] UN News Centre (2016) Afghanistan: UN mine clearance officials strongly condemn murder of four de-miners. http://www.un.org/apps/news/story.asp?NewsID=53107&Kw1=Afghanistan+&Kw2=&Kw3=#.V_9EYY997cs. Accessed 20 February 2017.

[10] UN News Centre (2016) Afghanistan: UN condemns attack targeting Logar judicial officials. http://www.un.org/apps/news/story.asp?NewsID=54141&Kw1=Afghanistan+&Kw2=&Kw3=#.V_9FnI997cs. Accessed 20 February 2017.

[11] UN News Centre (2016) UN mission in Afghanistan condemns Taliban attack on national police cadets. http://www.un.org/apps/news/story.asp?NewsID=54373&Kw1=Afghanistan+&Kw2=&Kw3=#.V_9GBI997cs. Accessed 20 February 2017.

[12] UN News Centre (2016) Afghanistan: UN mission condemns killings of worshippers in two Mosque attacks. http://www.un.org/apps/news/story.asp?NewsID=55272&Kw1=Afghanistan+&Kw2=&Kw3=#.V_9HK4997cs. Accessed 20 February 2017.

[13] Reuters (2016) Afghan elders killed in suicide attack on meeting. http://www.reuters.com/article/us-afghanistan-blast-idUSKBN12V1A6?il=0. Accessed 20 February 2017.

[14] Human Rights Watch (2016) Afghanistan: Taliban Child Soldier Recruitment Surges. https://www.hrw.org/news/2016/02/17/afghanistan-taliban-child-soldier-recruitment-surges. Accessed 13 February 2017.

also been used by the Taliban and by IS affiliated groups as military bases and have increasingly become the targets of attacks.[15] In addition to attacks carried out by anti-government groups, illegal militia recruited by the Afghan government are also responsible for a number of attacks on civilians.[16]

As of June, the United States (US) government pledged increased US support of the Afghan National Security Forces.[17] US airstrikes spiked to levels not seen since 2011, resulting in over 100 civilian casualties in the first six months of 2016.[18] The UN established a probe to investigate the alleged death of 32 civilians in a series of US military airstrikes in Kundaz on 3 November.[19]

8.1.2 Central African Republic

Following approximately three years of conflict between Muslim Séléka and Christian Anti-balaka groups, Faustin-Archange Touadéra won the presidential run-off election in February 2016.[20] While the international community pledged its

---

[15] Human Rights Watch (2016) "Education on the Front Lines" Military Use of Schools in Baghlan Province. https://www.hrw.org/report/2016/08/17/education-front-lines/military-use-schools-afghanistans-baghlan-province. Accessed 20 February 2017.

[16] Voa News (2016) Rights Group Demands Prosecution of Afghan Militia. http://www.voanews.com/a/rights-group-demand-prosecution-of-afghan-militia-forces-for-abuses/3442899.html. Accessed 20 February 2017; Human Rights Watch (2016) Afghanistan: Forces Linked to Vice President Terrorize Villagers. https://www.hrw.org/news/2016/07/31/afghanistan-forces-linked-vice-president-terrorize-villagers. Accessed 20 February 2017; UNAMA (2016) Afghanistan: Record Level of Civilian Casualties Sustained in First Half of 2016 – UN Report. https://unama.unmissions.org/afghanistan-record-level-civilian-casualties-sustained-first-half-2016-un-report. Accessed 20 February 2017.

[17] Human Rights Watch (2017) World Report 2017 – Events of 2016. https://www.hrw.org/world-report/2017. Accessed 9 July 2017, p. 70; Reuters (2016) Exclusive: Obama approves broader role for U.S. forces in Afghanistan. http://www.reuters.com/article/us-usa-afghanistan-obama-exclusive-idUSKCN0YW055. Accessed 9 March 2017.

[18] Reuters (2016) U.S. air strikes spike as Afghans struggle against Taliban, Islamic State. http://www.reuters.com/article/us-afghanistan-airstrikes-idUSKCN12Q0FH?il=0. Accessed 28 February 2017.

[19] UN News Centre (2016) Afghanistan: UN Mission probing air strikes that allegedly killed 32 civilians in Kundaz. http://www.un.org/apps/news/story.asp?NewsID=55487#.WJr5XW8rLIV. Accessed 28 February 2017.

[20] UN News Centre (2016) On visit to Central African Republic, UN rights expert urges support for new Government. http://www.un.org/apps/news/story.asp?NewsID=53454&Kw1=central+african+republic&Kw2=&Kw3=#.WIgVqRt9600. Accessed 24 January 2017; UN News Centre (2016) Ban commends peaceful holding of elections in the Central African Republic. http://www.un.org/apps/news/story.asp?NewsID=53282&Kw1=central+african+republic&Kw2=&Kw3=#.WIgVNRt9600. Accessed 24 January 2017; Dembassa-Kette C (2016) Ex-PM Touadera wins Central African Republic presidential vote. http://www.reuters.com/article/us-centralafrica-election-idUSKCN0VT0QX. Accessed 24 January 2017; Human Rights Watch (2016) Central African Republic: Prioritize Protection, Justice. https://www.hrw.org/news/2016/03/29/central-african-republic-prioritize-protection-justice. Accessed 24 January 2017.

support to the new administration, by June[21] the UN Multidimensional Integrated Stabilization Mission in the Central African Republic (MINUSCA) had noted new attacks in Ngaoundaye between Christian militias and Muslim herders and fighters.[22]

The second half of 2016 was marked by attacks on UN peacekeepers and aid workers,[23] an escalation in violent incidents across the Central African Republic, ongoing human rights violations,[24] and consequently the displacement of people

[21] UN News Centre (2016) UN joins partners in pledging support for President-elect of Central African Republic. http://www.un.org/apps/news/story.asp?NewsID=53371&Kw1=central+african+republic&Kw2=&Kw3=#.WIguMxt9600. Accessed 25 January 2017.

[22] UN News Centre (2016) Central African Republic: UN mission strongly condemns escalation of violence in country's west. http://www.un.org/apps/news/story.asp?NewsID=54257&Kw1=central+african+republic&Kw2=&Kw3=#.WIgoYht9600. Accessed 25 January 2017.

[23] UN News Centre (2016) Central African Republic: UN Humanitarian coordinator "outraged" at attacks on aid vehicles. http://www.un.org/apps/news/story.asp?NewsID=54272&Kw1=central+african+republic&Kw2=&Kw3=#.WIgo7ht9600. Accessed 25 January 2017; UN News Centre (2016) UN humanitarian wing condemns attacks on relief workers in Central African Republic. http://www.un.org/apps/news/story.asp?NewsID=55136&Kw1=central+african+republic&Kw2=&Kw3=#.WIgpXBt9600. Accessed 25 January 2017; UN News Centre (2016) UN aid wing cites 'deep concern' at surge in attacks on relief workers in Central African Republic. http://www.un.org/apps/news/story.asp?NewsID=55891&Kw1=central+african+republic&Kw2=&Kw3=#.WIgsaBt9600. Accessed 25 January 2017.

[24] UN News Centre (2016) UN rights chief warns of violence re-escalating in Central African Republic. http://www.un.org/apps/news/story.asp?NewsID=54396&Kw1=central+african+republic&Kw2=&Kw3=#.WIgpCRt9600. Accessed 25 January 2017; UN News Centre (2016) Thousands fleeing violent clashes in Central African Republic – UN refugee agency; http://www.un.org/apps/news/story.asp?NewsID=54417&Kw1=central+african+republic&Kw2=&Kw3=#.WIgpDBt9600. Accessed 25 January 2017; UN News Centre (2016) UN mission in Central African Republic condemns attack on villages, reinforces presence in affected areas. http://www.un.org/apps/news/story.asp?NewsID=54955&Kw1=central+african+republic&Kw2=&Kw3=#.WIgpSxt9600. Accessed 25 January 2017; UN News Centre (2016) Central African Republic needs support to tackle 'spoilers,' other challenges – UN peacekeeping chief. http://www.un.org/apps/news/story.asp?NewsID=55259&Kw1=central+african+republic&Kw2=&Kw3=#.WIgpZBt9600. Accessed 25 January 2017; UN News Centre (2016) UN provides emergency food aid to 8,000 people amid renewed violence in Central African Republic. http://www.un.org/apps/news/story.asp?NewsID=55351&Kw1=central+african+republic&Kw2=&Kw3=#.WIgpdht9600. Accessed 25 January 2017; UN News Agency (2016) UN mission condemns killings and increased violence in the Central African Republic. http://www.un.org/apps/news/story.asp?NewsID=55436&Kw1=central+african+republic&Kw2=&Kw3=#.WIgpfBt9600. Accessed 25 January 2017; UN News Centre (2016) Ban voices deep concerns over renewed violence in the Central African Republic. http://www.un.org/apps/news/story.asp?NewsID=55664&Kw1=central+african+republic&Kw2=&Kw3=#.WIgsTxt9600. Accessed 25 January 2017; UN News Centre (2016) Central African Republic: Arbitrary killings, sexual violence cited in new UN human rights report. http://www.un.org/apps/news/story.asp?NewsID=55804&Kw1=central+african+republic&Kw2=&Kw3=#.WIgsXht9600. Accessed 25 January 2017.

both internally and into nearby states.[25] In July, the UN Security Council extended the mandate of MINUSCA until 15 November 2017.[26]

New allegations relating to sexual abuse by UN peacekeepers emerged in January, February and March 2016.[27] This led to the appointment of Jane Holl Lute as the Special Coordinator on Improving United Nations Response to Sexual Exploitation and Abuse, as well as other measures such as the establishment of a Police-Force joint brigade and the repatriation of troops who allegedly committed offences.[28] In France, investigations are also underway in relation to the sexual abuse allegations against the French Sangaris military forces in the Central African

[25] UN News Centre (2016) Thousands fleeing violent clashes in Central African Republic – UN refugee agency. http://www.un.org/apps/news/story.asp?NewsID=54417&Kw1=central+african+republic&Kw2=&Kw3=#.WIgpDBt9600. Accessed 25 January 2017; UN News Centre (2016) UN refugee agency condemns rising violence against civilians in Central African Republic. http://www.un.org/apps/news/story.asp?NewsID=55286&Kw1=central+african+republic&Kw2=&Kw3=#.WIgpaxt9600. Accessed 25 January 2017; UN News Centre (2016) UN mission in Central African Republic steps up patrols after armed groups clash in Bria town. http://www.un.org/apps/news/story.asp?NewsID=55629&Kw1=central+african+republic&Kw2=&Kw3=#.WIgsSBt9600. Accessed 25 January 2017.

[26] UN News Centre (2016) Security Council extends UN Central African Republic Mission through 2017. http://www.un.org/apps/news/story.asp?NewsID=54564&Kw1=central+african+republic&Kw2=&Kw3=#.WIgpKxt9600. Accessed 25 January 2017.

[27] UN News Centre (2016) Fresh allegations of sexual abuse made against UN peacekeepers in Central African Republic. http://www.un.org/apps/news/story.asp?NewsID=52941&Kw1=central+african+republic&Kw2=&Kw3=#.WIgX3ht9600. Accessed 24 January 2017; UN News Centre (2016) New allegations of sexual abuse emerge against UN peacekeepers in Central African Republic. http://www.un.org/apps/news/story.asp?NewsID=53163&Kw1=central+african+republic&Kw2=&Kw3=#.WIgX8xt9600. Accessed 25 January 2017; UN News Centre (2016) UN team sent to Central African Republic to investigate new allegations of sexual exploitation. http://www.un.org/apps/news/story.asp?NewsID=53557&Kw1=central+african+republic&Kw2=&Kw3=#.WIgnuRt9600. Accessed 24 January 2017.

[28] UN (2016) Secretary-General Appoints Jane Holl Lute of United States as Special Coordinator on Improving United Nations Response to Sexual Exploitation and Abuse. http://www.un.org/press/en/2016/sga1634.doc.htm. Accessed 24 January 2017; UN News Centre (2016) Seasoned official appointed to coordinate UN efforts to curb sexual abuse by peacekeepers. http://www.un.org/apps/news/story.asp?NewsID=53185&Kw1=central+african+republic&Kw2=&Kw3=#.WIgX8ht9600. Accessed 24 January 2017; UN News Centre (2016) Fresh allegations of sexual abuse made against UN peacekeepers in Central African Republic. http://www.un.org/apps/news/story.asp?NewsID=52941&Kw1=central+african+republic&Kw2=&Kw3=#.WIgX3ht9600. Accessed 24 January 2017; UN News Centre (2016) "We must not allow protectors to become predators" – UN Field support chief. http://www.un.org/apps/news/story.asp?NewsID=53368&Kw1=central+african+republic&Kw2=&Kw3=#.WIgm-Rt9600. Accessed 24 January 2017; UN News Centre (2016) UN chief presents Security Council with special measures to curb sexual exploitation. http://www.un.org/apps/news/story.asp?NewsID=53409&Kw1=central+african+republic&Kw2=&Kw3=#.WIgnWht9600. Accessed 24 January 2017.

Republic.[29] In December, the UN announced the finalisation of its own internal investigations into sexual abuse by peacekeepers in Dekoa, Kemo prefecture, and it requested that national authorities in Gabon and Burundi continue these investigations.[30]

8.1.3 Colombia

In 2015, the Colombian government and the Revolutionary Armed Forces of Colombia/Fuerzas Armadas Revolucionarias de Colombia (FARC) leaders reached an agreement on a peace accord.[31] This was eventually signed on 26 September 2016 following a series of delays.[32] The accord brought to a formal end the 52-year conflict in Colombia between the government and FARC rebels. However, the peace accord was rejected by the people of Colombia when put to a referendum on 2 October.[33] While peace itself was welcomed by the majority of voters, some of the terms of the proposed agreement, such as the amnesties afforded to FARC leaders, were seen as too great a compromise and as possibly undermining peace through a lack of justice for victims.[34]

Following renewed peace talks, a new peace accord was reached on 12 November and signed on 24 November.[35] It was subsequently adopted by the government six days later without being put to a referendum.[36] In contrast to the original agreement, the second agreement includes provisions that set a ten-year time limit for the transitional justice process and requires the FARC to provide information on their assets to contribute to reparations for victims. Moreover, only the parts of the agreement, which relate to human rights and international humanitarian law will be entered into the Colombian constitution. The original

---

[29] AFP (2016) France disciplines five soldiers accused of abuse in Central African Republic. http://www.france24.com/en/20160604-france-disciplines-five-soldiers-accused-abuse-central-african-republic. Accessed 24 January 2017.

[30] UN News Centre (2016) Central African Republic: UN completes investigations into allegations of sexual abuse by peacekeepers. http://www.un.org/apps/news/story.asp?NewsID=55722&Kw1=central+african+republic&Kw2=&Kw3=#.WIgsVRt9600. Accessed 25 January 2017.

[31] The Guardian (2015) FARC peace talks: Colombia nears historic deal after agreement on justice and reparations. https://www.theguardian.com/world/2015/sep/24/farc-peace-talks-colombia-nears-historic-deal-after-agreement-on-justice-and-reparations. Accessed 2 March 2017.

[32] BBC News (2016) Colombia peace deal: Historic agreement is signed. http://www.bbc.com/news/world-latin-america-37477202. Accessed 13 February 2017.

[33] BBC News (2016) Colombia referendum: Voters reject FARC peace deal. http://www.bbc.com/news/world-latin-america-37537252. Accessed 20 February 2017.

[34] Ibid.

[35] Human Rights Watch (2017) World Report 2017 – Events of 2016, p. 201. https://www.hrw.org/world-report/2017. Accessed 9 July 2017.

[36] BBC News (2016) Colombian Senate backs new FARC peace deal. http://www.bbc.com/news/world-latin-america-38153932. Accessed 2 March 2017.

agreement had proposed depositing the entire accord as a "Special Accord of Common Article 3 of the Geneva Conventions, deposited before the Swiss Federal Council in Berne", which would have made the entire accord a "de facto" part of the Colombian Constitution.[37] The agreement will also create the "Special Jurisdiction for Peace" to try those responsible for gross human rights violations committed during the conflict, such as crimes against humanity or serious war crimes.[38]

A ceasefire pact was signed on 23 June.[39] To help the process of implementing the peace agreement, a tripartite monitoring body to oversee the ceasefire and the disarming by parties, was established by the UN Security Council, consisting of the UN, the Colombian government and the FARC.[40] Furthermore, in May an agreement was signed to separate and reintegrate the children of guerrilla forces into communities.[41] The UN tripartite mechanism, set up under the ceasefire pact, also found there had been a violation of the ceasefire by an incident on 13 November that resulted in the death of two FARC members.[42] On 6 December, FARC's troops began moving to demobilisation zones although a number of FARC leaders were later expelled for refusing to disarm as required by the peace accord.[43]

Notwithstanding the steps taken by the government and FARC in 2016, other armed groups remained actively engaged in hostilities in Colombia. However, the National Liberation Army/Ejército de Liberación Nacional (ELN), the second largest rebel group in Colombia,[44] also agreed to engage in formal peace talks in

---

[37] BBC News (2016) Colombian government and FARC to sign new peace deal. http://www.bbc.com/news/world-latin-america-38073899. Accessed 2 March 2017; for a full discussion of the changes to the peace accord see: Colombia Peace (2016) Key Changes to the Peace Accord. http://colombiapeace.org/2016/11/15/key-changes-to-the-new-peace-accord/, including a full comparison of the new and old peace agreements (available only in Spanish). Accessed 2 March 2017.

[38] Colombia Peace (2016) Key Changes to the Peace Accord. http://colombiapeace.org/2016/11/15/key-changes-to-the-new-peace-accord/. Accessed 2 March 2017.

[39] UN News Centre (2016) In Havana, Ban hails Colombia ceasefire pact as example of peace with dignity. http://www.un.org/apps/news/story.asp?NewsID=54312&Kw1=Colombia&Kw2=&Kw3=#.V_9kTI997cs. Accessed 2 March 2017; UN News Centre (2016) Colombia: UN Mission, Government and FARC-EP to start joint ceasefire monitoring and verification. http://www.un.org/apps/news/story.asp?NewsID=55483#.WCBHftUrLcs. Accessed 2 March 2017.

[40] UN News Centre (2016) UN Security Council approves mission to monitor peace deal between Colombia and FARC. http://www.un.org/apps/news/story.asp?NewsID=53091&Kw1=Colombia&Kw2=&Kw3=%20-%20.V_9KPY997cs#.WA3-_Ge7rcs. Accessed 2 March 2017.

[41] UN News Centre (2016) Colombia: agreement to reintegrate children from FARC welcomed by UN envoy. http://www.un.org/apps/news/story.asp?NewsID=53948&Kw1=Colombia&Kw2=&Kw3=%20-%20.V_9j3o997cs#.WA3_G2e7rcs. Accessed 2 March 2017.

[42] UN News Centre (2016) Colombia: Santa Rosa incident constituted ceasefire protocol violations, finds UN-led mechanism. http://www.un.org/apps/news/story.asp?NewsID=55688#.WEFBQdUrLcs. Accessed 2 March 2017.

[43] BBC News (2016) Colombia: FARC expels five leaders who "refused to accept peace". http://www.bbc.com/news/world-latin-america-38324186. Accessed 2 March 2017.

[44] BBC News (2016) Colombia and ELN rebels announce historic peace talks. http://www.bbc.com/news/world-latin-america-37614809. Accessed 20 February 2017.

October without agreeing to a ceasefire.[45] As of the end of 2016 these talks have not commenced due to disagreements concerning the release of hostages between the government and the ELN.[46] The ELN has continued to kidnap civilians and use anti-personnel landmines in 2016.[47]

8.1.4 Egypt

The conflict between Egyptian armed forces and insurgent armed groups opposing the government intensified in 2016, pp. 64–66.[48] Terrorist attacks were on the rise over the year and notably included the killing of eight police officers at gunpoint in a suburb of Cairo in May 2016[49] and a bomb attack on a church in Cairo targeting Coptic Christians that killed at least 25 people. Both attacks were claimed by IS.[50] Many of the attacks targeting security forces, government officials, the judiciary and civilians in North Sinai and other parts of the country throughout the year were claimed by Sinai Province,[51] an extremist armed group which has pledged allegiance to IS.[52] In May, the crash of an Egypt Air flight on route to Cairo from Paris in the Mediterranean Sea, killing 66 people, also raised suspicions of a terrorist attack.[53]

---

[45] Aljazeera (2016) Colombia to begin peace talks with ELN rebel. http://www.aljazeera.com/news/2016/10/colombia-peace-talks-eln-rebels-161011035944375.html. Accessed 20 February 2017.

[46] Colombia Reports (2016) Peace talks with Colombia's ELN rebels delayed until January: negotiator. http://colombiareports.com/peace-talks-colombias-eln-rebels-delayed-january-negotiator/. Accessed 20 February 2017.

[47] Human Rights Watch (2017) World Report 2017 – Events of 2016, p. 202. https://www.hrw.org/world-report/2017. Accessed 9 July 2017.

[48] Bellal A (2017) The War Report – Armed Conflicts in 2016, pp. 64–66. https://www.geneva-academy.ch/joomlatools-files/docman-files/The%20War%20Report%202016.pdf. Accessed 9 July 2017.

[49] Reuters (2016) Gunmen kill eight police in Cairo suburb, Islamic State claims attack. http://www.reuters.com/article/us-egypt-police-attack-idUSKCN0XZ00U. Accessed 14 April 2017.

[50] Amnesty International (2017) Amnesty International Report 2016/17 – The State of the World's Human Rights, p. 149. https://www.amnesty.org/en/latest/research/2017/02/amnesty-international-annual-report-201617/. Accessed 9 July 2017; Walsh D (2016) ISIS Claims Responsibility for Egypt Church Bombing and Warns of More to Come. https://www.nytimes.com/2016/12/13/world/middleeast/egypt-isis-bombing-coptic-christians.html?_r=0. Accessed 14 April 2017.

[51] Amnesty International (2017) Amnesty International Report 2016/17 – The State of the World's Human Rights, p. 146. https://www.amnesty.org/en/latest/research/2017/02/amnesty-international-annual-report-201617/. Accessed 9 July 2017.

[52] Previously called Ansar Beit al-Maqdis and initially inspired by al-Qaeda, Sinai Province changed its name in 2014 after pledging allegiance to IS. See Bellal A (2017) The War Report – Armed Conflicts in 2016, p. 66. https://www.geneva-academy.ch/joomlatools-files/docman-files/TheWarReport2016.pdf. Accessed 9 July 2017.

[53] The Guardian (2016) Traces of explosives found on EgyptAir crash victims, say authorities. https://www.theguardian.com/world/2016/dec/15/egyptair-crash-traces-explosives-found-flight-ms804-victims. Accessed 14 April 2017.

Meanwhile, the armed forces continued to carry out military operations against armed groups in North Sinai, allegedly killing dozens of "terrorists".[54] In August, the Egyptian military claimed to have killed Abu Duaa Al-Ansari, leader of the Sinai Branch of IS.[55] Many violations against civilians by members of the security forces were reported in 2016, including enforced disappearances of hundreds of people and the routine torture of detainees,[56] many of whom were accused of supporting the outlawed Muslim Brotherhood.[57] As many as 7 400 civilians were tried before military courts in 2016, often in the form of mass trials allegedly lacking guarantees of due process.[58]

8.1.5 Iraq

In 2016, there was an increase in clashes between government forces and IS through operations to retake key cities, such as Ramadi in February, Fallujah in June and Mosul, where the operation began in October.[59] Airstrikes continued in 2016 and killed a significant number of civilians.[60]

Revenge acts were reportedly carried out against civilians fleeing IS-held areas and these acts amounted to war crimes according to an Amnesty International report.[61] Enforced disappearances, torture and extrajudicial executions were carried out by Popular Mobilization Units (PMU) militias in operations to regain IS-held

[54] Amnesty International (2017) Amnesty International Report 2016/17 – The State of the World's Human Rights, p. 146. https://www.amnesty.org/en/latest/research/2017/02/amnesty-international-annual-report-201617/. Accessed 9 July 2017.

[55] Dearden L (2016) Abu Duaa al-Ansari: Leader of Isis' Sinai province killed in air strikes, Egyptian military says. http://www.independent.co.uk/news/world/africa/isis-leader-killed-air-strikes-bombed-egypt-military-sinai-province-wilayat-abu-duaa-doaa-al-ansari-a7172851.html. Accessed 15 April 2017; Bellal 2017, p. 67.

[56] Amnesty International (2017) Amnesty International Report 2016/17 – The State of the World's Human Rights, p. 148. https://www.amnesty.org/en/latest/research/2017/02/amnesty-international-annual-report-201617/. Accessed 9 July 2017.

[57] Ibid., p. 148; Human Rights Watch (2017) World Report 2017 – Events of 2016, pp. 233–234. https://www.hrw.org/world-report/2017. Accessed 9 July 2017.

[58] Human Rights Watch (2016) Egypt: 7,400 Civilians Tried in Military Courts. https://www.hrw.org/news/2016/04/13/egypt-7400-civilians-tried-military-courts. Accessed 15 April 2017; Amnesty International 2017, pp. 148–149; Amnesty International (2017) Amnesty International Report 2016/17 – The State of the World's Human Rights, p. 148. https://www.amnesty.org/en/latest/research/2017/02/amnesty-international-annual-report-201617/. Accessed 9 July 2017.

[59] Human Rights Watch (2017) World Report 2017 – Events of 2016, p. 341. https://www.hrw.org/world-report/2017. Accessed 9 July 2017.

[60] UN News Centre (2016) UN envoy voices alarm at ongoing violence, "unacceptable" loss of civilian lives, http://www.un.org/apps/news/story.asp?NewsID=53594&Kw1=Iraq&Kw2=&Kw3. Accessed 2 March 2017.

[61] Amnesty International (2016) Punished for Daesh's Crimes. https://www.amnesty.org/en/documents/mde14/4962/2016/en/. Accessed 2 March 2017.

territory.[62] Violations were also carried out by other forces against internally displaced people.[63] Amnesty International recorded various violations taking place in the Battle of Fallujah, including freedom of movement restrictions being applied to internally displaced persons.[64]

The Battle of Mosul started in October, as a major operation to regain the last remaining city in Iraq from IS control.[65] Turkish involvement in the Battle of Mosul has raised tensions with Baghdad and there have been calls for the withdrawal of Turkish troops.[66] Turkish troops and the training of anti-IS fighters are viewed by Iraq as an attack on its sovereignty.[67] Human Rights Watch reported allegations of war crimes with regard to the destruction and looting of civilian homes by troops fighting IS near Mosul from November 2016 due to a lack of military necessity and have called for an investigation to be carried out by the Iraqi authorities.[68] Under customary international humanitarian law, the displacement of civilians is prohibited except on security grounds or for imperative military reasons.[69] Reports have also emerged of abuses by government forces in the retaking of Mosul.[70] Amnesty International reported on allegations of summary executions, enforced disappearances and arbitrary detentions carried out by forces acting alongside the government military such as Kurdish forces.[71]

62 Ibid.

63 Amnesty International (2017) Amnesty International Report 2016/17 – The State of the World's Human Rights. https://www.amnesty.org/en/latest/research/2017/02/amnesty-international-annual-report-201617/. Accessed 9 July 2017 (Iraq).

64 Amnesty International (2016) Punished for Daesh's Crimes, p. 19 and following. https://www.amnesty.org/en/documents/mde14/4962/2016/en/. Accessed 2 March 2017.

65 The Guardian (2016) Mosul offensive: forces launch mass attack on Iraqi city to oust ISIS. https://www.theguardian.com/world/2016/oct/17/iraqi-forces-begin-assault-on-isis-stronghold-mosul. Accessed 9 March 2017.

66 Aljazeera (2016) ISIL captures Iraq town Ratba as Mosul battle rages. http://www.aljazeera.com/news/2016/10/isil-captures-iraq-town-ratba-mosul-battle-rages-161024191517704.html. Accessed 27 February 2017.

67 Aljazeera (2016) Battle for Mosul; Turkey confirms military involvement. http://www.aljazeera.com/news/2016/10/battle-mosul-turkey-confirms-military-involvement-161023144053661.html. Accessed 2 March 2017.

68 Human Rights Watch (2017) Iraq: Looting, Destruction by Forces Fighting ISIS. https://www.hrw.org/news/2017/02/16/iraq-looting-destruction-forces-fighting-isis. Accessed 2 March 2017.

69 Henckaerts and Doswald-Beck 2005, Rule 129, p. 457.

70 BBC News (2016) Mosul Battle: "Iraqi Forces" Tortured and Killed Civilians. http://www.bbc.com/news/world-middle-east-37930402. Accessed 2 March 2017.

71 Amnesty International (2016) Iraq: Banished and Disposed: Forced Displacement and Deliberate Destruction in Northern Iraq. https://www.amnesty.org/en/documents/mde14/3229/2016/en/. Accessed 2 March 2017.

Furthermore, reports documented flagrant violations of international humanitarian law (IHL) including the use of human shields,[72] summary executions[73] and the burning of a sulphur factory and oil fields[74] by IS. IS deliberately blocked civilians from leaving the city, in order to use them as human shields and brought others with them as they retreated from villages surrounding Mosul during the advance of Iraqi troops towards the city.[75] IS has continued to carry out attacks throughout Iraq in 2016 with suicide attacks and car bombs being used in cities and religious places of worship.[76] Reports have emerged of IS engaging in a scorched earth policy[77] and burning oil fields and a sulphur factory in a town south of Mosul in September and October.[78] Mass executions were reported and a mass grave was discovered in November in Hamman al-Alil as troops advanced towards Mosul.[79] Further mass graves were discovered across areas of Iraq previously held by IS.[80]

Attacks which continue to be carried out against members of the Yazidi minority, especially women and children, have been deemed war crimes and may also constitute crimes against humanity and genocide.[81] A UN-mandated human rights inquiry, the Independent International Commission of Inquiry on Syria, concluded that IS is committing genocide against the Yazidi community,[82] with a report by the UN Office of the High Commissioner for Human Rights (OHCHR)

---

[72] OHCHR (2016) Press Briefing notes on Iraq, Syria, and Saudi Arabia/Yemen. http://www.ohchr.org/EN/NewsEvents/Pages/DisplayNews.aspx?NewsID=20810&LangID=E. Accessed 2 March 2017.

[73] Reuters (2016) Iraqi army aims to reach site of Islamic State executions South of Mosul. http://www.reuters.com/article/us-mideast-crisis-iraq-mosul-idUSKCN12R1E0?il=0. Accessed 2 March 2017.

[74] Time (2016) Darkness at Noon: ISIS Sets Oil and Sulfur Fires in Battle for Mosul. http://time.com/4542032/iraq-mosul-isis-qayyarah-mosul-oil-fires-sulfur/. Accessed 2 March 2017.

[75] Reuters (2016) Battle for Mosul can shape or break Iraq further. http://www.reuters.com/article/us-mideast-crisis-iraq-mosul-insight-idUSKCN12N0QL. Accessed 2 March 2017; Reuters (2016) Islamic State using tens of thousands as human shields in Mosul: U.N. http://www.reuters.com/article/us-mideast-crisis-iraq-mosul-un-idUSKCN12S0ZV. Accessed 2 March 2017.

[76] Human Rights Watch (2017) World Report 2017 – Events of 2016, p. 361. https://www.hrw.org/world-report/2017. Accessed 9 July 2017.

[77] UN News Centre (2016) ISIL's "scorched earth policy" creating environment and health havoc in Mosul warns UN. http://www.un.org/apps/news/story.asp?NewsID=55411#.WBMXbdV97cs. Accessed 2 March 2017.

[78] Time (2016) Darkness at Noon: ISIS Sets Oil and Sulphur Fires in the Battle for Mosul. http://time.com/4542032/iraq-mosul-isis-qayyarah-mosul-oil-fires-sulfur/. Accessed 2 March 2017.

[79] BBC News (2016) Mosul battle: Experts probe IS mass grave at Hamam al-Alil. http://www.bbc.com/news/world-middle-east-37907811. Accessed 2 March 2017.

[80] Jerusalem Post (2016) UN says ISIS committing genocide following discovery of 50 mass graves in Iraq. http://www.jpost.com/Middle-East/ISIS-Threat/UN-says-ISIS-committing-genocide-following-discovery-of-50-mass-graves-in-Iraq-453410. Accessed 2 March 2017.

[81] UN News Centre (2016) UN human rights panel concludes ISIL is committing genocide against Yazidis. http://www.un.org/apps/news/story.asp?NewsID=54247&Kw1=Iraq&Kw2=&Kw3=#.WADuhI997cs. Accessed 2 March 2017.

[82] Ibid.

released in June outlining specific acts committed and containing accounts by survivors.[83]

8.1.6 *Israel/Palestine*

Following a new escalation of violence that began in the fall of 2015,[84] Israeli-Palestinian relations remained highly tense throughout 2016 as Israel maintained its military blockade of the Gaza Strip for a tenth consecutive year[85] and continued to promote and develop illegal settlements in the Occupied Palestinian Territory (OPT).[86] An Amnesty International report concluded that by 31 October, Israeli authorities had demolished 925 Palestinian homes in the West Bank[87] and forcibly displaced 1 283 Palestinian residents in areas under direct Israeli administrative control.[88] The situation triggered the adoption of a resolution from the UN Security Council in December calling on Israel to "immediately and completely cease all settlement activities in the Occupied Palestinian territory, including East Jerusalem",[89] which constitute an illegal transfer of its civilians in violation of IHL.[90] Furthermore, according to Human Rights Watch, the destruction of the houses of family members of persons who allegedly committed attacks on Israelis constitutes a collective punishment prohibited under IHL.[91]

Palestinians have reportedly committed a number of deliberate attacks on Israelis including stabbing, car-ramming and shooting in Israel and in the West Bank, killing 16 persons, mostly civilians, and armed groups have continued to fire

---

[83] UN News Centre (2016) New UN report lays bare widespread ISIL "atrocities" committed against Yazidis in Iraq. http://www.un.org/apps/news/story.asp?NewsID=54709&Kw1=Iraq&Kw2=&Kw3=#.WKLlW28rLIX. Accessed 2 March 2017; OHCHR (2016) "They came to destroy": ISIS Crimes Against Yazidis. http://www.ohchr.org/Documents/HRBodies/HRCouncil/CoISyria/A_HRC_32_CRP.2_en.pdf. Accessed 2 March 2017; OHCHR/UNAMI (2016) A Call for Accountability and Protection: Yezidi Survivors of Atrocities Committed by ISIL. http://www.ohchr.org/Documents/Countries/IQ/UNAMIReport12Aug2016_en.pdf. Accessed 2 March 2017.

[84] Human Rights Watch (2017) World Report 2017 – Events of 2016, p. 347. https://www.hrw.org/world-report/2017. Accessed 9 July 2017.

[85] Amnesty International (2017) Amnesty International Report 2016/17 – The State of the World's Human Rights, p. 202. https://www.amnesty.org/en/latest/research/2017/02/amnesty-international-annual-report-201617/. Accessed 9 July 2017.

[86] Ibid., pp. 201–202.

[87] Human Rights Watch (2017) World Report 2017 – Events of 2016, p. 353. https://www.hrw.org/world-report/2017. Accessed 9 July 2017.

[88] Ibid., p. 348.

[89] UN Security Council (2016m) Resolution 2334 (2016), UN Doc. S/RES/2334, p. 2.

[90] Human Rights Watch (2017) World Report 2017 – Events of 2016, p. 351. https://www.hrw.org/world-report/2017. Accessed 9 July 2017.

[91] Ibid., p. 353.

indiscriminate rockets into Israel from Gaza.[92] At the same time, Israeli forces reportedly killed 110 Palestinians[93] in Israel as well as in the OPT, some in air strikes and artillery fire,[94] others in what appears to have been extrajudicial executions.[95] Israeli forces also detained thousands of Palestinians throughout the year, including more than a hundred in administrative detention,[96] while Israel was criticised for its continued torture and other ill-treatment of detainees by the UN Committee against Torture.[97]

8.1.7 *Libya*

Continued clashes between several opposing governmental forces, other armed groups and militias in Libya plunged the country further into chaos in 2016, prolonging the new era of violence initiated in 2014.[98] The UN-backed Government of the National Accord (GNA), or "Unity Government", which was based on a political agreement signed on 17 December 2015[99] and struck a compromise between the two self-proclaimed governments in Tobruk and Tripoli,[100] failed to assert its authority. Its legitimacy remains contested by the Tripoli-based National Salvation Government which took control of the State Council building in October,[101]

---

[92] Amnesty International (2017) Amnesty International Report 2016/17 – The State of the World's Human Rights, p. 202. https://www.amnesty.org/en/latest/research/2017/02/amnesty-international-annual-report-201617/. Accessed 9 July 2017.

[93] Ibid., p. 201.

[94] Ibid., p. 202.

[95] Ibid., p. 203.

[96] Ibid., p. 201.

[97] Ibid., p. 203; See also UN News (2016) Committee against torture considers report of Israel. http://www.ohchr.org/EN/NewsEvents/Pages/DisplayNews.aspx?NewsID=19925&LangID=E. Accessed 16 April 2017.

[98] Bellal A (2017) The War Report – Armed Conflicts in 2016, p. 75. https://www.geneva-academy.ch/joomlatools-files/docman-files/TheWarReport2016.pdf. Accessed 9 July 2017.

[99] El Yaakoubi A (2015) Libyan factions sign U.N. deal to form unity government. http://www.reuters.com/article/us-libya-security-idUSKBN0U00WP20151217. Accessed 19 April 2017. The full text of the agreement can be accessed via the following link: https://unsmil.unmissions.org/LinkClick.aspx?fileticket=miXuJYkQAQg%3D&tabid=3559&mid=6187&language=fr. Accessed 19 April 2017.

[100] Bellal A (2017) The War Report – Armed Conflicts in 2016, p. 75. https://www.geneva-academy.ch/joomlatools-files/docman-files/TheWarReport2016.pdf. Accessed 9 July 2017.

[101] Human Rights Watch (2017) World Report 2017 – Events of 2016, p. 404. https://www.hrw.org/world-report/2017. Accessed 9 July 2017; and Elumami A (2016) Rival faction challenges Libya's UN-backed government in Tripoli. http://www.reuters.com/article/us-libya-security-idUSKBN12F051. Accessed 19 April 2017.

and by the House of Representatives (HoR), Libya's internationally recognised parliament based in Tobruk.[102]

The Libyan National Army (LNA) led by former army General Khalifa Haftar and affiliated to the HoR made important territorial gains in the Eastern part of the country, notably by capturing vital oil facilities from pro-GNA forces.[103] The year was also marked by the decline of IS's territorial control in Libya after it was successfully pushed out of the coastal city of Sirte, its most important stronghold outside of Iraq and Syria,[104] in December,[105] thanks to a coordinated offensive by the GNA and allied militias in May and US airstrikes in August.[106]

A UN report[107] published in February has documented since the beginning of 2014 "very serious violations and abuses that may, in many cases, amount to war crimes."[108] According to Amnesty International, war crimes were committed by all sides to the conflict,[109] including indiscriminate attacks and direct attacks on civilians, some of them targeting hospitals.[110] Some attacks by IS have included the

---

[102] Amnesty International (2017) Amnesty International Report 2016/17 – The State of the World's Human Rights, p. 233. https://www.amnesty.org/en/latest/research/2017/02/amnesty-international-annual-report-201617/. Accessed 9 July 2017; and Human Rights Watch (2017) World Report 2017 – Events of 2016, pp. 403–404. https://www.hrw.org/world-report/2017. Accessed 9 July 2017.

[103] Human Rights Watch (2017) World Report 2017 – Events of 2016, p. 404. https://www.hrw.org/world-report/2017. Accessed 9 July 2017; and Aljazeera, Rival Libyan factions battle over eastern oil ports. http://www.aljazeera.com/news/2016/09/rival-libyan-factions-battle-eastern-oil-ports-160918134102183.html. Accessed 19 April 2017.

[104] Human Rights Watch (2016) "We feel we are cursed" – Life under ISIS in Sirte, Libya. https://www.hrw.org/report/2016/05/18/we-feel-we-are-cursed/life-under-isis-sirte-libya. Accessed 20 April 2017.

[105] Al-Jazeera (2016) Libyan forces claim control of ISIL stronghold of Sirte. http://www.aljazeera.com/news/2016/12/libyan-forces-claim-control-isil-stronghold-sirte-161205140941343.html. Accessed 20 April 2017.

[106] Amnesty International (2017) Amnesty International Report 2016/17 – The State of the World's Human Rights, p. 233. https://www.amnesty.org/en/latest/research/2017/02/amnesty-international-annual-report-201617/. Accessed 9 July 2017; see also BBC News (2016) What's next for Islamic State in Libya after Sirte? http://www.bbc.com/news/world-africa-37188226. Accessed 20 April 2017.

[107] UN Human Rights Council (2016a) Investigation by the Office of the United High Commissioner for Human Rights on Libya: detailed findings, UN Doc. A/HRC/31/CRP.3.

[108] These are the words of UN High Commissioner for Human Rights Zeid Ra'ad Al Hussein: see OHCHR (2016) UN Reports documents litany of violations and abuses amid chaos in Libya. http://www.ohchr.org/EN/NewsEvents/Pages/DisplayNews.aspx?NewsID=17089&LangID=E. Accessed 22 April 2017.

[109] Amnesty International (2017) Amnesty International Report 2016/17 – The State of the World's Human Rights, p. 234. https://www.amnesty.org/en/latest/research/2017/02/amnesty-international-annual-report-201617/. Accessed 9 July 2017.

[110] Among many other deadly attacks, on 24 June a car bomb attack targeting al-Jalaa hospital killed five and injured 13. Amnesty International (2017) Amnesty International Report 2016/17 – The State of the World's Human Rights, p. 234. https://www.amnesty.org/en/latest/research/2017/02/amnesty-international-annual-report-201617/. Accessed 9 July 2017; for another example see Human Rights Watch (2016) Libya: Derna Air Strikes Hit Hospital – Civilians Killed, Extensive

use of improvised explosive devices and suicide bombings.[111] Unlawful killings, abductions, arbitrary detentions and torture and ill-treatment of members of opposing armed groups and civilians were also reported.[112] In June, 12 former regime officials accused of taking part in acts of repression during the 2011 uprising against Muammar Qaddafi were killed by gunmen the day after they were released from jail.[113]

Insecurity remained a serious issue in Libya, as illustrated by the fact that the Office of the Prosecutor of the International Criminal Court, which is investigating war crimes and crimes against humanity committed in Libya since 15 February 2011,[114] stated that instability in the country precluded it from conducting its investigations directly on the Libyan territory[115] and as a result it did not open any new investigation in 2016.[116] In December, the mandate of the UN Support Mission in Libya (UNSMIL) was extended until 15 September 2017 with the objective to support the implementation of the Libyan Political Agreement, the consolidation of governance and the transition process.[117]

8.1.8 Mali

Despite the conclusion of the Algiers Peace Accord in May 2015,[118] the north and centre of Mali continued to be plagued by violent clashes throughout the year

Damage. https://www.hrw.org/news/2016/02/17/libya-derna-air-strikes-hit-hospital. Accessed 22 April 2017.

[111] Amnesty International (2017) Amnesty International Report 2016/17 – The State of the World's Human Rights, p. 234. https://www.amnesty.org/en/latest/research/2017/02/amnesty-international-annual-report-201617/. Accessed 9 July 2017.

[112] Ibid., pp. 233–236.

[113] Al Arabiya English (by AFP) (2016) Twelve freed Qaddafi-era officials murdered. http://english.alarabiya.net/en/News/middle-east/2016/06/13/Twelve-freed-Qaddafi-era-officials-murdered-in-Libya.html. Accessed 22 April 2017.

[114] See UN Security Council (2011) Resolution 1970 (2011), UN Doc. S/RES/1970.

[115] Bellal A (2017) The War Report – Armed Conflicts in 2016, p. 79–80. https://www.geneva-academy.ch/joomlatools-files/docman-files/TheWarReport2016.pdf. Accessed 9 July 2017; ICC-OTP (2016) Twelfth Report of the Prosecutor of the International Criminal Court to the United Nations Security Council Pursuant to UNSCR 1970 (2011) para 13, www.icc-cpi.int/iccdocs/otp/16-11-10_OTP-rep-UNSCR-1970_ENG.pdf. Accessed 22 April 2017.

[116] Human Rights Watch (2017) World Report 2017 – Events of 2016, p. 407. https://www.hrw.org/world-report/2017. Accessed 9 July 2017.

[117] UN Security Council (2016l) Resolution 2323 (2016), UN Doc. S/RES/2323.

[118] The Accord for peace and reconciliation in Mali emanating from the Algiers process, also known as the Algiers Peace Accord, was signed in May 2015 by the Government and by two coalitions of armed groups: the Platform of Armed groups (the "Platform") and two groups part of the Coordination of Azawad Movements (CMA). Later on it was also signed by the remaining CMA groups. See Bellal A (2017) The War Report – Armed Conflicts in 2016, p. 82. https://www.geneva-academy.ch/joomlatools-files/docman-files/TheWarReport2016.pdf. Accessed 9 July 2017.

between armed groups affiliated to Al-Qaeda, ethnic Tuareg and Arab groups and government-supported militia.[119] The proliferation of armed groups, including the growing influence of those linked to Al-Qaeda and IS,[120] and the failure to disarm thousands of combatants from the 2012–2013 armed conflict,[121] seriously hampered the implementation of the peace accord which had been agreed by the government and a number of opposing armed groups.[122] Rising levels of violence spread instability to the centre of the country,[123] with attacks against UN personnel killing at least 29 peacekeepers and summary executions by Islamist groups killing 27 people throughout the year, including civilians.[124] Counterterrorism operations by Malian forces often resulted in arbitrary arrests, extrajudicial executions as well as torture and ill-treatment.[125] In the face of the deteriorating security situation, in July the Malian government extended the state of emergency until 29 March 2017.[126]

Meanwhile, terrorist attacks, notably in Ivory Coast and Burkina Faso, claimed by jihadist armed groups operating from northern Mali, including Al Qaeda in the Islamic Maghreb (AQIM),[127] were posing a direct threat to the security of neighbouring countries.[128] Expressing concern over the "transnational dimension of the

---

[119] Human Rights Watch (2017) World Report 2017 – Events of 2016, p. 420. https://www.hrw.org/world-report/2017. Accessed 9 July 2017.

[120] Irish J (2016) Mali Leader Warns U.N.: Qaeda, Islamic State Gaining Ground in Country. http://www.reuters.com/article/us-un-assembly-mali-idUSKCN11T1N0. Accessed 28 April 2017.

[121] Human Rights Watch (2017) World Report 2017 – Events of 2016, p. 419. https://www.hrw.org/world-report/2017. Accessed 9 July 2017. See also Human Rights Watch (2016) Mali: Islamist Group Abuses, Banditry Surge. https://www.hrw.org/news/2017/01/18/mali-islamist-group-abuses-banditry-surge. Accessed 28 April 2017.

[122] Amnesty International (2017) Amnesty International Report 2016/17 – The State of the World's Human Rights, p. 245. https://www.amnesty.org/en/latest/research/2017/02/amnesty-international-annual-report-201617/. Accessed 9 July 2017.

[123] Ibid.

[124] Human Rights Watch (2016) Mali: Islamist Group Abuses, Banditry Surge. https://www.hrw.org/news/2017/01/18/mali-islamist-group-abuses-banditry-surge. Accessed 28 April 2017.

[125] Ibid.

[126] Al Jazeera (2016) Mali extends state of emergency. http://www.aljazeera.com/news/2016/07/mali-extends-state-emergency-160731061324030.html. Accessed 28 April 2017; Bellal A (2017) The War Report – Armed Conflicts in 2016, p. 83. https://www.geneva-academy.ch/joomlatools-files/docman-files/TheWarReport2016.pdf. Accessed 9 July 2017.

[127] International Crisis Group (2016) The Sahel: Mali's Crumbling Peace Process and the Spreading Jihadist Threat. https://www.crisisgroup.org/africa/west-africa/mali/sahel-malis-crumbling-peace-process-and-spreading-jihadist-threat). Accessed 28 April 2017; The New York Times (2016) Al Qaeda's Branch in Africa Makes a Lethal Comeback. https://www.nytimes.com/2016/03/16/world/africa/al-qaedas-african-offshoot-makes-a-lethal-comeback.html?_r=1. Accessed 28 April 2017.

[128] Ibid. See also Irish J (2016) Mali Leader Warns U.N.: Qaeda, Islamic State Gaining Ground in Country. http://www.reuters.com/article/us-un-assembly-mali-idUSKCN11T1N0. Accessed 28 April 2017.

terrorist threat in the Sahel Region",[129] the UN Security Council voted in June to extend the mandate of the UN Multidimensional Integrated Stabilization Mission in Mali (MINUSMA) until 30 June 2017 and to increase the Mission's contingent to 13 289 military and 1 920 police personnel,[130] making it the UN's third largest peacekeeping force worldwide.[131] The Council also authorised the Mission to take all necessary means to carry out its mandate, which includes the protection of civilians,[132] and authorised French forces[133] to intervene in support of MINUSMA forces.[134]

The year also saw the beginning of the trial of General Amadou Haya Sanogi, leader of the 2012 coup that overthrew the elected president Amadou Toumani Touri in Bamako, and 17 co-defendants for abducting and killing 21 elite "red berets".[135]

8.1.9 Myanmar

In March, Myanmar's first civilian-led government in several decades took office after the landslide victory of the National League for Democracy (NLD) in the November 2015 elections.[136] However, fighting between the Burmese armed forces and various ethnic armed groups escalated throughout the year in the states of Rakhine, Kachin, Karen and Northern Shan, resulting in massive displacement and abuses against civilians.[137] Reports of violations of international human rights and international humanitarian law by government forces in areas of conflict included extrajudicial killings, torture, sexual violence, destruction of property, use of

---

[129] UN Security Council (2016h) Resolution 2295 (2016), UN Doc. S/RES/2295, p. 3.

[130] Ibid., p. 7; this represents approximately an additional 2500 personnel, see Human Rights Watch (2017) World Report 2017 – Events of 2016, p. 423. https://www.hrw.org/world-report/2017. Accessed 9 July 2017.

[131] Bellal A (2017) The War Report – Armed Conflicts in 2016, p. 84. https://www.geneva-academy.ch/joomlatools-files/docman-files/TheWarReport2016.pdf. Accessed 9 July 2017.

[132] UN Security Council (2016h) Resolution 2295 (2016), UN Doc. S/RES/2295, pp. 7–8.

[133] "Operation Barkhane" is a "3,000-strong French regional counterterrorism operation launched in 2014" with continued operations in Mali, Mauritania, Burkina Faso, Niger, and Chad. Human Rights Watch (2017) World Report 2017 – Events of 2016, p. 423. https://www.hrw.org/world-report/2017. Accessed 9 July 2017.

[134] Ibid., p. 423.

[135] Human Rights Watch (2016) Mali: "Red Berets": Trial Marks Progress in Tacking Impunity. https://www.hrw.org/news/2016/11/29/mali-red-berets-trial-marks-progress-tackling-impunity. Accessed 28 April 2017.

[136] Amnesty International (2017) Amnesty International Report 2016/17 – The State of the World's Human Rights, p. 263. https://www.amnesty.org/en/latest/research/2017/02/amnesty-international-annual-report-201617/. Accessed 9 July 2017.

[137] Human Rights Watch (2017) World Report 2017 – Events of 2016, p. 147. https://www.hrw.org/world-report/2017. Accessed 9 July 2017.

anti-personnel landmines and recruitment of child soldiers.[138] Furthermore, Human Rights Watch observed that "government shelling and airstrikes have been conducted against ethnic areas, in violation of the laws of war".[139]

The situation became particularly critical in the northern state of Rakhine after an attack on three border outposts that caused the deaths of nine police officers on 9 October led to the initiation of a "deadly crackdown" on the Rohingya Muslim minority.[140] "Clearance operations" by government security forces led to a number of reports of numerous abuses on Rohingya villagers,[141] triggering serious international concern[142] and calls for investigation[143] and causing 27 000 people to flee to neighbouring Bangladesh.[144] In November, renewed clashes between the army and the Rohingya militants resulted in the killing of nearly 70 so-called "attackers" by the government security forces,[145] while satellite imagery revealed by Human Rights Watch showed widespread destruction of 1 250 buildings in the state of Rakhine.[146] Restrictions imposed by the Burmese authorities and that were preventing humanitarian agencies from reaching people in need of assistance worsened an already critical

138 Ibid., pp. 147–149.

139 Ibid., p. 149; and Amnesty International (2017) Amnesty International Report 2016/17 – The State of the World's Human Rights, p. 264. https://www.amnesty.org/en/latest/research/2017/02/amnesty-international-annual-report-201617/. Accessed 9 July 2017.

140 Al Jazeera (2016) UN calls for probe into attacks on Rohingya in Myanmar. http://www.aljazeera.com/news/2016/10/calls-probe-attacks-rohingya-myanmar-161025063757177.html. Accessed 29 April 2017.

141 Human Rights Watch 2017, p. 150; see, among other things, the report from an OHCHR mission to Bangladesh documenting extrajudicial killings, enforced disappearances, rape and other forms of sexual violence, torture, arbitrary detention and destruction of property on Rohingyas that fled the violence in Myanmar: OHCHR (2017) Interviews with Rohingyas fleeing from Myanmar since 9 October 2016 – Flash Report. http://www.ohchr.org/Documents/Countries/MM/FlashReport3Feb2017.pdf). Accessed 29 April 2017.

142 OHCHR (2016) Press briefing note on Myanmar, Mosul and Syria. http://www.ohchr.org/EN/NewsEvents/Pages/DisplayNews.aspx?NewsID=20948&LangID=E. Accessed 29 April 2017.

143 See, e.g. Human Rights Watch (2016) Burma: Allow Access to Investigate Abuses in Rakhine State. https://www.hrw.org/news/2016/11/17/burma-allow-access-investigate-abuses-rakhine-state. Accessed 29 April 2017.

144 Amnesty International (2017) Amnesty International Report 2016/17 – The State of the World's Human Rights, p. 264. https://www.amnesty.org/en/latest/research/2017/02/amnesty-international-annual-report-201617/. Accessed 9 July 2017.

145 Al Jazeera (2016) Myanmar's army kills 69 "attackers" in Rakhine state. http://www.aljazeera.com/news/2016/11/myanmar-army-kills-69-attackers-rakhine-state-161115131026394.html. Accessed 29 April 2017; see also The Guardian (2016) Myanmar violence: dozens killed as army clashes with Rohingya in Rakhine state. https://www.theguardian.com/world/2016/nov/14/myanmar-rohingya-violence-dozens-killed-army-clashes. Accessed 29 April 2017.

146 Human Rights Watch (2016) Burma: New Wave of Destruction in Rohingya Villages. https://www.hrw.org/news/2016/11/21/burma-new-wave-destruction-rohingya-villages. Accessed 29 April 2017.

situation in the state of Rakhine,[147] with 30 000 internally displaced people having no access to sustained humanitarian aid by the end of the year.[148]

In August, the 21st Century Panglong Conference presided by Aung San Suu Kyi was attended by the military and the representatives of most ethnic armed groups as well as the UN Secretary-General in the aim of reaching a political settlement to the country's almost 70-year-long armed conflict.[149] Despite ending on some positive notes, the Conference did not produce tangible results[150] as fighting intensified through the end of the year.[151]

8.1.10 Pakistan

Pakistan has seen a decrease in the overall level of violence taking place as part of the conflict but attacks continued on universities[152] and courts,[153] with attacks carried out by the Taliban, Al Qaeda and affiliates targeting every area of Pakistani society, including hospitals[154] and a police academy attack claimed by IS.[155] On 27

---

[147] Human Rights Watch (2017) World Report 2017 – Events of 2016, p. 147. https://www.hrw.org/world-report/2017. Accessed 9 July 2017; and Amnesty International (2016) Myanmar: Lift restrictions immediately on humanitarian aid. https://www.amnesty.org/en/latest/news/2016/10/myanmar-lift-restrictions-immediately-on-humanitarian-aid/ Accessed 29 April 2017.

[148] Amnesty International (2017) Amnesty International Report 2016/17 – The State of the World's Human Rights, p. 265. https://www.amnesty.org/en/latest/research/2017/02/amnesty-international-annual-report-201617/. Accessed 9 July 2017; see also U.S. Embassy in Burma (2016) Joint Statement on Humanitarian Access to northern part of Rakhine State. https://mm.usembassy.gov/joint-statement-humanitarian-access-northern-part-rakhine-state/. Accessed 29 April 2017.

[149] Amnesty International (2017) Amnesty International Report 2016/17 – The State of the World's Human Rights, p. 264. https://www.amnesty.org/en/latest/research/2017/02/amnesty-international-annual-report-201617/. Accessed 9 July 2017.

[150] For more information on the peace process and its challenges, see The Economist (2016) Ending Myanmar's insurgencies – A long road. http://www.economist.com/news/asia/21706535-myanmars-new-government-sets-about-making-peace-its-many-ethnic-minorities-long-road. Accessed 29 April 2017; and International Crisis Group (2016) Myanmar's Peace Process: Getting to a Political Dialogue. https://www.crisisgroup.org/asia/south-east-asia/myanmar/myanmar-s-peace-process-getting-political-dialogue. Accessed 29 April 2017.

[151] Human Rights Watch (2017) World Report 2017 – Events of 2016, p. 149. https://www.hrw.org/world-report/2017. Accessed 9 July 2017.

[152] The Guardian (2016) Pakistan attacks: at least 30 dead in terror raid on Bacha Khan University. https://www.theguardian.com/world/2016/jan/20/bacha-khan-university-explosions-heard-as-gunmen-attack-pakistan. Accessed 9 March 2017.

[153] Dawn (2016) 16 killed in suicide blasts at courts in Shabqadar. https://www.dawn.com/news/1244260. Accessed 9 March 2017.

[154] BBC News (2016) Pakistan hospital bomb attack kills dozens in Quetta. http://www.bbc.com/news/world-asia-37007661. Accessed 2 March 2017.

[155] BBC News (2016) Quetta attack: Militants kill dozens at Balochistan Police College. http://www.bbc.com/news/world-asia-37757914. Accessed 2 March 2017.

March, there was a suicide bombing in a public park in Lahore targeting Christians celebrating Easter, killing at least 60 civilians and injuring over 100.[156]

The UN Committee on the Rights of the Child expressed concern in May regarding the effects of the conflict on the children of Pakistan.[157] Air strikes against the Taliban and other non-state armed groups have continued to take place in 2016, including the targeting of militants located near the border with Afghanistan.[158]

The UN Secretary-General[159] expressed concern due to the deterioration in relations between Pakistan and India with both countries accusing the other of facilitating unrest in the disputed Kashmir region.[160] A number of attacks have occurred in the region and cross border fire has been exchanged.[161]

8.1.11 South Sudan

Fighting continued in many areas of the country in 2016, including in Malakal, Western Bahr el Ghazal and Juba,[162] between the South Sudan armed forces loyal to President Salva Kiir and dissident South Sudan armed forces loyal to rebel leader Riek Machar.[163] After two years in exile, Machar returned to South Sudan in April to be sworn in as vice-president in the Transitional Government of National Unity

---

[156] UN News Centre (2016) Pakistan: Ban strongly condemns Sunday suicide bombing in Lahore. http://www.un.org/apps/news/story.asp?NewsID=53553&Kw1=Pakistan&Kw2=&Kw3=#. WATUGI997cs. Accessed 2 March 2017. See also Human Rights Watch (2017) World Report 2017 – Events of 2016, p. 470. https://www.hrw.org/world-report/2017. Accessed 9 July 2017.

[157] UN Committee on the Rights of the Child (2016) Concluding observations on the fifth Periodic report of Pakistan, CRC/C/PAK/CO/5, paras 63–64.

[158] First Post (2016) Nine terrorists killed in air strikes in Pakistan. http://www.firstpost.com/world/nine-terrorists-killed-in-air-strikes-in-pakistan-2967636.html. Accessed 2 March 2017; see also The New York Times (2016) Taliban Chief Targeted by Drone Strikes in Pakistan, Signalling a US Shift. http://www.nytimes.com/2016/05/23/world/asia/afghanistan-taliban-leader-mullah-mansour.html?_r=0. Accessed 2 March 2017.

[159] UN News Centre (2016) Ban "deeply concerned" about deteriorating situation along "Line of Control" in Kashmir. http://www.un.org/apps/news/story.asp?NewsID=55644#.WDvtOtUrLcs. Accessed 2 March 2017.

[160] Reuters (2016) India, Pakistan to expel diplomats amid Kashmir tension. http://www.reuters.com/article/us-pakistan-india-idUSKCN12R2DU?il=0. Accessed 9 March 2017.

[161] Reuters (2016) At least 19 killed in latest India-Pakistan border firing. http://www.reuters.com/article/us-india-pakistan-idUSKBN12W38H?il=0. Accessed 2 March 2017; Reuters (2016) At least four killed in India-Pakistan crossborder shelling. http://www.reuters.com/article/us-pakistan-india-kashmir-idUSKCN12O0LD?il=0. Accessed 2 March 2017.

[162] Amnesty International (2017) Amnesty International Report 2016/17 – The State of the World's Human Rights, p. 334. https://www.amnesty.org/en/latest/research/2017/02/amnesty-international-annual-report-201617/. Accessed 9 July 2017.

[163] Bellal A (2017) The War Report – Armed Conflicts in 2016, p. 87–88. https://www.geneva-academy.ch/joomlatools-files/docman-files/TheWarReport2016.pdf. Accessed 9 July 2017.

as part of a peace agreement signed in August 2015.[164] However, in July violence broke out again in Juba between governmental forces and opposition factions,[165] causing the collapse of the peace agreement as well as massive displacement and numerous abuses against civilians. Reports by international agencies detailed serious violations of IHL by both sides to the conflict, including widespread sexual abuses, deliberate killings, indiscriminate targeting of civilians and massive looting.[166] These added to previous reports of similar atrocities committed since the beginning of the conflict in December 2013 as part of what the UN described as a "government-operated 'scorched earth policy'" with "massive use of rape as an instrument of terror and weapon of war".[167]

International troops from the UN Mission in South Sudan (UNMISS) were criticised for failing to protect civilians and international workers from the violence during the July clashes.[168] In September, the UN Security Council authorised the creation of a Regional Protection Force of 4 000 members to support the 12 000 members of UNMISS already in place,[169] but the South Sudanese government rejected its deployment.[170] In December, despite warnings of escalation of ethnic

---

[164] Ibid., p. 88; and Amnesty International (2017) Amnesty International Report 2016/17 – The State of the World's Human Rights, p. 333. https://www.amnesty.org/en/latest/research/2017/02/amnesty-international-annual-report-201617/. Accessed 9 July 2017.

[165] Bellal A (2017) The War Report – Armed Conflicts in 2016, p. 88. https://www.geneva-academy.ch/joomlatools-files/docman-files/TheWarReport2016.pdf. Accessed 9 July 2017; and Human Rights Watch (2016) South Sudan: Killings, Rapes, Looting in Juba. https://www.hrw.org/news/2016/08/15/south-sudan-killings-rapes-looting-juba. Accessed 30 April 2017.

[166] See e.g. an Amnesty International report from October 2016: Amnesty International (2016) "We did not believe we would survive". Killings, rape and looting in Juba. https://www.amnesty.org/en/documents/afr65/5028/2016/en/; see also Human Rights Watch (2016) South Sudan: Killings, Rapes, Looting in Juba. https://www.hrw.org/news/2016/08/15/south-sudan-killings-rapes-looting-juba. Accessed 30 April 2017.

[167] OHCHC (2016) South Sudan: UN report contains "searing" account of killings, rapes and destruction. http://www.ohchr.org/EN/NewsEvents/Pages/DisplayNews.aspx?NewsID=17207&LangID=E. Accessed 30 April 2017.

[168] See e.g. The Guardian (2016) UN peacekeepers refused to help as aid workers were raped in South Sudan – report. https://www.theguardian.com/world/2016/oct/06/un-peacekeepers-refused-to-help-south-sudan-rebels-raped-aid-workers-report. Accessed 30 April 2017.

[169] Amnesty International (2017) Amnesty International Report 2016/17 – The State of the World's Human Rights, p. 334. https://www.amnesty.org/en/latest/research/2017/02/amnesty-international-annual-report-201617/. Accessed 9 July 2017; UN Security Council (2016j) Resolution 2304 (2016), UN Doc. S/RES/2304.

[170] Aljazeera (2017) South Sudan rejects 4000 additional UN peacekeepers. http://www.aljazeera.com/news/2017/01/south-sudan-rejects-4000-additional-peacekeepers-170111151623667.html. Accessed 30 April 2017; Bellal A (2017) The War Report – Armed Conflicts in 2016, p. 89. https://www.geneva-academy.ch/joomlatools-files/docman-files/TheWarReport2016.pdf. Accessed 9 July 2017.

violence and possible genocide,[171] the UN Security Council failed to adopt a resolution to impose an arms embargo on South Sudan.[172]

Counting from the start of the conflict in December 2013, the number of refugees from South Sudan in neighbouring countries reached 1 million in September, with a total of 1.83 million people internally displaced within the country.[173]

8.1.12 Sudan

Hostilities persisted throughout the year between government forces and armed opposition groups in the regions of Darfur, and, to a lesser extent, Blue Nile and South Kordofan.[174] A roadmap peace agreement proposed by the African Union High-Level Implementation Panel (AUHIP), which committed parties to engage in a national dialogue process concerning those three regions, was signed by the government of Sudan in March and by four opposition groups in August.[175] However, negotiations between the parties collapsed shortly after, owing partly to the failure of the government to agree with the Sudan People's Liberation Movement (SPLM-N) on the cessation of hostilities and humanitarian access, two key elements of the agreement, and the peace talks were suspended indefinitely.[176]

In Darfur, a large-scale military campaign launched in January and involving air and ground attacks in the rebel stronghold of Jebel Marra allegedly caused widespread violations of international humanitarian and human rights law.[177] Reported violations of international humanitarian law by government forces between January and September included indiscriminate attacks, unlawful killings, forced displacement of civilians, rape and pillage, which according to Amnesty International

---

[171] UN News Centre (2016) Risk of "outright ethnic war" and genocide in South Sudan, UN envoy warns. http://www.un.org/apps/news/story.asp?NewsID=55538#.WQZTOmV0WRt. Accessed 30 April 2017.

[172] Nichols M (2016) U.N. council fails to impose arms embargo on South Sudan. http://www.reuters.com/article/us-southsudan-security-un-idUSKBN14C1KY. Accessed 30 April 2017.

[173] Amnesty International (2017) Amnesty International Report 2016/17 – The State of the World's Human Rights, p. 334. https://www.amnesty.org/en/latest/research/2017/02/amnesty-international-annual-report-201617/. Accessed 9 July 2017.

[174] Ibid., pp. 342–343.

[175] Ibid., p. 342.

[176] Ibid., p. 342; and UN Security Council (2017) Final Report of the panel of experts on the Sudan established pursuant to resolution 1591 (2005), UN Doc. S/2017/22, p. 15.

[177] Amnesty International (2017) Amnesty International Report 2016/17 – The State of the World's Human Rights, pp. 342–343. https://www.amnesty.org/en/latest/research/2017/02/amnesty-international-annual-report-201617/. Accessed 9 July 2017; and Human Rights Watch (2017) World Report 2017 – Events of 2016, p. 561. https://www.hrw.org/world-report/2017. Accessed 9 July 2017.

amounted to war crimes.[178] Furthermore, the rights group argued that these attacks on civilians, particularly the unlawful killings and forced displacements, amounted to crimes against humanity as they were widespread and systematic and "appear[ed] to have been carried out as part of a government policy".[179] Additionally, evidence documented by the rights group suggested that government forces used chemical weapons in 32 attacks in the area of Jebel Marra during the same period, presumably causing the death of at least 200 people, mainly children,[180] and which also amounted to war crimes.[181]

Unilateral ceasefires in the Blue Nile and South Kordofan regions were announced in April by the Sudan Revolutionary Front, a coalition of four armed groups, and in June by President Omar al-Bashir.[182] Nevertheless, sporadic military attacks continued between government forces and the SPLM-N, including direct aerial and ground attacks by government forces on civilian objects, resulting in civilian casualties and the destruction of homes.[183] Government forces were also reported to have burned crops, looted food and displaced people from farming areas.[184]

Overall, humanitarian agencies continued to face serious restrictions of access in Darfur[185] and in Blue Nile and Southern Kordofan, where authorities have barred

[178] Amnesty International (2016) Scorched Earth, Poisoned Air. Sudanese Government Forces Ravage Jebel Marra, Darfur, p. 16. https://www.amnesty.org/en/documents/afr54/4877/2016/en/. Accessed 4 July 2017. See also Amnesty International (2017) Amnesty International Report 2016/17 – The State of the World's Human Rights, pp. 342–343. https://www.amnesty.org/en/latest/research/2017/02/amnesty-international-annual-report-201617/. Accessed 9 July 2017; Human Rights Watch (2017) World Report 2017 – Events of 2016, p. 561. https://www.hrw.org/world-report/2017. Accessed 9 July 2017; and UN General Assembly (2016c) Human Rights Council: Report of the Independent Expert on the situation of human rights in the Sudan, UN Doc. A/HRC/33/65, p. 9.

[179] Amnesty International (2016) Scorched Earth, Poisoned Air. Sudanese Government Forces Ravage Jebel Marra, Darfur, p. 18. https://www.amnesty.org/en/documents/afr54/4877/2016/en/. Accessed 4 July 2017.

[180] Ibid., p. 69.

[181] Ibid., p. 17.

[182] Amnesty International (2017) Amnesty International Report 2016/17 – The State of the World's Human Rights, p. 343. https://www.amnesty.org/en/latest/research/2017/02/amnesty-international-annual-report-201617/. Accessed 9 July 2017. See also UN General Assembly (2016c) Human Rights Council: Report of the Independent Expert on the situation of human rights in the Sudan, UN Doc. A/HRC/33/65, p. 11.

[183] Amnesty International (2017) Amnesty International Report 2016/17 – The State of the World's Human Rights, p. 343. https://www.amnesty.org/en/latest/research/2017/02/amnesty-international-annual-report-201617/. Accessed 9 July 2017.

[184] Human Rights Watch (2017) World Report 2017 – Events of 2016, p. 562. https://www.hrw.org/world-report/2017. Accessed 9 July 2017; see also UN General Assembly (2016c) Human Rights Council: Report of the Independent Expert on the situation of human rights in the Sudan, UN Doc. A/HRC/33/65, p. 11.

[185] UN Security Council (2017) Final Report of the panel of experts on the Sudan established pursuant to resolution 1591 (2005), UN Doc. S/2017/22, p. 23.

them from access to rebel-held areas[186] in an attempt by the government to reduce the role of the international humanitarian community in the country.[187] Both humanitarian workers and personnel and property of the UN – African Union Hybrid Operation in Darfur (UNAMID) were targeted by armed groups, although less frequently than in previous years.[188] Despite efforts by Sudanese authorities to restrict UNAMID's operations,[189] the UN Security Council decided to extend its mandate until 30 June 2017.[190]

Meanwhile, Sudanese authorities continued to refuse to execute an International Criminal Court arrest warrant against President Omar al-Bashir for war crimes, crimes against humanity and genocide.[191]

8.1.13 Syria

The conflict in Syria entered its fifth year in 2016.[192] Intra-Syrian peace talks concerning the conflict commenced but stalled in February 2016.[193] Brief ceasefires

---

[186] Human Rights Watch (2017) World Report 2017 – Events of 2016, p. 562. https://www.hrw.org/world-report/2017. Accessed 9 July 2017; restrictions on humanitarian access by the government notably included limitations on entry visas and renewal of residency permits, restrictions on movement and access denial. For more details on this, see UN General Assembly (2016c) Human Rights Council: Report of the Independent Expert on the situation of human rights in the Sudan, UN Doc. A/HRC/33/65, p. 10.

[187] UN General Assembly (2016c) Human Rights Council: Report of the Independent Expert on the situation of human rights in the Sudan, UN Doc. A/HRC/33/65, p. 10.

[188] UN Security Council (2017) Final Report of the panel of experts on the Sudan established pursuant to resolution 1591 (2005), UN Doc. S/2017/22, p. 24–25. For more details concerning attacks on UNAMID personnel and property, see UN Security Council (2016f) Report of the Secretary-General on the African Union – United Nations Hybrid Operation in Darfur, UN Doc. S/2016/1109, p. 7.

[189] Human Rights Watch (2017) World Report 2017 – Events of 2016, p. 566. https://www.hrw.org/world-report/2017. Accessed 9 July 2017.

[190] Ibid., p. 566; UN Security Council (2016i) Resolution 2296 (2016), UN Doc. S/RES/2296.

[191] Human Rights Watch (2017) World Report 2017 – Events of 2016, p. 566. https://www.hrw.org/world-report/2017. Accessed 9 July 2017; and Amnesty International (2017) Amnesty International Report 2016/17 – The State of the World's Human Rights, p. 343. https://www.amnesty.org/en/latest/research/2017/02/amnesty-international-annual-report-201617/. Accessed 9 July 2017.

[192] UN News Centre (2016) Syria: as conflict enters fifth year, UN-mediated peace talks resumed in Geneva. http://www.un.org/apps/news/story.asp?NewsID=53433&Kw1=Syria&Kw2=&Kw3. Accessed 2 March 2017.

[193] UN News Centre (2016) UN mediator suspends intra-Syrian talks for three weeks. http://www.un.org/apps/news/story.asp?NewsID=53159&Kw1=Syria&Kw2=&Kw3=#.WAYby4997cs. Accessed 2 March 2017.

were agreed in February[194] and September,[195] which led to a decrease in overall civilian deaths for the year.[196]

The Syrian conflict has had a significant effect on civilians. Alongside direct casualties of attacks, sieges and cities used as battlegrounds have been commonplace in the conflict leading to difficulties in providing humanitarian aid to civilians.[197] Numerous violations have been committed by all sides to the conflict including the targeting of civilians,[198] indiscriminate attacks[199] on civilian objects such as schools, hospitals and markets.[200] Numerous attacks have taken place against hospitals in 2016, which according to the UN are a gross disregard for civilian life and can amount to war crimes.[201] Numerous abuses have been carried out by Jabhat Al-Nusra and IS in Syria, including an attack against a Shia place of worship and a civilian neighbourhood on 21 February[202] and a series of car bombings and suicide attacks by IS near bus stations in Latakia governorate on 23 May.[203]

---

[194] UN News Centre (2016) Syria: diplomats agree "cessation of hostilities;" UN rights chief warns of dire situation in Aleppo. http://www.un.org/apps/news/story.asp?NewsID=53207&Kw1=Syria&Kw2=&Kw3=#.WAYeMY997cs. Accessed 2 March 2017.

[195] UN News Centre (2016) UN Special Envoy for Syria welcomes ceasefire understanding; pledges UN support. http://www.un.org/apps/news/story.asp?NewsID=54896&Kw1=Syria&Kw2=&Kw3. Accessed 2 March 2017.

[196] UN News Centre (2016) UN envoy: First full day of Syrian ceasefire sees "a significant drop in violence," but humanitarian access still needed. http://www.un.org/apps/news/story.asp?NewsID=54911&Kw1=Syria&Kw2=&Kw3. Accessed 2 March 2017.

[197] UN News Centre (2016) Civilians in embattled Yarmouk facing "starvation and dehydration," UN agency warns. http://www.un.org/apps/news/story.asp?NewsID=53700&Kw1=Syria&Kw2=&Kw3=#.WAYz3I997cs. Accessed 2 March 2017.

[198] UN News Centre (2016) UNICEF deplores "shocking" attacks in Northern Syria towns that leave scores of civilians dead. http://www.un.org/apps/news/story.asp?NewsID=54593&Kw1=Syria&Kw2=&Kw3=#.WAcwwI997cs. Accessed 2 March 2017.

[199] UN News Centre (2016) Syria: Deploring hostilities spreading across Aleppo, UN urges end to indiscriminate attacks. http://www.un.org/apps/news/story.asp?NewsID=54448&Kw1=Syria&Kw2=&Kw3=#.WAcu74997cs. Accessed 20 February 2017.

[200] UN News Centre (2016) UN chief condemns "abhorrent" attack on market in Syria's Idlib city. http://www.un.org/apps/news/story.asp?NewsID=54217&Kw1=Syria&Kw2=&Kw3=#.WAco_I997cs. Accessed 2 March 2017.

[201] UN News Centre (2016) "Monstrous disregard" for civilians, says UN rights chief, as hospitals bombed in Syria. http://www.un.org/apps/news/story.asp?NewsID=53818&Kw1=Syria&Kw2=&Kw3. Accessed 2 March 2017.

[202] Aljazeera (2016) ISIL car bomb attacks kill 129 in Damascus and Homs. http://www.aljazeera.com/news/2016/02/attacks-kill-scores-syria-damascus-homs-160221152344662.html. Accessed 2 March 2017.

[203] The Guardian (2016) Scores dead in ISIS attacks on Syrian coastal cities. https://www.theguardian.com/world/2016/may/23/explosions-hit-syrian-coastal-cities. Accessed 2 March 2017.

Reports continued to emerge of suspected use of toxic gas,[204] despite Syria becoming a member of the Organisation for the Prohibition of Chemical Weapons (OPCW) and the work carried out by the Joint Investigative Mechanism.[205] These include allegations concerning the use of chemical weapons against opposition forces and civilians by government forces in the battle of Aleppo.[206]

On 19 September, an airstrike was carried out on a humanitarian aid convoy and Syrian Red Crescent warehouse.[207] This would amount to a violation of international humanitarian law if deliberate and if it further exasperated the suffering of the civilians through the destruction of aid and the risk posed to those providing assistance.[208] The UN Secretary-General subsequently established a probe to investigate the attack.[209]

Government forces regained significant portions of Aleppo during 2016. However, the city and humanitarian situation have rapidly deteriorated.[210] Civilians feared reprisals if they fled to government held territories[211] and reports have emerged of disappearances and arrests of men and boys, as well as executions of civilians.[212] The Battle of Aleppo drew global outcry at the cost to civilians and the UN Security Council met for a special session to discuss the grave human rights situation in Aleppo but failed to adopt a resolution.[213] On 21 October, a Human Rights Council resolution was adopted mandating the Syrian Commission of Inquiry to conduct a "comprehensive, independent, special inquiry" into the events

---

[204] Human Rights Watch (2016) Syria: Coordinated Chemical Attacks on Aleppo. https://www.hrw.org/news/2017/02/13/syria-coordinated-chemical-attacks-aleppo. Accessed 2 March 2017.

[205] For further discussion of the use of toxic gas in Syria and the Joint Investigative Mechanism (JIM) findings, see Sect. 8.3.2.1 of this chapter.

[206] Human Rights Watch (2017) Syria: Coordinated Chemical Attacks on Aleppo. https://www.hrw.org/news/2017/02/13/syria-coordinated-chemical-attacks-aleppo. Accessed 2 March 2017.

[207] UN News Centre (2016) UN Officials condemn attack against aid convoy and warehouse in rural Aleppo. http://www.un.org/apps/news/story.asp?NewsID=54969&Kw1=Syria&Kw2=&Kw3=#.WAc1sY997cs. Accessed 2 March 2017.

[208] News24 (2016) UN suspends all humanitarian convoys in Syria after attack. http://www.news24.com/World/News/un-suspends-all-humanitarian-convoys-in-syria-after-attack-20160920. Accessed 2 March 2017.

[209] UN (2016) Secretary-General Creates Inquiry Board to Investigate Incident Involving United Nations-Syrian Arab Red Crescent Relief Convoy Near Aleppo. http://www.un.org/press/en/2016/sgsm18220.doc.htm. Accessed 2 March 2017.

[210] UN News Centre (2016) UN officials alarmed by closure of access route in Eastern Aleppo; call for humanitarian truce. http://www.un.org/apps/news/story.asp?NewsID=54526&Kw1=Syria&Kw2=&Kw3. Accessed 2 March 2017.

[211] Reuters (2016) Syrian general says Aleppo offensive in final stages. http://www.reuters.com/article/us-mideast-crisis-syria-idUSKBN1410LA. Accessed 2 March 2017.

[212] BBC News (2016) Aleppo battle: UN says hundreds of men missing. http://www.bbc.com/news/world-middle-east-38260388. Accessed 2 March 2017.

[213] UN News Centre (2016) Security Council fails to adopt resolutions on ending violence in war-torn Syria's eastern Aleppo. http://www.un.org/apps/news/story.asp?NewsID=55246&Kw1=Syria&Kw2=&Kw3=#.WAc5Oo997cs. Accessed 2 March 2017.

in Aleppo and identify the perpetrators of the alleged violations and attacks.[214] Intense aerial bombing of the city by Syrian and Russian forces destroyed all medical care facilities, wiped out market places and bakeries and resulted in thousands of civilian deaths.[215] This, in combination with the blockade on humanitarian access into rebel held areas, caused severe civilian suffering and possible violations of international humanitarian law. The Russian and Turkish governments eventually negotiated a ceasefire agreement at the start of December concerning the evacuation of civilians and rebels in Aleppo.[216]

Human Rights Watch recorded the use of internationally banned cluster munitions by government forces and Russian forces. Government forces also used incendiary weapons. However, Syria is not a party to the Convention on Certain Conventional Weapons protocol outlawing the use of these weapons.[217] The Syrian Network for Human Rights reported on the extensive use of barrel bombs in Syria in 2016, which is an indiscriminate weapon and causes civilian death and destruction. The Network recorded the use of 12 958 barrel bombs by government forces in 2016 in their monthly reports.[218]

Concern had been expressed regarding the YPG's (Kurdish forces) use of child soldiers. While they pledged to stop the practice[219] and there had been a decrease in use with disciplinary procedures against officials who recruit child soldiers, the practice still continued.[220]

8.1.14 Ukraine

The armed conflict between the government of Ukraine and pro-Russian separatist forces of the self-proclaimed People's Republics of Donetsk and Luhansk

---

[214] UN General Assembly (2016h) Resolution adopted by the General Assembly on 5 December 2016: 71/49. United action with renewed determination towards the total elimination of nuclear weapons, UN Doc. A/RES/71/49. Accessed 2 March 2017.

[215] Reuters (2016) Battle of Aleppo ends after years of bloodshed with rebel withdrawal. http://www.reuters.com/article/us-mideast-crisis-syria-idUSKBN1420H5; The Guardian (2016) Aleppo hospital bombed again as Assad vows to "clean" city. https://www.theguardian.com/world/2016/oct/14/syrian-regime-bombs-hospital-again-assad-vows-clean-aleppo. Accessed 2 March 2017.

[216] Ibid.

[217] Human Rights Watch (2016) Russia/Syria: War Crimes in Month of Bombing Aleppo. https://www.hrw.org/news/2016/12/01/russia/syria-war-crimes-month-bombing-aleppo. Accessed 2 March 2017.

[218] Syrian Network for Human Rights (2016) No less than 12,958 Barrel Bombs Dropped in 2016. http://sn4hr.org/blog/2017/01/09/30900/. Accessed 2 March 2017.

[219] Human Rights Watch (2015) Letter from YPG in Response to Human Rights Watch. https://www.hrw.org/news/2015/07/23/letter-ypg-response-human-rights-watch. Accessed 2 March 2017.

[220] Daily Sabah (2016) US-backed PYD abducts 6 children in north eastern Syria. https://www.dailysabah.com/war-on-terror/2016/05/16/us-backed-pyd-abducts-6-children-in-northeastern-syria. Accessed 2 March 2017.

continued in 2016 in the eastern part of the country.[221] Although the Minsk II Agreements signed in February 2015 resulted in a significant decrease in hostilities,[222] the situation remained tense throughout the year, as skirmishes and exchanges of artillery fire continued.[223] Violence peaked in the summer of 2016,[224] when the OHCHR recorded 188 civilian casualties, including 28 killed between 16 May and 15 August.[225] During that period, the OHCHR observed a "continued disregard for civilian protection by government forces and armed groups" and noted that both parties had been positioning their fighters and weapons and engaged in hostilities in residential areas.[226] Notably, the OHCHR observed that educational and health facilities had been used by government forces and armed groups and that hospitals had been frequently hit by artillery fire during the summer.[227]

On 21 September 2016, a few days after the announcement of a renewed ceasefire,[228] the government of Ukraine and representatives of certain areas of the Donetsk and Luhansk regions agreed to a Framework Decision to disengage their forces and hardware in three specific areas along the contact line.[229] The Organization for Security and Co-operation in Europe (OSCE) Special Monitoring Mission to Ukraine (SMM), which has seen its mandate extended until 31 March 2017,[230] was designated to monitor the disengagement process.[231] Despite an initial

---

[221] Bellal A (2017) The War Report – Armed Conflicts in 2016, p. 94. https://www.geneva-academy.ch/joomlatools-files/docman-files/TheWarReport2016.pdf. Accessed 9 July 2017.

[222] Human Rights Watch (2017) World Report 2017 – Events of 2016, p. 621. https://www.hrw.org/world-report/2017. Accessed 9 July 2017.

[223] Ibid., p. 621; See also Amnesty International (2017) Amnesty International Report 2016/17 – The State of the World's Human Rights, p. 376. https://www.amnesty.org/en/latest/research/2017/02/amnesty-international-annual-report-201617/. Accessed 9 July 2017.

[224] Bellal A (2017) The War Report – Armed Conflicts in 2016. https://www.geneva-academy.ch/joomlatools-files/docman-files/TheWarReport2016.pdf. Accessed 9 July 2017, p. 99; see also DW (2016) With fresh violence in Ukraine, is there hope for a solution? http://www.dw.com/en/with-fresh-violence-in-ukraine-is-there-hope-for-a-solution/a-19451997. Accessed 2 July 2017.

[225] OHCHR (2016) Report on the human rights situation in Ukraine, 16 May to 15 August 2016, p. 12. http://www.ohchr.org/Documents/Countries/UA/UAReport16th_EN.pdf. Accessed 2 July 2017.

[226] Ibid., p. 5 and 10.

[227] See ibid., p. 11. In its report, the OHCHR notes two incidents where hospitals were hit by artillery fire during the period under review, on 24 June and 23 July.

[228] DW (2016) New ceasefire announced for eastern Ukraine. http://www.dw.com/en/new-ceasefire-announced-for-eastern-ukraine/a-19550920. Accessed 2 July 2017.

[229] OSCE (2016) Special Representative of the OSCE Chairperson-in-Office in Ukraine Sajdik welcomes Framework Decision on Disengagement of Forces and Hardware, p. 12. http://www.osce.org/cio/266331. Accessed 2 July 2017.

[230] OSCE (2016) OSCE Chief Monitor in Ukraine welcomes extension of Special Monitoring Mission's mandate. http://www.osce.org/ukraine-smm/223406. Accessed 2 June 2017.

[231] Bellal A (2017) The War Report – Armed Conflicts in 2016, p. 100. https://www.geneva-academy.ch/joomlatools-files/docman-files/TheWarReport2016.pdf. Accessed 9 July 2017; see also DW (2016) Ukraine and Russian-backed rebels agree to pullback of troops. http://www.dw.com/en/ukraine-and-russian-backed-rebels-agree-to-pullback-of-troops/a-19567017. Accessed 2 July 2017.

de-escalation of hostilities in the area covered by the Framework Decision,[232] in the last months of the year exchange of fire continued in certain areas along the contact line, posing a great risk for civilians, who continued notably to suffer the consequences of damage to vital public infrastructure.[233] According to the UN Office for the Coordination of Humanitarian Affairs (OCHA), about 3.8 million people were in need of humanitarian assistance in Ukraine at the end of 2016, compared to 0.7 million earlier in the year.[234] Furthermore, the UN estimated that 9 598 people had been killed as a result of the armed conflict in Ukraine between mid-April 2014 and 30 November 2016,[235] of which at least 2000 were civilians.[236]

Meanwhile, the Dutch-led Joint Investigation Team (JIT) which had been examining the circumstances surrounding the crash of Malaysia Airlines flight MH17, downed over eastern Ukraine on 17 July 2014 while flying from Amsterdam to Kuala Lumpur and killing all 298 people on board, concluded that it was hit by a "Buk missile that came from the territory of the Russian Federation."[237] The JIT further concluded that this missile was fired from a territory controlled by the pro-Russian separatists.[238] These findings were denied by Russia.[239]

8.1.15 Yemen

Yemen has been involved in an armed conflict since March 2015 between the Houthi rebels and the pro-government forces.[240] In 2016, this conflict continued,

[232] OHCHR (2016) Report on the human rights situation in Ukraine, 16 August to 15 November 2016, p. 8. http://www.ohchr.org/Documents/Countries/UA/UAReport16th_EN.pdf. Accessed 2 July 2017.

[233] Ibid., p. 5 and 9.

[234] OCHA (2016) Humanitarian Bulletin, Ukraine, Issue 15, 1 October–31 December 2016, p. 1. http://reliefweb.int/sites/reliefweb.int/files/resources/ukraine_humanitarian_bulletin_issue_15_oct_dec_2016_en.pdf. Accessed 2 June 2017; see also UN News Centre (2016) Millions in Ukraine are in need of humanitarian assistance, UN relief wing reports. http://www.un.org/apps/news/story.asp?NewsID=55895#.WV1TEWV0WRs. Accessed 2 June 2017.

[235] OCHA (2016) Humanitarian Bulletin, Ukraine, Issue 15, 1 October–31 December 2016, p. 1–2. http://reliefweb.int/sites/reliefweb.int/files/resources/ukraine_humanitarian_bulletin_issue_15_oct_dec_2016_en.pdf. Accessed 2 June 2017.

[236] Ibid.; and OHCHR (2016) Report on the human rights situation in Ukraine 16 August to 15 November 2016. http://www.ohchr.org/Documents/Countries/UA/UAReport16th_EN.pdf. Accessed 2 June 2017.

[237] BBC News (2016) MH17 missile "came from Russia", Dutch-led investigators say. http://www.bbc.com/news/world-europe-37495067. Accessed 2 June 2017.

[238] Ibid.

[239] Ibid.

[240] BBC News (2016) Yemen crisis: Who is fighting whom? http://www.bbc.com/news/world-middle-east-29319423. Accessed 12 March 2017.

with increased airstrikes carried out by the Saudi-led coalition and concerns arising of human rights and international humanitarian law violations.[241] One of the deadliest strikes by the coalition took place on 9 October and killed 140 civilians attending a funeral.[242] Due to concerns expressed by various parties including the UN Secretary-General at the time, Ban Ki-Moon, an investigative body was subsequently set up to establish whether the strike amounted to a violation of international humanitarian law and potentially a war crime.[243] A report by the UN monitor on 17 October found the strike to be in violation of international humanitarian law.[244] Rights groups have raised concerns regarding another airstrike led by the Saudi-led coalition on a prison in Hudaydah on 30 October resulting in the deaths of 60 rebels and inmates.[245]

The Saudi-led coalition was added to the "list of shame" by the UN Secretary-General for grave violations against children during armed conflict. Saudi Arabia was, however, later removed on 6 June pending conclusions of a "joint-review".[246] Human rights groups have raised concerns about possible war crimes being committed by the Saudi-led coalition during its airstrikes on Yemen, through indiscriminate and disproportionate attacks and also the use of internationally banned cluster munition.[247] The OHCHR stated that the Saudi-led coalition is responsible for 60% of civilian deaths since the start of its airstrikes in March

[241] UN News Centre (2016) Yemen: civilian casualties top 8,100 as airstrikes and shelling continues, UN reports. http://www.un.org/apps/news/story.asp?NewsID=52938&Kw1=Yemen&Kw2=&Kw3=#.WAc-Y4997cs. Accessed 2 March 2017.

[242] Reuters (2016) Attack on mourners in Yemen kills more than 140, say local health officials. http://www.reuters.com/article/us-yemen-security-airstrike-idUSKCN1280OR/. Accessed 2 March 2017; BBC News (2016) More than 140 killed by air strikes at Yemen funeral. http://www.bbc.com/news/world-middle-east-37599433. Accessed 2 March 2017; Human Rights Watch (2016) Yemen: Saudi-Led Funeral Attack Apparent War Crime. https://www.hrw.org/news/2016/10/13/yemen-saudi-led-funeral-attack-apparent-war-crime. Accessed 2 March 2017.

[243] UN News Centre (2016) Latest horrific incident in Yemen demands "a full inquiry", Ban says, urging probe into funeral. http://www.un.org/apps/news/story.asp?NewsID=55255&Kw1=Yemen&Kw2=&Kw3=#.WAdtqY997cs. Accessed 2 March 2017.

[244] Reuters (2016) Saudi coalition violated law with Yemen funeral strike: U.N. monitors. http://www.reuters.com/article/us-yemen-security-saudi-un-idUSKCN12K2F1. Accessed 2 March 2017.

[245] BBC News (2016) Yemen conflict: Dozens killed as air strikes hit prison in Hudaydah. http://www.bbc.com/news/world-middle-east-37813569. Accessed 2 March 2017.

[246] The Telegraph (2016) UN removes Saudi-led coalition in Yemen from black list of childkillers under diplomatic pressure. http://www.telegraph.co.uk/news/2016/06/06/un-removes-saudi-led-coalition-in-yemen-from-black-list-of-child/. Accessed 2 March 2017.

[247] Human Rights Watch (2016) UN: Return Saudi-led Coalition to "List of Shame". https://www.hrw.org/news/2016/06/08/un-return-saudi-led-coalition-list-shame. Accessed 2 March 2017; The Telegraph (2017) UN experts say Yemen opponents may have committed war crimes. http://www.telegraph.co.uk/news/2017/01/31/un-experts-say-yemen-opponents-may-have-committed-war-crimes/. Accessed 9 March 2017.

2015.[248] The coalition defended its strikes in an August 2016 report by an investigative body which noted the presence of armed militiamen at civilian gatherings.[249] In May, the Obama administration suspended transfer of cluster munitions to Saudi Arabia after reports of use in civilian areas in Yemen. Yemen, Saudi Arabia and other coalition states are not party to the 2008 Convention on Cluster Munitions. Yemen was added to the US list of countries, where sale of arms is restricted by the US Child Soldiers Prevention Act.[250]

Although peace talks were conducted in an effort to bring the conflict to an end, these collapsed as the peace proposal was rejected by the Hadi government due to concessions made to rebels.[251] The Yemeni government considered the recognition of the Houthi government proposed in the peace proposal a "dangerous precedent" to encourage coups.[252] Fighting continued on the ground for the duration of the peace talks from April to August.[253]

Overall, attacks on civilians have been prevalent throughout Yemen during the conflict. On 15 March an airstrike was carried out on a Hajja market in Northern Yemen, killing at least 41 civilians.[254] The city of Taiz, in south-western Yemen, has been the subject of indiscriminate attacks carried out against civilians and militants on both sides of the conflict.[255] Mwatana Organisation for Human Rights, an independent Yemeni organisation, released a report in November documenting the international humanitarian law violations, including war crimes and a blockade preventing civilians from receiving food, water and medical supplies, which had

---

248 Reuters (2016) U.S. to halt some arms sales in Saudi, citing civilian deaths in Yemen campaign. http://www.reuters.com/article/us-usa-saudiarabia-yemen-exclusive-idUSKBN1421UK. Accessed 2 March 2017; Reuters (2016) Transparency, accountability, needed on Saudi airstrikes in Yemen: U.N. http://www.reuters.com/article/us-yemen-security-un-idUSKCN1100RP. Accessed 15 March 2017.

249 Reuters (2016) Saudi investigation largely defends deadly airstrikes in Yemen. http://www.reuters.com/article/us-yemen-security-saudi-airstrikes-idUSKCN10F23J. Accessed 15 March 2017.

250 BBC News (2016) Yemen conflict: US cuts arms sales to Saudi Arabia. http://www.bbc.com/news/world-us-canada-38310870. Accessed 2 March 2017.

251 Aljazeera (2016) Yemen peace talks collapse as fighting intensifies. http://www.aljazeera.com/news/2016/08/yemen-peace-talks-collapse-fighting-intensifies-160807042106210.html. Accessed 2 March 2017.

252 Reuters (2016) Yemen says U.N. roadmap to end conflict sets "dangerous precedent". http://www.reuters.com/article/us-yemen-security-un-idUSKBN13W03V. Accessed 9 March 2017.

253 UN News Centre (2016) Yemen: UN-mediated peace talks continuing amid "worrying" breaches of cessation of hostilities. http://www.un.org/apps/news/story.asp?NewsID=53866&Kw1=Yemen&Kw2=&Kw3=#.WAdrGY997cs. Accessed 2 March 2017.

254 BBC News (2016) Yemen conflict: "Dozens killed" in strike on Hajja market. http://www.bbc.com/news/world-middle-east-35816958. Accessed 2 March 2017.

255 UN News Centre (2016) Yemen: UN says shelling of Taiz leaves dozens of civilian casualties. http://www.un.org/apps/news/story.asp?NewsID=55202&Kw1=Yemen&Kw2=&Kw3=#.WAdtmY997cs. Accessed 2 March 2017.

taken place in Taiz between April 2015 and March 2016.[256] Human Rights Watch released a report in September condemning the use of anti-personnel landmines by Houthi forces due to the high number of civilian deaths.[257] Furthermore, attacks have also been carried out on the already struggling medical facilities in Yemen, including an airstrike on 15 August by the Saudi-led coalition airstrike, which hit a Médecins Sans Frontières-supported hospital in Hajja.[258] The denial of access to humanitarian assistance, unlawful detentions, and kidnappings and killings of aid workers is adding to the suffering being endured by the civilians of Yemen.[259] Houthis, government and pro-government forces have endangered schools[260] and used child soldiers. UNICEF estimates that around one third of fighters in the conflict are children.[261]

8.2 Tribunals and Courts

8.2.1 International Tribunals

8.2.1.1 International Criminal Tribunal for the Former Yugoslavia

In 2016, the President of the International Criminal Tribunal for the former Yugoslavia (ICTY) stated that the Tribunal "stands firm in its commitment to close its doors by the end of 2017", with only one case in the trial phase and one in the appellate phase at the end of 2016.[262] Contempt proceedings in the *Jojić et al.* case

[256] Mwatana (2016) Chapters from Hell: Violations of International Humanitarian Law in the Armed Ground Conflict in Taiz. http://mwatana.org/sites/default/files/pdf/Executive%20Summary%20-Chapters%20from%20Hell-%20Taiz.pdf. Accessed 2 March 2017.

[257] Human Rights Watch (2016) Yemen: Houthi Landmines Claim Civilian Victims. https://www.hrw.org/news/2016/09/08/yemen-houthi-landmines-claim-civilian-victims. Accessed 2 March 2017.

[258] Doctors without Borders (2016) Yemen: Death Toll Rises to 19 in Airstrike on MSF-Supported Hospital. http://www.doctorswithoutborders.org/article/yemen-death-toll-rises-19-airstrike-msf-supported-hospital. Accessed 2 March 2017.

[259] ICRC (2016) Yemen: Desperate situation for civilians trapped by intense fighting in Taiz. https://www.icrc.org/en/document/yemen-desperate-situation-civilians-trapped-intense-fighting-taiz. Accessed 2 March 2017.

[260] UN News Centre (2016) UN chief condemns attack on school in Yemen that killed at least 10 children. http://www.un.org/apps/news/story.asp?NewsID=54680&Kw1=Yemen&Kw2=&Kw3. Accessed 2 March 2017.

[261] The Independent (2016) Child soldiers make up a third of Yemeni fighters, says UNICEF. http://www.independent.co.uk/news/world/politics/child-soldiers-make-up-a-third-of-yemeni-fighters-says-unicef-a6861341.html. Accessed 9 March 2017.

[262] UN Security Council (2016e) Letter dated 17 November 2016 from the President of the International Tribunal for the Prosecution of Persons Responsible for Serious Violations of International Humanitarian Law Committed in the Territory of the Former Yugoslavia since 1991, addressed to the President of the Security Council, UN Doc. S/2016/976, paras 3 and 7.

likewise remained ongoing in the pre-trial phase, with President Agius informing the UN Security Council that Serbia had failed to execute arrest warrants in this case.[263] The *Hadžić* case was terminated this year following the death of Goran Hadžić on 12 July.[264] Mr. Hadžić had been on trial for crimes against humanity and was the former President of Serbian Krajina, a self-proclaimed republic located in Croatia.[265]

Trial Phase

On 24 March, Trial Chamber III convicted Radovan Karadžić of all but count 1 of the indictment and sentenced him to 40 years' imprisonment in a 2615-page judgment consisting of four volumes, in which the case itself was described as "unprecedented".[266] Mr. Karadžić was the President of the National Security Council of the Serbian Republic of Bosnia and Herzegovina in 1992, one of the Presidents of the Serbian Republic of Bosnia and Herzegovina in 1992, and he became the President and Supreme Commander of the armed forces of Republika Srpska in December 1992.[267] His indictment contained eleven counts, including two concerning genocide, five focusing on crimes against humanity, and four alleging violations of the laws or customs of war, and he was accused of participating in four related joint criminal enterprises (JCEs), namely, an "Overarching JCE", the "Sarajevo JCE", the "Hostages JCE" and the "Srebrenica JCE".[268]

In relation to the Overarching JCE, the Trial Chamber ultimately found that there was an armed conflict in Bosnia and Herzegovina that started in early April 1992 at the latest and saw Serb forces take over the Municipalities.[269] The Trial Chamber held that there "existed a widespread and systematic attack against the Bosnian Muslim and Bosnian Croat civilian populations [...] at all times relevant to the crimes charged in the indictment", including crimes such as murder, rape, torture and forced displacement.[270] It found, *inter alia*, that murder, extermination, deportation and inhumane acts (forcible transfer), and persecution as crimes against

[263] ICTY (2016) Address to the United Nations Security Council Judge Carmel Agius, President of the International Criminal Tribunal for the Former Yugoslavia, 8 December 2016, p. 3. http://www.icty.org/x/file/Press/Statements%20and%20Speeches/President/161208_president_agius_un_sc_en.pdf. Accessed 23 February 2017.

[264] ICTY, *Prosecutor v Goran Hadžić*, Order Terminating the Proceedings, 22 July 2016, Case No. IT-04-75-T.

[265] ICTY (2016) Proceedings against Goran Hadžić terminated following his death. http://www.icty.org/en/press/proceedings-against-goran-had%C5%BEi%C4%87-terminated-following-his-death. Accessed 23 February 2017.

[266] ICTY, *Prosecutor v Radovan Karadžić*, Public Redacted Version of Judgment Issued on 24 March 2016, Case No. IT-95-5/18-T (*Karadžić*), paras 6–7 and 6071–6072.

[267] Ibid., para 2.

[268] Ibid., paras 3 and 5.

[269] Ibid., para 2440.

[270] Ibid., paras 2443–2444.

humanity had taken place.[271] In determining whether Mr. Karadžić was criminally responsible for these crimes, factors such as his significant contribution to the JCE, which existed between October 1991 and November 1995 and aimed to remove Bosnian Muslims and Croats from Bosnian Serb claimed territory,[272] as well as his awareness that crimes may be committed in carrying out the JCE and his acceptance of that risk, were considered and ultimately held to give rise to his individual criminal responsibility.[273]

However, in relation to count 1, which concerned allegations of genocide in seven of the Municipalities, the Trial Chamber was "not satisfied that the evidence [...] [showed] an intent to physically destroy a part of [...]" the protected groups of Bosnian Muslims and Bosnian Serbs on behalf of the JCE.[274] The Trial Chamber noted, for example, that while the rhetoric used was "certainly highly inflammatory" and consistent with the "Bosnian Serb objective of ethnic separation and the forceful creation of an ethnically homogenous state", the evidence presented did not lead to the only reasonable inference that the members of the JCE sought to physically destroy these protected groups in the Municipalities.[275] Accordingly, Mr. Karadžić was acquitted on this count.[276]

In contrast to the findings with regards to the Municipalities, the Trial Chamber found sufficient evidence to prove that Bosnian Serb Forces intended to destroy the Bosnian Muslims, a protected group, in Srebrenica.[277] It concluded that Mr. Karadžić was responsible for this genocide as he significantly contributed to the common purpose of the JCE, namely the elimination of the Bosnian Muslims in Srebrenica, and subsequently did not punish his subordinates who also committed crimes.[278] Other members of this JCE included Ratko Mladić, Ljubiša Beara and Vujadin Popović.[279] Additional convictions in relation to the Sarajevo JCE, which existed between May 1992 and October 1995 and which used sniping and shelling to instil terror in civilians living in Sarajevo, and the hostage taking JCE, which existed between May and June 1995 and which aimed to take UN personnel hostage in order to compel NATO to halt air strikes, were also entered.[280] The Trial Chamber sentenced the accused to 40 years' imprisonment, and Judges Morrison

[271] Ibid., paras 2456, 2463, 2481, 2484, 2518, 2521, 2530, 2547, 2559 and 2570.
[272] Ibid., para 5996.
[273] Ibid., para 3524.
[274] Ibid., para 2596.
[275] Ibid., paras 2599, 2605 and 2626.
[276] Ibid., para 6071.
[277] Ibid., para 5673.
[278] Ibid., paras 5489 and 5850.
[279] Ibid., para 5998.
[280] Ibid., paras 4618–4619, 4628, 4635, 4937–4940, 5951, 5993–5991, 5997 and 5999.

and Baird appended dissenting opinions.[281] Mr. Karadžić subsequently appealed his convictions before the Mechanism for International Criminal Tribunals.[282]

The second judgment delivered during 2016 at trial level was the acquittal of Vojislav Šešelj on 31 March.[283] The judgment, which considered Mr. Šešelj's guilt in relation to committing, inciting, aiding or abetting three counts of crimes against humanity and six counts of war crimes,[284] received a mixed response amongst the international community[285] and included both a concurring and partially dissenting opinion.[286] The accused was the President of the Serbian Radical Party (SRS) and a Serbian parliamentarian, and the charges related to crimes "attributed to the Serbian protagonists in the conflict during the period from August 1991 to September 1993" and Mr. Šešelj's alleged membership in a JCE that included individuals such as Slobodan Milošević.[287]

In finding the accused not guilty, the majority of judges, *inter alia*, criticised the "maximalist" approach undertaken by the Prosecution in relation to charging and its choice of evidence,[288] found that the accused was not in control of recruited SRS volunteers during military operations nor in control of other paramilitary groups,[289] and held that the Prosecution had failed to prove that a general or systematic attack against non-Serb civilian populations in Croatia and Bosnia and Herzegovina had occurred, thus preventing a finding of crimes against humanity.[290] In relation to the war crimes charges, while the Trial Chamber found there had been an armed conflict in Croatia and Bosnia and Herzegovina in which crimes may have been committed by Serb forces,[291] it held that the Prosecution had failed to prove that

[281] Ibid., paras 6070 and 6074–6119.

[282] MICT, *Prosecutor v Radovan Karadžić*, Radovan Karadzic's Notice of Appeal, 22 July 2016, Case No. MICT-13-55-A (*Karadžić* Appeal); see discussion below in Sect. 8.2.1.2 of this chapter.

[283] ICTY, *Prosecutor v Vojislav Šešelj*, Jugement, 31 March 2016, Case No. IT-03-67-T (*Šešelj*).

[284] ICTY (2016) Trial Judgment in the case of Vojislav Šešelj delivered. http://www.icty.org/en/press/trial-judgement-in-the-case-of-vojislav-seselj-delivered. Accessed 22 February 2017.

[285] See, e.g., Milanovic M (2016) The Sorry Acquittal of Vojislav Seselj. http://www.ejiltalk.org/the-sorry-acquittal-of-vojislav-seselj/. Accessed 22 February 2017; Gordon G (2016) Vojislav Šešelj's Acquittal at the ICTY: Law in an Alternate Universe. http://www.jurist.org/forum/2016/04/gregory-gordon-seselj-acquittal.php. Accessed 22 February 2017; and Bowcott O (2016) Serb nationalist Vojislav Šešelj acquitted of war crimes at The Hague. https://www.theguardian.com/law/2016/mar/31/serb-nationalist-vojislav-seselj-acquitted-war-crimes-crimes-against-humanity-icty-the-hague. Accessed 22 February 2017.

[286] ICTY, *Prosecutor v Vojislav Šešelj*, Opinion Concordante du Judge Jean-Claude Antonetti, Président de la Chamber, Jointe au Jugement, 31 March 2016, Case No. IT-03-67-T; and ICTY, *Prosecutor v Vojislav Šešelj*, Opinion Partiellement Dissidente de la Juge Flavia Lattanzi – Version Corrigée, 31 March 2016, Case No. IT-03-67-T.

[287] ICTY (2016) Trial Judgement Summary for Vojislav Šešelj, p. 1. http://www.icty.org/x/cases/seselj/tjug/en/160331_judgement_summary.pdf. Accessed 22 February 2017.

[288] *Šešelj*, above n 283, paras 14–19 and 195.

[289] Ibid., paras 116 and 118–184.

[290] Ibid., para 192.

[291] Ibid., para 201.

certain crimes had occurred[292] and, for those crimes proven,[293] the Prosecution had not demonstrated the existence of a JCE[294] or the accused's individual criminal responsibility for these crimes via other modes of liability.[295] The Prosecution subsequently appealed this verdict at the Mechanism for International Criminal Tribunals.[296]

The only ongoing trial remaining at the ICTY is the *Mladić* case, which concerns Ratko Mladić's alleged responsibility via participation in JCEs for crimes against humanity and violations of the laws or customs of war.[297] In this case, closing arguments were heard in December and a judgment is expected in November 2017.[298]

Appeals Phase

The ICTY's Appeals Chamber delivered its judgment in the *Stanišić and Župljanin* case on 30 June, upholding Mićo Stanišić's and Stojan Župljanin's convictions and 22-year sentences of imprisonment.[299] Mr. Stanišić held various positions of authority in the Republika Srpska and Mr. Župljanin held leadership roles in security and crisis services in Banja Luka and the Autonomous Region of Krajina.[300] Both had been convicted, via their participation in a JCE, of persecution as a crime against humanity, and "murder and torture as violations of the laws or customs of war", with Mr. Župljanin receiving additional convictions for "extermination as a crime against humanity [...] and for ordering persecutions through plunder of property".[301] On appeal, Mr. Stanišić put forward 16 appellate grounds, arguing, *inter alia*, that the Trial Chamber had failed to provide a reasoned opinion, had made errors as regards its findings regarding the JCE and had failed to afford

[292] Ibid., paras 203–204.

[293] Ibid., paras 205–220.

[294] Ibid., para 281.

[295] Ibid., paras 285, 350 and 357.

[296] MICT, *Prosecutor v Vojislav Šešelj*, Prosecution's Notice of Appeal, 2 May 2016, Case No. MICT-16-99 (*Šešelj* Appeal); see discussion below in Sect. 8.2.1.2 of this chapter.

[297] ICTY (2016) Case Information Sheet: Ratko Mladić. http://www.icty.org/x/cases/mladic/cis/en/cis_mladic_en.pdf. Accessed 23 February 2017.

[298] ICTY (2016) Ratko Mladić Case – Key Information & Timeline. http://www.icty.org/en/cases/ratko-mladic-case-key-information-timeline. Accessed 23 February 2017; ICTY (2016) Address of Mr. Serge Brammertz, Prosecutor, International Criminal Tribunal for the Former Yugoslavia and Mechanism for International Criminal Tribunals to the United Nations Security Council, p. 1. http://www.icty.org/x/file/Press/Statements%20and%20Speeches/Prosecutor/161208_prosecutor_brammertz_un_sc_en.pdf. Accessed 22 February 2017.

[299] ICTY, *Prosecutor v Mićo Stanišić and Stojan Župljanin*, Judgment, 30 June 2016, Case No. IT-08-91-A (*Stanišić and Župljanin*); ICTY (2016) Appeals Chamber affirms Stanišić and Župljanin's sentences. http://www.icty.org/en/press/appeals-chamber-affirms-stanisic-and-zupljanin-sentences. Accessed 23 February 2017.

[300] *Stanišić and Župljanin*, above n 299, paras 2–3.

[301] Ibid., para 6.

him a fair trial.[302] Mr. Župljanin identified six grounds of appeal, concerning, *inter alia*, the Trial Chamber's findings regarding the JCE, his sentence and whether he received a fair trial.[303] The Prosecutor likewise raised two grounds of appeal, suggesting that the Trial Chamber had imposed an inadequate sentence and had failed to enter cumulative convictions for the other crimes for which they had been found responsible.[304]

In dismissing the majority of the grounds brought by Mr. Stanišić and Mr. Župljanin, the Appeals Chamber held, *inter alia*, that they had failed to prove that a reasonable observer would believe Judge Harhoff to be biased,[305] and that the Trial Chamber had not erred in its findings regarding the common criminal purpose of the JCE or the accused's membership in the JCE.[306] The Appeals Chamber found several errors in the Trial Chamber's reasoning concerning Mr. Stanišić's and Mr. Župljanin's participation in the JCE but held that these did not justify the alteration of their convictions or sentences.[307] It also upheld the Prosecutor's appeal with regard to cumulative convictions, but ultimately declined to enter the additional convictions.[308]

The ICTY's only other remaining case in the appeals phase is that of *Prlić et al.* which features seven appellants, including the Prosecution, and over 500 grounds and sub-grounds of appeal.[309] The six accused persons were originally convicted in May 2013 of "crimes against humanity and war crimes committed in Bosnia and Herzegovina between 1992 and 1994".[310] The appellate judgment in this case is expected in November 2017.[311]

8.2.1.2 Mechanism for International Criminal Tribunals

In 2016, the Mechanism for International Criminal Tribunals (MICT) continued its work, namely completing remaining judicial work, managing archives and witness protection, supervising sentences and assisting national jurisdictions, and it opened

[302] Ibid., para 7.
[303] Ibid., para 10.
[304] Ibid., para 13.
[305] Ibid., paras 57–58.
[306] Ibid., paras 71 and 87.
[307] See overview of findings in ICTY (2016) Appeal Judgement Summary for Stanišić and Župljanin. http://www.icty.org/x/cases/zupljanin_stanisicm/acjug/en/160630_summary.pdf. Accessed 23 February 2017, pp. 3–7; *Stanišić and Župljanin*, above n 299, paras 1191–1192.
[308] *Stanišić and Župljanin*, above n 299, para 1097.
[309] UN General Assembly and UN Security Council (2016) Report of the International Tribunal for the Former Yugoslavia, UN Doc. A/71/263-S/2016/670, para 35.
[310] Ibid., para 35.
[311] Ibid., para 35.

new premises in Arusha, Tanzania in November.[312] Serge Brammertz commenced his term as MICT Prosecutor on 1 March and Judge Theodor Meron's term as President was extended until June 2018.[313]

In the pre-trial phase, the *Stanišić and Simatović* case continued its initial proceedings. Following a decision of the ICTY Appeal Chamber in December 2015, a retrial was ordered with the indictment alleging the accused persons were "co-perpetrators in a joint criminal enterprise [...] [with the] alleged objective [being] [...] the forcible and permanent removal of the majority of non-Serbs from large areas in Croatia and Bosnia and Herzegovina".[314] During 2016, the Prosecutor and the accused persons filed their pre-trial briefs, and proceedings, including a pre-trial conference, are expected to continue in 2017.[315] This marks the first retrial in the history of the MICT, the International Criminal Tribunal for Rwanda (ICTR) and the ICTY.[316]

In its appellate jurisdiction, the MICT was seized by two new cases from the ICTY in 2016. The first of these is the *Karadžić* case, in which Mr. Karadžić and the Prosecution are appealing the ICTY's Trial Chamber judgment of 24 March 2016.[317] Mr. Karadžić and the Prosecutor both filed notices of appeal on 22 July and confidentially filed appeal briefs on 5 December.[318] The Prosecution advanced four grounds of appeal, including one in relation to the Trial Chamber's failure to find that Mr. Karadžić and other members of the JCE possessed genocidal intent, and another arguing that the Trial Chamber had erred by not imposing a life

[312] MICT (2016) Mechanism for International Criminal Tribunals opens its new premises of the Arusha branch. http://www.unmict.org/en/news/mechanism-international-criminal-tribunals-opens-its-new-premises-arusha-branch. Accessed 22 February 2017.

[313] MICT (2016) Serge Brammertz appointed Mechanism Prosecutor. http://www.unmict.org/en/news/serge-brammertz-appointed-mechanism-prosecutor. Accessed 22 February 2017; MICT (2016) Judge Theodor Meron appointed to new term as President of the Mechanism. http://www.unmict.org/en/news/judge-theodor-meron-appointed-new-term-president-mechanism. Accessed 22 February 2017.

[314] MICT (2016) Case Information Sheet: Jovica Stanišić and Franko Simatović. http://www.unmict.org/sites/default/files/cases/public-information/cis-stanisic-simatovic-en.pdf. Accessed 22 February 2017.

[315] MICT (2016) Case Information Sheet: Jovica Stanišić and Franko Simatović. http://www.unmict.org/sites/default/files/cases/public-information/cis-stanisic-simatovic-en.pdf. Accessed 22 February 2017; MICT (2016) Address to the UN Security Council: Judge Theodor Meron, President, Mechanism for International Criminal Tribunals, 8 December 2016, p. 3. http://www.unmict.org/sites/default/files/statements-and-speeches/161208-president-meron-sc-en.pdf. Accessed 22 February 2017.

[316] UN Security Council (2016d) Letter dated 17 November 2016 from the President of the International Residual Mechanism for Criminal Tribunals addressed to the President of the Security Council, UN Doc. S/2016/975, para 35.

[317] MICT (2016) Case Information Sheet: Radovan Karadžić. http://www.unmict.org/sites/default/files/cases/public-information/cis-karadzic-en_4.pdf. Accessed 22 February 2017; see discussion surrounding the Trial Chamber's judgment above in Sect. 8.2.1.1 of this chapter.

[318] Ibid.

sentence.[319] In his address to the UN Security Council on 8 December, Prosecutor Brammertz noted that the Prosecution was "intensively working on [the] [...] response to the fifty grounds of appeal raised by the Karadžić defence team".[320] These grounds focus on issues surrounding the accused's fair trial rights, including, *inter alia*, the prosecution's alleged failure to comply with its disclosure obligations, the admittance of certain evidence, and the alleged failure of the Trial Chamber to respect Mr. Karadžić's right to self-representation.[321] The MICT estimated that this case will take three years to complete.[322]

The MICT has also commenced work on the *Šešelj* case, following Mr. Šešelj's acquittal of "three counts of crimes against humanity and six counts of violations of the laws or customs of war" in March.[323] The Prosecution filed its notice of appeal on 2 May, in which it advanced two grounds of appeal: first, that the Trial Chamber failed to provide a reasoned judgment; and, second, that the Trial Chamber had erred by acquitting the accused.[324] It is requesting either that Mr. Šešelj be found guilty or that a retrial be ordered.[325] The Prosecution filed its appeals brief confidentially on 18 July and, at the end of 2016, the case remained in the pre-appeal phase.[326]

In addition, the MICT is still seeking eight fugitives who were indicted by the ICTR, five of whom will be transferred to the Rwandan national authorities for prosecution upon their arrest.[327] In February, Mr. Zdravko Tolimir, who was sentenced to life imprisonment by the ICTY, passed away of natural causes in the UN Detention Unit in Scheveningen.[328] In March, the MICT arrested Florence

[319] MICT, *Prosecutor v Radovan Karadžić*, Prosecution's Notice of Appeal, 22 July 2016, Case No. MICT-13-55-A, paras 16–25.

[320] ICTY (2016) Address of Mr. Serge Brammertz, Prosecutor, International Criminal Tribunal for the Former Yugoslavia and Mechanism for International Criminal Tribunals to the United Nations Security Council. http://www.icty.org/x/file/Press/Statements%20and%20Speeches/Prosecutor/161208_prosecutor_brammertz_un_sc_en.pdf. Accessed 22 February 2017, p. 2.

[321] *Karadžić* Appeal, above n 282, paras 2–12.

[322] UN Security Council (2016d) Letter dated 17 November 2016 from the President of the International Residual Mechanism for Criminal Tribunals addressed to the President of the Security Council, UN Doc. S/2016/975, para 36.

[323] MICT (2016) Case Information Sheet: Vojislav Šešelj. http://www.unmict.org/sites/default/files/cases/public-information/cis-seselj-en.pdf. Accessed 22 February 2017; see discussion surrounding the Trial Chamber's judgment above in Sect. 8.2.1.1 of this chapter.

[324] *Šešelj* Appeal, above n 296, paras I and II.

[325] UN Security Council (2016d) Letter dated 17 November 2016 from the President of the International Residual Mechanism for Criminal Tribunals addressed to the President of the Security Council, UN Doc. S/2016/975, para 37.

[326] MICT (2016) Case Information Sheet: Vojislav Šešelj. http://www.unmict.org/sites/default/files/cases/public-information/cis-seselj-en.pdf. Accessed 22 February 2017.

[327] UN Security Council (2016d) Letter dated 17 November 2016 from the President of the International Residual Mechanism for Criminal Tribunals addressed to the President of the Security Council, UN Doc. S/2016/975, para 55.

[328] MICT (2016) Autopsy confirms Tolimir died of natural causes. http://www.unmict.org/en/news/autopsy-confirms-tolimir-died-natural-causes. Accessed 22 February 2017.

Hartmann pursuant to an arrest warrant issued in November 2011, which related to her conviction for knowingly and wilfully interfering in the administration of justice.[329] On 5 October, the President of the MICT notified the UN Security Council of the arrest of MICT Judge Aydin Sefa Akay in Turkey, who remained detained at the end of 2016 despite the UN Secretary-General requesting his release due to his diplomatic immunity.[330] Judge Akay is a member of the Appeals Chamber that is hearing the *Ngirabatware* case and his detention has hindered these proceedings.[331] During 2016, the Appeals Chamber of the MICT also dismissed various appeals in relation to the decision to refer Jean Uwinkindi's case to Rwanda.[332]

8.2.1.3 International Criminal Court

The year 2016 proved to be an eventful year for the International Criminal Court (ICC), which included: the official opening of the ICC's new premises by King Willem-Alexander of the Netherlands;[333] the signing of agreements on cooperation, sentencing and witness protection with other international courts and States Parties;[334] the addition of a new State Party, El Salvador;[335] the release of a Policy Paper on Case Selection and Prioritisation by the Prosecutor;[336] the Presidency approving the request of the Democratic Republic of the Congo to prosecute

[329] MICT (2016) Mechanism arrests contempt convict. http://www.unmict.org/en/news/mechanism-arrests-contempt-convict. Accessed 33 February 2017.

[330] UN Security Council (2016d) Letter dated 17 November 2016 from the President of the International Residual Mechanism for Criminal Tribunals addressed to the President of the Security Council, UN Doc. S/2016/975, para 13; MICT (2017) The Mechanism orders Turkey to release Judge Aydin Sefa Akay. http://www.unmict.org/en/news/mechanism-orders-turkey-release-judge-aydin-sefa-akay. Accessed 22 February 2017.

[331] UN Security Council (2016d) Letter dated 17 November 2016 from the President of the International Residual Mechanism for Criminal Tribunals addressed to the President of the Security Council, UN Doc. S/2016/975, para 13.

[332] Ibid., para 39.

[333] ICC (2016) ICC Permanent Premises officially opened by His Majesty King Willem-Alexander of the Netherlands. https://www.icc-cpi.int/Pages/item.aspx?name=pr1208. Accessed 24 February 2017.

[334] See e.g. ICC (2016) International Criminal Court and Inter-American Court of Human Rights sign Memorandum of Understanding on cooperation. https://www.icc-cpi.int/Pages/item.aspx?name=pr1191. Accessed 24 February 2017; ICC (2016) Argentina and International Criminal Court sign an agreement on Witnesses' protection. https://www.icc-cpi.int/Pages/item.aspx?name=PR1258. Accessed 24 February 2017; and ICC (2016) ICC signs enforcement agreement with Norway. https://www.icc-cpi.int/Pages/item.aspx?name=pr1229. Accessed 24 February 2017.

[335] ICC (2016) El Salvador ratifies the Rome Statute and the Kampala Amendments on war crimes and the crime of aggression. https://www.icc-cpi.int/Pages/item.aspx?name=PR1193. Accessed 24 February 2017.

[336] ICC (2016) ICC Prosecutor, Fatou Bensouda, publishes comprehensive Policy Paper on Case Selection and Prioritisation. https://www.icc-cpi.int/Pages/item.aspx?name=pr1238. Accessed 24 February 2017.

Germain Katanga at the end of his ICC sentence;[337] and the announcement that three African States Parties, namely the Gambia, South Africa and Burundi, intended to withdraw from the ICC.[338]

Preliminary Examinations and Investigations

Two new preliminary examinations were opened in 2016: first, the Prosecutor opened an examination in Burundi in April in light of communications "detailing acts of killing, imprisonment, torture, rape and other forms of sexual violence, as well as cases of enforced disappearances";[339] and in September, Gabon referred the situation in Gabon since May 2016 to the ICC for examination.[340] Preliminary examinations remained ongoing into the situations in Iraq/UK, Palestine, Ukraine, Afghanistan, Colombia, Guinea, Nigeria and Comoros at the end of 2016.[341] In January, Pre-Trial Chamber I gave the Prosecutor permission to move from a preliminary examination to an investigation of the situation in Georgia.[342] In so doing, Pre-Trial Chamber I found there was a reasonable basis to believe that war crimes and crimes against humanity had been committed in South Ossetia from 1 July 2008 until 10 October 2008.[343]

Cases in the Trial Phase

- Central African Republic

In the situation concerning the Central African Republic (CAR), two trial judgments were delivered in 2016. On 21 March, Trial Chamber III delivered its verdict in the *Bemba* case, convicting Jean-Pierre Bemba Gombo of two counts of

---

[337] ICC (2016) ICC Presidency approves the prosecution of Mr Germain Katanga by national authorities of the Democratic Republic of the Congo. https://www.icc-cpi.int/Pages/item.aspx?name=pr1206. Accessed 24 February 2017.

[338] Agence France-Presse (2016) Gambia is latest African nation to quit international criminal court. https://www.theguardian.com/world/2016/oct/26/gambia-becomes-latest-african-nation-to-quit-international-criminal-court. Accessed 24 February 2017.

[339] ICC (2016) Statement of the Prosecutor of the International Criminal Court, Fatou Bensouda, on opening a Preliminary Examination into the situation in Burundi. https://www.icc-cpi.int/Pages/item.aspx?name=otp-stat-25-04-2016. Accessed 24 February 2017.

[340] ICC (2016) Statement of the Prosecutor of the International Criminal Court, Fatou Bensouda, concerning referral from the Gabonese Republic. https://www.icc-cpi.int/Pages/item.aspx?name=160929-otp-stat-gabon. Accessed 24 February 2017.

[341] See ICC (2016) Report on Preliminary Examination Activities 2016. https://www.icc-cpi.int/iccdocs/otp/161114-otp-rep-PE_ENG.pdf. Accessed 25 February 2017.

[342] ICC (2016) ICC Pre-Trial Chamber I authorises the Prosecutor to open an investigation into the situation in Georgia. https://www.icc-cpi.int/Pages/item.aspx?name=pr1183. Accessed 25 February 2017.

[343] ICC, *Situation in Georgia*, Decision on the Prosecutor's request for authorisation of an investigation, 27 January 2016, Case No. ICC-01/15, paras 1, 26–32, 59 and 64.

crimes against humanity and three counts of war crimes.[344] This case has been largely welcomed by commentators, who noted that it marks the ICC's first conviction on the basis of command responsibility as well as for rape as a war crime.[345] Mr. Bemba was the President of the Mouvement de Libération du Congo (MLC) and the Commander-in-Chief of the Armée de Libération du Congo (ALC), the military wing of the MLC.[346] Three battalions of the MLC were involved in the conflict in the CAR in 2002–2003 following a request by the President of the CAR to the MLC for assistance.[347]

The Trial Chamber found that between 26 October 2002 and 15 March 2003, there was an armed conflict in the CAR, and it concluded that the conflict "was not of an international character",[348] that it "was between the CAR governmental authorities, supported by forces including the MLC, an organised armed group, [...] and [...] the organised armed group of General Bozizé's rebels",[349] ultimately concluding that the contextual elements for war crimes had been met.[350] Pre-Trial Chamber III likewise concluded that the contextual elements for crimes against humanity were satisfied in this case.[351] Accordingly, during the armed conflict, the Chamber found that the MLC forces had committed: the war crime of murder and crime against humanity of murder;[352] the war crime of rape and the crime against humanity of rape;[353] and the war crime of pillaging.[354]

Mr. Bemba was held criminally responsible under Article 28(a) of the Rome Statute for the conduct of the MLC soldiers as he acted "effectively [...] as a military commander and had effective authority and control over the contingent of MLC troops in the CAR";[355] he "knew that the MLC forces under his effective

---

[344] ICC, *Prosecutor v Jean-Pierre Bemba Gombo*, Judgment Pursuant to Article 74 of the Statute, 21 March 2016, Case No. ICC-01/05-01/08-3343 (*Bemba*); ICC (2016) ICC Trial Chamber III declares Jean-Pierre Bemba Gombo guilty of war crimes and crimes against humanity. https://www.icc-cpi.int/Pages/item.aspx?name=pr1200. Accessed 12 September 2016.

[345] van Sweringen S (2016) ICC Conviction of Jean-Pierre Bemba: A Successful Effort to Combat Sexual Violence? http://jtl.columbia.edu/icc-conviction-of-jean-pierre-bemba-a-successful-effort-to-combat-sexual-violence/. Accessed 12 September 2016; Obara B (2016) "He will appeal. He's our President" – Reactions to Bemba's Sentencing. https://justicehub.org/article/he-will-appeal-hes-our-president-reactions-bembas-sentencing. Accessed 12 September 2016; Amnesty International (2016) International Criminal Court: Bemba verdict a historic step forward for victims of sexual violence. https://www.amnesty.org/en/latest/news/2016/03/international-criminal-court-bemba-verdict-a-historic-step-forward-for-victims-of-sexual-violence/. Accessed 12 September 2016.

[346] *Bemba*, above n 344, para 1.

[347] Ibid., paras 410 and 453–454.

[348] Ibid., para 656.

[349] Ibid., para 661.

[350] Ibid., para 668. See also paras 652–656, 661, 663 and 666–667.

[351] Ibid., paras 669–692.

[352] Ibid., para 630.

[353] Ibid., para 638.

[354] Ibid., para 648.

[355] Ibid., para 705.

authority and control were committing or about to commit [...] crimes";[356] Mr. Bemba "failed to take all necessary and reasonable measures within his power to prevent or repress the commission of crimes";[357] and, consequently, the crimes committed "in [...] the 2002–2003 CAR Operation were a result of Mr. Bemba's failure to exercise control properly".[358] Following his conviction, Mr. Bemba launched an appeal on 4 April[359] and on 21 June he was sentenced to 18 years' imprisonment by Trial Chamber III.[360]

The second trial judgment from the CAR situation was delivered in October and concerned the *Bemba et al.* case, which featured five co-accused individuals facing charges of offences against the administration of justice.[361] In the ICC's first case about evidence tampering, all five co-accused, which included Jean-Pierre Bemba Gombo, Aimé Kilolo Musamba, Jean-Jacques Mangenda Kabongo, Fidèle Babala Wandu and Narcisse Arido, were accused of "corruptly influencing witnesses, presenting false evidence and giving false testimony" in the *Bemba* case and were ultimately found guilty of differing charges.[362] The Decision on Sentencing in this case will be handed down in 2017.[363]

- Mali

In the Mali situation, Trial Chamber VIII delivered its judgment and sentence in the *Al Mahdi* case on 27 September.[364] Mr. Al Mahdi's charge, which concerned the destruction of historical and religious monuments in Timbuktu, was confirmed

---

[356] Ibid., para 717.

[357] Ibid., para 734.

[358] Ibid., para 741.

[359] UN General Assembly (2016d) Report of the International Criminal Court, UN Doc. A/71/342, para 40.

[360] ICC (2016) ICC Trial Chamber III sentences Jean-Pierre Bemba Gombo to 18 years' imprisonment for war crimes and crimes against humanity committed in the Central African Republic in 2002–2003. https://www.icc-cpi.int/Pages/item.aspx?name=PR1223. Accessed 25 February 2017.

[361] ICC (2016) Bemba et al. case: ICC Trial Chamber VII finds five accused guilty of offences against the administration of justice. https://www.icc-cpi.int/Pages/item.aspx?name=pr1245. Accessed 25 February 2017.

[362] Wakabi W (2016) Verdict in ICC's First Witness Tampering Trial Scheduled for October 19. https://www.ijmonitor.org/2016/09/verdict-in-iccs-first-witness-tampering-trial-scheduled-for-october-19/. Accessed 25 February 2017; ICC, *Prosecutor v Jean-Pierre Bemba Gombo, Aimé Kilolo Musamba, Jean-Jacques Mangenda Kabongo, Fidèle Babala Wandu and Narcisse Arido*, Judgment pursuant to Article 74 of the Statute, 19 October 2016, Case No. ICC-01/05-01/13, para 13 and pp. 455–457.

[363] ICC, *Prosecutor v Jean-Pierre Bemba Gombo, Aimé Kilolo Musamba, Jean-Jacques Mangenda Kabongo, Fidèle Babala Wandu and Narcisse Arido*, Order Scheduling the Delivery of the Decision on Sentencing, 23 February 2017, Case No. ICC-01/05-01/13.

[364] ICC (2016) ICC Trial Chamber VIII declares Mr Al Mahdi guilty of the war crime of attacking historic and religious buildings in Timbuktu and sentences him to nine years' imprisonment. https://www.icc-cpi.int/Pages/item.aspx?name=pr1242. Accessed 13 October 2016.

on 24 March 2016 by Pre-Trial Chamber I[365] and Mr. Al Mahdi earlier indicated his intention to plead guilty on 1 March,[366] following the finalisation of a plea agreement between the Prosecution and Mr. Al Mahdi in February.[367] Mr. Al Mahdi pleaded guilty to one charge of the war crime "of attacking protected objects under Article 8(2)(e)(iv) of the [Rome] Statute" at the trial,[368] which took place between 22 and 24 August 2016.[369]

Mr. Al Mahdi acknowledged his responsibility for "intentionally directing attacks against 10 buildings of a religious and historical character [...] between around 30 June 2012 and 11 July 2012".[370] The Trial Chamber provided some guidance regarding the interpretation of the crime, including: it held that "the element of 'direct[ing] an attack' encompasses any acts of violence against protected objects" and that the Rome Statute makes no "distinction as to whether it was carried out in the conduct of hostilities or after the object had fallen under the control of an armed group";[371] and it found that the attack on cultural property does not require "a link to any particular hostilities but only an association with the non-international armed conflict more generally".[372] Additionally, Trial Chamber VII reflected on guilty pleas and plea agreements before the ICC under Article 65 of the Rome Statute, noting the non-binding nature of such agreements, the oversight role that the Court plays in examining them and the benefits to the Court when accused persons plead guilty.[373] Mr. Al Mahdi was sentenced to nine years' imprisonment which has become final as no appeal was lodged.[374] Reparations proceedings have also commenced in this case.[375]

---

[365] ICC (2016) ICC Pre-Trial Chamber I confirms the charge against Ahmad Al Faqi Al Mahdi and commits him to trial. https://www.icc-cpi.int/Pages/item.aspx?name=pr1204. Accessed 13 October 2016; and ICC, *Prosecutor v Ahmad Al Faqi Al Mahdi*, Decision on the confirmation of charges against Ahmad Al Faqi Al Madhi, 25 March 2016, Case No. ICC-01/12-01/15-84-Red.

[366] ICC (2016) Statement of the Prosecutor of the International Criminal Court, Fatou Bensouda, following admission of guilt by the accused in Mali war crime case: "An important step for the victims, and another first for the ICC". https://www.icc-cpi.int/Pages/item.aspx?name=160324-otp-stat-al-Mahdi. Accessed 13 October 2016.

[367] ICC, *Prosecutor v Ahmad Al Faqi Al Mahdi*, Judgment and Sentence, 27 September 2016, Case No. ICC-01/12-01/15-171 (*Al Mahdi*), para 3.

[368] Ibid., para 2.

[369] Ibid., para 7.

[370] Ibid., paras 10–11.

[371] Ibid., para 15.

[372] Ibid., para 18.

[373] Ibid., paras 21–28.

[374] Ibid., para 109; ICC (2016) Presentation of the Court's annual report to the UN General Assembly by Judge Silvia Fernández de Gurmendi, President of the International Criminal Court. https://www.icc-cpi.int/Pages/item.aspx?name=161031-pres-UNGA-st. Accessed 25 February 2017.

[375] ICC (2016) Presentation of the Court's annual report to the UN General Assembly by Judge Silvia Fernández de Gurmendi, President of the International Criminal Court. https://www.icc-cpi.int/Pages/item.aspx?name=161031-pres-UNGA-st. Accessed 25 February 2017.

- Kenya

The *Ruto and Sang* case from the Kenya situation was ultimately terminated in April by Trial Chamber V(A) in response to "no case to answer" motions filed by the co-accused in October 2015, which followed the conclusion of the Prosecution's case in September 2015.[376] Mr. Ruto and Mr. Sang had been "accused of crimes against humanity (murder, deportation or forcible transfer of population and persecution) allegedly committed in the context of the 2007–2008 post-election violence in Kenya".[377] In a majority decision, Judges Fremr and Eboe-Osuji decided to vacate the charges without prejudice to future prosecution, with Judge Herrera Carbuccia dissenting.[378] In vacating the charges, Judge Fremr, who noted "that there was a disturbing level of interferences with witnesses [and] [...] inappropriate attempts at the political level to meddle with the trial", held that the evidence presented by the Prosecution could not sustain the charges levelled against Mr. Ruto or Mr. Sang, meaning there was no need for the defence teams to present their case.[379] Judge Eboe-Osuji, who agreed with Judge Fremr's findings with regards to the evidential review, preferred to declare a mistrial due to the "serious tainting of the trial process by way of witness interference and political intimidation of witnesses".[380] Earlier in February 2016, the Appeals Chamber had reversed Trial Chamber V(A)'s ruling on the admission of prior recorded testimony.[381]

[376] ICC (2016) Ruto and Sang case: ICC Trial Chamber V(A) terminates the case without prejudice to re-prosecution in future. https://www.icc-cpi.int/Pages/item.aspx?name=pr1205. Accessed 25 February 2017; ICC, *Prosecutor v William Samoei Ruto and Joshua Arap Sang*, Decision on Defence Applications for Judgments of Acquittal, 5 April 2016, Case No. ICC-01/09-01/11 (*Ruto and Sang*), paras 8–9.

[377] ICC (2016) Ruto and Sang case: ICC Trial Chamber V(A) terminates the case without prejudice to re-prosecution in future. https://www.icc-cpi.int/Pages/item.aspx?name=pr1205. Accessed 25 February 2017.

[378] *Ruto and Sang*, above n 376, p. 1.

[379] *Ruto and Sang*, above n 376, Reasons of Judge Fremr, paras 131 and 147; and ICC (2016) Ruto and Sang case: ICC Trial Chamber V(A) terminates the case without prejudice to re-prosecution in future. https://www.icc-cpi.int/Pages/item.aspx?name=pr1205. Accessed 25 February 2017.

[380] *Ruto and Sang*, above n 376, Reasons of Judge Eboe-Osuji, paras 1–2; and ICC (2016) Ruto and Sang case: ICC Trial Chamber V(A) terminates the case without prejudice to re-prosecution in future. https://www.icc-cpi.int/Pages/item.aspx?name=pr1205. Accessed 25 February 2017.

[381] ICC, *Prosecutor v William Samoei Ruto and Joshua Arap Sang*, Judgment on the appeals of Mr William Samoei Ruto and Mr Joshua Arap Sang on the decision of Trial Chamber V(A) of 19 August 2015 entitled "Decision on Prosecution Request for Admission of Prior Recorded Testimony", 12 February 2016, Case No. ICC-01/09-01/11 OA 10.

- Uganda

On 23 March, Pre-Trial Chamber II issued its judgment confirming charges against Dominic Ongwen from the Uganda situation.[382] The decision confirms 70 charges against Mr. Ongwen that relate to war crimes and crimes against humanity that occurred in Uganda between 2002 and 2005, including torture, sexual slavery, rape and the use of child soldiers.[383] Following the denial of a defence application to appeal the decision confirming the charges,[384] Mr. Ongwen's trial commenced before Trial Chamber IX on 6 December.[385] When presenting the annual report of the ICC to the UN General Assembly, President Fernández de Gurmendi noted that the trial marks a "significant development, more than ten years after arrest warrants were issued against Mr. Ongwen, Joseph Kony and others".[386] The trial was set to resume on 16 January with the presentation of the Prosecution's evidence.[387]

- Democratic Republic of the Congo

In the *Lubanga* case from the situation in the Democratic Republic of the Congo (DRC), Trial Chamber II requested further information on proposed reparations in February and it later approved a plan for symbolic collective reparations in October.[388] The Chamber indicated it would also issue a decision on collective reparations programmes.[389] Thomas Lubanga Dyilo was convicted of war crimes in March 2012 and is

---

[382] ICC, *Prosecutor v Dominic Ongwen*, Decision on the confirmation of charges against Dominic Ongwen, 23 March 2016, Case No. ICC-02/04-01/15 (*Ongwen*); and ICC (2016) ICC Pre-Trial Chamber II confirms the charges against Dominic Ongwen and commits him to trial. https://www.icc-cpi.int/Pages/item.aspx?name=pr1202. Accessed 25 February 2017.

[383] *Ongwen*, above n 382, pp. 71–104; ICC (2016) ICC Pre-Trial Chamber II confirms the charges against Dominic Ongwen and commits him to trial. https://www.icc-cpi.int/Pages/item.aspx?name=pr1202. Accessed 25 February 2017; and ICC (2016) Presentation of the Court's annual report to the UN General Assembly by Judge Silvia Fernández de Gurmendi, President of the International Criminal Court. https://www.icc-cpi.int/Pages/item.aspx?name=161031-pres-UNGA-st. Accessed 25 February 2017.

[384] ICC, *Prosecutor v Dominic Ongwen*, Decision on the Defence request for leave to appeal the decision on the confirmation of charges, 29 April 2016, Case No. ICC-02/04-01/15.

[385] ICC (2016) Ongwen trial opens at International Criminal Court. https://www.icc-cpi.int/Pages/item.aspx?name=pr1262. Accessed 25 February 2017.

[386] ICC (2016) Presentation of the Court's annual report to the UN General Assembly by Judge Silvia Fernández de Gurmendi, President of the International Criminal Court. https://www.icc-cpi.int/Pages/item.aspx?name=161031-pres-UNGA-st. Accessed 25 February 2017.

[387] ICC (2016) Ongwen trial opens at International Criminal Court. https://www.icc-cpi.int/Pages/item.aspx?name=pr1262. Accessed 25 February 2017.

[388] UN General Assembly (2016) Report of the International Criminal Court, UN Doc. A/71/342, para 34; ICC (2016) Lubanga case: ICC judges approve plan on symbolic reparations. https://www.icc-cpi.int/Pages/item.aspx?name=pr1247. Accessed 25 February 2017.

[389] ICC (2016) Lubanga case: ICC judges approve plan on symbolic reparations. https://www.icc-cpi.int/Pages/item.aspx?name=pr1247. Accessed 25 February 2017.

currently serving the remainder of his 14-year sentence in the DRC.[390] In the *Ntaganda* case, trial proceedings continued throughout 2016 after opening statements in September 2015.[391] Bosco Ntaganda is facing charges relating to war crimes and crimes against humanity committed in the DRC in the early 2000s.[392] In December, hearings relating to, *inter alia*, sexual violence and satellite images took place prior to the winter recess.[393]

- Côte d'Ivoire

In the situation in Côte d'Ivoire, trial proceedings in the *Gbagbo and Blé Goudé* case opened on 28 January 2016.[394] At the opening of the trial, Prosecutor Fatou Bensouda stated that the trial was "not driven by political considerations"[395] but instead was "about the individual criminal responsibility of the two [a]ccused for crimes committed in the 2010 post-election violence which fall under the jurisdiction" of the ICC.[396] Laurent Gbagbo and Charles Blé Goudé are accused of four counts of crimes against humanity that relate to post-electoral violence between 16 December 2010 and 12 April 2011 in Côte d'Ivoire.[397] Hearings continued until the winter recess and are expected to recommence in early 2017.[398]

---

[390] ICC (2017) Lubanga Case. https://www.icc-cpi.int/drc/lubanga. Accessed 25 February 2017.

[391] ICC (2016) Ntaganda trial opens at International Criminal Court. https://www.icc-cpi.int/Pages/item.aspx?name=pr1143. Accessed 25 February 2017; Wakabi K (2016) Ntaganda Trial Goes on Recess After Testimony of Expert Witness on Sexual Violence. https://www.ijmonitor.org/2016/12/ntaganda-trial-goes-on-recess-after-testimony-of-expert-witness-on-sexual-violence/. Accessed 25 February 2017.

[392] ICC (2017) Ntaganda Case. https://www.icc-cpi.int/drc/ntaganda. Accessed 25 February 2017.

[393] Wakabi W (2016) Ntaganda Trial Goes on Recess After Testimony of Expert Witness on Sexual Violence. https://www.ijmonitor.org/2016/12/ntaganda-trial-goes-on-recess-after-testimony-of-expert-witness-on-sexual-violence/. Accessed 25 February 2017; Wakabi W (2016) Analysis of Satellite Image Highlights Difficulties in Collecting Evidence Years After the Crimes. https://www.ijmonitor.org/2016/12/analysis-of-satellite-images-highlights-difficulties-in-collecting-evidence-years-after-the-crimes/. Accessed 25 February 2017.

[394] ICC (2016) Trial of Laurent Gbagbo and Charles Blé Goudé opens at International Criminal Court. https://www.icc-cpi.int/Pages/item.aspx?name=pr1184. Accessed 25 February 2017.

[395] ICC (2016) Statement of ICC-Prosecutor at the Commencement of Trial in the case against Messrs. Laurent Gbagbo and Charles Blé Goudé. https://www.icc-cpi.int/Pages/item.aspx?name=otp-stat-29-01-2016. Accessed 26 February 2017.

[396] Ibid.

[397] ICC (2016) Case Information Sheet: The Prosecutor v. Laurent Gbagbo and Charles Blé Goudé. https://www.icc-cpi.int/cdi/gbagbo-goude/Documents/LaurentGbagboandBleGoudeEng.pdf. Accessed 25 February 2017.

[398] Dubruelh C (2016) Last Day of Trial Before Recess. https://www.ijmonitor.org/2016/12/last-day-of-trial-before-recess/. Accessed 25 February 2017.

8.2.2 *Hybrid Tribunals*

8.2.2.1 Republic of Kosovo

EULEX

EULEX continued its work in Kosovo in 2016, adopting a new mandate in June[399] and with its new Head, Alexandra Papadopoulou, commencing in September.[400] The Basic Court of Mitrovica held Oliver Ivanović guilty of war crimes on 21 January.[401] The conviction related to Mr. Ivanović's participation as part of a group of paramilitaries or police who, in April 1999, led Albanian men, who had been forcibly removed from their homes, through a checkpoint and commenced killing them.[402] Mr. Ivanović, a Kosovo Serb politician, was held to have been "aware of the operation of expelling and killing Albanians [and] [...] he willingly complied with the plan, knowing that it would result in the killings".[403] He was sentenced to nine years' imprisonment.[404] Mr. Ivanović and his co-accused, Dragoljub Delibašić, Nebojša Vujačić, Ilija Vujačić and Aleksandar Lazović, were found not guilty of count 2 of the indictment that considered events that occurred on 3 February 2000.[405]

In August 2016, the Basic Court of Mitrovica found former Kosovo Liberation Army (KLA) member Xhemshit Krasniqi guilty of war crimes and unauthorised weapons charges, and sentenced him to eight years' imprisonment and a fine of 1 500 Euros.[406] Mr. Krasniqi "was found guilty of arrest, illegal detention, violation of bodily integrity, health and torture of several witnesses and unknown civilians in the KLA camps in Kukes and Cahan (Albania), as well as in Prizren during 1999".[407]

---

[399] EULEX Kosovo (2016) EULEX New Mandate. http://www.eulex-kosovo.eu/?page=2,10,437. Accessed 23 February 2017.

[400] EULEX Kosovo (2016) New Head of EULEX Assumes Her Duties. http://www.eulex-kosovo.eu/?page=2,10,460. Accessed 23 February 2017.

[401] EULEX Kosovo (2016) Verdict in Oliver Ivanovic Case Pronounced. http://www.eulex-kosovo.eu/?page=2,10,378. Accessed 23 February 2017.

[402] Ibid.

[403] Ibid; BBC (2016) EU judges convict Kosovo Serb politician Ivanovic of war crimes. http://www.bbc.com/news/world-europe-35374946. Accessed 23 February 2017.

[404] EULEX Kosovo (2016) Verdict in Oliver Ivanovic Case Pronounced. http://www.eulex-kosovo.eu/?page=2,10,378. Accessed 23 February 2017.

[405] Ibid.

[406] EULEX Kosovo (2016) Verdict pronounced in Krasniqi Trial. http://www.eulex-kosovo.eu/?page=2,10,450. Accessed 23 February 2017.

[407] Ibid.

Kosovo Specialist Chambers and Specialist Prosecutor's Office

Further progress was made on the establishment and the commencement of the work of the Kosovo Specialist Chambers and the Specialist Prosecutor's Office during 2016. The Specialist Chambers, which "have jurisdiction over crimes against humanity, war crimes and other crimes under Kosovo law in relation to allegations reported in the Council of Europe Parliamentary Assembly Report of 7 January 2011", is made up of two organs, namely the Chambers and the Registry.[408] The Specialist Prosecutor's Office "is an independent office for the investigation and prosecution of the crimes within the jurisdiction of the Specialist Chambers".[409] The seat of the Chambers is in The Hague and it will receive financial support from the European Union (EU), Canada, Norway, Switzerland, Turkey and the US.[410] 2016 saw a series of appointments to positions in the Specialist Chambers and the Specialist Prosecutor's Office. In April, Dr. Fidelma Donlon was appointed Registrar; in September, David Schwendiman was appointed as the Chief Prosecutor; and in December, Ekaterina Trendafilova was appointed as the President of the Specialist Chambers.[411] Going forward, the Chambers are awaiting the commencement of the Host State Agreement on 1 January 2017, and will then appoint judges who can adopt the Rules of Procedure and Evidence.[412] Subsequently, the Specialist Prosecutor's Office may begin to file indictments.[413]

8.2.2.2 Extraordinary Chambers in the Courts of Cambodia

The Extraordinary Chambers in the Courts of Cambodia (ECCC) continued its work throughout 2016. Notable developments included: the severance of proceedings concerning Im Chaem from Case 004 following the conclusion of judicial investigations in December 2015;[414] ongoing hearings in Case 002/02 against

[408] Kosovo Specialist Chambers & Specialist Prosecutor's Office (2017) Background. https://www.scp-ks.org/en/specialist-chambers/background. Accessed 23 February 2017.

[409] Ibid.

[410] Ibid.; Government of the Netherlands (2016) Kosovo court to be established in The Hague. https://www.government.nl/ministries/ministry-of-foreign-affairs/news/2016/01/15/kosovo-court-to-be-established-in-the-hague. Accessed 23 February 2017.

[411] Kosovo Specialist Chambers & Specialist Prosecutor's Office (2016) Appointment of Dr Donlon as Registrar of the Specialist Chambers. https://www.scp-ks.org/en/appointment-dr-donlon-registrar-specialist-chambers. Accessed 23 February 2017; Ristic M (2016) US Lawyer Appointed Kosovo Special Court Chief Prosecutor. http://www.balkaninsight.com/en/article/us-prosecutor-appointed-chief-prosecutor-of-kosovo-special-court-09-05-2016. Accessed 23 February 2017; Ristic M (2016) Kosovo Special Court Appoints First President. http://www.balkaninsight.com/en/article/kosovo-special-court-appoints-first-president-12-14-2016. Accessed 23 February 2017.

[412] Kosovo Specialist Chambers & Specialist Prosecutor's Office (2017) Frequently Asked Questions. https://www.scp-ks.org/en/frequently-asked-questions. Accessed 23 February 2017.

[413] Ibid.

[414] ECCC (2016) The Court Report – February, p. 3. https://www.eccc.gov.kh/en/publication/court-report-february-2016. Accessed 23 February 2017.

Khieu Samphân and Nuon Chea, including those on the topic of forced marriage and rape, and security centres and internal purges;[415] and in the case against Ao An, new charges concerning genocide, crimes against humanity and premeditated homicide were added in March, and the proceedings were severed from Case 004 in December following the completion of the judicial investigation.[416]

Following the conclusion of appeals hearings in Case 002/01 on 18 February,[417] the Supreme Court Chamber of the ECCC delivered its judgment in this case on 23 November.[418] Khieu Samphân, the "former Deputy Secretary of the Communist Party of Kampuchea",[419] and Nuon Chea, the "former Head of State of Democratic Kampuchea",[420] had previously been found guilty of "crimes against humanity (encompassing murder), persecution on political grounds, and other inhuman acts (comprising forced transfer, enforced disappearances and attacks against human dignity) committed within the territory of Democratic Kampuchea between 17 April 1975 and the end of 1977".[421] Nuon Chea had advanced 223 grounds of appeal, Khieu Samphân put forward 148 grounds of appeal and the Prosecutor also filed an appeal surrounding JCEs.[422]

In its 520-page judgment, the Supreme Court Chamber reversed convictions for: the crime against humanity of extermination in relation to Population Movement Phase One and for Population Movement Phase Two as the evidence before the Trial Chamber was insufficient to conclude beyond a reasonable doubt that the scale

---

[415] ECCC (2016) Trial Chamber will begin hearing evidence on the fourth trial topic in Case 002/02: Security Centres and Internal Purges. https://www.eccc.gov.kh/en/articles/trial-chamber-will-begin-hearing-evidence-fourth-trial-topic-case-00202-security-centres-an. Accessed 23 February 2017; Extraordinary Chambers in the Courts of Cambodia (2016) Trial Chamber to hear evidence on charges of forced marriage and rape. https://www.eccc.gov.kh/en/articles/trial-chamber-hear-evidence-charges-forced-marriage-and-rape. Accessed 23 February 2017.

[416] ECCC (2016) Additional charges announced against Ao An. https://www.eccc.gov.kh/en/articles/additional-charges-announced-against-ao. Accessed 23 February 2017; ECCC (2016) Press Release by the Office of the Co-Investigating Judges: Judicial investigation against Ao An concluded and severance from Case 004 ordered. https://www.eccc.gov.kh/en/articles/press-release-office-co-investigating-judges-judicial-investigation-against-ao-concluded-an. Accessed 23 February 2017.

[417] ECCC (2016) The Court Report – February. https://www.eccc.gov.kh/en/publication/court-report-february-2016. Accessed 23 February 2017; ECCC (2016) Supreme Court Chamber to resume Appeal Hearing in Case 002/01. https://www.eccc.gov.kh/en/articles/supreme-court-chamber-resume-appeal-hearing-case-00201. Accessed 23 February 2017.

[418] ECCC, *Case 002/01: Nuon Chea and Khieu Samphân*, Appeal Judgment, 23 November 2016, Case No. 002/19-09-2007-ECCC/SC (*Chea and Samphân*).

[419] ECCC (2016) Press Release: Supreme Court Chamber quashes part of the convictions, affirms life imprisonment for Nuon Chea and Khieu Samphan in Case 002/01. https://www.eccc.gov.kh/en/articles/supreme-court-chamber-quashes-part-convictions-affirms-life-imprisonment-nuon-chea-and-khie. Accessed 23 February 2017.

[420] Ibid.

[421] *Chea and Samphân*, above n 418, para 2.

[422] Ibid., para 4.

and intent elements had been met;[423] the crime against humanity of persecution in relation to the "New People", namely those living in Phnom Penh on 17 April 1975, in Population Movement Two as these population transfers involved both "Old" and "New People" and thus discriminatory intent was not sufficiently proved;[424] and "the crimes against humanity of extermination, murder and persecution on political grounds in respect of the events at Tuol Po Chrey",[425] as the evidence relied upon by the Trial Chamber was "of low probative value" and could not establish the common criminal purpose needed to prove the JCE.[426] However, the Supreme Court Chamber noted that, despite these alterations, this did not substantially alter the number of victims harmed by Nuon Chea and Khieu Samphân and that it had generally upheld the Trial Chamber's findings.[427] Accordingly, it confirmed the life sentences previously imposed upon both accused.[428]

8.2.2.3 Special Tribunal for Lebanon

In 2016, the presentation of evidence in the *Ayyash et al.* trial at the Special Tribunal for Lebanon (STL) continued. This case focuses on the attack on former Lebanese Prime Minister Rafik Hariri on 14 February 2005, which killed Prime Minister Hariri and 21 others.[429] In its seventh Annual Report, the Prosecution noted that this case is "a particularly complex terrorist case" with a "time-consuming nature".[430] As at 29 February 2016, the Prosecution had presented its first category of evidence and part of its second category.[431] By the end of 2016, the Prosecution was continuing to present evidence from its third category, which concerns "the identity of the Accused and their respective roles in the attack".[432] Proceedings before the Trial Chamber were interrupted briefly in June and July due to reports of the death of one of the accused persons, Mustafa Amine

[423] Ibid., paras 537, 539–541, 550, 556 and 560.

[424] Ibid., paras 683, 702 and 705–706.

[425] Ibid., para 1104.

[426] Ibid., paras 970–972.

[427] Ibid., para 1120.

[428] Ibid., para 1121.

[429] STL (2015–2016) Special Tribunal for Lebanon: Seventh Annual Report (2015–2016), p. 6. https://www.stl-tsl.org/en/documents/president-s-reports-and-memoranda/4833-seventh-annual-report-2015-2016. Accessed 7 July 2017.

[430] Ibid., p. 17.

[431] Ibid., p. 3 and 17.

[432] STL (2016) STL Bulletin – December 2016, p. 1. https://www.stl-tsl.org/en/media/stl-bulletin/5435-stl-bulletin-december-2016. Accessed 23 February 2017.

Badreddine.[433] While the Trial Chamber initially decided to continue proceedings due to a lack of evidence proving Mr. Badreddine's death, this was ultimately overturned by the Appeals Chamber, who found there was sufficient evidence that Mr. Badreddine had passed away and ordered that the case against him be terminated.[434]

The year 2016 also saw two judgments issued in relation to contempt cases at the STL. The first of these was the appellate decision of 8 March in the *Al Jadeed S.A.L. and Al Khayat* case.[435] This case focused on the broadcasting and online publication of information that allegedly revealed details about confidential witnesses in the *Ayyash et al.* case.[436] In the initial case, the company, Al Jadeed S.A.L., was acquitted on both counts and Ms. Al Khayat was convicted only on the second count, which concerned the failure to comply with the Pre-trial judge's order to remove material from the internet.[437] On appeal, the Appeals Panel overturned Ms. Al Khayat's conviction and her sentence, finding that the Contempt Judge had relied on circumstantial evidence without considering other plausible reasonable inferences in proving that Ms. Al Khayat had received, and subsequently wilfully ignored, the email with the Pre-trial judge's order.[438] Accordingly, Ms. Al Khayat's *mens rea* for the second count could not be proved and she was acquitted.[439] This marks the conclusion of this contempt case.[440]

---

433 STL (2016) Reports on the death of Mr Mustafa Badreddine. https://www.stl-tsl.org/en/news-and-press/press-releases/4995-reports-on-the-death-of-mr-mustafa-badreddine. Accessed 23 February 2017; STL (2016) The Appeals Chamber granted the request for suspensive relief pending resolution of the Appeal submitted by Defence Counsel for Mr Badreddine. https://www.stl-tsl.org/en/media/press-releases/5061-the-appeals-chamber-granted-the-request-for-suspensive-relief-pending-resolution-of-the-appeal-submitted-by-defence-counsel-for-mr-badreddine. Accessed 23 February 2017.

434 STL (2016) STL Judges: Trial continues pending further information on the death of Mustafa Badreddine. https://www.stl-tsl.org/en/news-and-press/press-releases/5022-stl-judges-trial-continues-pending-further-information-on-the-death-of-mustafa-badreddine. Accessed 23 February 2017; STL (2016) The Appeals Chamber orders termination of the proceedings against Mustafa Badreddine without prejudice. https://www.stl-tsl.org/en/news-and-press/press-releases/5078-the-appeals-chamber-orders-termination-of-the-proceedings-against-mustafa-badreddine-without-prejudice. Accessed 23 February 2017.

435 STL (2016) The Appeals Panel reverses Ms Karma Al Khayat's conviction and affirms Al Jadeed's acquittal. https://www.stl-tsl.org/en/appeals-judgment-in-stl-14-05. Accessed 23 February 2017; STL, *In the Case against Al Jadeed [CO.] S.A.L./NEW T.V. S.A.L. (N.T.V.) and Karma Mohamed Tahsin Al Khayat*, Public Redacted Version of Judgment on Appeal, 8 March 2016, Case No. STL-14-05/A/AP (*Al Jadeed*).

436 *Al Jadeed*, above n 435, para 2.

437 Ibid., paras 2 and 8.

438 Ibid., paras 166–170.

439 Ibid., para 173.

440 STL (2016) The Appeals Panel reverses Ms Karma Al Khayat's conviction and affirms Al Jadeed's acquittal. https://www.stl-tsl.org/en/appeals-judgment-in-stl-14-05. Accessed 24 February 2017.

The trial judgment in the second contempt case, which is linked to publishing information in the Al Akhbar newspaper on confidential witnesses in the *Ayyash et al.* case, was handed down on 15 July.[441] Both the company that owned the newspaper, Akhbar Beirut S.A.L., and Mr. Al Amin, the Editor-in-Chief and Chairman of the newspaper's Board of Directors, were charged with one count, under Rule 60 *bis* (A), of "knowingly and wilfully interfering with the administration of justice" via the publication of two articles in January 2013.[442] The Contempt Judge found that the publication of the two articles "created an objective likelihood that the public's confidence" in the STL would be undermined, satisfying the *actus reus* requirement.[443] Judge Lettieri likewise found the *mens rea* element made out as it held Mr. Al Amin had deliberately published the articles and that, in so doing, he "not only knew the impugned [a]rticles were objectively likely to undermine public confidence in the Tribunal, but intended such an outcome".[444] In considering the company's liability, the Contempt Judge noted that Mr. Al Amin was the Editor-in-Chief as well as Chairman of the Board, a director and general manager of Akhbar Beirut S.A.L., and that the company's by-laws hold members of the Board liable for failing to comply with legal requirements.[445] This qualified him as "an employee, representative and director of both the corporate Accused and its subsidiary newspaper", which permitted the Contempt Judge to also find Akhbar Beirut S.A.L. guilty of contempt.[446] Both Mr. Al Amin and the company were later sentenced in August to fines of 20 000 Euros and 6 000 Euros respectively.[447]

8.2.2.4 Extraordinary African Chambers

The Extraordinary African Chambers, within the courts of the Republic of Senegal (Chambres Africaines Extraordinaires, CAE) a "special court with international elements within the Senegalese judicial system",[448] started its operations in 2013 to prosecute and try the persons most responsible for genocide, crimes against humanity, war crimes and torture committed in Chad between 7 June 1982 and

---

[441] STL, *In the Case against Akhbar Beirut S.A.L. and Ibrahim Mohamed Ali Al Amin*, Public Redacted Version of the Judgment, 15 July 2016, Case No. STL-14-06/T/CJ, paras 1–8.

[442] Ibid., paras 1–5 and 32.

[443] Ibid., paras 120–121.

[444] Ibid., paras 146–148.

[445] Ibid., para 169.

[446] Ibid., paras 170–171.

[447] STL (2016) Sentencing judgment in the case against Mr Ibrahim Al Amin and Akhbar Beirut S.A.L. https://www.stl-tsl.org/en/news-and-press/press-releases/5181-sentencing-judgment-in-the-case-against-mr-ibrahim-al-amin-and-akhbar-beirut-s-a-l. Accessed 24 February 2017.

[448] International Crimes Database (2017) Courts – Hybrid – Extraordinary African Chambers. http://www.internationalcrimesdatabase.org/Courts/Hybrid#p7. Accessed 10 July 2017.

1 December 1990.[449] On 30 May 2016, the CAE in Dakar handed down a landmark judgment in the case of Chad's ex-President Hissène Habré,[450] finding him guilty of war crimes, crimes against humanity, torture and grave violations of Common Article 3 of the Geneva Conventions and Additional Protocol II,[451] and sentenced him to life imprisonment at the outcome of a ten-month trial.[452] The crimes committed under his rule of Chad between 1982 and 1990, when he fled to Senegal after being ousted in a coup,[453] include torture and ill-treatment, rape and sexual slavery, enforced disappearances, summary executions and murder[454] and killed 40 000 people.[455] Additionally, on 29 July, he was ordered to pay up to 34 000 dollars to the survivors of his crimes as well as to the family members of his victims.[456] His conviction and life sentence were upheld in appeal by the CAE on 27 April 2017,[457] marking the final stage of proceedings in that case.[458]

[449] Ibid.; Articles 3 and 4 of the CAE's Statute: Chambres Africaines extraordinaires (2012) Annexe, Statut des Chambres africaines extraordinaires au sein des juridictions sénégalaises pour la poursuite des crimes internationaux commis au Tchad durant la période du 7 juin 1982 au 1er décembre 1990. http://www.chambresafricaines.org/pdf/Accord%20UASenegal%20Chambres%20africaines%20extra%20Aout%202012.pdf. Accessed 10 July 2017.

[450] See e.g. The New York Times (2016) A Milestone for Justice in Africa. https://www.nytimes.com/2015/07/22/opinion/a-milestone-for-justice-in-africa.html?emc=edit_tnt_20150722&nlid=9510037&tntemail0=y&_r=0. Accessed 10 July 2017; and Al Jazeera (2016) The long road to justice for Chad's Hissene Habre. http://www.aljazeera.com/indepth/opinion/2016/05/long-road-justice-Chad-Hissene-Habre-160530143401443.html. Accessed 10 July 2017.

[451] CAE, *Ministère Public v Hissein Habré,* Judgment, 30 May 2016, p. 527; The full decision (in French) can be accessed via the following link: http://www.chambresafricaines.org/pdf/Jugement_complet.pdf. Accessed 10 July 2017.

[452] Human Rights Watch (2016) Chad's Ex-Dictator Convicted of Atrocities. https://www.hrw.org/news/2016/05/30/chads-ex-dictator-convicted-atrocities. Accessed 10 July 2017.

[453] Ibid.

[454] Ibid.

[455] BBC News (2016) Hissene Habre: Chad's ex-ruler convicted of crimes against humanity. http://www.bbc.com/news/world-africa-36411466. Accessed 4 May 2017.

[456] The Guardian (2016) Hissène Habré ordered to pay millions for crimes against humanity in Chad. https://www.theguardian.com/global-development/2016/jul/29/hissene-habre-compensation-90m-crimes-against-humanity-chad. Accessed 10 July 2017.

[457] The New York Times (2017) Hissène Habré, Ex-Ruler of Chad, Loses War Crimes Appeal. https://www.nytimes.com/2017/04/27/world/africa/court-habre-chad.html. Accessed 10 July 2017.

[458] Amnesty International (2017) Chad: Hissène Habré Appeal Ruling Closes Dark Chapter for Victims. https://www.amnesty.org/en/press-releases/2017/04/chad-hissene-habre-appeal-ruling-closes-dark-chapter-for-victims/. Accessed 10 July 2017.

8.2.3 *National Courts*[459]

8.2.3.1 Bangladesh

Prosecutions by the Bangladesh International Crimes Tribunal (ICT-BD) into genocide, war crimes, crimes against humanity and other international crimes committed during Bangladesh's independence war against Pakistan in 1971[460] continued in 2016 amidst sustained international scepticism. Criticism of the tribunal concern, notably, the exclusive focus on crimes committed by the leaders of the Islamist party Jamaat-e-Islami, which campaigned against the independence of Bangladesh from Pakistan in the early 1970s, and of the Bangladesh National Party, an opponent to the ruling Awami League party.[461]

Tribunal-1 handed down several death sentences throughout the year for genocide and crimes against humanity, including notably torture, rape, the abduction and killing of civilians and looting. Capital punishment was pronounced in separate judgments against Sakhawat Hossain;[462] Ashraf Hossain, Sharif Ahammed and Abdul Bari;[463] Mohibur Rahman;[464] Shamsuddin Ahmed;[465] Obaidul Haque and Ataur Rahman;[466] and Abdus Subhan.[467] Additionally, death

[459] Although it was already mentioned in the abstract of this chapter that this *Year in Review* cannot be comprehensive in scope, this goes *a fortiori* for the domestic context, where more and more cases on international humanitarian law and international criminal law are adjudicated. The current (domestic) section will therefore only select a few cases. Further analysis of national cases can be found at the T.M.C. Asser Instituut's International Crimes Database (http://www.Internationalcrimesdatabase.org), where one will also find analyses of cases adjudicated by hybrid and international tribunals.

[460] International Crimes Tribunal-1, Bangladesh (2016) About ICT-BD. http://www.ict-bd.org/ict1/indexdetails.php. Accessed 5 May 2017.

[461] International Crimes Database (2017) Courts – Domestic – International Crimes Tribunal Bangladesh. http://www.internationalcrimesdatabase.org/Courts/Domestic. Accessed 5 May 2017.

[462] AP (2016) Bangladesh sentenced ex-MP to death for war crimes in 1971. http://bigstory.ap.org/article/5332bd7d2c774920920ed3f63ea92eac/bangladesh-sentences-ex-mp-death-war-crimes-1971. Accessed 5 May 2017.

[463] ShanghaiDaily (2016) Three sentenced to death, five life in prison for Bangladesh 1971 war crimes. http://www.shanghaidaily.com/article/article_xinhua.aspx?id=331323. Accessed 5 May 2017.

[464] Jurist (2016) Bangladesh war crimes tribunal sentences man to death. http://www.jurist.org/paperchase/2016/06/bangladesh-war-crimes-tribunal-sentences-man-to-death.php. Accessed 5 May 2017.

[465] AP (2016) Bangladesh war crimes court sentences 4 to death. http://bigstory.ap.org/article/ecbfca1765414156aa556d9d4d0d316b/bangladesh-war-crimes-court-sentences-4-death. Accessed 5 May 2017.

[466] Aljazeera (2016) Bangladesh sentences two to death for war crimes. http://www.aljazeera.com/news/2016/02/bangladesh-sentences-death-war-crimes-160202130516749.html. Accessed 5 May 2016.

[467] Jurist (2016) Bangladesh Islamist leader sentenced to death. http://www.jurist.org/paperchase/2015/02/bangladesh-islamist-leader-sentenced-to-death.php. Accessed 5 May 2016.

sentences were delivered in absentia against Idris Ali Sardar;[468] Gazi Abdul Mannan; Hafiz Uddin and Nasiruddin Ahmed;[469] and Syed Mohammed Hasan Ali.[470] Others were sentenced to life in prison.[471]

Meanwhile, the Supreme Court of Bangladesh upheld the death sentences of Rahman Nizami, former head of the banned Jamaat-e-Islami party, on charges of genocide, rape, and murder[472] and Quasem Ali for murder and torture.[473] The two men were executed by hanging respectively in May and September,[474] despite repeated calls by international observers and human rights agencies to suspend executions due to concerns over guarantees of fair trial and due process.[475]

---

[468] Shaon AI (2016) Shariatpur Razakar Idris gets death penalty for war crimes. http://www.dhakatribune.com/bangladesh/2016/12/05/shariatpur-razakar-idris-gets-death-penalty-war-crimes/ Accessed 5 May 2017.

[469] AP (2016) Bangladesh war crimes court sentences 4 to death. http://bigstory.ap.org/article/ecbfca1765414156aa556d9d4d0d316b/bangladesh-war-crimes-court-sentences-4-death. Accessed 5 May 2017.

[470] Jurist (2016) Bangladesh war crimes tribunal sentences fugitive commander to death. http://www.jurist.org/paperchase/2015/06/bangladesh-war-crimes-tribunal-sentences-fugitive-commander-to-death.php. Accessed 5 May 2016.

[471] See e.g. ShanghaiDaily (2016) Three sentenced to death, five life in prison for Bangladesh 1971 war crimes. http://www.shanghaidaily.com/article/article_xinhua.aspx?id=331323. Accessed 5 May 2017; and Jurist (2016) Bangladesh war crimes tribunal sentences fugitive commander to death. http://www.jurist.org/paperchase/2015/06/bangladesh-war-crimes-tribunal-sentences-fugitive-commander-to-death.php. Accessed 5 May 2016.

[472] The Guardian (2016) Bangladesh court rejects Islamist leader's final death sentence appeal. https://www.theguardian.com/world/2016/may/05/bangladesh-court-islamist-leader-appeal-death-sentence-motiur-rahman-nizami. Accessed 5 May 2017.

[473] Jurist (2016) Bangladesh upholds death sentence for 1971 war crimes. http://www.jurist.org/paperchase/2016/03/bangladesh-upholds-death-sentence-for-1971-war-crimes.php. Accessed 5 May 2017.

[474] Aljazeera (2016) Bangladesh executes Motiur Rahman Nizami for war crimes. http://www.aljazeera.com/news/2016/05/bangladesh-hangs-nizami-1971-war-crimes-160510182253819.html. Accessed 5 May 2017; The New York Times (2016) Islamist Party Figure Executed in Bangladesh for '71 Atrocities. https://www.nytimes.com/2016/09/04/world/asia/bangladesh-execution-islamist.html?smprod=nytcore-iphone&smid=nytcore-iphone-share&_r=2. Accessed 5 May 2017.

[475] See UN News Centre (2016) UN rights experts call on Bangladesh to annul death sentence against opposition member. http://www.un.org/apps/news/story.asp?NewsID=54746#.WQxXoWV0WRt. Accessed 5 May 2017; Human Rights Watch (2016) Bangladesh: Halt imminent War Crimes Executions. https://www.hrw.org/news/2016/09/01/bangladesh-halt-imminent-war-crimes-executions. Accessed 5 May 2017; Amnesty International (2017) Amnesty International Report 2016/17 – The State of the World's Human Rights. https://www.amnesty.org/en/latest/research/2017/02/amnesty-international-annual-report-201617/. Accessed 9 July 2017, p. 81.

8.2.3.2 Bosnia and Herzegovina

In July, former Bosnian Serb policemen Goran Vujovic, Miroslav Duka and Zeljko Ilic were sentenced to six, 12 and five years of imprisonment respectively, for crimes against humanity for taking part in the abuse and torture of Bosnians and Croat civilians in Bileca in 1992. The Bosnian State Court "found that there was a widespread and systematic attack by Bosnian Serb army, police and paramilitary units on the civilian population of Bileca."[476]

Meanwhile, the trial of Naser Oric, the former Bosnian Muslim commander at Srebrenica who was extradited last year from Switzerland,[477] and Sabahudin Muhic started in January on nine counts in relation to the killings of three Serb prisoners in 1992 in the towns of Zalazje, Lolici and Kunjera.[478] Both accused pleaded not guilty.[479] In December, the ICTY rejected Oric's motion to order the Bosnian court to suspend proceedings in this case on the basis that he had already been tried and acquitted for war crimes by the Hague-based tribunal in 2008, observing that the new indictment was "significantly different" from the previous charges faced by Mr Oric (he was acquitted by the ICTY for command responsibility in relation to the murder of several people, and in Bosnia, he was accused of directly killing an individual and participating in the murder of two others).[480]

The year closed with the indictment in late December of Borislav Paravac, the Serb former member of Bosnia's tripartite presidency from 2003 to 2005, along with Andrija Bjelosevic and Milan Savic, for taking part in a "widespread and systematic attack" carried out by Serb police, military and paramilitary groups that killed hundreds of Bosnians and Croats in the early 1990s.[481] With 59 indictments issued in 2016 against 135 people, the state prosecution announced that it had now completed investigations in all cases that were transferred from the ICTY.[482] Earlier in July, however, an OSCE analysis had severely criticised the progress of Bosnia and Herzegovina's National War Crimes Strategy and highlighted the existence of a backlog of over 350 complex cases.[483]

---

[476] Balkan Transitional Justice (2016) Bosnian Serb Ex-Policemen Jailed for Abuse and Torture. http://www.balkaninsight.com/en/article/former-bosnian-serb-policemen-sentenced-for-bileca-crimes-07-08-2016. Accessed 4 May 2017.

[477] See Boutin et al. 2015, p. 264.

[478] B92 (2016) War Crimes trial of Naser Oric begins in Bosnia. http://www.b92.net/eng/news/region.php?yyyy=2016&mm=01&dd=26&nav_id=96816. Accessed 4 May 2017.

[479] Ibid.

[480] Ibid.

[481] Balkan Transitional Justice (2016) Bosnia Charges Former Presidency Member with War Crimes. http://www.balkaninsight.com/en/article/bosnia-charges-ex-presidency-member-for-war-crimes-12-31-2015. Accessed 4 May 2017.

[482] Ibid.

[483] OSCE (2016) Processing of War Crimes at the State Level in Bosnia and Herzegovina. http://www.osce.org/bih/247221. Accessed 4 May 2017.

8.2.3.3 Croatia

Prosecutions continued throughout the year concerning war crimes committed during the Croatian civil war of 1991–1995. Dragan Vasiljkovic, a former Serbian paramilitary leader who was extradited from Australia in 2015 to face war crime charges, was formally indicted in January by a Croatian Court for torturing and killing civilians as well as captive Croatian soldiers in 1991 and 1993.[484] He is also accused of planning an attack on a police station that caused many civilian casualties, looting and destruction of property.[485] He pleaded not guilty at the start of his trial in September, which was planned to take several months.[486]

In October, eight ex-Yugoslav military officers were charged with war crimes committed between 1991 and 1995 that include ordering attacks on civilian areas and failing to take the necessary measures to prevent rape, torture and murder of more than 100 civilians by soldiers under their command.[487] However in late July the eight-year prison sentence of Branimir Glavas, a former general and high-ranking politician convicted of war crimes in 2010 for abducting, torturing and murdering ten Serbs in 1991, was annulled by the Supreme Court on "procedural grounds" and sent to retrial, sparking outrage in Serbia.[488]

8.2.3.4 El Salvador

In July, the Supreme Court overturned on constitutional grounds a 1993 Amnesty Law that protected the military, paramilitary and guerrilla fighters from prosecution for crimes committed during El Salvador's 12-year civil war.[489] This ruling is considered a key development in the country's fight against impunity, opening the door to possible prosecutions against individuals who held high-ranking positions in the military command structure as well as current top officials, including the actual President Salvador Sanchez Ceren.[490] In October, a Salvadorian Court

[484] Reuters (2016) Croatia indicts Serb paramilitary commander for war crimes. http://www.reuters.com/article/us-croatia-warcrimes-idUSKBN0UM1ML20160108. Accessed 4 May 2017.

[485] Ibid.

[486] AP (2016) Ex-Serb commander pleads not guilty to war crime charges. http://bigstory.ap.org/article/ca5a3773e9734045aa65de7094acf637/ex-serb-commander-pleads-not-guilty-war-crimes-charges. Accessed 4 May 2017.

[487] Wildberger S (2016) Croatia prosecutor charges ex-Yugoslav military officers with war crimes. http://www.jurist.org/paperchase/2016/10/croatia-prosecutor-charges-ex-yugoslav-military-officers-with-war-crimes.php. Accessed 4 May 2017.

[488] Siddiqui SUR (2016) Croatian court orders retrial for ex-MP war crimes suspect. http://www.brecorder.com/2016/07/28/311257/. Accessed 4 May 2017.

[489] The Washington Times (2016) El Salvador scraps amnesty law, opens door for prosecutions. http://www.washingtontimes.com/news/2016/jul/14/el-salvador-scraps-amnesty-law-opens-door-for-pros/. Accessed 9 May 2017.

[490] Ibid.

accepted a request to reopen an investigation into the 1981 massacre of El Mozoto where 500 people died, allegedly at the hands of the country's military.[491]

8.2.3.5 France

On 6 July a Paris criminal Court convicted two Rwandan mayors, Octavien Ngenzi and Tito Barahira, of genocide and crimes against humanity for the 1994 massacre and killing of 2 000 people who had taken up refuge in a church in the Rwandan village of Kabarondo.[492] The two men, who had already been sentenced in absentia to life imprisonment in 2009 by a Gacaca Court under Rwanda's community justice system, appealed the verdict and their life imprisonment sentence.[493]

Meanwhile, an investigation is still ongoing into the activities of a French company suspected of aiding and abetting torture for selling surveillance equipment that may have been used by the Syrian regime to arrest, and subsequently, torture detainees.[494]

8.2.3.6 Germany

In July a radicalised German national was convicted[495] of "war crimes consisting of the degrading and humiliating treatment of protected persons"[496] after photographs circulated on social media of him posing with several heads of decapitated enemy combatants while in Syria.[497] He received a two-year imprisonment sentence.[498] In October, the trial of an alleged member of a jihadist rebel armed group accused of

---

[491] DW (2016) El Salvador to reopen probe into 1981 massacre. http://www.dw.com/en/el-salvador-to-reopen-probe-into-1981-massacre/a-35941387. Accessed 9 May 2017.

[492] The Guardian (2016) Two Rwandan mayors jailed for life over 1994 massacre. https://www.theguardian.com/world/2016/jul/06/two-rwandan-mayors-jailed-for-life-over-1994-massacre?CMP=share_btn_tw. Accessed 5 May 2017.

[493] Jeune Afrique (2016) Génocide au Rwanda: Tito Barahira et Octavien Ngenzi font appel de leur condamnation à perpétuité. http://www.jeuneafrique.com/339927/societe/genocide-rwanda-tito-barahira-octavien-ngenzi-appel-de-condamnation-a-perpetuite/. Accessed 5 May 2017.

[494] Human Rights Watch (2016) Q&A First Cracks to Impunity in Syria, Iraq. https://www.hrw.org/news/2016/10/20/qa-first-cracks-impunity-syria-iraq. Accessed 5 May 2017.

[495] Higher Regional Court, Frankfurt am Main, Germany, *Prosecutor v Aria Ladjedvardi*, Judgment, 12 July 2016, Case No. 5-3 StE 2/16 - 4 - 1/16.

[496] International Crimes Database (2016) Prosecutor v. Aria Ladjedvardi, Summary. http://www.internationalcrimesdatabase.org/Case/3276/Aria-Ladjedvardi/. Accessed 5 May 2017.

[497] Ibid.

[498] Ibid.

kidnapping a UN observer in 2013 in Damascus began on charges of war crimes.[499]

In what is likely to be one of Germany's last trial of Nazi war crimes, former death camp guard Reinhold Hanning was sentenced in June to five years of imprisonment by a German Court for being an accessory to the murder of 170 000 people at Auschwitz during the Second World War.[500] He appealed the verdict.[501] The trial of Hubert Zafke, a former Nazi SS medic indicted for his accomplice role in the killings of 3 861 persons at Auschwitz in 1944, resumed in October after being suspended many times throughout the year due to the health condition of the accused.[502] In November, a German federal court rejected former death camp guard Oskar Groening's appeal of his 2015 conviction for his role as an accessory to the murder of 300 000 Jews.[503]

8.2.3.7 Guatemala

Exactly two decades after the end of Guatemala's 36-year armed conflict, 2016 was marked by important albeit mostly symbolic progress in the fight against impunity for past violations in Guatemala. In a landmark judgment in February, High Risk Tribunal B sentenced two former military officers to 120 and 240 years of imprisonment for sexual enslavement of 15 Maya Q'Eqchi' women amounting to crimes against humanity in the village of Sepur Zarco in the 1980s.[504]

---

499 Human Rights Watch (2016) Q&A First Cracks to Impunity in Syria, Iraq. https://www.hrw.org/news/2016/10/20/qa-first-cracks-impunity-syria-iraq. Accessed 5 May 2017; and Huggle J (2016) Suspected Syrian jihadist arrested in Germany for "war crime". http://www.telegraph.co.uk/news/worldnews/europe/germany/12115037/Suspected-Syrian-jihadist-arrested-in-Germany-for-war-crime.html. Accessed 5 May 2017.

500 The Guardian (2016) Auschwitz guard jailed for five years in Holocaust murder trial. https://www.theguardian.com/world/2016/jun/17/auschwitz-guard-reinhold-hanning-jailed-holocaust-auschwitz. Accessed 5 May 2017.

501 CBS/AP (2016) Former Auschwitz guard to appeal verdict in murder trial. http://www.cbsnews.com/news/nazi-auschwitz-guard-reinhold-hanning-appeals-conviction/. Accessed 5 May 2017.

502 Trial International (2017) Hubert Zafke. https://trialinternational.org/latest-post/hubert-zafke/. Accessed 5 May 2017.

503 Moulson G (2016) German court denies appeal of ex-Auschwitz guard, sparking hope for other cases against suspected Nazis. http://www.nationalpost.com/m/wp/news/blog.html?b=news.nationalpost.com/news/world/german-court-denies-appeal-of-ex-auschwitz-guard-sparking-hope-for-other-cases-against-suspected-nazis&pubdate=2016-11-28. Accessed 5 May 2017.

504 The Guardian (2016) Justice at last for Guatemalan women as military officers jailed for sexual slavery. https://www.theguardian.com/world/2016/mar/01/guatemala-sexual-slavery-sepur-zarco-military-officers-jailed. Accessed 8 May 2017.

Proceedings remained ongoing in a number of other high-profile cases. Among them, the retrial of former General José Efraín Ríos Montt and his head of military intelligence, José Manuel Rodríguez Sánchez, for genocide and crimes against humanity against the Maya Ixil population during Ríos Montt's de facto rule of Guatemala in 1982–1983 began on 16 March before High Risk Tribunal B after suffering a long series of delays,[505] only to be suspended again in May by a decision of the First Court of Appeals.[506] Hearings in the case of Ríos Montt and his co-accused, which was sent back to the High Risk Tribunal after his criminal conviction was annulled by the Constitutional Court on procedural grounds in May 2013,[507] were being held behind closed doors and without the prospect of a criminal sanction against the ex-dictator due to his mental health condition, as was decided by the Tribunal in August 2015.[508] The decision of the Appeals Court, which was confirmed a month later, granted a request by the civil parties to the case claiming that the proceedings violated Guatemalan law and should be held in two separate trials.[509] At the time of writing a date for both new trials had yet to be set.[510]

In a case known as "Creompaz", High-Risk Tribunal A found on 7 June that there was enough evidence to allow a case against eight military officers for crimes against humanity allegedly committed between 1981 and 1987 to proceed to trial.[511] However, a certain number of appeals needed to be resolved before a trial could begin, including the Attorney-General's Office's Appeal to the Supreme

[505] Burt JM (2016) Ríos Montt Genocide Retrial Starts Amidst Controversy. https://www.ijmonitor.org/2016/03/rios-montt-genocide-retrial-starts-amidst-controversy/. Accessed 8 May 2017; see also NISGUA (2016) CALDH reports from the closed-door retrial of Ríos Montt. http://nisgua.org/caldh-reports-from-the-closed-door-retrial-of-rios-montt/. Accessed 8 May 2017.

[506] Burt JM (2016) Genocide Trial Suspended; Plaintiffs Claim Proceedings Illegal. https://www.ijmonitor.org/2016/05/genocide-trial-suspended-plaintiffs-claim-proceedings-illegal/. Accessed 8 May 2017.

[507] MacLean E (2013) Guatemala's Constitutional Court Overturns Ríos Montt Conviction and Sends Trial Back to April 19. https://www.ijmonitor.org/2013/05/constitutional-court-overturns-rios-montt-conviction-and-sends-trial-back-to-april-19/. Accessed 8 May 2017.

[508] Beaudoin S (2016) Court Orders Ríos Montt and Rodriguez Sanchez Retrial to Begin in January 2016. https://www.ijmonitor.org/2015/08/court-orders-rios-montt-and-rodriguez-sanchez-retrial-to-begin-in-january-2016/. Accessed 8 May 2017.

[509] More specifically, the Center for Human Rights Legal Action (CALDH) and the Justice and Reconciliation Association (AJR) claimed that the inclusion of the proceedings against Rodríguez Sánchez under Ríos Montt's closed doors trial violated the rights of victims to a public hearing. See Burt JM (2016) Appeals Court Upholds Suspension of Ríos Montt Genocide Trial. https://www.ijmonitor.org/2016/06/appeals-court-upholds-suspension-of-rios-montt-genocide-trial/. Accessed 8 May 2017.

[510] Human Rights Watch (2017) World Report 2017 – Events of 2016. https://www.hrw.org/world-report/2017. Accessed 9 July 2017, p. 295; Burt JM (2017) No Answers on Whether Ríos Montt Will Go to Trial for Dos Erres Massacre. https://www.ijmonitor.org/2017/02/no-answers-on-whether-rios-montt-will-go-to-trial-for-dos-erres-massacre/. Accessed 8 May 2017.

[511] NISGUA (2016) Creompaz: Eight former military officers to stand trial for forced disappearances. http://nisgua.org/creompaz-eight-former-military-officers-to-stand-trial-for-forced-disappearances/. Accessed 8 May 2017.

Court for the "Tribunal's failure to consider accusations of sexual violence and its refusal to characterise forced disappearance as a war crime in addition to a crime against humanity".[512] In another notorious case known as "Molina Theissen", five high-ranking military officers, including the former chief of the Guatemalan army Benedicto Lucas García were indicted in 2016 with charges of illegal detention, torture, sexual violence and enforced disappearances.[513] Among them, Mr. García (who is also being tried in the Creompaz case) is indicted for his role as intellectual author of these crimes[514] under the principle of command responsibility.[515] Critical hearings which are to be followed by the Judge's determination of whether the case should be allowed to proceed to trial were postponed to 2017.[516]

8.2.3.8 Rwanda

On 30 December 2015, Rwanda's High Court sentenced pastor Jean Uwinkindi to life in prison for his participation in attacks against members of the Tutsi minority in the 1994 genocide.[517] In October 2016, the MICT rejected Uwinkindi's various appeals concerning his request for the revocation of the referral of his case to Rwanda's High Court,[518] which was ordered in 2011 by the ICTR.[519] The year also saw a number of individuals extradited from European and North American

---

[512] Trial International (2016) Manuel Benedicto Lucas García – Creompaz case and Molina Theissen case. Legal Procedure. https://trialinternational.org/latest-post/manuel-benedicto-lucas-garcia/#section-2. Accessed 8 May 2017.

[513] Burt JM (2016) Judge Charges Former Army Chief Benedicto Lucas García in Molina Theissen Case. https://www.ijmonitor.org/2016/10/judge-charges-former-army-chief-benedicto-lucas-garcia-in-molina-theissen-case/. Accessed 8 May 2017.

[514] Trial International (2016) Manuel Benedicto Lucas García – Creompaz case and Molina Theissen case. Legal Procedure. https://trialinternational.org/latest-post/manuel-benedicto-lucas-garcia/#section-2. Accessed 8 May 2017.

[515] Burt JM (2016) Judge Charges Former Army Chief Benedicto Lucas García in Molina Theissen Case. https://www.ijmonitor.org/2016/10/judge-charges-former-army-chief-benedicto-lucas-garcia-in-molina-theissen-case/. Accessed 8 May 2017.

[516] Burt MJ (2016) Critical hearing in Guatemala's Molina Theissen case delayed again. https://www.ijmonitor.org/2016/12/critical-hearing-in-guatemalas-molina-theissen-case-delayed-again/. Accessed 8 May 2016.

[517] BBC News (2015) Rwanda genocide: Jean Uwinkindi sentenced to life in prison. http://www.bbc.com/news/world-africa-35202424. Accessed 9 May 2017.

[518] See, e.g., MICT, *Prosecutor v Jean Uwinkindi*, Decision on an appeal concerning a request for revocation of a referral, 4 October 2016, Case No. MICT-12-25-AR14.1; see also Sect. 8.2.1.2 of this chapter.

[519] ICTR, *Prosecutor v Jean Uwinkindi*, Decision on Prosecutor's request for referral to the Republic of Rwanda, 28 June 2011, Case No. ICTR-2001-75-R11bis.

countries to face charges of genocide and crimes against humanity in Rwanda. Those include Professor Leopold Munyakazi from the US,[520] Jean-Claude Iyamuremye and Jean-Baptiste Mugimba from the Netherlands,[521] and former military officer Jean Claude Seyoboka from Canada.[522]

8.2.3.9 Sri Lanka

The creation of a new court, announced in December 2015, to investigate alleged war crimes committed in the last phase of Sri Lanka's 26-year civil war did not materialise in 2016, contrary to expectations.[523] Nevertheless, progress was made through a public consultation process led by the Consultation Task Force on Reconciliation Mechanisms.[524] After months of discussion on the extent of foreign involvement,[525] the Task Force handed over its final report[526] in the first days of 2017, which recommended the establishment of a hybrid court involving both local and international judges,[527] a conclusion that was welcomed by international observers, including Human Rights Watch.[528]

---

[520] BBC News (2016) US deports Rwanda genocide suspect Leopold Munyakazi. http://www.bbc.com/news/world-africa-37493505. Accessed 9 May 2017.

[521] Le Monde (2016) Deux Rwandais vont être extradés des Pays-Bas vers le Rwanda. http://www.lemonde.fr/afrique/article/2016/11/12/deux-rwandais-vont-etre-extrades-des-pays-bas-vers-le-rwanda_5030104_3212.html. Accessed 9 May 2017; the two men pleaded not guilty to genocide and crimes against humanity-related charges on November 21. See Thomson Reuters Foundation (2016) Rwandan genocide suspects extradited from Netherlands face court. http://news.trust.org/item/20161121162014-yprn7/. Accessed 9 May 2017.

[522] New Times (2016) Canada deports Genocide suspect Seyoboka. http://www.newtimes.co.rw/section/article/2016-11-17/205456/. Accessed 9 May 2017; charges were officially brought against Seyoboka in December: See Uwiringiyimana C (2016) Rwandan tribunal charges ex-military officer over genocide. http://af.reuters.com/article/topNews/idAFKBN13Q4MS. Accessed 9 May 2017.

[523] See e.g. Reuters (2015) Sri Lanka to start up special court on alleged war crimes. http://www.reuters.com/article/us-sri-lanka-rights-idUSKBN0TK5E120151201. Accessed 4 May 2017.

[524] See Nafeel N (2016) Domestic mechanism consultation process to begin next week. http://www.dailynews.lk/?q=2016/01/08/local/domestic-mechanism-consultation-process-begin-next-week. Accessed 4 May 2017; for more details on this, see the Task Force's website: Secretariat for Coordinating Reconciliation Mechanisms (2017) Consultations. http://www.scrm.gov.lk/consultations. Accessed 4 May 2017.

[525] Ali I (2016) Sri Lanka could accept international actors in war crimes probe. http://www.reuters.com/article/usa-sri-lanka-court-idUSKCN0VZ01D. Accessed 4 May 2017.

[526] See the final report: Consultation Task Force on Reconciliation Mechanisms (2016) Final Report. http://www.scrm.gov.lk/documents-reports. Accessed 4 May 2017.

[527] Jurist (2016) Sri Lanka panel backs hybrid courts for investigation of war crimes. http://www.jurist.org/paperchase/2017/01/sri-lankan-panel-backs-hybrid-courts-for-war-crimes.php/. Accessed 4 May 2017.

[528] Human Rights Watch (2017) Sri Lanka: Adopt Task Force's Justice Proposals. https://www.hrw.org/news/2017/01/12/sri-lanka-adopt-task-forces-justice-proposals. Accessed 4 May 2017.

8.2.3.10 Sweden

On 16 May, the Stockholm District Court sentenced Claver Berinkindi, a Rwandan national who also became a Swedish citizen in 2012, to life in prison for "genocide and gross crime(s) under international law consisting of murder, attempted murder and kidnapping" committed in Rwanda in 1994.[529] He had previously been convicted in absentia of similar crimes by a Rwandan Gacaca court in 2007.[530] His sentence was confirmed on 15 February 2017 by the Svea Court of Appeals in Stockholm.[531]

In August, the Stockholm Court of Appeal also confirmed the 2015 conviction of Mouhannad Droubi, a Syrian national and alleged member of the Free Syrian Army, for the torture of a prisoner in Syria, which amounted to a war crime.[532]

8.3 Arms Control and Disarmament

8.3.1 Conventional Weapons

At the 71st Session of the UN General Assembly, the focus of the First Committee (Disarmament and International Security) was on disarmament machinery, nuclear non-proliferation, international security and outer space.[533] A series of draft resolutions on these topics were tabled and adopted on 5 December.[534]

The Governmental Experts on the "Continuing operation of the United Nations Register of Conventional Arms and its further development" submitted a report in 2016.[535] This group was convened by the UN Secretary-General at the request of the UN General Assembly in 2013 to provide a report on the UN Register of Conventional Arms.[536] The report noted that 2016 marked the 25th anniversary of

---

[529] Reuters (2016) Sweden sentences man to life imprisonment. http://www.reuters.com/article/us-rwanda-warcrimes-idUSKCN0Y70XQ/. Accessed 8 May 2017.

[530] Ibid.

[531] Swedish Court of Appeal confirms life sentence for Claver Berinkindi condemned for Genocide. http://cnlg.gov.rw/news-details/?tx_ttnews%5Btt_news%5D=1254&cHash=f69443a0e6f599db16b892446a7af573#.WRCbq02wdMw. Accessed 8 May 2017.

[532] Trial International (2016) Mouhannad Droubi. https://trialinternational.org/latest-post/mouhannad-droubi/. Accessed 5 May 2017.

[533] UN (2016) Approving Work Programme, First Committee Will Focus on Disarmament Machinery, Nuclear Non-proliferation, International Security and Outer Space. http://www.un.org/press/en/2016/gadis3544.doc.htm. Accessed 25 February 2017.

[534] For a full list of discussions and resolutions adopted at the 71st session of the GA First Committee, see: https://www.un.org/disarmament/firstcommittee-71/. Accessed 25 February 2017.

[535] UN General Assembly (2016a) Report on the continuing operation of the United Nations Register of Conventional Arms and its further development, UN Doc. A/71/259.

[536] UN General Assembly (2013) Resolution adopted by the General Assembly on 5 December 2013: 68/43. Transparency in armaments, UN Doc. A/RES/68/43.

the adoption of the register, expressed concern at the decline in reporting since 2008, and put forward recommendations regarding the classification of weapons in the Register.[537]

The Second Conference of States Parties to the Arms Trade Treaty (ATT), which was adopted in 2014, was held from 22 to 26 August in Geneva.[538] Prior to the Second Conference, Amnesty International expressed concern at the number of states who had not fulfilled their reporting obligations under the treaty.[539] The ATT expanded in 2016 with Benin, Cabo Verde, Cyprus, Georgia, Greece, Guatemala, Lesotho, Madagascar, Peru, the Republic of Korea and Zambia ratifying the treaty and the accession of Monaco.[540]

At the Fifth Review Conference on the Convention on Conventional Weapons (CCW) held in Geneva from 12 to 16 December, the discussion focused on "lethal autonomous weapon systems".[541] There were concerns regarding these systems, which were discussed at length in a Human Rights Watch report published earlier in the year.[542]

The Democratic People's Republic of Korea (DPRK) carried out a long-range rocket launch on 7 February, which was condemned by the UN Security Council in their resolution of 2 March. The resolution extended existing measures imposed by UN Security Council Resolution 1718 (2006) and added additional measures, including "that all States shall prohibit public and private financial support from within their territories or by persons or entities subject to their jurisdiction for trade with the DPRK […] where such financial support could contribute to the DPRK's nuclear or ballistic missile programs or other activities prohibited by resolutions".[543]

---

[537] UN General Assembly (2016a) Report on the continuing operation of the United Nations Register of Conventional Arms and its further development, UN Doc. A/71/259.

[538] ATT (2016) The Arms Trate Treaty Second Conference of States Parties, Geneva, Switzerland, 22–26 August 2016 – Final Report. http://thearmstradetreaty.org/images/ATT_documents/Final_Report_ATT_CSP2_2016_5. Accessed 25 February 2017.

[539] Amnesty International (2016) UN: Zero tolerance for states who flout Arms Trade Treaty obligations. https://www.amnesty.org/en/latest/news/2016/08/un-zero-tolerance-for-states-who-flout-arms-trade-treaty-obligations/. Accessed 23 February 2017.

[540] UN Treaty Collection (2016) Status of the Arms Trade Treaty. https://treaties.un.org/pages/ViewDetails.aspx?src=TREATY&mtdsg_no=XXVI-8&chapter=26&clang=_en. Accessed 23 February 2017.

[541] Fifth Review Conference of the High Contracting Parties to the Convention on Prohibitions or Restrictions on the Use of Certain Conventional Weapons Which May Be Deemed to Be Excessively Injurious or to Have Indiscriminate Effects (2016) Report of the 2016 Informal Meeting of Experts on Lethal Autonomous Weapons Systems (LAWS). https://documents-dds-ny.un.org/doc/UNDOC/GEN/G16/117/16/PDF/G1611716.pdf. Accessed 25 February 2017.

[542] Human Rights Watch (2016) Making the Case: The Dangers of Killer Robots and the Need for a Pre-emptive Ban. https://www.hrw.org/report/2016/12/09/making-case/dangers-killer-robots-and-need-preemptive-ban. Accessed 20 February 2017.

[543] UN Security Council (2016g) Resolution 2270 (2016), UN Doc. S/RES/2270.

In light of the adoption of UN General Assembly Resolution 70/44 at its 70th session regarding conventional arms control at the regional and subregional level,[544] the UN Secretary-General released a note requesting state views on the matter on 8 February.[545] A report outlining the views received from ten Member States was compiled and published by the UN Secretary-General on 14 July.[546] This report outlined the activities carried out by the various States in this area and their general views on the current system in place.

8.3.2 Non-Conventional Weapons

8.3.2.1 Chemical Weapons

In 2015 and pursuant to UN Security Council Resolution 2235, the Joint Investigative Mechanism (JIM) of the UN and the Organisation for the Prohibition of Chemical Weapons (OPCW) was established to investigate allegations surrounding the use of chemical weapons in Syria.[547] The JIM released four reports in 2016, which outlined its method of investigation and published findings regarding the actors involved in the use of chemical weapons in certain incidences.[548] The first report of the JIM was considered by the Security Council on 22 February and it provided "an overview of the work of the Mechanism to date, the sources of information available to the Mechanism and the methodology behind the investigation".[549] The second report of the JIM was presented to the UN Security Council on 10 June, further outlining the operational guidelines of the JIM.[550]

---

[544] UN General Assembly (2015b) Resolution adopted by the General Assembly on 7 December 2015: 70/44. Conventional arms control at the regional and subregional level, UN Doc. A/RES/70/44.

[545] UN General Assembly (2016b) Conventional arms control at the regional and subregional levels: Report of the Secretary-General, UN Doc. A/71/154, para 2.

[546] See generally, ibid.

[547] UN Security Council (2015) Resolution 2235 (2015), UN Doc. S/RES/2235.

[548] UN (2016) Joint Investigative Mechanism Presents Its First Report to Security Council. http://www.un.org/press/en/2016/dc3608.doc.htm. Accessed 24 February 2017; UN Security Council (2016n) Second report of the Organization for the Prohibition of Chemical Weapons-United Nations Joint Investigative Mechanism, UN Doc. S/2016/530; UN Security Council (2016o) Third report of the Organization for the Prohibition of Chemical Weapons-United Nations Joint Investigative Mechanism, UN Doc. S/2016/738, paras 19 and 25.

[549] UN (2016) Joint Investigative Mechanism Presents Its First Report to Security Council. http://www.un.org/press/en/2016/dc3608.doc.htm. Accessed 24 February 2017; UN Security Council (2016a) First Report of the Organization for the Prohibition of Chemical Weapons-United Nations Investigative Mechanism, UN Doc. S/2016/142.

[550] UN Security Council (2016n) Second report of the Organization for the Prohibition of Chemical Weapons-United Nations Joint Investigative Mechanism, UN Doc. S/2016/530.

The final two reports considered substantive incidents where chemical weapons were allegedly used and the actors involved. The third report was submitted on 24 August and found that the Syrian Arab Armed Forces[551] in Talmenas and Sarmin and IS forces in Marea were responsible for the use of chemical weapons in a number of the situations investigated.[552] The fourth report of the JIM was discussed by the UN Security Council at its meeting on 27 October.[553] It provided assessments and conclusions in the three pending cases from the third report, namely that of Kafr Zita on 18 April 2014, Qmenas on 16 March 2015 and Binnish on 24 March 2015. The Panel concluded that there was sufficient evidence in the case of Qmenas to determine that the Syrian Arab Armed Forces were responsible for the attack.[554] The findings in the remaining two cases, Kafr Zita and Binnish, which were examined in the fourth report were determined to be inconclusive by the Panel.[555] The Syrian government was highly critical of the JIM reports and considered the JIM to be "completely flawed", especially due to its reliance on findings of the "politicised" fact-finding mission, inconsistencies in testimonies acquired and the inconclusive nature of some of the evidence referred to.[556]

The JIM identified actors involved in carrying out chemical weapons attacks in four out of the nine cases investigated, with other cases considered inconclusive due to a lack of evidence.[557] The use of chlorine was suspected in eight cases and the use of sulphur mustard was investigated in one case.[558] Furthermore, the JIM was concerned by the number of allegations it received, 15 in total, of possession, movement and/or intent of use of toxic substances, including the use of chemical weapons by non-state actors in the Syrian Arab Republic.[559] The JIM mandate was extended for a further year from 17 November by UN Security Council Resolution 2319.[560] The US representative to the Security Council "noted that the Joint

---

[551] The Syrian Arab Armed Forces are the national armed forces of the Syrian Arab Republic.

[552] UN Security Council (2016o) Third report of the Organization for the Prohibition of Chemical Weapons-United Nations Joint Investigative Mechanism, UN Doc. S/2016/738.

[553] UN (2016) Security Council Considers Fourth Report by Joint Investigative Mechanism. https://www.un.org/press/en/2016/dc3668.doc.htm. Accessed 23 February 2017.

[554] UN Security Council (2016b) Fourth report of the Organization for the Prohibition of Chemical Weapons-United Nations Joint Investigative Mechanism, UN Doc. S/2016/888, paras 19 and 25.

[555] Fourth report of the Organization for the Prohibition of Chemical Weapons-United Nations Joint Investigative Mechanism, UN Doc. S/2016/888, para 34.

[556] UN Security Council (2016c) Letter dated 10 October 2016 from the Permanent Representative of the Syrian Arab Republic to the United Nations addressed to the President of the Security Council: Responses and main observations regarding the third report of the Joint Investigative Mechanism, UN Doc. S/2016/844.

[557] Fourth report of the Organization for the Prohibition of Chemical Weapons-United Nations Joint Investigative Mechanism, UN Doc. S/2016/888, para 47.

[558] Third report of the Organization for the Prohibition of Chemical Weapons-United Nations Joint Investigative Mechanism, UN Doc. S/2016/738, para 32.

[559] Fourth report of the Organization for the Prohibition of Chemical Weapons-United Nations Joint Investigative Mechanism, UN Doc. S/2016/888, para 51.

[560] UN Security Council (2016k) Resolution 2319 (2016), UN Doc. S/RES/2319.

Investigative Mechanism's work was not complete and must continue" and "it was the only body given the mandate to identify those involved in the use of chemicals as weapons."[561]

In September, Amnesty International published the results of its investigations into the alleged use of chemical weapons in Darfur, Sudan.[562] This report provides evidence that chemical weapons have been used against civilians in Sudan, with experts suggesting "exposure to vesicants, or blister agents, such as the chemical warfare agents sulphur mustard, lewisite or nitrogen mustard".[563] Amnesty International believes that the Sudanese government may be responsible for these alleged attacks.[564]

8.3.2.2 Biological Weapons

The Preparatory Meetings for the Eighth Review Conference of the States Parties to the Convention on the Prohibition of the Development, Production and Stockpiling of Bacteriological (Biological) and Toxin Weapons and on Their Destruction took place from 26 to 27 April and from 2 to 12 August,[565] with the Conference taking place in Geneva from 7 to 25 November 2016.[566] The Conference decided to have annual meetings of up to five days before the next Review Conference in 2021, which "will seek to make progress on issues of substance and process for the period before the next Review Conference, with a view to reaching consensus on an intersessional process."[567]

On 18 January, Council Decision (CFSP) 2016/51 was adopted by the EU in support of the Biological and Toxin Weapons Convention (BTWC) in the framework of the EU Strategy against Proliferation of Weapons of Mass Destruction. This highlighted the EU's support of the BTWC, which also included support for

---

[561] UN (2016) Unanimously Adopting Resolution 2319 (2016), Security Council Extends Mandate of Mechanism to Identify Perpetrators Using Chemical Weapons in Syria. https://www.un.org/press/en/2016/sc12594.doc.htm. Accessed 2 March 2017.

[562] Amnesty International (2016) Sudan: Credible evidence of the use of chemical weapons to kill and maim hundreds of civilians including children in Darfur revealed. https://www.amnesty.org/en/latest/news/2016/09/sudan-credible-evidence-chemical-weapons-darfur-revealed/. Accessed 25 February 2017.

[563] Ibid.

[564] Ibid.

[565] Preparatory Committee (2016) Report of the Preparatory Committee to the Review Conference. http://unog.ch/80256EDD006B8954/DB0D23DED41F63D1C1258018003259DD/$file/Advance+version+proc+report+and+summary+report.pdf. Accessed 25 February 2017.

[566] Eighth Review Conference of the States Parties to the Convention on the Prohibition of the Development, Production and Stockpiling of Bacteriological (Biological) and Toxin Weapons and on Their Destruction (2016) Final Document of the Eighth Review Conference. http://unog.ch/80256EDD006B8954/F277FA6A2B96BA98C125807A005B2F59/$file/2016-1129+Final+report+adv+vers.pdf. Accessed 25 February 2017.

[567] Ibid.: see "B. Intersessional Programme 2017–2021", para 1.

six projects which promote the universalisation and implementation of the Convention.[568]

8.3.2.3 Nuclear Weapons

On 5 January[569] and 8 September,[570] the DPRK conducted tests of its nuclear weapons in violation of its international obligations.[571] These tests were condemned by the international community at large[572] and, in March, the UN Security Council adopted Resolution 2270 condemning the testing and imposing new sanctions on the DPRK.[573] In its 71st session, the UN General Assembly urged the DPRK to fulfil its commitments under the Six-Party Talks, to return to the Treaty on the Non-Proliferation of Nuclear Weapons (NPT) and to adhere to the International Atomic Energy Agency (IAEA) safeguard agreements.[574] In response to the nuclear tests carried out by the DPRK, the US provided the Republic of Korea with a Terminal High Altitude Area Defence System; this decision received criticism from China.[575]

The UN General Assembly decided to convene a meeting of the UN Open-Ended Working Group (OEWG) in Geneva in 2016.[576] It was tasked with

---

568 Official Journal of the European Union (2016) Council Decision (CFSP) 2016/51 of 18 January 2016 in support of the Biological and Toxin Weapons Convention (BTWC) in the framework of the EU Strategy against Proliferation of Weapons of Mass Destruction. www.eur-lex.europa.eu/legal-content/EN/TXT/PDF/?uri=CELEX:32016D0051&from=EN. Accessed 25 February 2017.

569 The Guardian (2016) North Korea claims successful hydrogen bomb test in "self-defence against US". https://www.theguardian.com/world/2016/jan/06/north-korean-nuclear-test-suspected-as-artificial-earthquake-detected. Accessed 23 February 2017.

570 New York Times (2016) North Korea's Nuclear Blasts Keep Getting Stronger. https://www.nytimes.com/2016/09/10/world/asia/north-korea-nuclear-weapons-tests.html?action=click&contentCollection=Asia%20Pacific&module=RelatedCoverage&region=EndOfArticle&pgtype=article. Accessed 23 February 2017.

571 European Union External Action (2016) Statement on the nuclear test in the DPRK. https://eeas.europa.eu/headquarters/headquarters-homepage/9582/statement-on-the-nuclear-test-in-the-dprk_en. Accessed 1 March 2017.

572 Aljazeera (2016) North Korea nuclear test: World leaders react. http://www.aljazeera.com/news/2016/09/north-korea-nuclear-test-world-leaders-react-160909055255360.html. Accessed 1 March 2017.

573 UN Security Council (2016g) Resolution 2270 (2016), UN Doc. S/RES/2270.

574 UN General Assembly (2016f) Report of the Open-ended Working Group taking forward multilateral nuclear disarmament negotiations, UN Doc. A/71/37, para 15.

575 Reuters (2016) U.S. to deploy THAAD anti-missile battery in South Korea in 8–10 months: commander. http://www.reuters.com/article/us-southkorea-usa-thaad-idUSKBN12Z028. Accessed 25 February 2017.

576 UN General Assembly (2015a) Resolution adopted by the General Assembly on 7 December 2015: 70/33. Taking forward multilateral nuclear disarmament negotiations, UN Doc. A/RES/70/33. http://www.unfoldzero.org/wp-content/uploads/UN-Resolution-70-33-establishing-the-2016-UN-OEWG.pdf. Accessed 23 February 2017.

taking forward multilateral nuclear disarmament negotiations and substantively addressing the legal measures that would need to be concluded in order to attain and maintain a world without nuclear weapons.[577] On 19 August, the OEWG adopted its report which contained suggestions, such as to hold a conference in 2017 of "all States, with the participation and contribution of international organizations and civil society, to negotiate a legally binding instrument to prohibit nuclear weapons",[578] to move towards nuclear disarmament.[579]

The Joint Comprehensive Plan of Action, signed by the P5+1, the EU and Iran in 2015 to ensure Iran's nuclear programme remains exclusively peaceful, has come under pressure in 2016. Iran alleged violations of the agreement by the US through an extension of the sanctions regime against Iran.[580] Consequently, Iran released a statement in which it stated it will develop nuclear ships.[581] As part of the agreement, nuclear sanctions on Iran were to be lifted once Iran met its key nuclear-related measures under the agreement and these had been verified by the IAEA.[582]

The 20-year anniversary of the opening for signature of the Comprehensive Nuclear Test Ban Treaty (CTBT) was commemorated in 2016 at the ministerial meeting in Vienna in June and at the eighth ministerial meeting in support of the Treaty in New York in September.[583] However, this treaty has not yet entered into force due to the absence of key state signatures and ratifications from nuclear states as required by Annex II of the treaty.[584] The UN General Assembly urged the remaining Annex II states in Resolution 71/49 to sign and ratify the treaty and to

---

[577] Ibid.

[578] UN General Assembly (2016e) Report of the Open-ended Working Group taking forward multilateral nuclear disarmament negotiations, UN Doc. A/71/37, para 67.

[579] UN General Assembly (2016e) Report of the Open-ended Working Group taking forward multilateral nuclear disarmament negotiations, UN Doc. A/71/37.

[580] Reuters (2016) Iran says U.S. extension of sanctions act violates nuclear deal. http://www.reuters.com/article/us-iran-nuclear-usa-idUSKBN13R0MO?il=0%20/. Accessed 23 February 2017.

[581] BBC News (2016) Iran says it will develop nuclear-powered ships after US extends sanctions. http://www.bbc.com/news/world-middle-east-38299179. Accessed 23 February 2017.

[582] UN (2015) Security Council, Adopting Resolution 2231 (2015), Endorses Joint Comprehensive Agreement on Iran's Nuclear Programme. https://www.un.org/press/en/2015/sc11974.doc.htm. Accessed 25 February 2017.

[583] UN General Assembly (2016g) Resolution adopted by the General Assembly on 5 December 2016: 71/54. Towards a nuclear-weapon-free world: Accelerating the implementation of nuclear disarmament commitments, UN Doc. A/Res/71/54, para 15.

[584] UN News Centre (2016) Nuclear tests: 20 years after its adoption, the test ban treaty is yet to get into force. http://www.un.org/apps/news/story.asp?NewsID=54807&Kw1=Pakistan&Kw2=&Kw3=#.WATUsY997cs. Accessed 23 February 2017.

continue endorsing other measures in place to prevent nuclear testing.[585] Myanmar and Swaziland have become the latest states to ratify the CTBT on 21 September, increasing the number of total ratifications to 166.[586] Additionally, the UN Security Council adopted Resolution 2310 on nuclear non-proliferation and disarmament on 23 September and, while it does not contain a legal prohibition on the conducting of nuclear weapon testing, it does endorse the broader objectives of the CTBT.[587]

In 2016, the Advisory Board on Disarmament Matters met for its 65th and 66th sessions in January and July respectively.[588] The 65th session focused on the challenges faced by the NPT, especially in the Middle East and in light of the withdrawal of North Korea and its recent nuclear testing. The Board highlighted the need for a precise agenda on disarmament and for the implementation of Resolution 2270 to demonstrate the impact of non-compliance.[589] It further recommended the establishment of a Middle East zone free of nuclear weapons.[590]

8.4 Miscellaneous

8.4.1 New ICRC Commentary on the First Geneva Convention

In March 2016, the latest Commentary on the First Geneva Convention (Convention (I) for the Amelioration of the Condition of the Wounded and Sick in Armed Forces in the Field)[591] was published by the ICRC.[592] This Commentary is part of a broader project commissioned by the ICRC to provide a comprehensive update of the original Commentaries to the four Geneva Conventions of 1949 that were published between 1950 and 1960 under the editorship of Jean Pictet,[593] with

---

[585] UN General Assembly (2016) Resolution adopted by the General Assembly on 5 December 2016: 71/49. United action with renewed determination towards the total elimination of nuclear weapons, UN Doc. A/RES/71/49, para 19.

[586] CTBTO Preparatory Commission (2017) Status of Signature and Ratification. https://www.ctbto.org/the-treaty/status-of-signature-and-ratification/. Accessed 25 February 2017.

[587] UN News Centre (2016) Security Council adopts resolution on nuclear non-proliferation and nuclear disarmament. http://www.un.org/apps/news/story.asp?NewsID=55068&Kw1=Pakistan&Kw2=&Kw3=#.WATcRY997cs. Accessed 23 February 2017.

[588] UN General Assembly (2016i) Work of the Advisory Board on Disarmament Matters: Report of the Secretary-General, UN Doc. A/71/176.

[589] Ibid., paras 23 and following.

[590] Ibid., para 19.

[591] See ICRC 2016.

[592] ICRC (2016) ICRC launches new guidance bolstering relevance of Geneva Conventions. https://www.icrc.org/en/document/ihl-icrc-launches-new-guidance-bolstering-relevance-geneva-conventions. Accessed 6 July 2017.

[593] Pictet 1952, 1958, 1960a and 1960b.

the objective of promoting a better understanding of, and respect for the rules of international humanitarian law.[594]

The updated Commentaries reflect the developments in law and practice that have occurred in the past six decades since the publication of the original Commentaries and build on "experience gained in applying and interpreting the Conventions [...] [which] has generated a detailed understanding of how they operate in armed conflicts all over the world in contexts very different to those that led to their adoption."[595] The updated Commentaries aim to serve as a tool notably for practitioners, including military commanders and officers, judges of national and international courts and tribunals, academics, governments and international organisations in the aim of reaffirming the continued relevance of the Geneva Conventions, generating respect for them and enhancing the protection for victims of armed conflicts.[596]

The article-by-article Commentary to the First Geneva Convention has been reviewed by humanitarian law practitioners and academics from all parts of the world[597] and provides important clarifications on fundamental legal aspects of the protection of the wounded and sick in armed conflict.[598] In addition to the ICRC's interpretation of international humanitarian law, it presents diverging views as well as issues subject to further discussion and clarification and provides for a contextualisation of the Convention's rules.[599]

References

Articles, Books and Other Documents

Bellal A (2017) The War Report – Armed Conflicts in 2016. https://www.geneva-academy.ch/joomlatools-files/docman-files/The%20War%20Report%202016.pdf. Accessed 9 July 2017, pp. 64–66

Boutin B, Pitcher K, Güven O (2015) Year in Review 2015. Yearbook of International Humanitarian Law 18: 225–286

[594] See ICRC 2016, Preface.

[595] ICRC (2016) Updated Commentaries bring fresh insights on continued relevance of Geneva Conventions. https://www.icrc.org/en/document/updated-commentaries-first-geneva-convention. Accessed 6 July 2017.

[596] Ibid.

[597] See ICRC 2016, Preface.

[598] Dorsey J (2016) Introducing the First Multi-Blog Series on the Updated Geneva Conventions Commentaries. http://opiniojuris.org/2016/06/22/introducing-the-first-multi-blog-series-on-the-updated-geneva-conventions-commentaries/. Accessed 6 July 2017.

[599] ICRC 2016, Foreword by Peter Maurer, p. xii.

Henckaerts J-M, Doswald-Beck L (2005) Customary International Humanitarian Law, Volume I: Rules. Cambridge University Press, Cambridge

ICRC (2016) Commentary on the First Geneva Convention – Convention (I) for the Amelioration of the Condition of the Wounded and Sick in Armed Forces in the Field. Cambridge University Press, Cambridge

Pictet JS (1952) The Geneva Conventions of 12 August 1949 – Commentary. Geneva Convention (I) for the amelioration of the condition of the wounded and sick in armed forces in the field. ICRC, Geneva

Pictet JS (1958) The Geneva Conventions of 12 August 1949, Commentary, Geneva Convention (IV) relative to the protection of civilian persons in time of war: Commentary. ICRC, Geneva

Pictet JS (1960a) The Geneva Conventions of 12 August 1949 – Commentary. Geneva Convention (II) for the amelioration of the condition of wounded, sick and shipwrecked members of armed forces at sea. ICRC, Geneva

Pictet JS (1960b) The Geneva Conventions of 12 August 1949 – Commentary, Geneva Convention (III) relative to the treatment of prisoners of war. ICRC, Geneva

UN Committee on the Rights of the Child (2016) Concluding observations on the fifth periodic report of Pakistan. CRC/C/PAK/CO/5

UN Human Rights Council (2016) Investigation by the Office of the United High Commissioner for Human Rights on Libya: Detailed findings. UN Doc. A/HRC/31/CRP.3

UN General Assembly (2013) Resolution adopted by the General Assembly on 5 December 2013: 68/43. Transparency in armaments. UN Doc. A/RES/68/43

UN General Assembly (2015a) Resolution adopted by the General Assembly on 7 December 2015: 70/33. Taking forward multilateral nuclear disarmament negotiations. UN Doc. A/RES/70/33

UN General Assembly (2015b) Resolution adopted by the General Assembly on 7 December 2015: 70/44. Conventional arms control at the regional and subregional level. UN Doc. A/RES/70/44

UN General Assembly (2016a) Report on the continuing operation of the United Nations Register of Conventional Arms and its further development. UN Doc. A/71/259

UN General Assembly (2016b) Conventional arms control at the regional and subregional levels: Report of the Secretary-General. UN Doc. A/71/154

UN General Assembly (2016c) Human Rights Council: Report of the Independent Expert on the situation of human rights in the Sudan. UN Doc. A/HRC/33/65

UN General Assembly (2016d) Report of the International Criminal Court. UN Doc. A/71/342

UN General Assembly (2016e) Report of the Open-ended Working Group taking forward multilateral nuclear disarmament negotiations. UN Doc. A/71/37

UN General Assembly (2016f) Resolution adopted by the General Assembly on 5 December 2016: 71/54. Towards a nuclear-weapon-free world: Accelerating the implementation of nuclear disarmament commitments. UN Doc. A/Res/71/54, para 15

UN General Assembly (2016g) Resolution adopted by the General Assembly on 5 December 2016: 71/49. United action with renewed determination towards the total elimination of nuclear weapons. UN Doc. A/RES/71/49

UN General Assembly (2016h) Resolution adopted by the Human Rights Council on 21 October 2016, S-25/1. The deteriorating situation of human rights in the Syrian Arab Republic, and the recent situation in Aleppo. UN Doc. A/HRC/RES/S-25/1

UN General Assembly (2016i) Work of the Advisory Board on Disarmament Matters: Report of the Secretary-General. UN Doc. A/71/176

UN General Assembly and UN Security Council (2016) Report of the International Tribunal for the Former Yugoslavia. UN Doc. A/71/263-S/2016/670

UN Security Council (2011) Resolution 1970 (2011). UN Doc. S/RES/1970

UN Security Council (2015) Resolution 2235 (2015). UN Doc. S/RES/2235

UN Security Council (2016a) First Report of the Organization for the Prohibition of Chemical Weapons-United Nations Investigative Mechanism. UN Doc. S/2016/142

UN Security Council (2016b) Fourth report of the Organization for the Prohibition of Chemical Weapons-United Nations Joint Investigative Mechanism. UN Doc. S/2016/888

UN Security Council (2016c) Letter dated 10 October 2016 from the Permanent Representative of the Syrian Arab Republic to the United Nations addressed to the President of the Security Council: Responses and main observations regarding the third report of the Joint Investigative Mechanism. UN Doc. S/2016/844

UN Security Council (2016d) Letter dated 17 November 2016 from the President of the International Residual Mechanism for Criminal Tribunals addressed to the President of the Security Council. UN Doc. S/2016/975

UN Security Council (2016e) Letter dated 17 November 2016 from the President of the International Tribunal for the Prosecution of Persons Responsible for Serious Violations of International Humanitarian Law Committed in the Territory of the Former Yugoslavia since 1991, addressed to the President of the Security Council. UN Doc. S/2016/976

UN Security Council (2016f) Report of the Secretary-General on the African Union – United Nations Hybrid Operation in Darfur. UN Doc. S/2016/1109

UN Security Council (2016g) Resolution 2270 (2016). UN Doc. S/RES/2270

UN Security Council (2016h) Resolution 2295 (2016). UN Doc. S/RES/2295

UN Security Council (2016i) Resolution 2296 (2016). UN Doc. S/RES/2296

UN Security Council (2016j) Resolution 2304 (2016). UN Doc. S/RES/2304

UN Security Council (2016k) Resolution 2319 (2016). UN Doc. S/RES/2319

UN Security Council (2016l) Resolution 2323 (2016). UN Doc. S/RES/2323

UN Security Council (2016m) Resolution 2334 (2016). UN Doc. S/RES/2334

UN Security Council (2016n) Second report of the Organization for the Prohibition of Chemical Weapons-United Nations Joint Investigative Mechanism. UN Doc. S/2016/530

UN Security Council (2016o) Third report of the Organization for the Prohibition of Chemical Weapons-United Nations Joint Investigative Mechanism. UN Doc. S/2016/738

UN Security Council (2017) Final Report of the panel of experts on the Sudan established pursuant to resolution 1591 (2005). UN Doc. S/2017/22

Case Law

CAE, *Ministère Public v Hissein Habré*, Judgment, 30 May 2016

ECCC, *Case 002/01: Nuon Chea and Khieu Samphân*, Appeal Judgment, 23 November 2016, Case No. 002/19-09-2007-ECCC/SC

Higher Regional Court, Frankfurt am Main, Germany, *Prosecutor v Aria Ladjedvardi*, Judgment, 12 July 2016, Case No. 5-3 StE 2/16 - 4 - 1/16

ICC, *Prosecutor v Ahmad Al Faqi Al Mahdi*, Decision on the confirmation of charges against Ahmad Al Faqi Al Madhi, 25 March 2016, Case No. ICC-01/12-01/15-84-Red

ICC, *Prosecutor v Ahmad Al Faqi Al Mahdi*, Judgment and Sentence, 27 September 2016, Case No. ICC-01/12-01/15-171

ICC, *Prosecutor v Dominic Ongwen*, Decision on the confirmation of charges against Dominic Ongwen, 23 March 2016, Case No. ICC-02/04-01/15

ICC, *Prosecutor v Dominic Ongwen*, Decision on the Defence request for leave to appeal the decision on the confirmation of charges, 29 April 2016, Case No. ICC-02/04-01/15

ICC, *Prosecutor v Jean-Pierre Bemba Gombo*, Judgment Pursuant to Article 74 of the Statute, 21 March 2016, Case No. ICC-01/05-01/08-3343

ICC, *Prosecutor v Jean-Pierre Bemba Gombo, Aimé Kilolo Musamba, Jean-Jacques Mangenda Kabongo, Fidèle Babala Wandu and Narcisse Arido*, Judgment pursuant to Article 74 of the Statute, 19 October 2016, Case No. ICC-01/05-01/13

ICC, *Prosecutor v Jean-Pierre Bemba Gombo, Aimé Kilolo Musamba, Jean-Jacques Mangenda Kabongo, Fidèle Babala Wandu and Narcisse Arido*, Order Scheduling the Delivery of the Decision on Sentencing, 23 February 2017, Case No. ICC-01/05-01/13

ICC, *Situation in Georgia*, Decision on the Prosecutor's request for authorisation of an investigation, 27 January 2016, Case No. ICC-01/15

ICC, *Prosecutor v William Samoei Ruto and Joshua Arap Sang*, Decision on Defence Applications for Judgments of Acquittal, 5 April 2016, Case No. ICC-01/09-01/11

ICC, *Prosecutor v William Samoei Ruto and Joshua Arap Sang*, Judgment on the appeals of Mr William Samoei Ruto and Mr Joshua Arap Sang on the decision of Trial Chamber V(A) of 19 August 2015 entitled "Decision on Prosecution Request for Admission of Prior Recorded Testimony", 12 February 2016, Case No. ICC-01/09-01/11 OA 10

ICTR, *Prosecutor v Jean Uwinkindi*, Decision on Prosecutor's request for referral to the Republic of Rwanda, 28 June 2011, Case No. ICTR-2001-75-R11bis

ICTY, *Prosecutor v Goran Hadžić*, Order Terminating the Proceedings, 22 July 2016, Case No. IT-04-75-T

ICTY, *Prosecutor v Mićo Stanišić and Stojan Župljanin*, Judgment, 30 June 2016, Case No. IT-08-91-A

ICTY, *Prosecutor v Radovan Karadžić*, Public Redacted Version of Judgment Issued on 24 March 2016, Case No. IT-95-5/18-T

ICTY, *Prosecutor v Vojislav Šešelj*, Jugement, 31 March 2016, Case No. IT-03-67-T

ICTY, *Prosecutor v Vojislav Šešelj*, Opinion Concordante du Judge Jean-Claude Antonetti, Président de la Chambre, Jointe au Jugement, 31 March 2016, Case No. IT-03-67-T

ICTY, *Prosecutor v Vojislav Šešelj*, Opinion Partiellement Dissidente de la Juge Flavia Lattanzi – Version Corrigée, 31 March 2016, Case No. IT-03-67-T

MICT, *Prosecutor v Jean Uwinkindi*, Decision on an appeal concerning a request for revocation of a referral, 4 October 2016, Case No. MICT-12-25-AR14.1

MICT, *Prosecutor v Radovan Karadžić*, Prosecution's Notice of Appeal, 22 July 2016, Case No. MICT-13-55-A

MICT, *Prosecutor v Radovan Karadžić*, Radovan Karadzic's Notice of Appeal, 22 July 2016, Case No. MICT-13-55-A

MICT, *Prosecutor v Vojislav Šešelj*, Prosecution's Notice of Appeal, 2 May 2016, Case No. MICT-16-99

STL, *In the Case against Al Jadeed [CO.] S.A.L./NEW T.V. S.A.L. (N.T.V.) and Karma Mohamed Tahsin Al Khayat*, Public Redacted Version of Judgment on Appeal, 8 March 2016, Case No. STL-14-05/A/AP

STL, *In the Case against Akhbar Beirut S.A.L. and Ibrahim Mohamed Ali Al Amin*, Public Redacted Version of the Judgment, 15 July 2016, Case No. STL-14-06/T/CJ

Final Report ILA Study Group on the Conduct of Hostilities

The Conduct of Hostilities Under International Humanitarian Law

Challenges of 21st Century Warfare

Members: Terry Gill (Chair); Robin Geiß (Rapporteur); Robert Heinsch (Rapporteur); Louise Arimatsu; Jeroen van den Boogaard; Geoffrey Corn; Robert Cryer; Paul Ducheine; Charles Garraway; Laurent Gisel; Wolff Heintschel von Heinegg; Jann Kleffner; Heike Krieger; Oluwabunmi Lar; Thilo Marauhn; Kazuhiro Nakatani; Hector Olasolo Alonso; Eric Pouw; Yaël Ronen; Aurel Sari; Kirsten Schmalenbach; Michael Schmitt; Sandesh Sivakumaran; Gabriella Venturini; Ken Watkin; Gentian Zyberi.

Final Report

Presented at the 77th ILA Conference in Johannesburg, South Africa

General introduction: The work of the Study Group between 2012 and 2016

The Study Group on the Conduct of Hostilities in the 21st Century (hereinafter the SG) was established in 2011 and conducted its first meeting in Sofia in 2012. It conducted a workshop in Leiden in November 2013. During this workshop, three general topics were explored. These were the relationship of International Humanitarian Law (IHL) and International Human Rights Law in the conduct of military operations, technological challenges posed by new weapons systems and the function of the basic principles of IHL in the conduct of hostilities. An interim report on these topics was published and presented at the April 2014 Washington D.C. joint meeting of the ILA and the American Society of International Law. These topics were discussed further at a subsequent workshop held in Berlin at the Freie Universität in November of the same year. Attention was also devoted to the relationship of IHL with general international law and the place of IHL within the legal 'pluriverse' surrounding modern multinational military operations. The SG was unable to arrive at a consensus on a number of issues which arose, but the discussions were nevertheless extremely useful in highlighting some of the central questions related to the conduct of hostilities and focusing attention on the core area of the mandate; the legal challenges *within* IHL relating to the conduct of hostilities.

T.D. Gill et al. (eds.), *Yearbook of International Humanitarian Law 2016*,
Yearbook of International Humanitarian Law 19,
https://doi.org/10.1007/978-94-6265-213-2

It was decided in Berlin to refocus the work of the SG and the final report on those challenges and leave the broader questions of how IHL relates to other bodies of international law to further exploration in other forums.

Three working groups were established in Berlin to prepare working papers for the next meeting to be held in Oslo on 19–20 October 2015. Each working group had a coordinator and between 7–8 members and each of them produced a working paper for discussion at the Oslo meeting, which was hosted by the Norwegian Centre for Human Rights (University of Oslo). These three working papers were thoroughly discussed during the two-day meeting and all members subsequently had the opportunity to provide additional comments. These working papers and the subsequent comments form the basis for this final report. Working Group I focused on the issue of 'The Military Objective' under IHL, Working Group II on 'Precautions in Attack' and Working Group III on 'Proportionality under IHL'. These three topics were unanimously determined to be core issues within IHL in relation to the conduct of hostilities in modern warfare and each topic contained a number of sub-topics set out in the three working papers.[1] These working papers were edited and revised in consultation with the SG members by the three SG officers (Terry Gill, Chair; Robin Geiß, Rapporteur; and Robert Heinsch, Rapporteur). It is these revised and edited papers which together comprise the final report. Again, all members of the SG had the opportunity to comment on the final report.

The Mandate of the Study Group

Armed conflicts evolve dynamically and the way wars are fought has changed significantly over time. The majority of contemporary armed conflicts involve a multitude of different actors with varying military capabilities. This asymmetry creates an incentive for the inferior party to use war tactics which violate rules of international humanitarian law[2] in order to make up for disadvantages in matters relating to materiel, resources and fighting capacity. This links in with the observation that today's armed conflicts ('new wars') are often characterized not only by the objective to gain territory or military victory in the classical sense, but are rather often (also) about achieving independence, identity, ethnic cleansing, or spreading terror and gaining publicity. This being said, the traditional objectives of defeating enemy forces and gaining or maintaining control over territory are still highly relevant, including for non-State parties. For example, for the so-called Islamic State (IS) territorial control is a strategic priority. For State parties engaged in conflict with such groups, the objective is often to contain the threat posed by such tactics, regain and hold territories that such groups may have captured, degrade their ability to mount effective operations and

---

[1] Other core issues such as precautions against the effects of attacks or the prohibition of indiscriminate attacks were considered equally important by the SG but were not discussed in depth for lack of time and because of the limited page number allowed for ILA Reports.

[2] For coherence purposes, this report mainly uses the term International Humanitarian Law (IHL) in order to denote the area of law which deals with the rules and principles governing armed conflict. This area of law is also regularly called Law of Armed Conflict (LOAC), Law of War, or *Jus in Bello*.

ultimately to defeat them, which includes but is often not limited to a traditional military victory, whereby one side is forced to submit by superior force.

Although international humanitarian law has already adapted in certain ways, e.g. by providing rules for non-international armed conflicts (NIAC), one needs to keep in mind that IHL was originally designed to deal with interstate wars. What is more, in modern asymmetric armed conflicts the conduct of hostilities increasingly seems to take place in parallel with law enforcement operations. Thus, the central question is the extent to which the rules governing the conduct of hostilities need to be clarified, both in terms of their scope of application and their substantive aspects. Although some sub-aspects of this issue have been examined before, what is still missing is a coherent and more principled approach to the challenges of 21st century warfare. The central focus of the SG lies on the actual rules governing the conduct of hostilities, taking into account the three main areas highlighted above. In this context, it was not the aim of the SG to comprehensively deal with all of the various issues arising in relation to the conduct of hostilities, but to focus on selected issues where the SG felt that there is a need and/or potential for further clarification.

Whereas API's scope of application is limited by virtue of Art. 49(3) API, the SG agreed that today it is widely accepted that the customary law rules governing the conduct of hostilities are applicable in all domains of warfare, i.e. land, air, sea as well as outer-space and cyber-space.[3]

Therefore, the SG decided to focus on three main issues related to the rules governing the conduct of hostilities: I. The meaning and interpretation of the term 'Military Objectives'; II. 'The Principle of Proportionality'; and III. 'Precautions'.

Part I: Military Objectives[4]

Outline

1. Art. 52(2) API: the two-pronged test
2. The first prong: objects making an 'effective contribution' to military action

   2.1. Military objectives by nature

      2.1.1. On Rule 23 HPCR Manual

---

[3] L. Doswald-Beck, J.M. Henckaerts, International Committee of the Red Cross, *Customary International Humanitarian Law*, (vol 1, CUP 2005) Rules 7, 8 (ICRC Customary IHL) p. xxxvi: 'The general rules contained in the manual [San Remo Manual on Naval Warfare] were nevertheless considered useful for the assessment of the customary nature of rules that apply to all types of warfare.' (emphasis added); see also M.N. Schmitt (ed) *Tallinn Manual on International Law Applicable to Cyber Warfare* (CUP 2013) (Tallinn Manual) and Program on Humanitarian Policy and Conflict Research at Harvard University, 'Manual on International Law Applicable to Air and Missile Warfare' (Harvard University 2009) http://ihlresearch.org/amw/HPCR%20Manual.pdf accessed 21 April 2017 (HPCR Manual).

[4] This part of the report was initially drawn up by the members of working group 1 of the 2015 Oslo meeting: Gabriella Venturini (Group Coordinator), Robert Cryer, Paul Ducheine, Laurent Gisel, Wolff Heintschel von Heinegg, Oluwabunmi Lar, Gentian Zyberi. All members of the Study Group had a role in commenting upon the initial draft and the entire SG is responsible for the final version of all parts of the report.

1. Art. 52(2) API: the two-pronged test

Art. 52(2) API was determined to be the logical starting point for any discussion on military objectives. This is due to the fact that it not only provides the definition of a military objective in contemporary treaty law, but more especially, because of its status as customary international humanitarian law in both international armed conflicts (IAC) and non-international armed conflicts.[5]

In accordance with Art. 52(2) API the definition of military objective consists of a two-pronged test. The first prong is that by its nature, location, purpose or use, the object must make an effective contribution to military action. The second prong is that its destruction must give a definite military advantage in the circumstances ruling at the time. These two prongs are cumulative.

[5] ICRC Customary IHL (n 3); Tallinn Manual (n 3) 125, Rule 38.

The two-pronged test in Art. 52(2) API has generated heated debates in the literature. One view, not shared within the SG, is that the total or partial destruction of an objective making an effective contribution to military action will 'almost automatically' offer a definite military advantage.[6] According to this argument, the second part of the test would be deprived of any significant meaning.[7] Some members of the SG were of the opinion that this could arguably apply for military objectives by 'nature', while other members did not share this position. However, the SG rejected such a broad interpretation for the other categories of military objectives. It is widely recognized that the second prong of the definition 'purports to radically limit the category of legitimate objectives of military operations'.[8]

It is true that there are more situations in which both prongs are simultaneously fulfilled than situations in which only one prong is fulfilled and not the other; however, this should not lead to mistakenly assume that when one is fulfilled the other is also necessarily fulfilled.[9] There are probably not many examples of objects that make an effective contribution to military action but the destruction of which would not offer a definite military advantage; one that may be suggested is the physical infrastructure of cyber space, such as cables and routers. The entire cyber-infrastructure is regularly used for both civilian and military purposes, hence rendering it a military objective because of its military applications. However, if a router or a cable is destroyed, cyberspace is so built that the data will simply be rerouted instantaneously and automatically through other paths within the networks. One could thus argue that such destruction would bring no military advantage, and that therefore, contrary to other dual-use objects, internet infrastructure actually does not constitute a military objective—unless it can be shown that the foreseen destruction or neutralization does indeed offer a definite military advantage because of the specific characteristic of that object or its location in the cyberspace.[10]

The second prong of the definition requires that whether an object constitutes a military objective be assessed on a case-by-case basis in view of the circumstances ruling at the time, rather than at some hypothetical future time. Sweeping or anticipatory classification of objects would be inconsistent with this element of assessment whether an object is military and would negate the obligation to

---

[6] Y. Dinstein, *The Conduct of Hostilities under the Law of International Armed Conflict* (3rd edn, CUP 2016) 91.

[7] R. Geiß and H. Lahmann, 'Cyberwarfare: Applying the Principles of Distinction in an Interconnected Space' (2012) 45(3) Israel Law Review 381, 388.

[8] S. Oeter, 'Methods and Means of Combat' in D. Fleck (ed) *The Handbook of International Humanitarian Law* (3rd edn, OUP 2013) 115, 169.

[9] A. Boivin, 'The Legal Regime Applicable to Targeting Military Objectives in the Context of Contemporary Warfare' (CUDH/UCHL, Research Paper Series/Collection des travaux de recherche No. 2, 2006) 15–16.

[10] M. Roscini, *Cyber Operations and the Use of Force in International Law* (OUP 2014) 190; ICRC Report, 'International humanitarian law and the challenges of contemporary armed conflicts' (32nd International Conference of the Red Cross and Red Crescent, Geneva, 8–10 December 2015, ICRC 2015) https://www.icrc.org/en/download/file/15061/32ic-report-on-ihl-and-challenges-of-armed-conflicts.pdf accessed 21 April 2017 (ICRC 2015 IHL Challenges report) 42.

continually validate the nature of a proposed target. For example, it would be clearly contrary to IHL if all objects somewhat related to, owned by, or associated with the enemy were collectively considered military objectives. Art. 52(2) API has a clear temporal dimension, which works both ways. An object, which is normally used for civilian purposes, may turn into a military objective if it is used for military purposes. An object, which has been used militarily, becomes (again) a civilian object when the military use is abandoned. Thus, timely and reliable information of the military situation is an important element in the target selection and essential for the implementation of the principle of distinction.

2. The first prong: objects making an 'effective contribution to military action'

The first prong of the test is in turn divided into two elements: first, the nature, location, purpose or use of the object; and second, the effective contribution of the object to military action. While 'effective contribution to military action' requires a proximate nexus between the object and the fighting, it is not limiting the notion of military objectives to only those of a purely 'military nature'. Hence, targeting of objects such as fuel production facilities, bridges or the electrical grid can be permissible provided the object in question makes an effective contribution to military action.

2.1. Military objectives by nature

'Nature' refers to the intrinsic character of an object. For example, a weapon system or a missile launching site are objects that make an effective contribution to military action by their very nature. It is not only a question of use because the qualification of military objective by nature may remain even if the object is not actually used at the time of the attack (a military plane in a hangar remains a military objective). However, a military object which is used in such a manner that its nature can be said to have changed (e.g. a deserted military barracks housing refugees) will no longer be a military objective unless it would remain so because of purpose or location.[11]

2.1.1. On Rule 23 HPCR Manual Applicable to Air and Missile Warfare[12]

---

[11] Dinstein (n 6) 94.

[12] Rule 23 HPCR Manual (n 3): 'Objects which may qualify as military objectives through the definition in Rules 1 (y) and 22 (a) include, but are not limited to, factories, lines and means of communications (such as airfields, railway lines, roads, bridges and tunnels); energy producing facilities; oil storage depots; transmission facilities and equipment.'
Rule 1(y) HPCR Manual (n 3): ''Military objectives', as far as objects are concerned, are those objects which by their nature, location, purpose or use, make an effective contribution to military action and whose total or partial destruction, capture or neutralization, in the circumstances ruling at the time, offers a definite military advantage.'
Rule 22(a) HPCR Manual (n 3): 'In the definition of objects as military objectives (see Rule 1 (y)), the following criteria apply: (a) The 'nature' of an object symbolizes its fundamental character. Examples of military objectives by nature include military aircraft (including military UAV/UCAVs); military vehicles (other than medical transport); missiles and other weapons; military equipment; military fortifications, facilities and depots; warships; ministries of defence and armaments factories.'

While Rule 1(y) of the HPCR Manual repeats literally the definition of military objective given by Art. 52(2) API, Rule 22 enumerates some examples of military objectives by nature (Rule 22(a)) or by location (Rule 22(b)). Rule 23 provides a further list of military objectives by nature. The Commentary to the HPCR Manual explains that in the view of the majority of the Group of Experts which drafted the HPCR Manual, 'military objectives by nature were to be divided into two subsets. The first, reflected in Rule 22(a), consists of military objectives by nature at all times. By contrast, the second subset (reflected in Rule 23) consists of objects which become military objectives by nature only in light of the circumstances ruling at the time.'[13] The objects listed in Rule 23 were subject to debate. Some disagreement emerged among the Group of Experts and the suggestion of a new subcategory of 'temporary military objectives by nature' was criticized by the ICRC.[14] According to this opinion, objects falling into the categories mentioned in Rule 23 do not constitute military objectives by nature, while they may become military objectives by use or purpose, provided they fall under Art. 52(2) API definition in the circumstances ruling at the time. The members of the SG unanimously concluded that there was no basis in law for a subset of military objectives by nature in light of the circumstances ruling at the time and therefore this subset should be regarded as covered by 'use'.

2.2. Military objectives by location

The generally accepted view is that 'location' refers to a site which is of importance for military operations, either because it is a site that must be seized or because it is important to prevent the enemy from seizing it.[15] It should be noted that in the view of a number of Western States a specific area of land may be a military objective if, because of its location or other reasons specified in Art. 52(2) API, its total or partial destruction, capture or neutralization in the circumstances ruling at the time offers definite military advantage (see e.g. the declarations made on Art. 52 at the time of ratification of API by Italy, Germany, the United Kingdom, Canada, the Netherlands, New Zealand and France). This should be clearly distinguished from a

---

[13] Program on Humanitarian Policy and Conflict Research at Harvard University, 'Commentary on Manual on International Law Applicable to Air and Missile Warfare' (Harvard University 2010) 109 http://ihlresearch.org/amw/Commentary%20on%20the%20HPCR%20Manual.pdf accessed 21 April 2017 (HPCR Commentary).

[14] The ICRC's position on Rule 23 of the HPCR Manual states: 'According to the ICRC, there are no subsets of military objectives by nature. In its view, it has no foundation in the existing law of international armed conflict. The Commentary to Rule 22 (a) clearly indicates that an object is a military objective by nature only if it has an 'inherent characteristic or attribute which contributes to military action'. An 'inherent characteristic or attribute' cannot be conceived of on a merely temporary basis. By definition it has to be permanent. In the opinion of the ICRC, Rule 23 — for illustration purposes — includes categories of objects which, depending on the circumstances, may qualify as military objectives through use, purpose or location. In other words, every object falling into the categories mentioned in Rule 22 (a) is a military objective by nature, whereas the objects falling into the categories cited in Rule 23 may only under certain circumstances qualify as military objectives.' See HPCR Commentary (n 13) 109, n 261.

[15] Y. Sandoz, C. Swinarski and B. Zimmermann (eds) *The Commentary on the Additional Protocols of 8 June 1987* (ICRC 1987) 636, para 2021 (ICRC 1987 Commentary).

situation in which several military objectives (by nature, purpose or use) are located in the same area. In any case, 'the legality of target area bombing depends on the application of the principle of distinction and the proportionality principle',[16] but the targeting of several distinct military objectives located in the same area (as opposed to a military objective by location) is governed in particular by the prohibition of indiscriminate attacks and, in populated area, of area bombardments (Art. 51(5)(a) API).

2.3. Military objects by purpose

The SG agreed that the criterion of 'purpose' is concerned with the intended future use of an object.[17] However, what does 'intended future use' encompass? Clearly, if the mere possibility that an object might be converted into some military use would be sufficient, then almost no limits in target selection would exist. As a limiting factor it has been suggested that purpose is predicated on intentions which are based on reasonable certainty and not on those figured out hypothetically in contingency plans based on a 'worst case scenario'. In practice, military commanders rely on intelligence assessments to make such judgments. This practice corresponds to the notion of 'reasonable certainty' which is far more than mere speculation or conjecture.[18]

For military objectives by purpose, as for any other military objective, all feasible precautions must be taken to verify that the objective to be attacked is a military objective (Art. 57(1) API). While this provision in no way imposes an obligation of result, it does require that, in case of doubt, additional information must be obtained before an attack is launched.[19] This obligation obviously requires that close attention be paid to the gathering, assessment and rapid circulation of information on potential targets. These activities are naturally dependent on the availability and quality of the belligerents' technical resources.

2.3.1. What information is needed to conclude that there is intent to use an object for military purposes?

In IHL, objective criteria must be relied upon to determine whether an object will be used in the future to make an effective contribution to the enemy's military action.

First, there must be clear indications that the enemy will use an object for military action. Second, the information must be objective and allow a reasonable commander to conclude that a specific object will, in the future, be used for contributing to the enemy's military action. This can be the case, for example, when the enemy

[16] T. Marauhn and S. Kirchner, 'Target Area Bombing' in N. Ronzitti and G. Venturini (eds) *The Law of Air Warfare. Contemporary Issues* (1st edn, Eleven International 2006) 87, 102–03.
[17] ICRC 1987 Commentary (n 15) 636, para 2022.
[18] Dinstein (n 6) 100; W.H. Boothby, *The Law of Targeting* (OUP 2012) 103; M.N. Schmitt, 'Targeting in Operational Law' in T.D. Gill and D. Fleck (eds) *The Handbook of the International Law of Military Operations* (2nd edn, OUP 2015) 269, 280. A bombing raid that is carried out on the basis of mere suspicion as to the military nature of the target amounts *ipso facto* to a violation of the principle of distinction.
[19] ICRC 1987 Commentary (n 15) 620, para 1952.

has taken the decision to use it, but such decision has not yet been implemented.[20] This information must refer to a specific object (and not a class of objects), as each object must individually fulfill the definition of military objective to become a lawful target.[21] Third, the evidence need not be 'beyond any reasonable doubt' in a criminal law sense. It suffices if a reasonable commander who bases her/his decision on the information from all sources which are available to him/her concludes that he/she has sufficiently reliable information to determine that an object will, in the future, make an effective contribution to the enemy's military action.[22]

2.4. Military objectives by use

The generally accepted view is that 'use' refers to the current function of an object. This category comprises all objects directly used by the armed forces as well as those having a dual function that are of value for the civilian population, but also for the military in a manner that makes them fall under the definition of military objective.[23]

2.4.1. Defining the limits of the object

An object has to be strictly defined. Each object needs to be looked at individually.[24] For the purpose of the notion of military objective, an object should be defined by its 'material/physical element', namely one building/a single structure for immovable objects. Whether or not a word exists that encompasses it (a school, a compound, a factory, etc.) cannot be a relevant criterion for defining an object for the rules on the conduct of hostilities. When a school (or a compound, a factory, etc.) is formed of several buildings, only the building(s) used for military purposes constitutes the specific, distinct object which becomes a military objective(s), provided it/they meet the two-pronged test definition of Art. 52(2) API.[25]

---

[20] For instance, in the course of the Falklands/Malvinas conflict (1982) the British government used merchant vessels to transport troops and materiel to the islands. That was based on an Order-in-Council according to which the government was entitled to require British merchant vessels to assist in the military effort. Certainly, those 'ships taken up from trade' (STUFTs) were military objectives as soon as they were used to transport military personnel and materiel. The question is, whether and at what point in time merchant vessels could have been considered military objectives by purpose. Assuming that the Order-in-Council mentioned in a general manner that the government was entitled to require merchants vessels to assist, this would not have made them military objective by purpose unless and until it could be possible to determine (on the basis of the Order or otherwise) which specific ship(s) the government was going to require.

[21] ICRC 1987 Commentary (n 15), para 2028.

[22] ICRC Customary IHL (n 3) Rule 15.

[23] ICRC 1987 Commentary (n 15) 636, para 2023.

[24] For example, a school comprising of several buildings is not one object for the purpose of the definition of military objective.

[25] C. Droege, 'Get off my cloud: cyber warfare, international humanitarian law, and the protection of civilians' (2012) 94(866) International Review of the Red Cross 533, 562. This is not precluded by the fact that 'school' is mentioned as an object in Art. 52(3) API, as a school can well be a single building depending on the situation. Of course, when all the buildings that form the compound (or school, or factory, etc.) are used for military purposes, the entire compound (school, factory etc.) becomes a military objective.

In reality, it might nevertheless remain difficult to draw a clear line on what is one building as opposed to two/several. Are two contiguous houses one or two buildings? To be a distinct building, does a minaret need to be separated from the rest of the mosque? Such situations can only be answered in a case-by-case analysis, and in view of the object and purpose of the rules governing the conduct of hostilities, namely to ensure respect for and protection of the civilian population and civilian objects. The delimitation of the building/structure should therefore be understood as narrowly as is reasonably possible in view of the circumstances of the case. Otherwise, buildings/structures should be considered as separate/distinct whenever reasonably possible.

2.4.1.1. Partial use of a building

Modern weapons technology will often enable the parties to an armed conflict which possessed such capabilities to target only that part of, e.g., a building that was in fact being used for military action. However, the majority of the SG took the position that if a given floor of a building can be attacked, this does not mean that only that floor is a military objective and that the remaining parts of the building remain civilian objects. When looking at one individual object partly used for military purposes, for example a multi-story building when only the roof or one apartment is used for military purposes, today's prevailing understanding of the notion of military objective is that once an object is used in such a way as to fulfill the definition of military objective, the entire object becomes a lawful target.[26] Some members of the SG, however, felt that to the extent a party had the capability to identify a specific portion of a building or structure as a military objective and direct an attack upon it, this would affect the classification of the other portions of the structure not being so used and result in them remaining civilian. The determination of whether an object qualifies in whole or in part as a military objective has clear implications for the prohibition of indiscriminate attacks. However, it might have less relevance for the obligation to take precautions in attack and for the prohibition of excessive collateral damage. Indeed, and while some members of the SG disagreed with this position, the majority of the SG considered the damage to the parts of the structure used for civilian purposes would in any case have to be factored into the proportionality assessment and requirement to take feasible precautions. In addition, (for proportionality) the concrete and direct military advantage would stem only from the destruction of the part used for military purposes. Furthermore, injury to civilians and damage to civilian objects located within those parts of the building that are used for civilian purposes would remain relevant even if the building has become a military objective (see below subsection 2.4.2.).

The technological capabilities of different actors are not and should not in the view of the SG be determinative of the definition of military objectives. It would run

[26] United States Department of the Navy, 'The Commander's Handbook on the Law of Naval Operations' (US Navy, US Marine Corps, US Coast Guard 2007) para 8.3 http://www.jag.navy.mil/documents/NWP_1-14M_Commanders_Handbook.pdf accessed 21 April 2017 (The Commander's Handbook); Tallinn Manual (n 3) 134–35.

counter to the equal application of IHL to all parties to an armed conflict that armed forces of technologically advanced States would come under stricter rules than those of less technologically advanced States. This is different with regard to precautions in attack, including precautions in the identification of a military objective, because of the criterion of 'feasibility'. However, the definition of military objectives does not refer to either 'feasibility' or military capabilities of the respective party to the conflict.

2.4.2. Dual use, simultaneous use

The expression 'dual use', which is not identical to the meaning of the same term in arms control law, is commonly employed to refer to objects serving both military and civilian uses. This can be the case of an object of which distinct parts are used for military and civilian purposes respectively (see the example in subsection 2.4.1.1 of a multi-story building in which one apartment/floor is used for military purposes). This can also be the case of an object which in its entirety simultaneously fulfills both functions (such as a single power plant providing electricity to both a military camp and a hospital). The term 'dual use' has no specific place within international humanitarian law, which only recognizes two categories of objects: military or civilian. However, for purposes of discussion, the term 'dual use' referring to a military objective which is also (simultaneously) used for civilian purposes is often used in a descriptive sense, which is the way it is used here.

As mentioned above, and provided that the military objective has been properly identified (cf. subsection 2.4.1.1. above), today's prevailing understanding of the notion of military objective is that once an object is used in such a way as to fulfill the definition of military objective, the entire object becomes a lawful target. For the purpose of identifying whether the object fulfills the definition of military objective, it is irrelevant whether such use amounts to more than 50%. Beyond the question of the identification of the object, the principles of proportionality and precautions in attack remain obviously applicable when targeting such a dual-use object. In this context it is important to emphasize that an object used for military action qualifies as a military objective but that it still may not be attacked if collateral damage to civilians is expected to be excessive.

A problematic aspect is the (incidental) damage to that (non-separable) part of the object that remains being used for civilian purposes. A literal reading of the law could lead to the conclusion that, as the entire object has become a military objective, the destruction of the part that is not used for military purposes does not need to be factored into the proportionality assessment and precautionary measures as incidental damage.[27] According to Shue and Whippman, however, 'state practice suggests that governments are uncomfortable with the notion that the civilian function of a dual-use facility can be ignored.'[28] The position that the destruction of

[27] W.H. Parks, 'Asymmetries and the identification of Legitimate military objectives' in W. Heintschel von Heinegg and V. Epping (eds) *International Humanitarian Law Facing New Challenges* (Springer Publications 2007) 65, 106.

[28] H. Shue and D. Whippman, 'Limiting Attacks on Dual Use Facilities Performing Indispensable Civilian Functions' (2002) 35(3) Cornell International Law Journal 559, 565.

the 'civilian use' of a dual-use object must be considered as incidental damage under the proportionality and (less often mentioned) precautions principles appears in official documents talking of dual-use objects[29] as well as in the doctrine,[30] and the SG deemed it to be the better view while recognizing that the opposite view exists as well.[31] Furthermore, the reverberating effects of an attack must be included in the collateral damages[32] and while the destruction of a dual-use object constitutes the destruction of a military objective, the fact that the part of that military objective which was used for civilian purposes has been destroyed obviously prevents the civilians from using it, which is thus to be counted as incidental harm (see below Part II, subsection 1.1.1. on reasonably foreseeable indirect effects).

2.4.3. Dual use of cyber-infrastructure: does Art. 52(2) API still lead to adequate results if applied in cyberspace?

Although there is a growing consensus that IHL applies to cyber operations in armed conflict, the unique technological dimension of cyberspace raises the question whether the application of IHL rules can adequately meet the specific humanitarian concerns of cyber warfare. In particular, the application of the principle of distinction is problematic.[33] Since the Internet is used for both civilian and military purposes, in times of armed conflict basically every component might qualify as a military objective if its destruction offered a definite military advantage.[34] However, as discussed above (subsection 1.), the second prong of the definition of military objective might not be fulfilled because of the resilient character of the Internet.[35] Furthermore, as mentioned above (see subsection 2.4.2.), the incidental civilian harm caused by the damage to a dual-use object has to be

[29] The Commander's Handbook (n 26) para 8.3; C.D. Guymon (ed) 'Digest of United States Practice in International Law' (Office of the Legal Adviser, United States Department of State 2014) 737 http://m.state.gov/mc67643.htm accessed 21 April 2017.

[30] Shue and Whippman (n 28) 563; M. Sassòli and L. Cameron, 'The Protection of Civilian Objects: Current State of the Law and Issues de lege ferenda' in Ronzitti and Venturini (n 16) 35, 57–58; HPCR Commentary (n 13) 109; N. Lubell, 'Current challenges with regard to the notion of military objective – legal and operational perspectives' in E. Greppi, G.L. Beruto (eds) *Conduct of Hostilities: the Practice, the Law and the Future, Proceedings of San Remo Round Table 4–6 September 2014* (Franco Angeli 2014) 79, 84; M.N. Schmitt and E.W. Widmar, 'On Target: Precision and Balance in the Contemporary Law of Targeting' (2014) 7(3) Journal of National Security and Policy 379, 393.

[31] W.H. Parks, 'Asymmetries and the identification of Legitimate military objectives' in W. Heintschel von Heinegg and V. Epping (eds) *International Humanitarian Law Facing New Challenges* (Springer Publications 2007) 65, 106.

[32] Boothby (n 18) 414; ICRC 2015 IHL Challenges report (n 10) 52; Tallinn Manual (n 3) 160.

[33] Droege (n 25) 566; Geiß and Lahmann (n 7) 391.

[34] Droege (n 25) 562–63; Geiß and Lahmann (n 7) 384.

[35] See n 10 above and text in relation thereto. Very often there may not be a definite military advantage because the respective data can be rerouted. This, however, does not always hold true. Consider a network of a company that is not connected to the Internet and used for both civilian and military purposes. Hence, any statement on whether cyber infrastructure qualifies as a military objective should be made with great caution.

considered, which would also apply to specific dual-use objects belonging to the cyber infrastructure. It has also to be noted that mere intrusion into a cyber system or downloading of the information resident therein do not qualify as attacks.

In any case, Art. 54 API prohibits rendering objects indispensable to the survival of the population useless, which would apply for example to attacks against the cyber infrastructure of a water network, subject to the purpose requirement of Art. 54 API.

To ensure a more comprehensive protection of cyber infrastructure and avoid the humanitarian cost of attacks against it, *de lege ferenda* alternatives could rely on Art. 56(1) API and exclude certain vital cyber infrastructure from attack because of the humanitarian consequence the attack might lead to[36] or alternatively consider the whole of cyber infrastructure as an object indispensable for the survival of the population (Art. 54 API) in view of the havoc that an attack on the global cyber infrastructure as such could bring about to the food supply logistic chain in major cities; or to extend the presumption established by Art. 52(3) API to part of or the whole cyber infrastructure.

2.4.3.1. Is data an object?

As regards the on-going debate on whether the notion of 'object' includes data two different views were expressed in the SG.

According to the majority of the group of experts drafting the Tallinn Manual—and one body of opinion within the SG—there is, at present, not sufficient evidence that data may be considered as an object. In this context, it was opined that since data is intangible it does not qualify as an object, and certain members emphasized that the approach taken in the Tallinn Manual already stretches the law to its limits. Of course, States may, by subsequent practice or otherwise, agree that data qualify as objects.[37]

In some literature[38] and in the opinion of other members of the SG this view seems to overly rely on a passage in the ICRC 1987 Commentary which is meant to distinguish the term 'objects' from notions like the 'aim' or 'purpose' of a military operation, not between tangible and intangible goods.[39] In this view the danger is that failure to view data as an object would leave without protection a whole range of civilian data, such as social security data, tax records, bank accounts, companies'

[36] Geiß and Lahmann (n 7) 391.

[37] Tallinn Manual (n 3) 127. In many domestic legal orders new provisions were adopted in order to characterize the theft of electricity a crime because the original rules on theft only applied to 'objects'. See also M.N. Schmitt, 'The notion of 'objects' during cyber operations: a riposte in defence of interpretive and applicative precision' (2015) 48 Israel Law Review, 81–109.

[38] K. Macak, 'Military Objectives 2.0: The Case for Interpreting Computer Data as Objects under International Humanitarian Law' (2015) 48 Israel Law Review 55; H.H. Dinniss, *Cyber Warfare and the Laws of War* (CUP 2012) 181.

[39] ICRC 1987 Commentary (n 15) 634, para 2010.

client files or election lists or records.[40] Deleting or tampering with such data could quickly bring government services and private businesses to a complete standstill. The conclusion that operations with these effects are not prohibited by IHL in today's ever more cyber-reliant world seems difficult for those members of the SG to reconcile with the object and purpose of this body of norms.[41] As a consequence, the interpretation of the term 'object' today, in its context and in view of the object and purpose of the rules on the conduct of hostilities, should in their view lead to the conclusion that data is an object to which the definition of military objective and the prohibition of directing attacks against civilian objects apply.[42] Some other members of the SG pointed out, however, that this interpretation would mean that many types of cyber operations, such as intelligence and information operations which routinely alter or destroy data currently undertaken by a number of States on a regular basis, would be illegal and could potentially constitute a war crime. At present, the matter is probably unsettled in international law and the SG could reach no consensus on it as a general matter.

On the other hand, the SG as a whole agreed that the special protection afforded to certain classes of objects (medical units, cultural property, water systems, etc.) should be understood as extending to data pertaining to them and thus prohibiting operations directed at deleting, damaging, manipulating or otherwise tampering with such data.[43] For instance, the obligation to respect and protect medical facilities must be understood as extending to medical data stored in a hospital's network or otherwise belonging to it; they will be immune from attack or other hostile military operations because of their importance for medical treatment. Similarly, the prohibition to 'render useless' objects indispensable to the survival of the population will prohibit operations directed against the data that enable their proper functioning. A similarly special protection may apply to culturally important data.

2.5 The controversy concerning the notion of 'war sustaining' objects as military objectives

[40] The commentary to Rule 38 of the Tallinn Manual explains that a minority of the international group of experts was of the opinion that, for the purposes of targeting, data *per se* should be regarded as an object. The majority characterized this position as *de lege ferenda*, Tallinn Manual (n 3) 125–34.

[41] ICRC 2015 IHL Challenges report (n 10) 43. Furthermore, this would leave open the question of whether all data could be the lawful target of cyber operations, or whether another criterion exists —or should be developed—to distinguish protected data from that which could be attacked.

[42] N. Melzer, 'Cyberwarfare and International Law' (UN Institute for Disarmament Research, Resources Paper 2011) 31; N. Lubell, 'Lawful Targets in Cyber Operations – Does the Principle of Distinction Apply?' (2013) 89 International Law Studies, US Naval War College 252, 255–56, 271.

[43] M.N. Schmitt (ed) *Tallinn Manual 2.0 on the International Law Applicable to Cyber Operations* (2nd ed, CUP 2017) 515, Rule 132; ICRC 2015 IHL Challenges report (n 10) 43. For instance, the obligation to respect and protect medical facilities must be understood as extending to medical data stored in a hospital's network or otherwise belonging to it; they will be immune from attack or other hostile military operations because of their importance for medical treatment. Similarly, the prohibition to 'render useless' objects indispensable to the survival of the population will prohibit operations directed against the data that enable their proper functioning.

To constitute a military objective, an object must make an 'effective contribution' to 'military action'. The contribution must be directed towards the actual war-fighting capabilities of a party to the conflict. The generally accepted view is that 'to qualify as a military objective, there must exist a proximate nexus to military action (or 'war-fighting').'[44]

The discussion related to 'war-sustaining' objects largely concerns the question to what extent economic targets can be the object of an attack. Until recently, the discussion was associated with the US Commander's Handbook on the Law of Naval Operations, which substitutes the words 'military action' with the formulation 'war-fighting or war-sustaining'.[45] The June 2015 US DoD Law of War Manual endorses the wording used in the CCW protocols,[46] identical to that of Art. 52(2) API, though it explains later on that 'the United States has interpreted the military objective definition to include these concepts ['war-fighting', 'war-supporting', and 'war-sustaining'].'[47] This position seems to be inspired by the experience of the American Civil War and by the practice of economic warfare in the Law of Naval Warfare and possibly the intention to apply a rather flexible standard of lawful military objectives. However, US practice is far from consistent.[48]

The connection between military action and exports required to finance the war effort is too remote, as almost every civilian activity might be construed by the enemy as indirectly sustaining the war effort.[49] There is only one legal method of warfare which allows a party to an international armed conflict to 'target' the enemy's war-sustaining effort, i.e. a blockade. But even in naval warfare measures of economic warfare may only be directed against goods destined to the enemy's war fighting effort (blockade law). There is no indication in State practice that objects contributing to the enemy's war-sustaining effort qualify as such as military objectives and the SG believes that this position has no basis in the law as it stands today and should be clearly rejected.

Having said that, an object that makes an effective contribution to military action ('war-fighting') might also, depending on the circumstances, be a 'war-sustaining' object (for example an oil production facility which both generates revenue for the war effort ('war-sustaining') and provides fuel for the armed forces ('war-fighting'). It is the latter aspect that makes the object a military objective.). However, in the

---

[44] Dinstein (n 6) 95–96; Schmitt (n 18) 279.
[45] The Commander's Handbook (n 26) para 8.2.
[46] US Department of Defense, 'Law of War Manual' (Office of General Counsel Department of Defense 2015) para 5.7.2 http://archive.defense.gov/pubs/law-of-war-manual-june-2015.pdf accessed 21 July 2016.
[47] Ibid., para 5.7.6.2.
[48] For instance, the US government condemned the sinking of (neutral) outbound oil tankers during the Iran-Iraq War (1980–88) as a violation of IHL although both parties to the conflict could have argued that, by destroying the oil exports, they would deprive the respective enemy of important revenues that enabled it to continue its war effort.
[49] L. Doswald-Beck (ed) *San Remo Manual on International Law Applicable to Armed Conflicts at Sea* (CUP 1995) Explanations, para 60.27; HPCR Manual (n 3) Rule 24; HPCR Commentary (n 13) 110; Tallinn Manual (n 3) 130–31, commentary on Rule 38, para 16.

view of the SG an object that merely contributes towards the 'war-sustaining' capability of a party to the conflict, i.e., its war effort, does not qualify as a military objective.[50] The application of the definition of military objective in this situation would in itself violate the principle of distinction.

2.5.1. Are there any grounds for concluding that States not party to API have a greater latitude of discretion in this respect?

Since the customary rule is identical to the definition in Art. 52(2) API, the question is thus fundamentally one of interpretation of that norm.[51] This rule essentially filled the gap that may have been created by some states not acceding to the Protocols. Non-parties to API have very little State practice to rely upon to support the view that there is a wider latitude for them. There is therefore no reason to believe that States not party to API have greater latitude of discretion in this respect.

3. The second prong: the 'definite military advantage'

The second prong of the test establishes that an object qualifies as a military objective only if its destruction, capture or neutralization would offer a 'definite military advantage' in the circumstances ruling at the time.

With regard to the adjective 'definite', the ICRC 1987 Commentary explains that 'According to the Rapporteur, the adjective 'definite' was discussed at length. The adjectives considered and rejected included the words: 'distinct' (distinct), 'direct' (direct), 'clear' (net), 'immediate' (immédiat), 'obvious' (évident), 'specific' (spécifique) and 'substantial' (substantiel). The Rapporteur of the Working Group added that he was not very clear about the reasons for the choice of words that was made.'[52]

A 'definite' military advantage has been defined as 'concrete and perceptible' rather than 'hypothetical and speculative'.[53] Even when the military advantage is derived from the 'attack as a whole' (as stated by two States in their military manuals[54]) it bears

[50] But see Ryan Goodman's account of reportedly long-standing operational practice targeting war-sustaining infrastructure by the US and other States, R. Goodman, 'The Obama Administration and Targeting 'War-Sustaining' Objects in Non-International Armed Conflicts' (2016) 110 American Journal of International Law 663–79.

[51] This definition has been used consistently in subsequent treaties, namely in Protocol II to the Convention on Certain Conventional Weapons, Art. 2(4); Amended Protocol II to the Convention on Certain Conventional Weapons, Art. 2(6); Protocol III to the Convention on Certain Conventional Weapons, Art. 1(3); Second Protocol to the Hague Convention for the Protection of Cultural Property, Art. 1(f).

[52] ICRC 1987 Commentary (n 15) 635, para 2019.

[53] W.A. Solf, 'Art. 52 API' in M. Bothe, K.J. Partsch and W.A. Solf (eds) *New Rules for Victims of Armed Conflicts* (2nd edn, Martinus Nijhoff Publishers 2013) 367, para 2.4.6.

[54] Several States made declarations upon ratification of API according to which the military advantage relevant for the principle of proportionality is the military advantage offered by 'the attack as a whole' (see below subsection 3.1.2); while none of these declarations apply to the definition of military objective, the military manual of Germany (para 407) and the UK (para 5.4.4 (j) express this view also for the definition of military objective.

emphasis that the attack as a whole constitutes a finite operation (an attack) with defined limits and must not be confused with the entire war effort.[55]

The adjective 'military' limits lawful targets to those that serve a military purpose. Military advantage generally consists in ground gained and in annihilating or weakening the enemy armed forces.[56] It also can include targets which are used for direct logistical support, for military communications and maneuver, as well as production facilities engaged in producing arms or goods for military use. Objects do not, however, become military objectives because there would simply be a political or economic advantage to their destruction. Similarly, forcing a change in the negotiating attitudes of an adverse Party cannot be deemed a proper military advantage.[57]

In interpreting the expression 'definite military advantage' the Eritrea-Ethiopia Claims Commission (EECC) held in a majority decision that 'a definite military advantage must be considered in the context of its relation to the armed conflict as a whole at the time of the attack' and that 'there can be few military advantages more evident than effective pressure to end an armed conflict'.[58] This interpretation must be rejected since it admits that the advantage gained from an attack may be purely political instead of essentially military.[59]

3.1. The distinction between 'definite' and 'concrete and direct' military advantage

Art. 51(5)(b) and 57(2)(a)(iii) API on the principle of proportionality refer to the 'concrete and direct' military advantage anticipated. "Concrete' means specific, not general; perceptible to the senses;' 'direct' means 'without intervening condition or agency'.[60] A remote advantage to be gained at some unknown time in the future is not to be included in the proportionality equation.[61]

The ICRC Commentary on the Additional Protocols explains that 'The expression 'concrete and direct' was intended to show that the advantage concerned should be substantial and relatively close, and that advantages which are hardly perceptible

---

[55] K. Dörmann, 'Obligations of International Humanitarian Law' (2012) 4(2) Military and Strategic Affairs 15; Dinstein (n 6) 94–95, para 232; K. Watkin, 'Military Advantage: A Matter of 'Value', Strategy and Tactics' (2014) 17 Yearbook of International Humanitarian Law 277, 289ff, 339.

[56] ICRC 1987 Commentary (n 15) 685, para 2218.

[57] Schmitt (n 18) 253–54.

[58] Eritrea-Ethiopia Claims Commission, 'Partial Award, Western Front, Aerial Bombardment and related claims – Eritrea's Claims 1, 3, 5, 9–13, 14, 21, 25 & 26' (Permanent Court of Arbitration, State of Eritrea vs Federal Democratic Republic of Ethiopia, 2005) paras 113, 121 https://pcacases.com/web/sendAttach/757 accessed 21 April 2017. The discussion related to the attack of the Hirgigo power plant. The Commission considered that the power plant was making an effective contribution to military action by purpose, because it was intended to provide electricity to a major port and naval facility, at Massawa (para 120). It then stated that '[i]n general, a large power plant being constructed to provide power for an area including a major port and naval facility certainly would seem to be an object the destruction of which would offer a distinct military advantage' (para 121). So it would appear that the Commission considered first the actual military advantage that the destruction of the power plant offered, before turning to these additional—and mistaken—considerations related to 'putting pressure to end an armed conflict'.

[59] Dinstein (n 6) 93.

[60] Solf, 'Art. 57 API' in Bothe, Partsch, Solf (n 53) 407, para 2.7.2.

[61] Ibid. See also Doswald-Beck (n 49) 124.

and those which would only appear in the long term should be disregarded.'[62] Hence there do not seem to be well-founded reasons to believe that the terms 'definite' and 'concrete and direct' should be given different meanings in this regard. Both will similarly exclude hypothetical, indirect, and political advantages from being relevant for the selection of targets as well as for the rule of proportionality.

On the other hand, it has been argued that 'concrete and direct' adds a further element of specificity to the notion of 'definite military advantage'. According to this opinion 'at the stage of target selection, it is sufficient for an attacking Party to determine that the object is capable of yielding a definite military advantage; whereas in the context of assessing proportionality, the military advantage anticipated must be established with more certainty and is also then qualified in relation to potential collateral damage.'[63] This view found support in the ICRC Commentary[64] and in Bothe, Partsch and Solf,[65] and has been endorsed by the Inter-American Commission on Human Rights.[66] This reading is consistent with the principle of effectiveness in the interpretation of treaties whereby all provisions of a treaty should have a meaning.

3.2. On the implication of Art. 8 ICC Statute

Art. 8(2)(b)(iv) of the Rome Statute for the establishment of the International Criminal Court includes among the serious violations of the laws and customs applicable in international armed conflict launching an attack in the knowledge that it will cause collateral damage which would be clearly excessive in relation to the 'concrete and direct overall military advantage' anticipated. This provision seems to broaden the concept of military advantage by adding the term 'overall' to the 'concrete and direct military advantage'. In a footnote to the text adopted for the elements of crimes under the ICC Statute, which was the result of very controversial discussions, includes the following statement: 'The expression 'concrete and direct overall military advantage' refers to a military advantage that is foreseeable by the perpetrator at the relevant time. Such advantage may or may not be temporally or geographically related to the object of the attack.'[67] There is a risk that this

[62] ICRC 1987 Commentary (n 15) 684, para 2209.

[63] Boivin (n 9) 21.

[64] ICRC 1987 Commentary (n 15) 685, para 2218: '[I]t should be noted that the words 'concrete and direct' impose stricter conditions on the attacker than those implied by the criteria defining military objectives in Art. 52 (General protection of civilian objects) paragraph 2.'

[65] Solf, 'Art. 57 API' in Bothe, Partsch, Solf (n 53) 407, para 2.7.2: "Concrete' means specific, not general; perceptible to the senses. Its meaning is therefore roughly equivalent to the adjective 'definite' used in the two pronged test prescribed by Art. 52(2). 'Direct', on the other hand, means 'without intervening condition or agency'. Taken together the two words of limitation raise the standard set by Art. 52 in those situations where civilians may be affected by the attack.'

[66] Inter-American Commission on Human Rights, 'Third Report on the Human Rights Situation in Colombia' (OEA/Ser.L/V/II.102, Doc. 9 rev. 1, 1999) ch IV, para 78.

[67] International Criminal Court, 'Elements of Crimes' (ICC 2011) 19 http://www.icc-cpi.int/nr/rdonlyres/336923d8-a6ad-40ec-ad7b-45bf9de73d56/0/elementsofcrimeseng.pdf accessed 21 April 2017.

explanation may invite unjustifiably expansive interpretations of the concept 'concrete and direct military advantage'. However, in 'informal consultations the need for this sentence was highlighted to cover attacks where the military advantage is planned to materialize at a later time and in a different place.'[68] This should be kept in mind when one tries to understand the meaning of the footnote.

The fact that the Rome Statute has a different wording than the IHL rule does not modify the latter.[69] While the criteria of international criminal responsibility do not necessarily coincide with the elements of the substantive rules of international law, there cannot be a war crime without a violation of IHL. After the adoption of API some States declared that military advantage means the advantage anticipated from the attack considered as a whole and not from isolated or particular parts of the attack.[70] Based on these declarations some commentators conclude that the relative military value of the specific purpose of an individual attack must be assessed in the framework of the more complex overall campaign plan of a belligerent.[71] However, no official explanation is given by these States as to the meaning of 'attack as a whole'. In any case, it must however constitute a finite operation (an attack) with defined limits,[72] and certainly does not mean the whole conflict. Such an interpretation could hardly be reconciled with the meaning of the words 'concrete and direct' and it would confuse 'proportionality' as required by the *ius ad bellum* rules of self-defense with the rules of proportionality in attack in the *ius in bello*.[73]

---

[68] K. Dörmann, *Elements of War Crimes under the Rome Statue of the International Criminal Court, Sources and Commentary* (ICRC, CUP 2002) 163. By way of example, reference was made to feigned attacks during World War II to permit the allied forces to land in Normandy as mentioned by Solf: Solf, 'Art. 52 API' in Bothe, Partsch, Solf (n 53) 366, para 2.4.4.

[69] In this regard, the ICRC submitted at the Rome Conference that *'the inclusions of the word 'overall' is redundant'*, as the understanding that an attack against a particular target may offer an important military advantage felt over a lengthy period of time and in an area other than the vicinity of the target '*is already included in the existing wording of Additional Protocol I.*' (UN Doc. A/CONF.183/INF/10, 13 July 1998).

[70] See e.g. the Declarations on Art. 51 and 57 API by Italy (1986), Germany (1991), the United Kingdom (1992) and France (2001), Reservation/Declarations to API https://www.icrc.org/applic/ihl/ihl.nsf/States.xsp?xp_viewStates=XPages_NORMStatesParties&xp_treatySelected=470 accessed 21 April 2017.

[71] Oeter (n 8) 175–76.

[72] See reference in n 55 above.

[73] US Secretary of Defense, 'The Conduct of the Persian Gulf War: Final Report to Congress, Pursuant to Title V of the Persian Gulf Conflict Supplemental Authorization and Personnel Benefits Act of 1991' (Public Law 102–25, 1992) at 611 seems to reflect such confusion: 'An uncodified but similar provision is the principle of proportionality. It prohibits military action in which the negative effects (such as collateral civilian casualties) clearly outweigh the military gain. This balancing may be done on a target-by-target basis, as frequently was the case during Operation Desert Storm, but also may be weighed in overall terms against campaign objectives.'

Similarly, the addition of the word 'clearly' before 'excessive' in Art. 8 of the ICC Statute does not change the standard under IHL in that regard.[74]

4. The relationship between Art. 23(g) Hague Regulations and Art. 52(2) API

Art. 23(g) Hague Regulations (HR) prohibits 'To destroy or seize the enemy's property, unless such destruction or seizure be imperatively demanded by the necessities of war.' This is a long-standing rule of customary international law applicable in both international and non-international armed conflicts.[75]

The definition of military objectives set forth in Art. 52(2) API is also deemed to have achieved the status of customary law applicable in both international and non-international armed conflicts, since it has been used consistently in subsequent treaties and military manuals and it is supported by official statements, including those of states not being party to API.[76]

4.1. The concept of 'enemy's property'

Some ambiguity surrounds the concept of enemy's property, which is not defined by the Hague Regulations or by other international IHL instruments. It is interpreted to encompass both private and State property or property belonging to the enemy's authorities, movable or immovable.[77] The scope of the prohibition in the Hague Regulations would clearly appear to be broader than simply during attack and includes destruction of enemy property in occupied territory (Art. 53 GCIV) and other situations not directly connected with the conduct of hostilities.[78]

4.2. Is Art. 52(2) API posterior and special?

While Art. 52(2) API is clearly *lex posterior* compared to Art. 23(g) HR, specialty implies that two provisions govern the same subject-matter, which in our case is questionable. It is true that, in a broad perspective, both rules aim at regulating the conduct of hostilities by restricting destruction to what is militarily necessary;[79] their different formulation and setting mainly depend on historical patterns (Art. 23(g) HR) and on negotiating compromises (Art. 52 API). Nevertheless, when taking into consideration the key constituent elements of the two provisions further differences emerge.

---

[74] During the Rome Conference, the ICRC stressed that '[t]he addition of the words 'clearly' and 'overall' in this provision relating to proportionality in attacks must be understood as not changing existing law.' See International Committee of the Red Cross, 'Statement of 8 July 1998 relating to Bureau Discussion Paper in Document A/CONF.183/C.1/L.53' (UN Doc. A/CONF.183/INF/10) 1.

[75] ICTY, *Prosecutor vs Hadzihanasanovic and Kubura* (Case No IT-01-47-AR73.3, 11 March 2005); ICRC Customary IHL (n 3) Rule 50.

[76] ICRC Customary IHL (n 3) Rule 8.

[77] Solf, 'Art. 52 API' in Bothe, Partsch, Solf (n 53) 361–62; L.C. Green, *The Contemporary Law of Armed Conflict* (Manchester University Press 2008) 178; Dinstein (n 6) 252; J. Pictet (ed) *Commentary IV Geneva Convention* (ICRC 1958) 301; H.G. Dederer, 'Enemy Property' in *Max Planck Encyclopedia of Public International Law* (2013) 2.

[78] ICRC Customary IHL (n 3) Rule 50.

[79] Boivin (n 9) 17.

4.3. Is Art. 23 HR broader in scope?

Art. 23(g) HR prohibits destruction of property both as a military objective and a collateral damage, as well as seizure; hence it seems to clearly apply also *outside* situations of hostilities. In this respect, its scope of application is broader than that of Art. 52(2) API, which covers only attacks and the latter would therefore be *lex specialis* compared to the former. Within the scope of application of Art. 52 API, namely during situations of hostilities, Art. 23(g) HR cannot be considered to allow the destruction of objects which are protected against direct attack. During hostilities, only those objects that fulfill the criteria of the definition contained in Art. 52(2) API can be qualified as military objectives and attacked.

On the other hand, Art. 23(g) HR does not aim at defining what is a military objective or a civilian object, but merely exempts a specific category of property from destruction. Although in practice civilian objects will be for the most part publicly or privately owned, they are not limited to enemy's property; furthermore, Art. 52(2) API protects also the civilian objects belonging to the belligerents' own civilians. From this point of view, the material scope of application of Art. 52(2) API is broader than that of Art. 23(g) HR.

In conclusion, Art. 23(g) HR and Art. 52(2) API, if considered singularly, are quite distinct. As was usual at the time of its adoption, Art. 23(g) HR lays down a general rule in a very succinct way. Subsequently, the principle underlying that rule was the basis of more detailed provisions, such as Art. 53 GCIV (on prohibited destruction in occupied territories) and Art. 52 and 57 API (on the protection of civilian objects from attacks and precautions to avoid or minimizing collateral damages caused by attacks). As the customary norm is identical to Art. 52(2) API we must conclude that today in the conduct of hostilities any destruction due to attacks against property is exclusively regulated by the rule contained in Art. 52(2) API. Put otherwise, in situations of hostilities, imperative military necessity does not allow attacking an object that does not constitute a military objective under Art. 52(2) API and the corresponding rule of customary law.

Part II: The Principle of Proportionality[80]

Outline

1. The different elements of the principle of proportionality
   1.1. Incidental loss of civilian life, injury to civilians and damage to civilian objects
      1.1.1. Effects of an attack
      1.1.2. Damage to civilian objects

[80] This part of the report was initially drawn up by the members of working group 3 of the 2015 Oslo meeting: Thilo Marauhn (Group Coordinator), Kazuhiro Nakatani, Eric Pouw, Ken Watkin, Kirsten Schmalenbach, Hector Olasolo Alonso, Jeroen van den Boogaard. All members of the Study Group had a role in commenting upon the initial draft and the entire SG is responsible for the final version of all parts of the report.

- 1.1.3. Civilian taking direct part in hostilities, hors de combat, and military medical doctors
- 1.1.4. Mental injury
- 1.1.5. Human shields
- 1.1.6. Environmental damage
- 1.2. Concrete and direct military advantage
- 1.3. Excessiveness

1. The different elements of the principle of proportionality[81]

The principle of proportionality is a fundamental principle of the law of armed conflict. It is central to the protection of the civilian population during the conduct of hostilities. Violating the principle of proportionality constitutes an indiscriminate attack. According to Art. 51(5)(b) API and Art. 57(2)(a)(iii) and (3) API, the principle of proportionality prohibits attacks

> 'which may be expected to cause incidental loss of civilian life, injury to civilians, damage to civilian objects, or a combination thereof, which would be excessive in relation to the concrete and direct military advantage anticipated.'

By virtue of customary international law parties to an armed conflict are under an obligation to abide by the principle of proportionality in both international as well as non-international armed conflicts.[82] The importance and applicability of the proportionality principle in both types of armed conflict is uncontroversial. Nevertheless, the SG found that a number of the aspects of the proportionality analysis could benefit from further clarification in order to improve the protection of the civilian population.[83] Examples include: the kind of expected incidental harm that must be considered and factored into the proportionality analysis; the concept of the anticipated concrete and direct military advantage; the effect of considerations of force protection; whether criteria exist that indicate excessiveness and which may be applied in a manner as objective as possible; and whether the application of the principle of proportionality could or should differ in different types of conflicts.

---

[81] For an overview on the principle of proportionality, see: W. Fenrick, 'Applying IHL Targeting Rules to Practical Situations: Proportionality and Military Objectives' (2009) 27 Windsor Yearbook of Access to Justice 271; R. Barber, 'The Proportionality Equation: Balancing Military Objectives with Civilian Lives in the Armed Conflict in Afghanistan' (2010) 15 Journal of Conflict and Security Law 467; R. Geiß and M. Siegrist, 'Has the armed conflict in Afghanistan affected the rules on the conduct of hostilities?' (2011) 93(881) International Review of the Red Cross 11, 29–35; J. van den Boogaard, 'Fighting by the Principles: Principles as a Source of International Humanitarian Law' in: M. Matthee, B. Toebes, M. Brus (eds) *Armed Conflict and International Law: In Search of the Human Face - Liber Amicorum in Memory of Avril McDonald* (T.M.C. Asser Press 2013) 3–32.

[82] ICRC Customary IHL (n 3) Rule 14.

[83] Sloane labeled the standard of proportionality as a 'singularly subjective and indeterminate legal standard', See R.D. Sloane, 'Puzzles of Proportion and the 'Reasonable Military Commander': Reflections on the Law, Ethics and Geopolitics of Proportionality' (2015) 6 Harvard National Security Journal 299, 301–02.

1.1. Incidental loss of civilian life, injury to civilians and damage to civilian objects

The principle of proportionality requires a balancing of different considerations. Obviously, different factors will be at stake in different scenarios and depending on the circumstances of each specific case. But even before applying the principle of proportionality to any specific case in concreto, it is important to clarify in the abstract which factors must and/or may be taken into consideration when applying the principle of proportionality.

1.1.1. Effects of an attack

With regard to the question as to what kind of effects of an attack have to be taken into account with regard to the principle of proportionality, there are mainly two views which can be put forward: (i) that proportionality only concerns direct effects of the attack; (ii) that indirect effects of attacks must also be considered because if only direct effects were intended, the rule would have included the word 'direct' (as is the case with regard to military advantage). Therefore, the prevailing view is that indirect effects must also be considered alongside direct ones. The follow-on question that arises from this finding is where and how to draw the line between indirect effects that are relevant for purposes of the principle of proportionality and those that are too remote, if any.

Direct effects of an attack are consequently to be taken into account as part of the incidental harm to be considered for the proportionality analysis. For example: if an explosive weapon is used, it usually causes blast, fragmentation, thermal, cratering and penetration effects. As far as the effects of an attack on the civilian population are concerned, one could think of death, physical injury, caused by the blast wave, by fragments from the weapon or secondary fragmentation (such as glass fragments caused by the blast wave), by burns or by collapsed buildings and damaged vehicles.[84]

Indirect effects on the civilian population, or 'reverberating effects' (also referred to as 'knock on effects'), have been defined as 'the effects that are not directly or immediately caused by the attack, but are nonetheless a consequence of it.'[85] Indirect effects of an attack describe especially its long-term consequences, e.g., the long-term consequences of damaged essential civilian infrastructure.[86] This could include effects on the health care system and level of hygiene that the civilian population is able to maintain during hostilities and after they have ended. According to an ICRC expert medical adviser:

> 'health-care facilities may be directly affected by the blast or fragmentation effects of explosive weapons; electricity and water supplies may be cut off; health-care staff may be killed, injured or unable to get to work; and blood stocks may decrease because regular blood donors are unable to access health-care facilities. One or a combination of these

[84] Ibid., 14.

[85] ICRC Report, 'Expert Meeting, Explosive Weapons in Populated Areas: Humanitarian, Legal, Technical and Military Aspects' (24–25 February 2015 Chavannes-De-Bogis, Switzerland, ICRC 2015) 21 https://www.icrc.org/eng/assets/files/publications/icrc-002-4244.pdf accessed 21 April 2017 (ICRC Expert Meeting).

[86] Ibid., 5.

> factors usually means that the capacity of health-care facilities is weakened at precisely the time that they are most needed – that is, in the aftermath of an attack when hospitals are faced with multiple patients, often with multiple injuries.'[87]

Regarding the consideration of indirect effects of an attack for purposes of the principle of proportionality, the main question that may be asked is whether it is an issue of how far the indirect incidental damage is actually (geographically or temporally) removed from the original attack (site), or whether it is rather a question of foreseeability. The SG agreed that foreseeability is the relevant criterion and that accordingly there is an obligation to take into account all indirect harm that can reasonably be foreseen by a reasonably well-informed person. As stated in the ICTY *Galic* case, that also requires that the 'a reasonably well-informed person in the circumstances of the actual perpetrator, making reasonable use of the information available to him or her, could have expected excessive civilian casualties to result from the attack'[88] In addition, 'the information necessary for reaching an assessment for purposes of the principle of proportionality shall emanate from all sources available at the relevant time.'[89] From this it follows, that reverberating effects that are unforeseeable need not be taken into account.

There is, however, no basis in IHL to impose a certain (absolute) time limit on those indirect effects that need to be taken into account. Various military manuals and statements by States indicate that long-term effects, i.e. indirect effects that occur long after the actual attack, must also be taken into consideration in so far as these are reasonably foreseeable.[90] Therefore, when considering indirect effects the focus should not primarily be on the timeframe in which these effects will materialize, but on their *foreseeability*.[91] It is important to point out that indirect effects can be as or even more severe than the direct effects of an attack. For example, the reverberating effects on objects that are indispensable for the health care system may have a foreseeable and deep impact in terms of loss of civilian life and injury to civilians caused by a planned attack. That is not to say that the law prohibits mere

[87] Ibid., 14.

[88] ICTY, *Prosecutor vs Galić* (Judgement, Trial Chamber, Case No IT-89-29-T, 5 December 2003) para 58; see also ICRC Expert Meeting (n 85) 22.

[89] See e.g. United Kingdom declaration upon ratification of API (2002): '(c) Military commanders and others responsible for planning, deciding upon, or executing attacks necessarily have to reach decisions on the basis of their assessment of the information from all sources which is reasonably available to them at the relevant time.' https://www.icrc.org/applic/ihl/ihl.nsf/Notification.xsp?action=openDocument&documentId=0A9E03F0F2EE757CC1256402003FB6D2 accessed 21 April 2017. Similar declarations were made notably by Australia, Ireland, Italy and New Zealand.

[90] See e.g. Department of Defence, 'Australian Defence Doctrine Publication 3.14 Targeting' (Canberra, Defence Publishing Service 2009) para 1.21; UK Ministry of Defence, *The Manual of the Law of Armed Conflict* (OUP 2004) para 5.33.4; The Commander's Handbook (n 26) para 8.11.4; UN Office of Disarmament Affairs, 'Third Review Conference of the High Contracting Parties to the Convention on Prohibitions or Restrictions on the Use of Certain Conventional Weapons Which May Be Deemed to Be Excessively Injurious or to Have Indiscriminate Effects' (Final Document, CCW/CONF.III/11, Part II, 2006) 4, preambular para 11; see also Tallinn Manual (n 3) 160, commentary on Rule 51, para 6.

[91] This is also the ICRC position; see ICRC 2015 IHL Challenges report (n 10) 52.

inconvenience for the civilian population that is caused by hostilities—as mere inconvenience will usually not be excessive in comparison to the concrete and direct military advantage anticipated, but it does mean that commanders need to balance the concrete and direct military advantage they seek to achieve with more than only the direct incidental harm they expect their planned attack to cause. Parties to an armed conflict can and should enhance their capability to anticipate foreseeable reverberating effects of a planned attack for example through military training of commanders and staff-officers, the consideration of previous battlefield experience and computer-driven simulation programs.

Against this backdrop, the SG unanimously agreed that the interpretation that only immediate effects need be taken into account is too narrow and highlighted the importance of reasonable foreseeability in relation to determining indirect effects.

Incidental harm must therefore be assessed from the attacker's perspective based on what was known—or should have been known on the basis of information available from all sources—at the time of the attack and what was reasonably foreseeable in that situation.

1.1.2. Damage to civilian objects

The definition of 'damage to civilian objects' as part of the principle of proportionality necessarily has to take into account the concept of 'military objective' (see also above Part I of this report), as according to Art. 52 API civilian objects are 'all objects which are not military objectives'. As far as the scope of harm to objects within the principle of proportionality is concerned, the term to use is 'damage', which in the view of the SG also includes the loss of functionality of objects.[92]

The SG discussed the suggestion that an object that does not qualify as a military objective because its destruction offers no definite military advantage in the circumstances ruling at the time, may nevertheless be taken into account—for purposes of the proportionality analysis—as contributing to the military advantage expected from an attack on another military objective if it is expected that this object could become a military objective in the future. The SG concluded that this suggestion has no basis in law. Objects, which could potentially become military objectives in the future, remain civilian objects as long as they have not yet actually become military objectives and any incidental damage to them must be included on the civilian side of the proportionality principle.[93]

---

[92] For several views of the debate concerning the loss of functionality, see ICRC 2015 IHL Challenges report (n 10) 41; ICRC Report, 'International Humanitarian Law and the challenges of contemporary armed conflicts' (31st International Conference of the Red Cross And Red Crescent, Geneva, 28 November–1 December 2011, ICRC 2011) 37; Droege (n 25) 557–59; M.N. Schmitt, 'Rewired warfare: rethinking the law of cyber attack' (2014) 96(893) International Review of the Red Cross 189–206; H.H. Dinniss, 'The Nature of Objects: Targeting Networks and the Challenge of Defining Cyber Military Objectives' (2015) 48(01) Israel Law Review 39–45.

[93] This has to be distinguished from the question of when an intended future use may make the object a military objective by purpose (see above Part I, subsection 2.3.); if it is already established at the time of the attack that the object is a military objective by purpose, then obviously incidental damage to this object does not constitute incidental damage to a civilian object.

Another question discussed by the SG was the application of the principle of proportionality in relation to so-called 'dual-use objects',[94] i.e. objects which in the circumstances ruling at the time fulfill the definition of a military objective (e.g. because of the way in which they are used) but simultaneously also serve civilian functions (see discussion above Part I, subsection 2.4.). A case in point is an electric power station that supplies the civilian population but that is temporarily also used to supply a military compound in a manner that makes this power station fulfill the definition of military objective. The SG agreed that all foreseeable (direct and indirect) effects that an attack on a dual-use object might cause on the civilian use of this object must be taken into account as incidental civilian harm.[95] With respect to the above-mentioned example of the electric power station this means that the loss of electricity for the civilian population and other resultant foreseeable effects on civilians that an attack on this power station might cause must be taken into account as relevant incidental harm for purposes of the proportionality analysis despite the fact that the power station itself is a military objective.

1.1.3. Civilians taking direct part in hostilities, persons *hors de combat*, and military medical personnel

Civilians taking direct part in hostilities

It is clear that persons who at the time of the attack may lawfully be attacked do not factor into the proportionality analysis as relevant civilian harm. If anything, the loss of fighting capacity that would result from an attack on such persons may be factored into the military advantage that is to be obtained from the attack in

---

[94] Notion that has been discussed in the first report, see ILA Study Group, 'The conduct of hostilities under international humanitarian law - challenges of 21st century warfare' (ILA Study Group Report 2014) 11–12 http://www.ila-hq.org/index.php/study-groups accessed 21 April 2017.

[95] ICTY, *Prosecutor vs. Prlić and al* (Judgment, Trial Chamber, Case No IT-04-74-T, 29 May 2013) paras 1582–4; US Joint Chiefs of Staff, 'Joint publication 3–60, Joint Targeting' (CJCS 2013) A-5; see also C.D. Guymon (ed) 'Digest of United States Practice in International Law 2014' (US Department of State 2014) 737 https://www.state.gov/documents/organization/244504.pdf accessed 21 April 2017; The Commander's Handbook (n 26) para 8.3; Inspecteur Militair Juridische Dienst, 'Humanitair Oorlogsrecht' (Koninklijke Landmacht 2005) VS 27-412; Royal Army of the Netherlands, 'The Humanitarian Law of War: A Manual' (official in Dutch, English unofficial translation, ICRC library, 2005) para 0546; Norway, 'Manual i krigens folkerett' (2013) para 2.22; Pentagon briefing on February 5, 2003 arguing that attacks on dual use facilities are considered as automatically producing incidental damage, M. Knights, 'Infrastructure Targeting and Postwar Iraq' (The Washington Institute 14 March 2003) http://www.washingtoninstitute.org/policy-analysis/view/infrastructure-targeting-and-postwar-iraq accessed 21 April 2017; HPCR Commentary (n 13) 109, Rule 22(d), para 7; Tallinn Manual (n 3) 134–35, commentary on Rule 39, para 2; C. Greenwood, 'Customary International Law and the First Geneva Protocol of 1977 in the Gulf Conflict' in P. Rowe (ed) *The Gulf War 1990–91 In International And English Law* (London, Routledge 1993) 73ff; Schmitt and Widmar (n 30) 393; M. Sassoli and L. Cameron: 'The Protection of Civilian Objects: Current State of the Law and Issues de lege ferenda' in N. Ronzitti and G. Venturini (n 16) 57–58; Shue and Whippman (n 28) 559, 565–66; H. Durham, 'Keynote address' in E. Greppi (ed.) *Conduct of hostilities: The Practice, the Law and the Future* (International Institute of Humanitarian Law, Franco Angeli 2015) 31.

question. Civilians directly participating in hostilities remain civilians but temporarily—for as long as they directly participate in hostilities—lose protection from direct attack. During such time they may not only be directly attacked but logically also do not count as relevant civilian harm for purposes of the principle of proportionality. It is equally clear, however, that civilians who are known to be sympathetic to the attacked party and who have participated directly to the hostilities in the past (but not at the time of the attack, cf. the so-called 'revolving door' controversy),[96] remain protected against direct attack and any loss of life or injury to them must be taken into consideration for purposes of the principle of proportionality.

Persons hors de combat, and military medical personnel

The SG noted that both the treaty-based and the customary law rule on proportionality refer to loss of life and injury to 'civilians'. Other categories of protected persons who lack civilian status, namely combatants *hors de combat* and military medical personnel find no explicit mentioning. This raises the question of whether expected incidental harm to such persons may render an attack on a military objective unlawful, and if so on what legal basis.

These categories of persons enjoy strong protection under IHL. In the case of military medical personnel, it may be added that they fulfill an important medical function, potentially of benefit to all sides of the armed conflict. What is more, in light of the increasingly common presence of civilian medical personnel and facilities in areas of armed conflict, it may often be impossible or difficult to distinguish between civilian medical personnel which is undoubtedly protected by the principle of proportionality and military medical personnel. If indeed incidental harm to protected persons other than civilians did not need to be considered in the proportionality assessment, and considering that in such a case the expectation to cause them incidental harm—however extensive—could never render an attack unlawful, this position would undermine the special protection that IHL affords to these persons. In particular, the SG noted that parties to an armed conflict must respect and protect medical personnel, and that this obligation has been understood notably by the ICRC as encompassing a prohibition on attacks that would be expected to cause excessive harm to protected persons other than civilians.[97] Furthermore, the SG noted that notwithstanding the narrow formulation of the proportionality rule in the ICRC Customary Law Study—referring only to civilians

---

[96] Regarding the so-called 'revolving door controversy': see K.W. Watkin, 'Combatants, Unprivileged Belligerents and Conflicts in the 21st Century' (International Humanitarian Law Research Initiative, Harvard Program on Humanitarian Policy and Conflict Research 2003) 11–12 http://www.hpcrresearch.org/sites/default/files/publications/Session2.pdf accessed 21 April 2017 and N. Melzer, 'Keeping the Balance Between Military Necessity and Humanity: A Response to Four Critiques of the ICRC's Interpretive Guidance on the Notion of Direct Participation in Hostilities' (2010) 42(831) New York University Journal if International Law and politics 831, 888ff.

[97] For the ICRC position, see ICRC 2015 IHL Challenges report (n 10) 31–32. See also L. Gisel, 'Can the incidental killing of military doctors never be excessive?' (2013) 95(889) International Review of the Red Cross 215–30.

—the customary law rule comprising the principle of proportionality might actually be broader comprising also protected persons other than civilians. Indeed, several States' military manuals[98] as well as experts' reports and manuals refer to 'protected persons' (i.e. not only civilians) either when stating the principle of proportionality,[99] or in their definition of collateral damage which then applies to all the conduct of hostilities rules addressing incidental harm, including proportionality. While some members of the SG initially favored a literal reading of the proportionality rule, the SG agreed that incidental killings of or injury to protected persons other than civilians render the attack prohibited if it is excessive compared to the concrete and direct military advantage anticipated—whether one anchors this finding in the rules on the protection of medical mission (and in particular the obligation to protect and respect medical personnel including military medical personnel), in the rules on the conduct of hostilities, or in both.

It was also suggested that even if one would not recognize such an obligation through the application of specific norms, as a minimum, the Martens Clause would demand a constant effort to spare these actors and facilities from unnecessary risk and assess proportionality when operationally feasible.[100]

1.1.4. Mental injury

The question whether and in how far 'mental injury' has to be taken into consideration when assessing civilian impact for purposes of the principle of proportionality was also discussed. One opinion expressed within the SG was that mental injury falls within the notion of 'injury' to civilians and that it is relevant when conducting the proportionality analysis. In this context reference was made to the Tallinn Manual on Cyber Warfare where, in the context of the definition of a cyber

[98] Australia: Australian Defence Headquarters, 'Australian Defence Doctrine Publication 06.4 Law of Armed Conflict' (Canberra, Defence Publishing Service 2006) para 2.8; Canada: Office of the Judge Advocate General, 'The Law of Armed Conflict at the Operational and Tactical Levels' (Chief of Defence Staff 2001) para 204.5: New Zealand: New Zealand Defence Force, Headquarters, 'Interim Law of Armed Conflict Manual' (DM 112, Wellington, Directorate of Legal Services 1992) para 207; Philippines: Philippine Air Force, Headquarters, 'Air Power Manual' (Office of Special Studies 2000) paras 1–6.4. A contrary view is expressed in: US Department of Defense, 'Law of War Manual' (Office of General Counsel of the Department of Defense 2015, updated 2016) para 5.10.1.2 https://www.hsdl.org/?view&did=797480 accessed 21 April 2017.

[99] See Final Report to the Prosecutor, the Committee Established to Review the NATO Bombing Campaign Against the Federal Republic of Yugoslavia that speak of 'injury to non-combatants' (and not 'injury to civilians') under the principle of proportionality, ICTY Office of the Prosecutor, 'Final Report to the Prosecutor by the Committee Established to Review the NATO Bombing Campaign Against the Federal Republic of Yugoslavia' (2000) paras 49, 50 http://www.icty.org/en/press/final-report-prosecutor-committee-established-review-nato-bombing-campaign-against-federal accessed 21 April 2017. Doswald-Beck (n 49) 9, para 13(c); see also Doswald-Beck (n 49) 87, para 13.9. With regard to objects, see also HPCR Manual (n 3) Rule 1(l).

[100] For a detailed analysis of this issue, cf G.S. Corn and A. Culliver, 'Wounded Combatants, Military Medical Personnel, and the Dilemma of Collateral Risk' (Social Science Research Network 2016) https://ssrn.com/abstract=2884854 accessed 21 April 2017.

attack, serious illness and severe mental suffering are considered to be included in the notion of injury.[101] Such a position would seem to require the consideration of similarly serious illness and severe mental suffering caused incidentally to civilians as relevant incidental injury under the principle of proportionality. This could be the case for example with regard to post-traumatic stress disorder.[102] At the same time it was suggested within the SG that psychological harm should be distinguished from such mental harm and that psychological harm should be excluded from the proportionality analysis, noting that in the domestic criminal law of some States mental injury constitutes grievous bodily harm whilst psychological harm does not. It was put forward that mental injury is often seen as a biological condition that requires medical treatment whereas psychological disorders are usually treated through psychotherapy and psychological and behavioral interventions. Some members of the SG however raised concerns about how military commanders could be expected to evaluate this distinction. The question of proving a causal link between the attack and the mental injury in question also arose within the SG.[103]

Various members of the SG agreed on the importance of this issue, bearing in mind however that mental harm could only be included within the proportionality analysis when it is measurable and when a causal link to a specific attack can be established (war is intrinsically harmful). The SG noted that acts or threats of violence the primary purpose of which is to spread terror among the civilian population, and which may and often will cause mental harm, are clearly prohibited.[104]

1.1.5. Human shields[105]

The SG also discussed the issue of 'human shields'. The SG agreed that involuntary human shields remain protected, and that therefore any expected incidental harm to involuntary human shields is relevant under the principle of proportionality. The controversial issue with regard to human shields concerns the question whether *voluntary* shields are civilians protected against direct attack,[106] or whether the act

---

[101] Tallinn Manual (n 3) 108, commentary on Rule 30, para 8.

[102] E. Lieblich, 'Beyond Life and Limb: Exploring Incidental Mental Harm Under International Humanitarian Law' in D. Jinks et al (eds) *Applying International Humanitarian Law in Judicial and Quasi-Judicial Bodies* (The Hague, T.M.C Asser Press 2014) 185–218.

[103] Stanford International Human Rights and Conflict Resolution Clinic and Global Justice Clinic at NYU School of Law, 'Living Under Drones: Death, Injury and Trauma to Civilians from US Drone Practices in Pakistan' (Stanford Law School & NYU School of Law 2012) http://chrgj.org/wp-content/uploads/2012/10/Living-Under-Drones.pdf accessed 21 April 2017.

[104] See Art. 51(2) API and Art. 13(2) APII; ICRC Customary IHL (n 3) Rule 2.

[105] See A. Rubinstein and Y. Roznai, 'Human Shields in Modern Armed Conflicts: The Need for a Proportionate Proportionality' (2011) 22 Stanford Law & Policy Review 93; N. Al-Duaij, 'The Volunteer Human Shields in International Humanitarian Law' (2010) 12 Oregon Review of International Law 117; M.N. Schmitt, 'Human Shields in International Humanitarian Law' (2009) 47 Columbia Journal of Transnational Law 292.

[106] For the arguments supporting this position, see ICRC, *Interpretive Guidance on the notion of direct participation in hostilities under International Humanitarian Law* (ICRC 2009) 56 and Melzer (n 96) 869–72.

of voluntary shielding amounts to direct participation in hostilities leading to a temporary loss of protection from attack. Going even further, there are some voices in the literature which claim that civilians who do not heed a precautionary warning prior to an attack and who remain in the area, factually become voluntary shields; while others have rightly pointed out that there might be many other reasons for being unable or unwilling to leave an area in spite of the warning. The SG considered that the view that civilians who do not heed to a warning would lose their protection has no basis in law.[107] It therefore agreed that a party that issues an effective advance warning is not relieved from its obligation to take all other feasible precautions including to avoid or minimize civilian harm, including with respect to those civilians who have not heeded to the warning (see below Part III, subsection 6.). The SG also agreed that the only manner in which civilians lose their protection is for such time as they directly participate in hostilities. Opinions within the SG remained split, however, with regard to the question whether voluntary human shielding could amount to directly participating in hostilities, and if so whether this could be the case for any voluntary human shield or only depending on specific circumstances. In this regard, the SG took note of the December 2016 amendment of the US DoD Law of War manual, which considers that (voluntary and involuntary) human shields remain protected civilians unless they take a direct part in hostilities.[108]

[107] See e.g. UN Commission in Human Rights, 'Report of the Commission of Inquiry on Lebanon pursuant to Human Rights Council Resolution S-2/1' (A/HRC/3/2, UN General Assembly 2006) para 158 ('A warning to evacuate does not relieve the military of their ongoing obligation to 'take all feasible precautions' to protect civilians who remain behind, and this includes their property. By remaining in place, the people and their property do not suddenly become military objectives which can be attacked. The law requires the cancelling of an attack when it becomes apparent that the target is civilian or that the civilian loss would be disproportionate to the expected military gain'); P.S. Baruch and N. Neuman 'Warning Civilians Prior to Attack under International Law' in R.A. Pedrozo and D.P. Wollschlaeger (eds) *International Law Studies – Vol 87, International Law and the Changing Character of War* (Naval War College Press 2011) 359ff, 395: 'One of the concerns raised with regard to warnings is that after advising civilians to evacuate a certain area, military forces might consider anyone who did not evacuate as forfeiting civilian status and becoming a lawful attack objective. This, of course, is not the case and civilians who have not left the area must be taken into account in the proportionality analysis.'

[108] The manual as amended in December 2016 states that 'If civilians are being used as human shields, provided they are not taking a direct part in hostilities, they must be considered as civilians in determining whether a planned attack would be excessive, and feasible precautions must be taken to reduce the risk of harm to them', US Department of Defense, 'Law of War Manual 2016' (n 98) para 5.12.3.4; the original text, no longer valid, held that: 'Harm to the following categories of persons and objects would be understood not to prohibit attacks under the proportionality rule: (…) human shields', see Department of Defense, 'Law of War Manual 2015' (n 46) para 5.12.3.

1.1.6. Environmental damage[109]

According to Art. 52(1) API and customary international humanitarian law,[110] any object, which is not a military objective, is a civilian object. The SG agreed that as the environment does not fulfill the definition of a military objective, it must be considered a civilian object (or rather many civilian objects). Therefore, the principle of distinction applies to the natural environment and it is prohibited to attack any part of the natural environment unless it has become a military objective in the circumstances ruling at the time. Incidental damage to the environment or to specific objects forming part thereof constitutes relevant incidental civilian harm for the principles of proportionality and precaution (unless these objects have become military objectives). Such incidental harm may, alone or in combination with other incidental harm to civilians or civilian objects, render an attack unlawful.

1.2. Concrete and direct military advantage

In the context of the principle of proportionality, the 'military advantage anticipated' is traditionally understood to consist of ground gained and a weakening of enemy forces.[111] In some modern armed conflicts especially in certain NIACs military advantages other than territorial gain may also—depending on the circumstances—be of relevance. It has been suggested that the notion of military advantage should be construed more broadly to encompass 'any consequences of an attack which directly enhance friendly military operations or hinder those of the enemy',[112] or 'all sorts of tactical gains and military considerations, and that different advantages that need not necessarily derive from the destruction of the specific object under attack may be considered cumulatively'.[113] Some members of the SG considered these views as too broad. In any case, the SG agreed that the notion of military advantage does not include advantages that are only political, psychological, economic, financial, social, or moral in nature.[114] As the wording makes clear, the advantage sought must be a military one. This is adequately reflected in the definition put forward in Rule 1(w) of the Air and Missile Warfare Manual according to which: "Military advantage'

[109] See E.T. Jensen, 'The International Law of Environmental Warfare: Active and Passive Damage during Armed Conflict' (2005) 38 Vanderbilt Journal of Transnational Law 145; C. Thomas, 'Advancing the Legal Protection of the Environment in Relation to Armed Conflict: Protocol I's Threshold of Impermissible Environmental Damage and Alternatives' (2013) 82 Nordic Journal of International Law 83; A. Leibler, 'Deliberate Wartime Environmental Damage: New Challenges for International Law' (1992) 23 California Western International Law Journal 67; C. Droege and M.L. Tougas, 'The Protection of the Natural Environment in Armed Conflict – Existing Rules and Need for Further Legal Protection' in R. Rayfuse (ed) *War and the Environment* (Leiden, Brill Nijhoff 2014) 11, 33ff.

[110] ICRC Customary IHL (n 3) Rule 9.

[111] ICRC 1987 Commentary (n 15) 685, para 2218.

[112] HPCR Commentary (n 13) 45.

[113] K. Watkin, 'Assessing Proportionality: Moral Complexity and Legal Rules' (2005) 8 Yearbook of International Humanitarian Law 19; R. Geiß, 'The Principle of Proportionality: Force Protection as a Military Advantage' (2012) 45(1) Israel Law Review 71, 77.

[114] HPCR Commentary (n 13) 45.

means those benefits of a military nature that result from an attack. They relate to the attack considered as a whole and not merely to isolated or particular parts of the attack.'[115] This implies that there must be a measurable (while not necessarily calculable in a mathematical way) effect,[116] with a 'close connection between the action and the attainment of the military purpose'.[117] However, even when States view the relevant military advantage as that anticipated from the 'attack as a whole',[118] the 'attack as a whole' involves a finite, delimitable event, and should not be confused with the entire war.[119]

It is important to be clear whether one speaks of 'military advantage' in a general sense, or of a 'military advantage' that is relevant for the principle of proportionality (or the definition of a military objective), namely only the 'concrete and direct military advantage' (or 'definite military advantage', respectively). The military advantage that may justify civilian loss, injury and damages for purposes of the principle of proportionality must be (1) concrete, (2) direct and (3) military. The limiting qualifiers 'concrete and direct' fulfil different important functions. 'Concrete' means that there has to be a *real* (i.e. a tangible or measurable) effect, while 'direct' refers to the chain of causation. The expected military advantage must be sufficiently tangible. As such, it cannot be 'based merely on hope or speculation'.[120] The qualifiers 'concrete' and 'direct' mean that the military advantage should be 'substantial and relatively close'.[121] Advantages that are vague, hypothetical, indirect, long-term, including possible military advantages that might indirectly derive from advantages in the political, economic, moral or financial realms are therefore excluded.[122] Clear examples of military advantageous results that may be expected from an attack are the ground that is conquered by the attack or the effects it has on opposing forces, both in terms of casualties and damage to the military objects and installations of the enemy.[123] Typical examples include the destruction of an enemy stronghold, military headquarters, or military equipment.

The concept of 'military advantage' is part both of the principle of proportionality and the definition of a military objective (for the latter, see above Part I.). The SG agreed that the meaning of 'military advantage' is identical with regard to both rules.[124] The question remains, however, whether the different qualifiers,

---

[115] HPCR Manual (n 3) 5, Rule 1(w).
[116] Watkin (n 113) 22.
[117] F. Hampson and Y. Dinstein, 'Proportionality and Necessity in the Gulf Conflict' (1992) 86 Proceedings of the American Society of International Law 45, 47.
[118] Australia, Belgium, Canada, France, Germany, Italy, the Netherlands, New Zealand, Spain, the United Kingdom and the United States. For example UK declaration upon ratification of API (n 89) para (i). Statements made by the other States are similar, see Reservation/Declarations to API (n 70).
[119] See reference in n 55 above.
[120] HPCR Commentary (n 13) 92.
[121] ICRC 1987 Commentary (n 15) 684, para 2209.
[122] Ibid.; UK Ministry of Defence (n 90) para 5.33.3; Tallinn Manual (n 3) 161, commentary on Rule 51, para 8
[123] ICRC 1987 Commentary (n 15) 685, para 2218.
[124] See, for example, Watkin (n 113) 3, 18.

namely the requirement of a 'definite' military advantage for purposes of defining a military objective, and the requirement of a 'concrete and direct' military advantage for purposes of the principle of proportionality, lead to different results with regard to the military advantages that may ultimately be taken into consideration under these different rules.

The qualifier 'definite' may be understood to mean that the military advantage must be of some substance and it must be highly likely that the military advantageous effect will be attained.[125] In this regard, the Bothe/Partsch/Solf Commentary on API indicates that the qualifier 'concrete', meaning 'specific, and not general', can be seen as more or less comparable to the adjective 'definite' used in Art. 52(2) API.[126] The manner in which the Air and Missile Warfare Manual defines 'definite' picks up on this interpretation, indicating that the term 'definite' is employed to exclude advantages which are merely potential, speculative or indeterminate, and thus renders it very similar to the understanding of 'concrete'.[127] The additional qualifier 'direct', understood as requiring the absence of an 'intervening condition or agency',[128] shows that the military advantage relevant for the proportionality analysis is more restrictive than the one required to make an object a military objective in the first place: the military advantage must be 'concrete *and* direct', thus more than just any 'remote advantage to be gained at some unknown time in the future'.[129] It thus seems that therefore the threshold is higher for the military advantage that is relevant to the proportionality rule. The ICRC Commentary notes that the words 'concrete and direct' are 'intended to show that the advantage concerned should be substantial and relatively close, and advantages which are hardly perceptible and those which appear only in the long term should be disregarded';[130] while the 2004 UK Military Manual stipulates that "concrete and direct' means that the advantage to be gained is identifiable and quantifiable and one that flows directly from the attack, not some pious hope that it might improve the military situation in the long term'.[131] The aspect which seems to be crucial is that 'definite' and 'concrete and direct' both exclude advantages that are hardly

[125] See the ICRC 1987 Commentary (n 15) 635, para 2019: 'According to the Rapporteur, the adjective 'definite' was discussed at length. The adjectives considered and rejected included the words: 'distinct' (distinct), 'direct' (direct), 'clear' (net), 'immediate' (immédiat), 'obvious' (évident), 'specific' (spécifique) and 'substantial' (substantiel). The Rapporteur of the Working Group added that he was not very clear about the reasons for the choice of words that was made.'; Solf, 'Art. 52 API' in Bothe, Partsch, Solf (n 53) 367, para 2.4.6: 'It may, however, be concluded that the adjective is a word of limitation denoting in this context a concrete and perceptible military advantage rather than a hypothetical and speculative one.'

[126] Cf Solf, 'Art. 57 API' in Bothe, Partsch, Solf (n 53) 407, para 2.7.2.

[127] HPCR Commentary (n 13) 49, Rule 1(y), para 7.

[128] Cf Solf, 'Art. 57 API' in Bothe, Partsch, Solf (n 53) 407, para 2.7.2.

[129] Ibid.; see also ICRC 1987 Commentary (n 15) 685, para 2218.

[130] ICRC 1987 Commentary (n 15) 684, para 2209.

[131] UK Ministry of Defence (n 90) para 5.33.3.

perceptible or those which would only appear in the long run or advantages that are merely potential, speculative, indeterminate or based on hope.[132]

The SG also discussed the issue of 'force protection' within the context of the principle of proportionality and in light of the notion of a 'concrete and direct military advantage'.[133] The concept of force protection is not legally defined, but might be understood as referring to minimizing risks and losses to preserve combat capability. The majority of the SG, agreed that the notion of force protection is relevant for the implementation of the proportionality principle at least in certain circumstances. Whether military commanders are under a duty to protect their subordinates derived from the domestic law of their respective State is irrelevant in this regard. What matters is that under IHL preventing losses among ones' own troops constitutes a military advantage, and provided this military advantage is sufficiently concrete and direct it may be considered for purposes of the principle of proportionality. For example, the military advantage of saving troops which are under enemy fire would amount to a concrete and direct military advantage that is to be factored into the proportionality analysis when attacking the source of enemy fire. Saving one's own forces is the very purpose of fire support to troops in contact. It should, however, also be noted that while force protection is a relevant military consideration, it does not automatically trump other considerations. The relative value of protecting ones' own forces is not necessarily higher than the expected incidental harm to civilians.

The debates turn on the relevance of force protection (or force preservation) when comparing various (alternative) means or methods to achieve a specific military advantage. In that regard, there is no doubt that an attack cannot take place if the only means and methods considered feasible for force protection are such that the incidental civilian casualties and damages expected would be excessive in relation to the anticipated concrete and direct military advantage. The more complicated issue is whether the protection of one's own force that results from choosing a safer means or method of attack, e.g. a high altitude attack that under the circumstances is considered 'safer', constitutes a concrete and direct military advantage of that attack, relevant for the principle of proportionality.

The SG agreed that the military advantage resulting from 'force protection' may only be included in the proportionality analysis if it is concrete and direct.[134] This

---

[132] Cf Solf, 'Art. 57 API' in Bothe, Partsch, Solf (n 53) 407, para 2.7.2; ICRC 1987 Commentary (n 15) 684, para 2209; HPCR Commentary (n 13) 92, Rule 14, para 9; Tallinn Manual (n 3) 161, commentary on Rule 51, para 8.

[133] For a general overview see N. Neuman, 'Applying the Rule of Proportionality: Force Protection and Cumulative Assessment in International Law and Morality' (2004) 7 Yearbook of International Humanitarian Law 79–112; Geiß (n 113) 71. The SG also discussed how the issue of force protection relates to precautions. The SG agreed that force protection considerations are relevant 'military considerations' for the application of the principle of precautions; see also discussion on force protection in the context of precautions at Part III, subsection 2.2.2 below. Some members of the SG indicated that the main relevance of the issue of force protection lies in the context of precautions rather than in the context of the principle of proportionality.

[134] Geiß (n 113) 88.

means that in circumstances where a decision is being made to adopt a method or means of attack anticipated to be more protective for the attacking forces, but also expected to result in greater incidental damage, the difference in terms of 'force protection' between the two means or methods of attack cannot be factored into the assessment of the military advantage of the less secure attack. This is because the advantage becomes apparent only when the safer method of attack is compared to a hypothetical less secure course of action that was never carried out. As such, the advantage is too remote or hypothetical to qualify as a 'concrete and direct military advantage', as required by the principle of proportionality. Furthermore, if force protection could be considered as a military advantage in such a situation, the proportionality test could be one-sidedly manipulated. Indeed, the excessiveness requirement for a specific operation would depend of the consideration of other hypothetical operational options and the danger to one's own troops in these other operations. In any case, the idea that the armed forces' own soldiers could be ascribed a greater value in the balancing exercise than civilians is incompatible with the principle of proportionality, and in fact would undermine this principle.

1.3. Excessiveness

The word that has been codified in the principle of proportionality to determine the difference between a lawful attack and an unlawful attack is the word 'excessive'. The original draft drawn up by the ICRC contained the word 'proportionate', but this wording appeared to be unacceptable to some States during the negotiations. Frits Kalshoven has claimed to have proposed the use of the word 'excessive' during these debates, which was subsequently accepted.[135]

Some commentators have pointed out that the expected 'concrete and direct military advantage' and the 'incidental loss of civilian life, injury to civilians, damage to civilian objects, or a combination thereof' are incomparable as incommensurate factors.[136] It should be noted, however, that the balancing of different considerations in the realm of the principle of proportionality is nothing unusual at all. It is the rule rather than the exception and it should not be viewed as an obstacle to carry out a sound proportionality analysis. For example, under human rights law, the principle of proportionality typically requires the balancing of public order maintenance on the one hand with certain limitations on individual freedoms on the other hand.

When determining excessiveness for purposes of the principle of proportionality in the realm of IHL, quantitative and qualitative factors play a role. This part of the proportionality analysis requires the (difficult) attribution of certain values to the

[135] As indicated by Frits Kalshoven during a presentation by Jeroen van den Boogaard on 'Controversial issues surrounding the principle of proportionality in international humanitarian law' at a research meeting of the Kalshoven-Gieskes Forum on International Humanitarian Law at Leiden Law School on 27 November 2012.

[136] See, for example, K. Anderson, 'The Ethics of Robot Soldiers?' (Law of War and Just War Theory Blog 4 July 2007) http://kennethandersonlawofwar.blogspot.nl/2007/07/ethics-of-robot-soldiers.html accessed 21 April 2017; Sloane (n 83) 299, 321.

anticipated military advantage and expected civilian damages. As an example for the combination of qualitative and quantitative factors one might think of the military advantage anticipated from an attack killing three ordinary soldiers, which must be deemed to be in principle lower than the advantage anticipated from killing three high-ranking commanders due to the military importance of the different functions fulfilled. But of course the assessment will necessarily always be situational, depending on the circumstances of each specific case. It could be the case that under the given circumstances the three ordinary soldiers are fulfilling a centrally important military task in which case the military advantage of defeating these soldiers could be seen as higher as the military advantage anticipated from an attack on higher-ranking soldiers. Conversely, the military advantage offered by attacking high-ranking officers assigned to administrative tasks might be quite low. The assessment of the expected civilian harm is similarly situational. The relative value of an abandoned shepherd-shed in a rural area would seem to be relatively low but this assessment may change if the shed is used as shelter by civilians. A quasi-mathematical assessment may sometimes be possible; for example, when a planned attack is directed against one hundred enemy combatants but expected to cause the death of three civilians.

Whether an attack qualifies as excessive is to be determined from the perspective of a 'reasonable military commander'.[137] According to the ICTY Trial Chamber: 'In determining whether an attack was proportionate, it is necessary to examine whether a reasonably well-informed person in the circumstances of the actual perpetrator, making reasonable use of the information available to him or her, could have expected excessive civilian causalities to result from the attack'.[138] It is important to note that while the determination of excessiveness from the perspective of a reasonable military commander necessarily leaves commanders with a certain margin of discretion, it is an objective standard. Incidental harm may be proportionate from the perspective of a reasonable military commander even if an individual commander might regard it as excessive; conversely incidental harm may be excessive from the perspective of a reasonable military commander even if an individual commander might regard it as proportionate. The principle of proportionality thus accommodates operational realities. In addition, while it allows for a certain spectrum of decisions that would be in line with the law, at the same time the principle of proportionality also sets an objective limit whenever a reasonable military commander would consider the expected civilian damages to be excessive.

Furthermore, the armed forces may strive for more objectivity in the application of the principle of proportionality by institutionalizing procedures for the purpose of targeting that include the obligation to conclude a proportionality analysis with clear guidance on the understanding of the factors that need to be taken into account.

---

[137] Sloane (n 83) 299, 302: 'At best, its [the principle of proportionality's] implementation in the field is guided by the nebulous standard of the good-faith and optimally informed 'reasonable military commander.'

[138] ICTY, *Prosecutor vs Galić* (n 88) para 58.

The objectivity of the process may also be further enhanced by ensuring that as far as possible military commanders have access to well-trained (military) legal advisers throughout the 'targeting cycle'.

It was suggested by some members of the SG that a (large-scale) survey assessing where military operators and civilians would 'draw the line', i.e. at which point they would consider civilian casualties and damages to be excessive, in a number of different scenarios would be useful.[139] This empirical research could then feed into military doctrine and training modules and inform operational decision-making in the application of the principle of proportionality.

Part III: Precautions[140]

Outline

1. Precautions in attack
2. When are precautions 'feasible'?
   - 2.1. Scope and content of the feasibility caveat
   - 2.2. Factors to be taken into consideration when determining feasibility
     - 2.2.1. Financial implications as a relevant factor in the determination of feasibility
     - 2.2.2. Force Protection as a relevant consideration when determining feasibility
3. Increasing incentives for compliance
4. The obligation to take constant care
5. The obligation to verify
6. Feasible precautions in the choice of means and methods of attack: No general obligation to use the most precise or modern technology
7. The obligation to take effective advance warning

1. Precautions in attack

The obligation to take all feasible precautions to avoid or minimize the risk to civilians resulting from military operations is a fundamental principle of the law of

[139] See Janina Dill, *Legitimate Targets? Social Construction, International Law and US Bombing* (Cambridge Studies in International Relations 133, CUP 2014). See, L. Blank, G.S. Corn and E. Jensen's rather critical post, 'Surveying Proportionality: Wither the Reasonable Commander?' (Just Security 25 March 2015) https://www.justsecurity.org/21474/surveying-proportionality-reasonable-commander/ accessed 21 April 2017, and J. Dill's answer, "Proportionate' Collateral Damage and Why We Should Care About What Civilians Think' (Just Security 27 March 2015) https://www.justsecurity.org/21529/meaning-proportionate-collateral-damage-care-civilians/ accessed 21 April 2017.

[140] This part of the report was initially drawn up by the members of working group 2 of the 2015 Oslo meeting: Charles Garraway (Coordinator), Mike Schmitt, Jann Kleffner, Heike Krieger, Sandesh Sivakumaran, Aurel Sari, Yaël Ronen, Louise Arimatsu, Geoffrey Corn. All members of the Study Group had a role in commenting upon the initial draft and the entire SG is responsible for the final version of all parts of the report.

armed conflict.[141] Precautions are of central importance to the protection of the civilian population. Nevertheless, compared to the principle of distinction and the principle of proportionality, the issue of precautions has remained under-researched and more problematically under-emphasized.

The principal legal regime governing precautions in attack during an international armed conflict is laid out in Art. 57 API. As mentioned above, the customary law rules governing the conduct of hostilities are applicable in all domains of warfare.[142] To the extent that Art. 57(4) API had imposed through the use of the term 'reasonable' a standard 'a little less far-reaching' than 'all feasible precautions',[143] the customary rules pertaining to precautions in attack today impose the requirement of taking all feasible precautions in all domains of warfare.[144]

It is now generally accepted that the obligation to take 'precautions in attack' also applies to NIAC by virtue of customary international law.[145] Although the obligation as such does not appear in APII (nor in Common Art. 3 GC I–IV), Art. 13(1) APII requires that 'the civilian population and individual civilians shall enjoy general protection against the dangers arising from military operations'. As the ICRC Customary IHL Study commentary to Rule 15 states: 'it would be difficult to comply with this requirement without taking precautions in attack'.[146]

By virtue of customary international law, parties to an armed conflict are under an obligation to take precautions in attack in both international as well as non-international armed conflicts.

It follows from the humanitarian rationale and structure of Art. 57 API, which starts out with a general obligation to exercise constant care to spare the civilian population, that the provision imposes a presumptive obligation to take precautions and that the feasibility caveat provides the basis for a possible rebuttal. In other

---

[141] See G.S. Corn, 'War, Law, and the Oft Overlooked Value of Process as a Precautionary Measure' (2014) 42 Pepperdine Law Review 419; G.S. Corn, 'Precautions to minimize civilian harm are a fundamental principle of the law of war' (Just Security 8 July 2015) https://www.justsecurity.org/24493/obligation-precautions-fundamental-principle-law-war accessed 21 April 2017. On precautions, see generally J.F. Quéguiner, 'Precautions under the law governing the conduct of hostilities' (2006) 88(864) International Review of the Red Cross 793–821; Dinstein (n 6); Oeter (n 8); I. Henderson, *The Contemporary Law of Targeting* (Brill 2009) ch 7; Boothby (n 18) ch 7; M. Sassoli and A. Quintin, 'Active and Passive Precautions in Air and Missile Warfare' (2014) 44 Israel Yearbook on Human Rights 69–123.

[142] See text in relation to n 3 above.

[143] ICRC 1987 Commentary (n 15) 687–88, para 2230.

[144] See also in this sense HPCR Manual on International Law Applicable to Air and Missile Warfare where it precisely discusses this and states that 'the Group of Experts reached the conclusion that, as a general principle, the same legal regime applies equally in all domains of warfare (land, sea or air)', HPCR Commentary (n 13) 124–25, Rule 30, para 2.

[145] ICRC Customary IHL (n 3) Rules 15–21; B.J. Egan, 'International Law, Legal Diplomacy, and the Counter-ISIL Campaign: Some Observation' (2016) 92 International Law Studies, US Naval War College. See also S. Sivakumaran, *The Law of Non-International Armed Conflict* (OUP 2012) ch 2.5.1. Both, Art. 3(10) of the Amended Protocol II to the Conventional Weapons Convention and Art. 7 of the Second Protocol to the Cultural Property Convention, apply in NIAC.

[146] ICRC Customary IHL (n 3) Rule 15.

words, the obligation to take precautions is the rule and it may only be dispensed with in exceptional cases.

2. When are precautions feasible?

The feasibility qualifier is linked to several specific obligations, namely the obligations laid out in Art. 57(2)(a)(i) and (ii) API, usually referred to as precautions in attack. Rules 16–19 in the ICRC Customary Law Study also include the feasibility qualifier. Similarly, the relevant obligations regarding precautions against the effects of attacks, namely Art. 58(a), (b), (c) API and customary IHL Rules 22–24 also include the feasibility qualifier. The SG noted that the general understanding of feasibility is the same for both precautions in attack and precautions against the effects of attacks.

2.1. Scope and content of the feasibility caveat

Understanding the full effect of the feasibility qualifier in relation to these obligations is perhaps the most complicated aspect of implementing precautions. Unfortunately, neither the text of these provisions nor the associated 1987 ICRC Commentary provides much insight into the meaning of this qualifier.[147]

'Feasible' is an inherently variable concept and the obligation is always context dependent, i.e. what is feasible will not only be contingent on the environment in which the attack is to be carried out but will also depend on a range of factors including time, terrain, weather, capabilities, available troops and resources, enemy activity and civilian considerations.[148] It is against this backdrop that the obligation to take precautions in attack is often described as 'relative'.[149]

The word 'feasible' has indeed been defined as 'those precautions which are practicable or practically possible taking into account all circumstances ruling at the time, including humanitarian and military considerations'. This text is found in Art. 3(10) of Amended Protocol II and Art. 1(5) of Protocol III to the 1980 Convention on Certain Conventional Weapons (CCW) and is reflected in reservation b) which the United Kingdom made on ratification of API.[150] Similar wording was used by

[147] For example, when discussing the target verification obligation, the Commentary provides that, '[o]nce again the interpretation will be a matter of common sense and good faith. What is required of the person launching an offensive is to take the necessary identification measures in good time in order to spare the population as far as possible. It is not clear how the success of military operations could be jeopardized by this.' See ICRC 1987 Commentary (n 15) 682, para 2198.
[148] The phraseology has been discussed in many separate contexts including the ICRC Customary International Humanitarian Law Study, see ICRC Customary IHL (n 3) Rule 15; ICTY, *Prosecutor vs Galić* (n 88) para 58, n 105; UK Ministry of Defence (n 90) paras 5.32.2–5.32.10.
[149] There is also the comment by the chair in Session 2 of the ICRC Expert Meeting on Explosive Weapons in Populated Areas: Humanitarian, Legal, Technical and Military Aspects which reads: 'While the rules prohibiting indiscriminate attacks and requiring attacks to respect proportionality are absolute, the requirement to take precautions is relative, based on what is feasible', see ICRC Expert Meeting (n 85) 18.
[150] The text of the reservation made by the UK (n 89).

other States such as France and Spain.[151] This understanding has received widespread acceptance and was also supported by the SG.

The 2015 US Department of Defense Manual deals with the matter in less detail and is somewhat controversial. According to the manual '[t]he standard for what precautions must be taken is one of due regard or diligence, not an absolute requirement to do everything possible. A wanton disregard for civilian casualties or harm to other protected persons and objects is clearly prohibited.'[152] 'Wanton disregard' implies that no precautions have been taken and so it is almost otiose to say that it is clearly prohibited. It is also somewhat surprising given that the US has stated that Art. 57(2)(a)(ii) API is an 'accurate statement of the fundamental law of war principle of discrimination'.[153] The question is whether the assessment of feasibility was, under the circumstances, one that a reasonable commander in the same situation would have made.

The Harvard Air and Missile Warfare Manual has taken the view that the standard for precautions required in the air domain is 'feasibility' (and not 'reasonableness'),[154] defined as per the abovementioned CCW definition;[155] precisely in the chapter on precautions, 'the Group of Experts [drafting the Air and Missile Warfare Manual] reached the conclusion that, as a general principle, the same legal regime applies equally in all domains of warfare (land, sea or air).'[156] The Rules in the Tallinn Manual also use 'feasible'.[157] Some of the experts in the 2013 Tallinn Manual stated that the difference between the term 'reasonable' and 'feasible' is tenuous and 'that the distinction is so highly nuanced as to be of little practical relevance, and that the applicable legal standard is operationally the same.'[158] Under this view, 'the attacker must perform those precautionary measures that are both technically possible and militarily feasible'.[159] The SG agreed with this finding. The Tallinn Manual 2.0 simply deleted this discussion and any reference to the fact that the standard might be different, which further supports the position that the standard of 'all feasible precautions' applies in all domains.[160]

---

[151] According to the interpretative declaration submitted by Spain: 'It is the understanding [of the Government of Spain] that in Art. 41, 56, 57, 58, 78 and 86 the word 'feasible' means that the matter to which reference is made is practicable or practically possible taking into account all circumstances at the time when the situation arises, including humanitarian and military considerations.' (1989) https://www.icrc.org/applic/ihl/ihl.nsf/Notification.xsp?action=openDocument&documentId=FC622F31C9E2236EC1256402003FB660 accessed 21 April 2017.

[152] US Department of Defense, 'Law of War Manual 2015' (n 46) para 5.3.3.2.

[153] Harold Koh, Legal Adviser, Department of State, 'Letter to Paul Seger, Legal Adviser of Switzerland regarding Switzerland's Position on the US Reservation to Protocol III of the Convention on Certain Conventional Weapons' (30 December 2009) quoted in: US Department of Defense, 'Law of War Manual 2015' (n 46) para 5.11, n 279.

[154] See HPCR Manual (n 3) 12, 16, 18–20, 26, 34, Rules 20, 31, 32, 39, 40, 42–44, 46, 68(d) and 95(c).

[155] See HPCR Manual (n 3) 4, Rule 1(q).

[156] HPCR Commentary (n 13) 124–25, Rule 30, para 2.

[157] See Tallinn Manual (n 3) 167–68, 176, Rules 53–54 and 59.

[158] Tallinn Manual (n 3) 165.

[159] Ibid.

[160] Tallinn Manual 2.0 (n 43).

The Group noted that feasibility is to be determined from an *ex ante* perspective, i.e. prior to (and if possible during) the attack and on the basis of the information available at the time; not with hindsight. As United Kingdom Reservation (c) to Additional Protocol I stipulates, '[m]ilitary commanders and others responsible for planning, deciding upon, or executing attacks necessarily have to reach decisions on the basis of their assessment of the information from all sources which is reasonably available to them at the relevant time.'[161]

2.2. Factors to be taken into consideration when determining feasibility

According to Art. 3(10) of the 1996 Amended Mine Protocol of the UN Weapons Convention, the circumstances to be included in the feasibility determination include but are not limited to: (a) the short- and long-term effect of mines upon the local civilian population for the duration of the minefield; (b) possible measures to protect civilians (for example, fencing, signs, warning and monitoring); (c) the availability and feasibility of using alternatives; and (d) the short- and long-term military requirements for a minefield. More generally, the UK Military Manual states that:

> '[A] commander should have regard to the following factors: a. the importance of the target and the urgency of the situation; b. intelligence about the proposed target – what it is being, or will be, used for and when; c. the characteristics of the target itself, for example, whether it houses dangerous forces; d. what weapons are available, their range, accuracy, and radius of effect; e. conditions affecting the accuracy of targeting, such as terrain, weather, night or day; f. factors affecting incidental loss or damage, such as the proximity of civilians or civilian objects in the vicinity of the target or other protected objects or zones and whether they are inhabited, or the possible release of hazardous substances as a result of the attack; g. the risks to his own troops of the various options open to him.'[162]

According to the 2015 US Department of Defense Manual relevant circumstances may include:

> 'the effect of taking the precaution on mission accomplishment; whether taking the precaution poses a risk to one's own forces or presents other security risks; the likelihood and degree of humanitarian benefit from taking the precaution; the cost of taking the precaution, in terms of time, resources, or money; or whether taking the precaution forecloses alternative courses of action.'[163]

Few could dispute that 'feasible' e.g. in relation to the target verification obligation certainly factors in the capability of a commander to gather and assess information. For example, while it would be 'feasible' for a commander with eyes on the target (through human intelligence on the ground) or with access to real-time imagery from an unmanned aerial vehicle to continue to gather information on a potential target up to the moment of the actual attack decision (and even while the attack was in progress), it would not be 'feasible' for a commander lacking this capability to do the same. In this sense, the feasibility qualifier is relatively

161 UK declaration upon ratification of API (n 89) para (c).
162 UK Ministry of Defence (n 90) para 5.32.5; generally see also Oeter (n 8) 200, para 460.
163 US Department of Defense, 'Law of War Manual 2015' (n 46) para 5.3.3.2.

uncontroversial; a commander cannot be required to do that which is simply practically impossible under the given circumstances. Resources and capacity are thus relevant factors in the determination of feasibility.

However, it bears emphasis that even if some options may not be available due to a lack of resources, the military commander in charge will have to explore other options. As the wording of Art. 57(2)(a)(i) and (ii) API makes clear, those planning an attack have to do *everything* feasible to verify the military nature of the target and take *all* feasible precautions in the choice of their means and methods. If lack of resources or capacity does not allow ascertaining that the proposed target is actually a military objective, the attack must not take place.

2.2.1. Financial implications as a relevant factor in the determination of feasibility

The question whether financial costs can be factored into the feasibility assessment is controversial. The 2015 US Department of Defense Manual explicitly refers to 'money' as a circumstance to be taken into consideration when assessing feasibility.[164] The SG found this position controversial and agreed with the view put forward in the literature that '[t]here is no basis in international humanitarian law for factoring expense into feasibility assessments. Once a belligerent purchases equipment and supplies it to its forces in the field, it must be used if it is available, makes good military sense and will minimize civilian impact'.[165] The SG noted that financial considerations should not be confused with specific resources considerations, e.g. when a military commander has the intention to save up a weapon/ammunition in short supply for a later occasion where it is expected that the use of this weapon would be more appropriate from a military or humanitarian perspective, knowing that it is in short supply and cannot easily be replaced. Such resources considerations are recognized factors in the determination of feasibility. Conversely, allowing financial and economic considerations as such to enter the equation is risky given that they may be abstract and remote and could easily be invoked so as to manipulate the obligation to take feasible precautions.

2.2.2. Force protection as a relevant consideration when determining feasibility

The relevance of the protection of one's own forces is also controversially debated. Much of the controversy, however, concerns the question whether (and how) force protection may be factored in the proportionality calculus (see Part II above).[166] With regard to precautions, it is beyond doubt that in times of armed conflict force protection is a priority concern of every military commander and as such it is a standard 'military consideration' that may be taken into account when assessing the

[164] Ibid.
[165] M.N. Schmitt, 'Precision attack and international humanitarian law' (2005) 87(859) International Review of the Red Cross 462.
[166] Part II (1.2), text in relation to n 132 and n 133.

feasibility of a given precautionary measure.[167] It bears emphasis, however, that force protection is only one among many factors determining feasibility and it does not automatically trump relevant humanitarian considerations. Indeed, the accepted definition of feasible precautions recalled above, makes humanitarian considerations as relevant as military ones.

3. Increasing the incentives for compliance

The SG noted a structural problem regarding the operational implementation of precautionary measures, namely that they may often be perceived as compromising the tactical gains and anticipated military advantages of a given attack. When the obligation is emphasized exclusively in terms of mitigating civilian risk, there is, as the 1987 ICRC Commentary notes, a risk that commanders will view the obligation in competition with military operational considerations. In contrast, the obligation should be understood as one that typically—albeit not always—operates symmetrically with military operational interests of maximizing situational awareness, as the 1987 ICRC Commentary highlights.[168] Commanders should constantly seek to maximize the effect of using the finite combat power available, and therefore typically have a constant operational interest in avoiding the use of such power against targets that do not in fact qualify as military objectives. In other words, commanders and operational planners should instinctively seek to maximize the use of intelligence, surveillance and reconnaissance (ISR) assets to gain the best situational awareness possible. Framing precautionary obligations in general and the obligation to verify in particular in these terms would highlight the convergence of military and humanitarian consideration in maximizing the use of available ISR assets.[169] If commanders perceive situational awareness as a force multiplier, it leads to choose not to utilize available ISR resources only as the result of genuine considerations of military necessity. These could include, *inter alia*, concerns over loss of surprise; concerns over losing ISR assets considered essential for future missions; prioritizing ISR efforts towards other anticipated targets; and the risk that information overload might dilute combat initiative. All of these considerations arguably influence a military 'feasibility' judgment, but when a commander views situational awareness as an operational advantage, and not merely as a humanitarian measure, it is less likely that these considerations will be prematurely or unjustifiably invoked.

4. The obligation to take constant care

According to Art. 57(1) API '[i]n the conduct of military operations, constant care shall be taken to spare the civilian population, civilians and civilian objects.' With reference to NIAC, note should be taken of Art. 13(1) APII, which reads:

---

[167] Sassoli and Quintin (n 141) 69–123; see the definition of 'feasible' recalled above: '*those precautions which are practicable or practically possible taking into account all circumstances ruling at the time, including humanitarianand military considerations*' (emphasis added).
[168] ICRC 1987 Commentary (n 15) 680–81, para 2195.
[169] Corn, 'War, Law, and the Oft Overlooked Value of Process as a Precautionary Measure' (n 141) 430.

'The civilian population and individual civilians shall enjoy general protection against the dangers arising from military operations.' The ICRC Customary IHL Study confirms that the constant care obligation applies in both international and non-international armed conflicts.[170]

Although Art. 57 is located among the rules related to the employment of combat power—commonly referred to within military circles as the 'targeting process', there is no indication that the general obligation is limited to this process. The SG agreed that in spite of Art. 57's title 'Precautions in attack', the obligation to take constant care to spare the civilian population applies to the entire range of military operations and not only to attacks in the sense of Art. 49 API. This follows from the clear wording of the provision and from the fact that reducing its scope of application to that of attacks would deprive the provision of most of its meaning given that relevant scenarios would already be covered by Art. 57(2)–(5) API.[171] The scope of application of the general obligation laid out in Art. 57(1) API therefore is broader than that of the specific obligations contained in paragraphs 2–5, which only apply to attacks. Such a broad reading of Art. 57(1) is supported *inter alia* by the UK Manual which distinguishes between Art. 57(1) and Art. 57(2), pointing out that the phrase 'military operations' 'has a wider connotation than 'attacks' and would include the movement or deployment of armed forces' (footnote 187 to para 5.32.). The text goes on to say that: 'So the commander will have to bear in mind the effect on the civilian population of what he is planning to do and take steps to reduce that effect as much as possible. In planning or deciding on or carrying out attacks, however, those responsible have more specific duties.'[172] Art. 57(2)–(5) API should thus be understood as derivative specifications of the general obligation stipulated in Art. 57(1) API.[173] They can be derived from and partially overlap with Art. 57(1) API without, however, exhausting the broader meaning of this provision.

According to the ICRC Commentary to Art. 57 API, '[t]he term 'military operations' should be understood to mean any movements, maneuvers and other activities whatsoever carried out by the armed forces with a view to combat.'[174] The SG agreed with such a broad understanding of the term 'military operations'.

The term 'constant care' is not defined under IHL. Even the 1987 ICRC Commentary refers to it only as a 'general principle'.[175] Constant care is, of course, a quite general obligation. But generality need not dilute its significance. The use of

---

[170] ICRC Customary IHL (n 3) Rule 15.

[171] Quéguiner (n 141) 796.

[172] UK Ministry of Defence (n 90) para 5.32.1. As shown by Rule 30 and its commentary, the Harvard Air and Missile Warfare Manual consider that the obligation of constant care applies at all times and places and with no exception, HPCR Commentary (n 13) 124–25, Rule 30, para 2.

[173] According to the 1987 ICRC Commentary, 'the other paragraphs [of Art. 57 API] are devoted to the practical application of this principle', see ICRC 1987 Commentary (n 15) 680, para 2191.

[174] Ibid.

[175] Ibid.

the word 'shall' in Art. 57(1) API indicates that whatever it is that this provision entails is binding upon the parties to the Protocol. It has been said to apply to all domains of warfare[176] and all levels of operations.[177] The obligation to take constant care is best understood as an obligation of conduct, i.e. a positive and continuous obligation aimed at risk mitigation and harm prevention and the fulfillment of which requires the exercise of due diligence.[178] As such it is relative in character, i.e. what precisely the obligation requires depends on the circumstances of each specific case. As a general rule, the higher the risks for the civilian population in any given military operation, the more will be required in terms of care. Naturally, risks for the civilian population are particularly high, whenever the military is executing an attack. It is for this reason, that Art. 57(2–5) lists a number of 'attack-specific' obligations, in addition to the general obligation contained in Art. 57(1).

5. The obligation to verify

According to Art. 57(2)(a)(i) API 'those who plan or decide upon an attack *shall do everything feasible to verify* that the objectives to be attacked are neither civilians nor civilian objects and are not subject to special protection but are military objectives [...] and that it is not prohibited by the provisions of this Protocol to attack them.'[179] According to the ICRC Customary IHL Study in both international and non-international armed conflicts, '[e]ach party to the conflict must do everything feasible to verify that targets are military objectives.'[180]

The obligation to verify is crucial for two reasons: first, it functions to minimize the risk that a target will be mistakenly assessed as qualifying for deliberate attack; second, it functions to maximize the probability that attacks will only be directed at targets that genuinely contribute to bringing the enemy into submission. In other words, the obligation to verify not only gives expression to a central humanitarian rationale, it is also in line with the dictates of military logic. The obligation can usefully be regarded as the procedural corollary to the general obligation to distinguish civilians and civilian objects from military objectives.[181] The obligation requires verification that the target is a 'combatant',[182] or a civilian taking a direct

[176] HPCR Commentary (n 13) 124–25, Rule 30, para 2.
[177] Corn, 'Precautions to Minimize Civilian Harm are a Fundamental Principle of the Law of War' (n 141): 'a requirement to take 'constant care' to mitigate the risk to civilians and civilian property must animate all strategic, operational, and tactical decision-making (...)'.
[178] The commentary on Rule 52 of the Tallinn Manual suggests that 'in cyber operations, the duty of care requires commanders and all others involved in the operations to be continuously sensitive to the effects of their activities on the civilian population and civilian objects, and to seek to avoid any unnecessary effects thereon.' See Tallinn Manual (n 3) 166, commentary on Rule 52, para 4.
[179] Emphasis added.
[180] ICRC Customary IHL (n 3) Rule 16.
[181] W.G. Schmidt, 'The Protection of Victims of International Armed Conflict: Protocol 1 additional to the Geneva Conventions' (1984) 24 Air Force Law Review 189, 235.
[182] Combatant is used here in a generic sense encompassing privileged and unprivileged belligerents, including fighters of an organized non-State armed group.

part in hostilities, or a military objective in line with the definition in Art. 52(2) API and that it is not prohibited by IHL to attack them.[183] It is a continuous obligation subject to the feasibility-qualifier and therefore context dependent.[184] The wording 'shall do everything feasible to verify' indicates a requirement to maximize the utilization of available intelligence, surveillance and reconnaissance assets to gain the most comprehensive situational awareness possible under the circumstances; and where possible utilize analytical processes to transform this battlefield information into intelligence.[185] The United Kingdom Manual lists different factors to which any commander selecting a target will have to pay regard, namely:

> 'a. whether he can personally verify the target; b. instructions from higher authority about objects which are not to be targeted; c. intelligence reports, aerial or satellite reconnaissance pictures, and any other information in his possession about the nature of the proposed target; d. any rules of engagement imposed by higher authority under which he is required to operate; e. the risks to his own forces necessitated by target verification.'

While the specific aspects that are to be taken into consideration will always depend on the given situation, other factors that can play a role are: the level of risk for civilians in case of an erroneous identification of the target; the type of target and the basis for its identification as a lawful target; the likelihood of confusion with civilians or civilian objects—e.g. there is a greater risk of confusion if target identification is based mainly on 'patterns of life'; or past errors in target identification in similar situations, on the basis of similar sources of intelligence and/or with regard to similar types of targets.

6. Feasible precautions in the choice of means and methods of attack: no general obligation to always use the most precise or modern technology

According to Art. 57(2)(a)(ii) API 'those who plan or decide upon an attack shall take all feasible precautions in the choice of means and methods of attack with a view to avoiding, and in any event to minimizing, incidental loss of civilian life, injury to civilians and damage to civilian objects.' According to the ICRC Customary IHL Study in both international and non-international armed conflicts '[e]ach party to the conflict must take all feasible precautions in the choice of means

[183] ICRC Customary IHL (n 3) Rule 8.

[184] The United Kingdom Manual deals with verification, it states: 'The problem of verification is obviously different for the air or artillery commander drawing up target lists from a distance than it is for a tank troop commander who has enemy armored vehicles in his sights. The former has more time to make up his mind; the latter is more easily able to verify the target.' See UK Ministry of Defence (n 90) para 5.32.2.

[185] The Report to the ICTY Prosecutor about the NATO Bombing Campaign held that '[a] military commander must set up an effective intelligence gathering system to collect and evaluate information concerning potential targets. The commander must also direct his forces to use available technical means to properly identify targets during operations. Both the commander and the aircrew actually engaged in operations must have some range of discretion to determine which available resources shall be used and how they shall be used', see ICTY Office of the Prosecutor (n 99) para 29.

and methods of warfare with a view to avoiding, and in any event to minimizing, incidental loss of civilian life, injury to civilians and damage to civilian objects.'[186]

According to the Air and Missile Warfare Manual '[t]here is no specific obligation on Belligerent Parties to use precision guided weapons. There may however be situations in which the prohibition of indiscriminate attacks, or the obligation to avoid—or, in any event, minimize—collateral damage, cannot be fulfilled without using precision guided weapons'.[187] The SG agreed with this finding. There is no obligation to acquire the most precise or modern technology (or any particular technology) on the market nor is there a general obligation for a party to an armed conflict to use in all situations the most precise technology that it has in its arsenal.

In this regard it should be kept in mind that even though a weapon may be classed as 'precision-guided', it may still be more destructive than other weapons (e.g. in the case of a 1000 lb. precision guided munitions (PGM) versus a 250 lb. dumb bomb).

At the same time, it bears emphasis that all precautionary obligations are 'technology neutral', i.e. they apply irrespective of the weapons technology used, including PGMs. Thus, if the use of a PGM will avoid or minimize incidental civilian casualties compared to another means or method of warfare and provided its use is *feasible* under the given circumstances (i.e. taking into account both military and humanitarian considerations), then using such a PGM is compulsory. Similarly, if the only way to carry out an operation without violating the prohibitions of indiscriminate or disproportionate attacks is to use a PGM, then the attacker is faced with only two options: to use the PGM; or not carry out the attack at all.

It bears emphasis that this reasoning applies not only to the issue of PGMs but to all methods and means of warfare, including 'modern' technologies such as cyber-attacks, drone strikes and the possible future use of increasingly autonomous weapons systems.

7. The obligation to take effective advance warning

Providing advance warnings to civilians in order to mitigate the risk of attack is one of the most commonly debated precautionary measures.[188] Art. 57 specifically requires that 'effective advance warning shall be given of attacks which may affect the civilian population, unless circumstances do not permit.' Israel's 2014 operations in Gaza, and the extensive efforts to provide such warnings, have elevated the discourse on this warnings precaution to unprecedented levels: some worry that the Israeli Defense Forces (IDF) created an unrealistically high bar on when and how to provide warnings; conversely, some condemn the IDF because the warnings did not produce their intended effects; finally, some suggest that the extent of warnings were the result of policy decisions, and not legal obligation.

---

[186] ICRC Customary IHL (n 3) Rule 17.

[187] HPCR Manual (n 3) Rule 8.

[188] See P.S. Baruch and N. Newman, 'Warning civilians prior to attack under international law - theory and practice' (2011) 41 Israel Yearbook of Human Rights 359ff.

It is important to note the way that the provision is phrased. It indicates that the presumption (subject to the exception) is that a warning shall be given.[189]

Generally speaking, advance warnings may include but are not limited to leaflets, signals, phone calls, text messages, as well as passing warnings to village elders and others likely to influence decision to take shelter or temporarily leave the area. Whether they can be qualified as 'effective' depends on the circumstances of each given case. As is the case with all the precautionary obligations the assessment has to be made *ex ante*, on the basis of the information available prior to the attack and not with hindsight. The military commander taking the relevant decision must thus be assessed, objectively, on whether the warning efforts could have reasonably been expected to produce the intended protective effect in the circumstances ruling at the time, in view of information available from all sources to the commander.

It is clear that warnings that leave civilians with no means of, or time to, escape cannot be considered 'effective'. Similarly, military operations that qualify as an attack cannot simultaneously qualify as a warning. In this regard, so-called 'roof knock operations' were controversially discussed within the SG.[190] Some members of the SG argued that so-called 'roof knock operations' amount to an attack, because they involve an act of violence against the adversary and that it is therefore prohibited to direct such tactics against a civilian object. On the other hand, it was argued that when used against a military objective in order to warn civilian bystanders, it may constitute a precaution in the choice of means and methods of warfare to avoid or minimize civilian casualties.[191]

Both Art. 57(2)(c) API as well as the corresponding customary law rule take into consideration that issuing an effective advance warning may not always be possible or 'feasible'. Unlike other precautionary obligations, however, these provisions do not use the word 'feasible' but speak of an obligation to give effective advance warning 'unless circumstances do not permit'. The explanation of this qualifier in the 1987 ICRC Commentary is cursory and somewhat cryptic.[192] This is unfortunate, as when, where, and why this qualifier is legitimately applicable to rebut the presumptive obligation to provide warnings is critically important, as foregoing warnings can substantially contribute to civilian risk.

It is clear that whenever a force is objectively incapable of providing an advance warning, the circumstances do not permit such a warning. Such scenarios, however, will presumably be quite rare. In most situations, providing some form of warning,

---

[189] Quéguiner (n 141) 807.

[190] The US reportedly used this method in Iraq, see Y. Torbati and I. Ali, 'U.S. military' used 'roof knock' tactic in Iraq to try to warn civilians before bombing' (Reuters 26 April 2016) http://www.reuters.com/article/us-mideast-crisis-usa-airstrike-idUSKCN0XN2NK accessed 21 April 2017.

[191] Israel's report on operation protective edge discusses roof knocking in para 313 on page 180, that is in Part VI D 2 c on choice of means and methods and not in Part VI D 2 b on advance warnings, see State of Israel, 'The Gaza Conflict 7 July–26 August 2014, Factual and legal Aspects' (2015) 180, para 313 http://mfa.gov.il/ProtectiveEdge/Documents/2014GazaConflictFullReport.pdf accessed 21 April 2017.

[192] ICRC 1987 Commentary (n 15) 686–87, paras 2222–25.

even if cursory, will be possible. If by nothing other than a bullhorn or yelling towards a group of civilians, or 'buzzing' a town before launching an air attack, some warning effect may result. Such a type of warning may not be the most effective warning but it is likely to have some effect in terms of civilian risk mitigation, and if circumstances do not allow for any alternatives it is certainly better than no warning at all, and therefore this kind of warning would be obligatory. Conversely, whenever a military commander has different options to warn, he must—as far as circumstances permit—opt for the most effective warning. This follows from the object and purpose of the warning requirement, namely to mitigate risks for the civilian population, as well as the general, overarching obligation to take constant care to spare the civilian population.

The 1987 ICRC Commentary references loss of necessary surprise when it is a condition of the attack's success as the motive for including the qualifier in the rule.[193] This is logical, as it would contradict basic military logic to require commanders to provide warnings when doing so would seriously undermine the effect of an anticipated attack by providing the enemy the opportunity to effectively prepare for the attack. In that regard, military manuals refer to both the success of the attack and the preservation of the forces.[194] Beyond these, some members of the SG submitted that reduction of the anticipated military advantage, and possibly the protection of civilians where it is clear that a warning would lead to the use of human shields may also be relevant considerations.

At the same time, it is important to note that such considerations do not automatically set aside the obligation to warn. Any warning prior to an attack carries the risk of somehow mitigating the attack's effectiveness or endangering the attacking forces. Allowing any loss of tactical initiative to justify dispensing with the warning requirement would therefore result in an exception that swallows the rule.

If the warning requirement is to have any meaning, the expected effects of the warning in terms of protecting civilians and the presumptive nature by which it was established in Art. 57(2)(c) API and the corresponding customary law rule must weigh against dispensing with it for any slight loss of tactical advantage or other military disadvantage. The ICRC Customary IHL Study captures this point quite well by referring to 'cases where the element of surprise is *essential* to the success

---

[193] Ibid., para 2223.

[194] UK Ministry of Defence (n 90) para 5.32.8; US Department of Defense, 'Law of War Manual 2015' (n 46) 5.11.1.3. While the 2015 DOD Law of War Manual reinforces the application of the qualifier to attacks requiring surprise, it also suggests that circumstances that would not permit for warnings include 'legitimate military reasons, such as exploiting the element of surprise in order to provide for mission accomplishment and preserving the security of the attacking force.' The term 'such as' indicates that surprise is not the exclusive justification for dispensing with the presumptive requirement to provide warnings, although the Manual does not provide insight into other justifications.

of an operation.'[195] This is reflected in military manuals.[196] Warnings must therefore be required unless providing them will produce a compromise to the mission that creates a genuine risk of failure. Ultimately, assessing when it is appropriate to forego a warning is highly situational and depends on what an objective, reasonable commander would have decided under the given circumstances. The determination whether circumstances do not permit a warning is a balancing exercise in which different considerations must be weighted rather than a simple yes or no answer. It would seem that where issuing a warning is likely to lower civilian casualties by 90% but where the warning would have a slight impact on the tactical advantage sought, any reasonable commander would choose to warn. In any case, what seems clear is that commanders should be trained to assume warnings will be provided, and demand significant tactical and operational justification for dispensing with them. Otherwise, the benefit of the warning precaution will be substantially diluted.

Finally, it is important to bear in mind that civilians not heeding to a warning and remaining behind do not lose their protection from direct attack under the rules relevant to the conduct of hostilities. While they will be subject to a heightened (factual) risk of becoming collateral damage, legally they remain protected civilians. Not heeding a warning cannot be equated with a direct participation in hostilities. Therefore, an effective advance warning does not relieve the attacker from the obligation to take all other feasible precautionary measures to avoid and in any event to minimize civilian harm.

---

195 ICRC Customary IHL (n 3) Rule 20.

196 UK Military Manual, 'where the element of surprise is crucial to the success of the military operation', see UK Ministry of Defence (n 90) para 5.32.8; Australia Military Manual: an action that 'is likely to be seriously compromised by a warning', see Australian Defence Force Warfare Center, 'Law of Armed Conflict' (Canberra, Defence Publishing Service 2006) para 5.56; US Commander's Handbook: if the success of the mission is 'placed in jeopardy', it may justify resorting to a general warning instead of a specific warning, see The Commander's Handbook (n 26) para 8.9.2; The US Operational Law Handbook, 'where surprise is a key element', see US International and Operational Law Department, 'Operational Law Handbook' (Charlottesville, Virginia, The Judge Advocate General S Legal Center & School, US Army 2015) 24 https://www.loc.gov/rr/frd/Military_Law/pdf/operational-law-handbook_2015.pdf accessed 21 April 2017; US response to ICRC memorandum regarding the 1990–91 Gulf conflict, '[w]here surprise is important to mission accomplishment and allowable risk to friendly forces, a warning is not required', see S.J. Cummins and D.P. Stewert (eds) 'Digest of United States Practice in International law 1991–1999' (US Department of State 1991–1999) 2064; all emphasis added.

Table of Cases*

INTERNATIONAL

European Court of Human Rights

Extraordinary African Chambers

Inter-American Court of Human Rights

International Court of Justice

---

* The Table of Cases was compiled by Ms C.C. Diepeveen, Middelburg, The Netherlands, e-mail: cdiep@zeelandnet.nl

T.D. Gill et al. (eds.), *Yearbook of International Humanitarian Law 2016*,
Yearbook of International Humanitarian Law 19,
https://doi.org/10.1007/978-94-6265-213-2

International Criminal Court

International Criminal Tribunal for the former Yugoslavia

International Criminal Tribunal for Rwanda

Lebanon Special Tribunal

Mechanism for International Criminal Tribunals

Nuremberg International Military Tribunal

Permanent Court of Arbitration

Index**

** The Index was compiled by Ms C.C. Diepeveen, Middelburg, The Netherlands, e-mail: cdiep@zeelandnet.nl

T.D. Gill et al. (eds.), *Yearbook of International Humanitarian Law 2016*,
Yearbook of International Humanitarian Law 19,
https://doi.org/10.1007/978-94-6265-213-2

M

N

O

FSC
www.fsc.org
MIX
Papier | Fördert gute Waldnutzung
FSC® C083411

Kolibri 360 GmbH
Ferdinand-Jühlke-Straße 7
99095 Erfurt, Deutschland
produktsicherheit@kolibri360.de